D0724245

FOUR EASY STEPS TO UNDERSTANDING YOUR DREAMS

1. Write down your dream
2. Look up the entry that best describes the opening scene
3. Look up the symbols and the situations that occurred in your dream
4. Discover what your dream actually means

DID YOU KNOW . . .

. . . A dream can be a forewarning of things to come?

. . . Dreams can help you solve problems in your everyday life?

. . . Women dream more during PMS?

. . . Revelatory dreams are more common in men?

. . . Sleepwalking occurs most frequently in adolescence?

. . . You can control your dreams?

You can find the key to your inner life in the . . .

DREAM DICTIONARY

Dream Dictionary

A GUIDE TO DREAMS AND SLEEP EXPERIENCES

Tony Crisp

A DELL BOOK

Published by
Dell Publishing
a division of
Bantam Doubleday Dell Publishing Group, Inc.
1540 Broadway
New York, New York 10036

This work was first published in Great Britain by Macdonald Optima, a division of Macdonald & Co. (Publishers) Ltd.

ISBN: 0-440-20861-0

Reprinted by arrangement with Macdonald Optima, London, England

Printed in the United States of America

Published simultaneously in Canada

December 1991

20 19 18 17 16 15 14

OPM

To Quentin
Who awoke in the cellar
and has had the courage
to stay awake

Contents

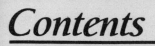

Introduction

Dreams are one of nature's miracles, not the result of a wandering mind in sleep. A dream is an interface between the process of life and our conscious personality. Life existed quite capably for millions of years before the self-aware human personality came on the scene. Life's age old processes are still the major part of our being, yet we seldom consciously meet them—except in dreams. As our physical and psychological health depends upon a reasonable co-operation between the spontaneous processes of life and our conscious decisions and actions, the encounter in dreams is vital.

A dream is a meeting between the most ancient and the most recent in evolution. It is also much more. In an overview of the study and research concerning dreams, there is evidence that a dream can be:

- An expression of what is happening in the physical body; some doctors consider dreams to show signs of illness long before they are evident consciously.
- A way of balancing the physiological and psychological activities in us. When a person is deprived of dreaming in experiments, a breakdown in mind and body quickly occurs.
- An enormously original source of insight and information. Dreams tap our memory, our experience, and our mental functions of scanning information and forming new ideas.
- An expression of human supersenses. Humans have an unconscious ability to read body language—so can assess other humans very quickly. Humans have an unimaginable ability to absorb information, not simply from books, but from everyday events; with it they constantly arrive at new

1

insights and realisations. Humans frequently correctly predict the future, not out of a bizarre ability, but from the information gathered about the present. All these abilities and more show in our dreams.

- A means of solving problems, not only in our personal life, but also in relationships and work.
- A way of reaching beyond the known world of experience and presenting intimations from the unknown.

We all dream every night, so we each have what could be called a magical dream machine. If we imagine ourself locked in a dark mechanism, hardly moving, with no sounds or light from outside disturbing us, our mind relaxed—this is sleep. But now, in the darkness a light glimmers. Gradually it takes shape. The shape of a woman is suggested. In the time that follows she evolves form, moves, and we have full sensory experience of her. We are totally involved, with all our emotions and sexuality responding. Changes occur and we love, fight, fear, murder and bring to life again the woman, who can become an animal, a devil, God or a bodiless voice lost in a sombre countryside.

If we had been in such a machine and, on coming out of the total involvement of these moving experiences, were told that we had created it all ourself—that on the black screen we had, out of our fears, habits, secret longings and passion, out of our immense store of memories, with our unbelievable range of feelings and creativity, through giving form to urges and processes in our body, we had made this rich world of experience, what would we feel? Would we disclaim responsibility? Would we consider it meaningless? Would we realise what amazing creativity and potential we have?

Your dreams are such a magical place. Do you discount them? Do you see that you create your own world of experience in them? If you do, have you wondered why you may have a propensity for creating what you do? Or why, with such creative potential, you might still lack self confidence?

Just as we create our surroundings in dreams, we also create the psychological world we live in. Understanding our dreams can help us to clarify why we create what does not satisfy us, and show us how to generate a whole new world of experience. We can take charge of our creativity and ride with it instead of being at its mercy. Such power, after all, can as easily produce misery and ill health as pleasure and ability— unless we learn to direct it.

So how can we get into this magical world of our dreams and start to harvest the possibilities held there? The following pages of this book are designed to help, guide and inform on how to do this. The book is also a counsellor on what you may find in your dream adventure.

What Is Offered in This Book

The information about dreams presented in this book has been gathered during 22 years of working with and studying dreams and the dream process. It synthesises the experience of helping hundreds of individuals explore their dreams. From a collection of 3,000 dreams put on to a computer filing system, the examples used have been taken. The filing system was also used to define general associations with commonly used dream images.

In the entries in the *Dictionary* are explanations of the many different types of dreams and dream images. Despite some people's attempts to explain dreams in one simple formula, dreams cover a huge range of phenomena and human experience. Amongst subjects covered in the book are **thousands of entries on the researched meaning of the things, people, creatures and places we dream about**. There are also many entries on special subjects such as symbols and dreaming, dream interpretation, recurring dreams, nightmares, sex while asleep, predictive dreams, sleep talking, dream as an adventure, science and dreams, and many more.

Therefore, if you have dreamt of such things as your teeth

3

falling out, being chased, or your marriage partner dying, you will find an explanation of your dream in the following pages.

Using the Book

The *Dictionary* contains explanations on almost any type of dream subject. The entries are placed in alphabetical order for easy reference, but some, like dog or running, are placed in certain categories such as **animals** and **posture, movement, body language.** So, if you dreamt of a flying saucer landing in a field and aliens getting out and taking sheep and a dog back into the saucer, you could look up each of these subjects in the text. Turn to the F entries for **flying saucer**; the **animals** entry for *dog* and *sheep,* and so on.

Each entry gives the general meaning of the dream subject, just as an encyclopaedia or dictionary does for a word. Several possible meanings are given, as in the example below.

> **perfume, scent, smell** Example: 'I went back in time in circles, almost as if going unconscious. I went back and back and then there came this awful smell such as I've never experienced. I always felt it was the smell of death. I would wake terrified. One night my husband, a practical and down to earth man, said he would read me to sleep to see if it helped me not have the dream. It made no difference. I still had the nightmare. Imagine my surprise though. He said "I knew you'd had the dream again for there was an awful smell in the room for a minute" ' (Mrs EC). Frequently in dreams a smell expresses an intuition of something rotten in one's life if the smell is bad. Rotten might mean 'bad' emotions felt in a relationship; a hunch or feelings about something, as in the example; memories. <u>Good smell</u>: good feelings; non-verbalised intimations or love. <u>Idioms</u>: on the right scent; throw someone off the scent. See *nose* under **body.**

The above entry is typical of most entries. The example it contains is within quotes and illustrates the entry, or an aspect of it. In general, the description of what the dream image means is set out as the part which reads 'Rotten might mean "bad" emotions felt in a relationship; a hunch or feelings about something, as in the example; memories.' The insertion of the semicolon (;) means that a separate suggestion for the meaning of the dream image is being given. We could therefore read it as saying 'Perfume or smell might mean "bad" emotions felt in a relationship. It might depict a hunch or feelings about something. It might mean memories of something—depending on the smell.' To pack as much information into the available space, the semicolons have been used to shorten statements. Therefore, in using the entries to find meanings of dream images, consider each suggestion given.

Many entries, as with the above, also give variations, as with <u>Good smell</u>. The headings for these are underlined to make them easier to find. Because many dream images depict our unconscious thought processes, as used in language, the section <u>Idioms</u>, also underlined, is frequently given. Standing in a pink room might well be our dream's way of saying we feel 'in the pink'. Coming down from a tall building to street level might be quickly understood by the idiom 'coming down to earth'.

'See' suggests the reading of other entries which might be useful. In this section when it says *nose* under **body**, this means look for the entry called **body,** and then find the sub-entry *nose* which is just below it. Sometimes a suggestion is made to 'see' an example. This is because the example has in it mention of the symbol dealt with. Occasionally there is a 'see also'; this gives entries which might be interesting further reading but are not as directly linked as the 'see' references.

A dream has in it many sources of information. Not only should you consider the basic dream images, but what is happening, how people are dressed and their posture, and what the dream environment is. A dream is often like a film. The background provides a lot of information that gives the fore-ground action meaning. There is a great difference between a scene taking place in a farmyard and one in a bedroom. So even things such as what hand was used, left or right, should be referred to. Entries in the *Dictionary* such as **settings** and **posture** help to understand this aspect of dreams.

Lastly, it must be remembered that where sex or sexuality is mentioned, I am not simply referring to the sex act. I mean sexuality in its overall aspect, which includes the urge towards parenthood, and the love and caring connected with it.

Getting to Work on Your Dream

An example will be used to show how to arrive at a dream's meaning from use of the entries. It is important first to write the dream down as fully as possible; don't stint on the use of words; be descriptive. Then take the very opening scene of the dream and look it up in the appropriate entry.

> Example: 'I was standing in the back garden of a house—one of a row of terraced houses. Each garden was fenced and ran down to a large drainage ditch. It seemed to be raining and water was filling the drainage ditch. The water was backing up into the gardens because something was blocking the ditch. It started rising up my legs. It was quite hot. I realised this was because hot water was running out of the baths and sinks in the houses. I felt I must get out of the gardens. Not only because of the water, but because of how people might feel if they saw me in their garden. I managed to find a way into a farmyard where I felt relaxed' (Ted F).

The first scene here is garden. On a piece of paper separate to the dream, write 'garden' with space for notes to be put beside it. The entry on **garden** in the *Dictionary* says 'The inner life of the dreamer; the area of growth or change in your life; what you are trying to cultivate in yourself; feelings of peace; being near to one's natural self; meditative attitude'.

The words 'houses', 'raining', 'hot water', 'fences', 'farm-yard' need to be looked up and relevant comments written down next to each word. In doing this with his dream, Ted ended up with the following:

- Garden—The growth and changes occurring in my life at present.
- Row of houses—Other people.
- Raining—Depressed feelings or difficulties; emotions which take away enthusiasm and act as a barrier to action; tears and emotional release, an outpouring; other people's emotions 'raining' on me.
- Hot water—Emotions. In the idioms is 'hot water', suggesting I have got myself in trouble.
- Fences—Social boundaries.
- Farmyard—Where my natural drives such as sexuality, parenthood, love of fellowship, are cared for or expressed.

When Ted added his own associations to this the dream became fully understandable to him and read like this. 'I am going through a lot of changes at the moment—the garden. These are to do with allowing myself to have a warm but non-sexual relationship with women. I have always been too dragged along by my sexuality in the past. Just a few days before the dream I was in a "growth" group. I had made friends with a woman there, Susan, who I was warm with, but not sexually. The group work required some close physical contact, and I and another man worked with Susan. It seemed to me to go without complications. A while afterwards a woman in the group came to me and, with evident emotion, said I had made love publicly to my lover, meaning Susan. I had certainly been physically close to her and had felt at ease, but the viewpoint and feelings of the woman's accusations, coupled with her threat to expose me to the authority figure in

7

the group, bowled me over. This is the hot water in the dream. The fences are the boundaries people erect between their personal life and what is socially acceptable. For some days, up until understanding the dream, I felt really blocked up emotionally—the blocked drainage ditch. I cut off any friendship towards Susan. When I realised that in the farmyard—the acceptance of natural feelings without neat little boundaries—I could feel at peace, I was able to allow my natural warmth again.'

After writing the comments next to each dream image or setting, add any personal memories, feelings or associations, as Ted has. Put down anything which amplifies what has been dreamt. For instance a car is said to be one's drive and motivation in the entry on **car**. But it is helpful to add what personal feelings one has about one's car. Try imagining what the absence in one's life of the car, or house, etc., would mean; a friend recently told me the absence of her car would mean loss of independence—this was her personal association.

Deepening Dream Understanding

The method described above will throw light on most dreams, even if one does not take time to write out fuller associations. When the insights gained in this way become useful, one may wish to increase one's skill still further. Therefore, below, and throughout the book, additional information is given on how to draw out the wisdom in dreams. A working attitude towards them is also outlined.

Although the dream process might not be a direct attempt to present meaning, a dream may nevertheless have a great deal of information in it. This becomes clearer if we remember that not many years ago it would have appeared highly superstitious or suspect to claim to be able to tell a person details of their health and parentage from a sample of their urine or blood. Today it is common practice. We accept that a growing amount of information can be gained from these unlikely sources. Blood doesn't contain meaning, but we can gain information from it. In a similar way a sample of our dreams can also tell us an enormous amount. Sometimes this data is obvious, sometimes it needs processing in order to uncover it, as with urine and blood.

The following dream needs no deep techniques of processing. (The word 'processing' is used throughout the book instead of analysis. Analysis has the connotation of giving our own thoughts or opinions to the dream: processing is used to suggest extraction of information which leads to insight.) With this particular dream, all it needs is a few facts brought to it to make clear what information it holds. The dream is that of a young woman, Mrs CL.

It is a bright sunny day. I am walking across a large concrete car park. It is empty except for a huge trailer from a truck. It has Boots written on the side, and stands high off the ground. Being 4 feet 9 inches tall myself I decide to walk underneath. As I am half way the trailer starts to be lowered on top of me. I try to shout but cannot. I get on to my hands and knees and the trailer still kept coming down. I am now lying on my stomach, convinced it is going to crush me. Then it suddenly stops a couple of inches from my head. I wake feeling terrible.

The dream is interesting, although the information it holds may at first not be obvious. But with a minimum of processing, the dream information will become clear. The first technique of processing the dream is to recognise some of the key statements within it. These are 'I am walking', 'I try to shout', 'convinced it is going to crush me'. The reason these are key statements is because the dreamer is saying '*I* am walking', '*I* try to shout', '*I* am convinced'.

This form of processing has not added anything to the dream. It has simply drawn attention to the information already there in the dreamer's description of her experience—

this is why it is useful to write the dream out fully. If we add a little more information which the dreamer herself connects with the dream, then it becomes even clearer. Mrs CL says 'I work for Boots the chemist. The employees at the shop I work in were told at the beginning of the year that Boots are selling our shop. When that happens I will be made redundant. We were supposed to finish on May 26. It is now the end of July. The deal fell through so we are now just left hanging indefinitely until a new buyer comes along. I feel very unsettled as I can't make any plans for the future.'

Having read these comments, it would be difficult not to see the dream as relating to the woman's work, and to her strong anxiety connected with it. She says—through her dream—she is 'convinced it (the situation) is going to crush' her. She also feels her strong emotions about this, expressed in her attempt to shout, are not being expressed or 'heard'. From just this one dream we can be forgiven if we assume that dreams may express in dramatic form our feelings and reactions to the circumstances of our everyday life. Taking this dream as information, Mrs CL could see she is feeling crushed by the situation, yet not stating her feelings loudly enough to be heard. She might therefore speak to the manager to clarify the situation for herself.

Here is an even shorter and less complex dream. It has been left just as it was written so its information is immediately apparent. The key words here might be 'trying to contact him' and 'not understanding why he left me'. The dream is from Mrs CJ.

Years ago I lost my first husband at 29. I had the same dream continually of being in a phonebox trying to contact him, not understanding why he had left me. He died of cancer. Later I remarried and this husband died of a heart attack. Once again the same dream came back so much.

On speculating about the dream from what is immediately apparent, we might say that, although it is irrational to try to contact her husband, nevertheless her desire to be with him continues year after year. This same part of her cannot understand why he died. We might put such feelings into words— 'But what had he done to die so young? Why should it happen to me twice?' We can also assume that her desire to understand these questions, which is what contacting her husband represents, is expressed in the dream as the telephone. The dream process has dramatised her situation and inner feelings, given them form and made them experiential. Looking at this dream helps us see how an image, such as the telephone, performs exactly the same sort of function as a spoken word, although in a different way; namely, it represents feelings and thoughts. That the woman's questions remain, that her problem is unsolved, is apparent from the fact she does not make contact on the telephone, and does not find peace. Understanding her dream shows her the importance of the questions she continually asks herself, and the need to release the emotions behind them. With this she could be free of the dream.

It is to the possibility of finding this, and even greater degrees of information, in dreams that this book is devoted. It will do so accepting that, for whatever reason, dreams do give form not only to our inner feelings but also to our habits, our intuitions, our physical processes and our variety of mental states and functions. Therefore, although the entries about dream subjects or images may describe what the theme and meaning of your dream is, it must be remembered that your dream is an expression of the way you feel at the time of the dream. Dreams do not express your fate or future, only inasmuch as you might perpetuate the attitudes or feelings the dream may express. The woman who had the 'Boots' dream is not *fated* to be crushed by her feelings about her work; but she might very well continue to feel crushed if she carries on

11

believing her whole future well-being depends on her part-time job at Boots, or continues without stating her feelings.

The World of Dreams

When we sleep and dream we enter a completely different realm of experience than when we are awake. It would be foolish to try to breathe under water in the physical world, but in dreams this is not only possible but lots of dreamers do it. In dreams we can fly. We can make love to men or women as we please, without fear of social or physical consequences. While dreaming we can die over and over. The dead can be reborn, and the world around us can be changed simply by changing our attitude. A monster pursuing us one moment can in an instant become a warm friend because we change our fear to love.

In the world of dreams our most intimate fears and longings are given an exterior life of their own in the form of the people, objects and places of our dream. Therefore our sexual drive may be shown as a person and how we relate to them; or given shape and colour as an object; or given mood as a scene. Our feeling of ambition might thus be portrayed as a business person in our dream, our changing emotions as the sea or a river; while the present relationship we have with our ambition or emotions is expressed in the events or plot of the dream.

A dream portrays a part of us, such as our ambition, as being exterior to us, because a thought or an emotion is something we experience, not something we are. By showing our urges or fears as people or places exterior to us, our dreams are able to portray the strange fact that while, for instance, the love we have for another person is intimately our own, we may find such a feeling difficult to bear, as when one is married and falls in love with someone else. While we dream, the subtleties of such dilemmas are given dramatic form. To observe our dilemma as if we were watching it as a play has very real advantages. The different factors of our situation, such as our feelings for our marriage partner, our love of the new person, and social pressures such as our family's reactions, might all be shown as different people in the dream. We can therefore not only experience these as separate from our central self, but we define in the dream's action how we relate to them. Most important, we can explore safely the possible ways of living within, or changing, the factors involved.

This exteriorisation of internal feelings is clear in the dream of the unanswered telephone, and in that of the sinking Boots trailer. Dreams might do this because they frequently portray intimate parts of ourself which have never been made fully conscious or verbalised. Put in another way, because some parts of our feelings may never have been consciously felt or recognised, they cannot be grasped by us as a thinking or perceiving being. We cannot see them with our eyes, touch them with fingers, or smell them, let alone think about them. After all, they are unknown and formless. But a dream can portray what has not yet been put into words or organised into conscious thought by portraying it in images and drama. The woman who dreams of trying to contact her dead husband may not have fully acknowledged her question: Why did he leave me?' Being able to 'think' in story form, about subtle areas of our experience is a great additional faculty when added to our other modes of gaining information and insight. In this way dreams are able to bring to our notice areas of our being which might otherwise never be known. The dream is thus another sense organ, looking into areas we might not have any other way of examining.

That the external person or object in the dream is actually the dreamer's own internal feelings and mental structure is difficult for many people to believe or even grasp. The following unusual dream helps us to develop a conception of this. I say it is unusual because very seldom can a dreamer admit to themselves while asleep that the world which in their dream appears as exterior is actually their own internal thoughts, feelings and psychobiological functions. The dreamer, AB, is a man in his 50s and dreams he has found a huge thistle in his garden which is as big as a tree.

> I look at the trunk of the thistle, examining it. At this point it seems like a giant hardwood tree. I snap a twig and it smells very nice—a perfumed wood. Other branches are going rotten. Walking around to the back of the tree to see if the bark is rotten I notice a hole where bees or wasps have a colony. I put my left hand up to touch the bark and as I do so notice there is also a hole in the back of my hand, in and out of which wasps are flying. With great shock I look in the hole and see wasps eating my flesh away, so my hand is almost hollow. I wake with the feeling of being old and decrepit.

What is of particular importance in this dream is the point of transition where the dreamer moves from seeing the hole in the tree to seeing the hole in himself. But this transition continues, for the dreamer then moves to the feeling of being old and decrepit. These points of transition mark the stages of realisation that what seems exterior is not. Some of the key statements in the dream are 'examining', 'I notice', 'a hole', 'look in' and 'see', 'the feeling of being old' and 'decrepit'. If we put this into a flowing sentence we have, 'In examining myself I notice "a hole" or emptiness in myself. When I look into this I find a sense of being old and decrepit.'

In looking at his hand and realising there was a hole in his life, AB took note of what he felt. Just prior to the dream he had experienced a lot of anxiety about whether his marriage was breaking up. The dream made him realise that niggling thoughts and emotions were eating away at his self confidence, leading him to feelings of being near to the scrap heap, having outlived his usefulness. The dream had depicted these emotions and thoughts as wasps. This enabled him to see that if he entertained such feelings, they would certainly eat away his grasp of life. He could see that as a person he only entertained thoughts and emotions. They were simply what he thought and felt about reality, not reality itself. It was up to him as to what he wanted reality to be. Did he want to entertain the reality of the tired aging man who could no longer satisfy his wife's need for love and companionship, having nothing worthwhile to contribute to others? That could certainly become reality if he allowed such feelings to dominate him. He had thought that his life was like a giant thistle, but on closer inspection he saw it was a giant hardwood. It did have branches which needed pruning, but the rest of the tree was good and perfumed, giving of good feelings to others. So he decided to put love and care into his life and marriage instead of self doubt and a sense of defeat.

When we realise each aspect of the dream, each emotion, each landscape and environment are materialisations of our own feeling states, we begin to see how we live in the midst of a world—the world of our thoughts, feelings, values, judgments, fears—largely of our own making. Whatever we think or feel, even in the depths of our being, becomes a material fact of experience in our dream. It is almost certainly this inner universe that religion speaks of as heaven or hell. Finding some degree of direction, mastery or harmony within this world of our own being is the great work of human life.

A

abandoned A sense of how others, particularly our parents, felt about us while we were a child. This feeling of not being wanted may have become habitual. It may not be true that we are not wanted, but our feelings are saying it is. Example: 'My mother asked me to go and buy some butter for her. A chain on my left leg prevented me from going very far. I look down the road and see my mum, dad and my four brothers in the back of a car. I wave and call and they drive right past me, going over the chain I am wearing on my leg' (Lorraine). Lorraine's dream illustrates not only her feelings of being left out of family life, but also the chain on her leg shows her not fully independent. We often feel 'abandoned' while we are trying to become more independent. Being abandoned in the sense of <u>allowing sexual and emotional liberty</u>: finding a new freedom; dropping usual social codes and unashamedly expressing ourselves. <u>Also</u>: it can be an example of one of the functions of dreams, which is to release held back sexuality and emotion. See **alone; functions of dreaming; hero**.

abnormal Even if parts of one's body or face are shown in a dream to be distorted or abnormal, such a dream is not usually referring to the physical body. Our own idea or image of what sort of person we are is translated in dreams into our body form. We might dream our face looks subnormal mentally, or our body has strange areas. This refers to an internal sense of ourself not having developed to our full potential, or of psychological hurts having distorted some aspect of ourself, such as our ability to reach out for help. See **body**.

17

aboriginal   The part of self which still has contact with the natural life processes within, and feels unified with, the rest of nature and the cosmos. See **African; black person; natives**.

abortion   Suggests one has aborted an idea, a direction, or an area of one's feelings such as might surround a love affair. If <u>dream connects with actual abortion</u>: the emotions surrounding a woman's actual experience of abortion; sense of guilt; the fears of damage to future possibility of childbearing; the feelings about loss of the baby. All these need to be healed in some measure. <u>Also</u>: the body was in the midst of a process if the abortion was induced. The body has powerful feeling reactions which need acknowledgment, and are frequently presented in dreams.

above   See **positions**.

abreaction   Example: 'For some considerable time I have been troubled by a nightmarish dream which is so realistic sometimes I think I am going to die. In my dream I have swallowed something which is literally choking me or is going to poison me. I wake up and rush down the stairs to the kitchen, spitting and choking, holding my throat and making all sorts of disturbing noises which frighten my wife. I have had this dream as many as five or six times a night. My doctor says it could be to do with the last war. I was a child then and my dad constantly had to wake me up to take us down to the shelter, sometimes as many as four times a night, and we were bombed out twice. I cannot recall having any fears about this at the time' (Mr KT).

Abreaction is a re-experiencing of painful or traumatic events or situations. In many dreams it is obvious that the process underlying dreams is attempting to trigger an abreaction. This suggests the dream process, as Jung and Hadfield say, is a self-regulatory one in our psyche. In many cases where a person explores the feeling content of their dreams in a confident way, abreaction occurs. Although it has been given different names in recent years, such as primal therapy, rolfing, discharge, catharsis, abreaction is still a basic psychological healing process. Parts of our experience become repressed because there is an automatic reaction in us to avoid pain. Therefore painful experience may never be fully felt or understood at the time. Reliving them allows us to review and integrate vital information about ourselves. Frequently all the analysis in the world cannot relieve a neurotic pattern until the repressed emotion holding it in place is released and understood.

The strength with which we hold out against allowing our being to abreact spontaneously is seen in the above example. Mr KT is brought to the brink of reliving his very stressful childhood again and again. Yet he manages to avoid actual memory and, in particular, the experiencing of any childhood emotions and fears. The opposite is shown in this account by Clive, who explored with me a dream about being shot in the arm in his father's shop. 'For several hours I could find nothing about the dream. My mind simply wandered. But with help I persisted. Suddenly I seemed to break through, first to seeing how the shop was a place in which I have unconsciously experienced great emotional pain. My father was always criticising. Never a word of encouragement. Then I burst into powerful sobbing as I felt the pain of wanting my father to love me, instead of criticising all the time, and help me grow into somebody capable of meeting life. And then, something I just had not wanted to see, the 30 years of my life I had wasted by avoiding any contact with authority. My father was the original authority in my life. I had cut off from him because of the lack of support, and I had done the same with school and other authority situations. But what a relief to understand myself, and to meet that young vulnerable boy I used to be. How I loved him and understood him/myself.'

abroad   General: your feelings about that country. If <u>you have lived in that country</u>: overall experience of that place. Were you happy there, lonely? What characteristics of the people did you take in?

absorb   Dreams often represent learning as an organic process. Ideas are taken in, digested, then form part of an organic whole in an integrated system. Seeing something absorbed in a dream may represent the taking in of ideas, or even poisonous feelings, depending upon what the dream images are.

abyss   <u>If feared</u>: fear of losing control, failure; loss of identity; death. <u>Without fear</u>: going beyond the boundaries of one's own limitations, concepts, present experience. Literally it is an entrance into enormous potential, the as yet unformed. The ability to do this gives tremendous liberation to the dreamer, freeing them from restricting rigid concepts or habits of thinking, responding and relating. See **falling**.

accident   Example: 'I was standing in a hospital corridor looking through a glass partition. I could see a man having what I thought was a heart attack. Nurses and doctors came rushing to him and he was vomiting blood. I was on holiday in Canada at the time, staying in a hotel. I thought this dream was a bad omen and wouldn't leave my bedroom for ages. But this was five years ago' (Mrs F). The woman in the example was having her heart (feelings) massively attacked by anxiety, so much so she is laid low (unable to go out of the room and lead a normal life). Many people have strong feelings of anxiety about any dream which shows them having an accident or being injured. If we could have a record of every dream each person had, we would see that everyone dreams of being injured, murdered, killed, again and again. Because these are common themes, some dreams are going to coincide with an actual accident or plane crash. Many dreams in the files are attempts on the part of the dreamer to link the dream with a later event. But such dreams are about psychological injury or anxiety. General: anxiety; self punishment or introverted aggression. An accident to someone else: could be hidden aggression. Idioms : accidentally on purpose; chapter of accidents.

acid Something burning away at our feelings or confidence; our own vitriolic attack on someone else. Idioms: acid tongue; the acid test.

acorn Considering that our being has emerged from the tiny combination of sperm and ovum, a huge growth has emerged from a tiny beginning. This potential is frequently represented by the acorn or a seed. Even when adult, there is still enormous potential.

active imagination Carl Jung several times described a technique for using imagination which allowed the spontaneous expression of the unconscious. Jung described active imagination as a putting aside of conscious criticism while we allow our irrational to play or fantasise. In relationship to a dream, this technique can be extraordinarily helpful and revealing. A way to learn the technique is to take a dream in which a fairly defined person appears. It can be a child or adult. One then sits in a quiet situation alone, or with a sympathetic listener, and imagines or feels oneself back in the dream. One does not need to develop clear images unless these come easily. Just holding the idea of the dream is often sufficient. Then in a playful way develop a conversation with the dream person. Ask them what they are doing; why they appear in your dream; what do they represent of yourself? With a little practice the dream characters can come to life for you if you can let yourself play or free-wheel a little.

As we learn active imagination, it can give us other ways of entering into the life of our dreams. We can imagine ourself as the dream character, or even as the objects or animals, and allow ourself to experience and speak from their viewpoint. We can enter the dream and carry it forward from where it stopped, imagining what would satisfy us, thus becoming more active in dealing with our own inner and outer life. See **dream processing**.

active/passive   Example: 'I was in a house that I lived in many years ago. How I got there I do not know, but I saw myself sitting in an ordinary chair just behind the closed front street door. It was very quiet, and I was afraid, but I did not make any effort to move' (Mrs J).

When we are an inactive observer in our dream, are all the time on the receiving end of dream action, or as in the example make no effort to move from discomfort, we are in a passive role. If this occurs frequently in our dreams, we are probably passive in our waking life. This can gradually be changed by such techniques as active imagination. It is our own emotions, fears and sexuality we are meeting in our dreams, so it is wise to take charge of our being rather than be a victim. The following dream illustrates an active dreamer: 'As I walked toward a house a number of demons or devils came at me menacingly, trying to stop me getting near the house. Although they made all the ghostly noises, I wasn't at all afraid of them. I felt they were a damned nuisance, and to show them I meant business I grabbed one and with my right hand I gripped its flesh and squeezed. It started to squeak in pain and I squeezed harder' (Clive J).

active sleep   During experiments to monitor the brain activity of animals and humans while asleep, it was noted that the brain seemed to move through a series of levels of activity. In deep sleep there are slow rhythmic brainwaves. These at times would give way to faster rhythms of a more dynamic nature. This was at first called 'desynchronised' sleep because during it the muscular system relaxed deeply, even though the brain was active. It was also known as paradoxical sleep, but more recently has become internationally known as 'active sleep'. During active sleep the rapid eye movements (REM) characteristic of dreaming occur. The brain's activity was found to be a better indicator of dreaming in animals than REM because some creatures, such as owls, do not move their eyes. In this way, all mammals were seen to exhibit active sleep or dreaming. Birds also dream, and, measured in this way, so do many types of fish, reptiles and some amphibians. See **science, sleep and dreams**.

actor and actress   See **roles**.

adder   See **reptiles**.

addicted   Anxiety that something or someone is getting a hold on us. Sometimes fear of something is the power which actually dominates us, not the thing itself. Each of us have areas dominated by such fears or feelings, and the dream action will point to what they are.

address   Oneself; way one lives; one's present style of life. To forget or lose your address: to lose sight of your goals or standards in life. Past address: the person you were, the traits you developed, what you faced in life at that time. Another person's address: contact with that person.

Adler, Alfred (1870–1937)   Born in Vienna, Austria. Studied medicine, later became a disciple of Freud. Diverged from Freud over the sexual impulse being all important in human behaviour. Adler saw people as goal oriented, with an urge toward personal growth and wholeness. He stated that in dreams we can clearly see our aggressive impulses and desire for fulfilment. Dreams can also help the dreamer define two often conflicting aspects of their experience—their image or sense of themselves, and their sense of what is socially acceptable. Because we strive from our earliest years to have some control over ourself and surroundings, we may develop a style of life around a sense of inferiority or lack of power. So a person who feels vulnerable may become aggressive to compensate. Adler therefore felt that in our dreams we not only see what we think of ourself, and what our environmental situation is, but also find a definition of our techniques for satisfying our drive to deal with and succeed in the world.

adolescent Example: 'My lover and I were going to try and make love, both with our own hurts and being aware of each other's difficulties. We were both very gentle with each other. A young girl came in under the bedclothes with us. I thought it would interfere, but I could see it wasn't worrying her. She was playing hide and seek. We were in bed out in the open countryside' (Hilary). Whether the young person is your own child, someone you know, or a stranger, it is usually an expression of oneself at that age. The dream above shows Hilary taking her teenage feelings into her lovemaking. This is because Hilary had no chance during those years to mature sexually, so, as an older woman, she now finds herself meeting a young girl's feelings with her lover.

If dreamt by a child, the adolescent depicts their feelings or assessment of their own future, or ways of meeting future relationships. See **boy**; **girl**; **woman**; **man**.

adoration See **worship**.

adultery See **affair**.

adventure of the dreamworld Dreams give us a doorway into a strange and wonderful world. Although it appears to have many of the features of our waking world, such as people, animals, objects and places, it is nevertheless full of subtle surprises and differences. To enter this world while asleep leaves us largely unaware of its possibilities. To take waking awareness into our entrance, as happens when we explore a dream through dream processing, unfolds the magic impact of what we meet.

When we open the door of dreams in this way we begin a journey. It has stages, problems to surmount and things to learn, just like any journey. Many people have already travelled before us, and there are books such as *Alice in Wonderland, The Odyssey, Exploring Inner Space,* and *Altered States of Consciousness* which describe journeys and the terrain.

Although we might meet the heights of religious experience as well as the depths of human despair on the journey, in simple terms it is primarily a journey into a confrontation with our own potential, our own fear, our own prison bars of thought and habit, our own ability to lift perception beyond what we have known before and look at the world, and our life in it, from new perspectives. It is a journey towards greater maturity in which we face the humbling vision of our own littleness; the moving encounter with the vulnerable child we once were; the cleaning out of the store cupboards of resentment, hurt and anger; the DIY of conscious renewal of our identity; and the meeting with Love as we experience ourself as a living participator in the wonder of life. We look at birth, we meet death, we gaze into the vast depths of space out of which our being has arisen. Then we find ourselves seeing the faces of the other human beings we live with, and recognising we are all on the journey, and we only have each other. Realising we are all waves on a shoreless sea—from no port we move to no destination—we understand our self responsibility, and consider what we will to do with the momentum of our life.

advertisement   A desire to have others know something about yourself; a way of bringing something to your attention.

advice   Conscience; sense of 'ought' or 'should'; what you desire to say but haven't. See **voice; talking**.

aesculapius   The Roman form of the Greek god of healing, Asclepius. See **Asclepius**.

affair   Example: 'I was on board a pleasure cruiser with my wife. As I stood on a high deck I looked down and saw her sitting below with very tight knickers on and nothing else. As a man walked towards her the knickers came off or slipped down. The man was sexually aroused and started attempting to penetrate her. She only put up a token resistance, mewing a bit, but not fighting him off. I rushed towards them and kicked him off' (Andrew P). In this dream Andrew's fear of his wife's desire for another man is being expressed, but the dream really depicts Andrew's feelings of sexual inadequacy. Adultery dreams may also express release of sexual feelings; desire for another partner; desire for one's partner to have sex with someone else. See **sex in dreams**; last example in **dark**.

African   This may refer to one's own feelings about coloured people or racial prejudices; Africa may have been the birthplace for the human race. In dreams we still use primitive Africans or Australian aborigines to represent our own natural inner life. See **aboriginal**; **black people**; **native**.

aggression   See **hostility**.

aim   Suggests directing attention or desire towards what is represented by target or goal. Gun being aimed: directing anger, sexuality or attention.

air   See **wind**.

airplane   Example: 'I saw a biplane fly overhead. Its pilot was performing daring new stunts. I ran into a house to tell a man who was in bed to run out and see the plane' (David R). The example clearly shows one aspect of what a plane means, being daring in a new area, taking risks in life, braving a new work area or relationship. Sometimes the plane in the sky represents us feeling threatened by something new or unknown; thus one dreamer dreamt of <u>bombs being dropped from a plane</u> when she was offered a new job which would take her into the public eye. The <u>crashed plane</u>: can be anxiety bringing down our ambition or adventurousness; a loss of self confidence or mental equilibrium. The <u>plane journey</u>: shows a move towards independence; leaving home or friends; success. Being <u>grounded</u>: sense of not getting anywhere and frustration. An <u>attacking aircraft</u>: feeling attacked either by our own doubts and self criticism, or that of others.

airport   Making new departures; changes; being en route to something new in life; a checking of one's own values, identity, a sort of self assessment in regard to independence and moving to new opportunities. Self doubts and uncertainties at this stage stop us from attempting the new.

air raid   Example: 'I am in a house and planes are dropping bombs on it' (Mrs SM). We feel under attack, the severity depending on the dream damage. The attack might be emotional, from people, or feelings we have about events around us. Things may be going badly at work, and comments be felt like bombshells. Very often, though, the threats are purely mental. We may read of an illness such as AIDS and the anxiety we connect with the idea has a devastating effect. <u>Idioms</u>: I feel blitzed. See **airplane; war**.

alcohol   An influence which changes the way we feel, moving us towards negative or positive feelings; prelude to friendliness or intimacy; an allowing into our life of another influence we do not immediately feel is our own conscious will; in a religious sense the wine represents a life-changing influence.

alien   Urges or feelings we find difficult to identify with; feelings of being an outsider in a group or society; can also be something very new and previously not experienced in regard to one's own potential or mind.

alligator   See **animals**.

alone   Expresses one's sense of isolation; feelings of loneliness; independence, depending on dream feelings. Idioms: go it alone. See **abandoned**.

altar   Self giving—this can be a very positive action, or a sort of self punishment out of guilt; place of death, but also of rebirth. See **archetypes**.

ambulance   See **accident**.

America   See **abroad**.

American Indian   Natural wisdom. See: **Iroquoian dream cult**.

amnesia   Example: 'I am sleeping rough in a garden with a woman I do not love. I think I should try to make the best of the situation, but my feelings against it are too strong. Then I decide I don't ever want to live like that again and tear up the mattress we slept on. As I do this I realise, as if waking from amnesia, that Pat lives just across the road. She has specially moved there because of our love. I realise with horror I had forgotten and may have lost her' (David H). The dream says only too clearly how we often forget things that are so important to us, and fall into old habits. The woman David was sleeping with was someone from his past he was unhappy with.

amplification method   An approach suggested by Carl Jung. In essence it is to honour what the dream states. In the dream quoted above under **amnesia**, David is sleeping on a mattress, but it could have been a bed or a hammock, or even a sleeping bag. So why a mattress and why in the garden, and why not alone? Having noted the specifics of our dream, we then amplify what we know about them. We ask ourself such questions as 'What does sleeping on a mattress on the floor mean? Have I ever done it? When? Why? Where? In what circumstances? Does it represent some condition?' In other words we bring out as much information as we can about each dream specific; this includes memories, associated ideas, anything relevant. In the case of David, he was sleeping on a mattress on the floor in his present relationship. But he had slipped back into attitudes which damaged this old relationship. P.W. Martin emphasises it is **amplification** not free association which is sought. Free association may lead to an interesting 'interpretation' which may not be connected to the dream specifics. See **dream processing; postures, movement and body language; word analysis of dreams; settings**.

amputation   To lose whatever the limb represents; loss of adequacy, sexual or otherwise. See **body**.

anaesthetic   Death; avoiding painful emotions; entering the unconscious; feeling overpowered.

analysis, dream   See **dream processing**.

analyst   An analyst, psychologist, psychiatrist in our dream depicts our self assessment. Our mind can transform itself in a number of ways. Sometimes one new piece of information, or a new mental discipline, can change the quality of all mental life. The analyst represents such power to transform, as well as the often avoided self awareness.

angel   The positive side of relationship with your mother; religious concepts; sometimes feelings about death; a need for a parent figure to guide or instruct in decision making. <u>Idioms</u>: guardian angel; like an angel; on the side of the angels; fools rush in where angels fear to tread. See **religion and dreams**.

anger   See **hostility**.

animals   Like any other animal, human beings have developed certain physical and behavioural traits. Some of these traits, such as a newborn baby attempting to suckle the breast, are rooted in millions of years of past experience and can be thought of as instinctive. We can observe such traits in a dog in such behaviour as cocking of the leg in male dogs. We can see some of our own traits in such things as the human desire to elect leaders. Many of these habits are physiological or social. In our dreams we represent these drives or habits in the form of various animals. Our restrained sex drive or aggression may be shown in our dream as a dog on a lead. The power of drives such as the urge to parenthood via sex might be shown as a horse which we are trying to control. More than anything else, though, our dream animal represents our powerful reactions to situations, reactions developed through centuries of human experience in frequently terrible situations. This aspect of ourself is rooted in the older portions of the brain.

The animal in our dreams has commonly been seen only as the sex drive. A careful examination of animal dreams, though, shows this to be untrue. The animal represents *all* our biological needs and responses, which include survival and hunger; reproduction; parental urges; need for exercise and rest; social drives; fear reactions; anger; urge to provide (for young and mate); home/nest building; territory protection; social hierarchy, etc. If these aspects in an individual are damaged or traumatised, we see parents who have lost their natural bonding and caring for their child; individuals who have no sense of social status or responsibility, enabling them to be criminally violent; disturbed and misplaced sexuality. Dominating or attempting to kill out the animal in us can cause tension, depression and illness. The common escape into dry intellectualism is a cause of internal conflict. Complete permissiveness is no answer either; our higher brain functions need expression too. So one of the challenges of maturing is how to meet and relate to our 'animals', and perhaps bring them into expression in a satisfying way. Such drives are fundamentally a push towards life.

It must be remembered that where sex or sexuality is mentioned, I am not simply referring to the sex act. I mean sexuality in its overall aspect, which includes the urge towards parenthood, and the love and caring connected with it. (Brain damage or certain drugs or chemicals can diminish the 'human' levels of function and only the animal and lizard levels are expressed.) Below are listed some common ways animals are used in our dreams.

animal situations   Example: 'I am given an animal to look after (usually somebody's pet) while they are away on holiday. I then completely forget the animal, go away and when I return the animal is either dead or very dried up or has been got at by another animal and is in the throes of dying. When I wake from the dream I feel most dreadful and it is only when I am fully awake and realise it is not true do I feel better' (Lynda E). Neglect , mutilation or killing our 'animal' is a common theme. Lynda's feelings show how she senses what she is doing to her inner nature, but she dismisses this by convincing herself such feelings are not 'true'. We have a responsibility to care for our animal drives, to see our sexual, nutritional and body needs are met. Eating the animal: integrating our natural wisdom and energy. Hiding from or trapped by an animal: see *wolf* in this entry. Animal with its young: parental feelings; one's basic childhood needs. Baby

31

animal: oneself when young; baby feelings; desire for babies; see example in **eating**. Talking, shining , holy or wise animals: important intuitive information; a meeting with the gathered wisdom we have unconsciously. This is one of the sources of religious inspiration, and many older cultures represent their origin of great learning or holiness as animals or animal headed beings. See *ape* in this entry; **birds**; **pets**; **reptiles, lizards and snakes**; **unconscious**.

ape Can represent a world of experience human beings have lost and feel sorrow at its absence. In developing self consciousness, with its labyrinth of ideas and decisions, humans lost a sense of oneness with life around them. Animals have enormous *remembered* wisdom; remembered through instincts and complex social codes. This wisdom is still accessible to humans who can listen to the unconscious, and discover the enormous wealth of information they have about such things as social behaviour and body language. The ape can depict this wisdom, especially if it is white haired. Or it might show the personal folly of trying to let instincts dominate us now we have self awareness. Idioms: he is just aping.

ass The basic life processes in the body, which uphold or carry us through the years; the plodding long suffering body.

bear Power of our feeling reaction and traits; possessiveness, as or by a parent or lover; the 'animal' side of our relationship with our parent(s).

bull With Taureans, may depict their innate characteristics and how they are dealing with them. Sex drive; the basic drives towards parenthood, and caring and providing via sex. The aggressive bull often shows the frustration arising from these basic drives being taunted or thwarted; for instance a person may wish for a family, yet be frustrated by a form of sexuality in their partner which does not care for the instinctive drive for children. The killed bull is a killing of these drives; if sacrificed, though, it may show self-giving. The rid-den bull in dreams shows a harmony between self awareness and its decision making, and the basic 'animal' drives. Idioms: like a bull at a gate; bull in a china shop; red rag to a bull; score a bull's eye; take the bull by the horns.

cat Example: 'I went to the fridge to get out some mince meat to feed the cat. It came in, and as it fed I had a strong urge to touch it, such strong feelings of love were pouring out of me. The animal looked up at my face as I wanted to kiss it. The lips had pink lipstick on. I kissed it, its paw came up around my arm, I could see the black claws. We were rolling around on the floor, it felt very sexual' (Monica). Refined female sexuality, unless the cat is markedly a tom; can be our intuition, warning us through its sensitivity to moods or unseen dangers. Idioms: copy cat; bell the cat; cat and mouse; cat's whiskers; cat out of the bag; cat and dog life; cat on hot bricks; something the cat brought in; a cat's paw; cat among the pigeons; while the cat's away. See example in **kiss**.

cow Similar to the bull, but representing the female side of one's nature, especially the easy self-giving of oneself and body to others, or a baby; one's mother or the mother role. Idioms: sacred cow; milch cow; till the cows come home.

dinosaur Exploring dreams is like uncovering different strata of human psychological history, history we all share. The dinosaur represents our very basic urges of life such as fear, reproduction and survival; this does not make these 'brutal'—they are fundamental and necessary in today's life. Because these aspects of ourself are so old, and have survived so long, there is often great wisdom in them to be made conscious.

dog Easy expression of such aspects of ourself as aggression —maybe because dogs show their teeth easily—sexuality, friendship; our easy flowing natural feelings; devotion, perhaps to a lover or child. For some people a dog was the only source of expressive love in their childhood, so may well depict this. <u>Dog on lead</u>: restrained or controlled urges. The dog appears more often than other animals in dreams.

Example: 'I continue on my path, and suddenly the nettles disappear and the path is clear. Ahead the wall has curved round to face me, but there is a gate in it, and I can see my dog waiting for me on the other side' (Mrs MG). In the dream of this elderly woman the dog is leading the way through the experience of meeting death. Mythology has often shown the dog in this light, as an inner sense of knowing how to find transformation through death—or as the ravaging threat of death. <u>Idioms</u>: die like a dog; dirty dog; dog eared; dog eat dog; dog in the manger; gay dog; go to the dogs; let sleeping dogs lie; etc.

elephant The enormous potential power of life, in growth and activity. If we run from the elephant we are afraid of our own strength or inner drive. <u>Idioms</u>: white elephant; pink elephants; rogue elephant. See *the self* under **archetypes**.

frog The deeply unconscious psychobiological life processes which transformed us from a tadpole/sperm into an air-breathing frog/adult. The enormous information such symbols hold if we explore them gives them their power.

goat A Capricornian's basic traits. Rutting sexuality; ability to climb socially. Sometimes connected with repressed natural drives which become reversed or evil/live.

hare Intuition; creative ideas; the crazy irrational notions we sometimes call intuition. The hare occasionally appears as a supernatural figure giving advice; or as a sacrificial animal. As such it depicts our ability to make great changes in life.

horse General: pleasurable energy and exuberance; dynamic sexual drive. Example: 'As I talked to the pale golden horse it felt more and more as if I were talking to a male companion who was in union with me' (Alison B). Alison's horse is obviously portraying her feelings for a man. The dream shows how easy and integrated she is with these. Controlling the horse or fear of it: fear of feelings of love and sexuality. If the horse dragged the dreamer along: impetuosity of such feelings; feeling dragged along by natural urges. Running away from a horse or horsemen: fear of sexuality, which includes responsibility for parenthood and relationship; fear of life drive. The winged horse: shows how our life or drive is not limited to sexuality or survival, but can lift into wider activities—a woman turning her love of her children into social caring. A horse race: one's life; everyday competition and where you rate yourself in it. A sick or dying horse: loss of health, energy, enthusiasm. Black horse: unaccepted passions. White horse: changing sexual drive into love and wider awareness; a meeting with our feelings about death. The mare: femininity, receptiveness, fertility. The stallion: masculinity, power and virility. Idioms: back the wrong horse; from the horse's mouth; horse sense; you can take a horse to water; wild horses. See **dream as spiritual guide**.

lamb The childlike, dependent, vulnerable part of self; innocence; Christ.

lion The power of our physical strength, of our temper, of our emotions or sexuality; love that has become anger through jealousy or pain. The story of Androcles and the lion shows how the pain felt by our 'animal' life process, if tended by the conscious personality, brings a loving relationship between conscious and unconscious. Idioms: brave the lion's den; lion's share; head in the lion's mouth.

monkey Foolishness; thoughtlessness; being ruled by impulse. But sometimes same as *ape* (see above in this entry). Idioms: make a monkey of; monkey business; monkey with; monkey tricks.

mouse Minor irritations; fears and worries; the mousy or timid part of self; the activities within us—our house—which go on unconsciously, which might be important though small, or gnaw away at one; the sexual organ, which goes in and out of a hole.

pig Physical appetites; life directed only by physical needs; sensuality. The sow represents giving of oneself and sustenance; lack of spiritual directive. <u>Idioms</u>: pig in a poke; happy as a pig in shit; make a pig of oneself; pig in the middle; pigs might fly; pig headed.

rabbit Sexuality, due to human associations with its rapid breeding; softness and non-aggression, sometimes to the point of depicting a victim or foolish passivity—may thus represent unworldly idealism. Perhaps because of its tendency to be the victim of predators, is often used as a sacrifice in dreams, which suggests the hurt we might experience to the soft, vulnerable parts of our nature as we experience the pain of meeting reality in the maturing process. <u>Rabbit hole</u>: Alice down the rabbit hole illustrates this—a going within self; into the unconscious; the womb.

rat What the dreamer senses as sick or negative inside self; physical sickness or anxieties about health; feelings of sexual repulsion, or using sex to gain material aims; intuitions about a person being a 'rat', doing things behind one's back or underhandedly, or deserting a relationship when difficulties arise; seeing the underhanded side of oneself. Also time gnawing away at our life. <u>Idioms</u>: rat on someone; rat race; smell a rat; feeling ratty.

sheep Sheep depict the way we might be led into situations, sometimes awful, by conforming to prevailing attitudes and social pressures. Example: 'I walked past a married couple who were walking up the hill too. As I passed I heard them say something about a shepherd. Looking up the hill I saw the sheep, then The Shepherd. A beautiful aura of many colours surrounded The Shepherd. I looked and felt joy and exuberance rise in me, and I ran to the couple saying it was The Shepherd' (Brian C). In the example Brian is not only aware of the sheep, but also The Shepherd. The sheep is his sense of being one of the crowd and The Shepherd is his sense of his own unique potential or love transforming his ordinariness.

wolf Although the wolf can depict our sense that 'things' are out to get us, the wolf is often just fear. Fear is one of our instinctive reactions to situations, so is depicted by an animal. We may find ourselves a prisoner of such feelings, as Anna in the following example: 'I was in a caravan in the middle of a field and in this field was a large black wolf. Every time I tried to run from the caravan to the edge of the field, the wolf chased me back, so I was a prisoner in the caravan. It all sounds so simple now, but at the time I was truly terrified.'

This next example from Oliver, a boy of six, illustrates how such fears can be met with a little courage. It is a dream which recurred several times, so his description is of a series of dreams: 'I am in my bed in my own room and I hear what I know to be a wolf wearing the sort of clogs worn in Lancashire. He (the wolf) gets to a certain point, there is a bang, and I wake terrified. My mother's reassurances do not help. Each night he gets a bit nearer before my panicky awakening. The night comes when I know he will reach me. Sure enough he arrives, and the bedroom door—in my dream—is flung wide open with a tremendous bang. There is no one there. I never dreamt it again.' Idioms: wolf at the door; wolf in sheep's clothing; cry wolf; throw to the wolves.

antique See **old**.

anxiety dreams One of the most frequent dream themes is that of anxiety in some form. This may not be because most dreams are about things we fear, but simply because we remember those dreams more than a bland dream. In our dreams the things we fear *are only our own feelings*. Of course, the dream may be about a snake, or car accident—things we fear which are not inside us. Even so, it is our feeling about the snake or situation which disturbs us, and these can change, even though the snake remains just what it is. If we cannot meet our feelings of fear or emotional pain we are controlled or trapped by them. Sometimes we need the help of a professional therapist to meet what we fear, but many fears can be met by using simple techniques. See *wolf* under **animal; dream processing; premenstrual tension.**

apparitions   See **ghost.**

applause   Desire for acclaim or giving oneself acclaim.

appointment   Reminder of something our unconscious feels we are about to meet, or something we ought to meet.

archetypes   Although the word archetype has a long history, Carl Jung used it to express something he observed in human dreams. He said the archetypes are a tendency or instinctive trend in the human unconscious to represent certain motifs or themes. As our instinctive urge to reproduce may show itself in consciousness as sexual fantasies, so archetypes show themselves as certain dream, fantasy, or story themes. Just as each individual animal does not create its own instincts, we do not create our own collective thought pattern. The influence these archetypes have upon our conscious self is varied. Partly they are supportive, as instincts are to an animal.

Some ancient cultures erected a pantheon of gods and goddesses. Many of these gods were expressions of archetypal themes, such as death, rebirth and womanhood. A sheepdog has in itself, unconsciously, a propensity to herd animals under direction. Through the worship of gods, perhaps ancient people touched similar reservoirs of strength and healing. Without such, the individual might find it more difficult to face the fact that death waits at the end of their life, or to allow sexuality to emerge into their life at puberty. The dream of a girl suffering from anorexia shows her cutting off her own breasts with scissors. Here her developing sexual traits and urges are unacceptable to her. Perhaps she 'cuts them off' by not eating, thus preventing her body and psyche from maturing. In the past it would have been recommended that she give offerings to a goddess, thus aligning her with an unconscious power to adapt and mature.

Some of these archetypal patterns of behaviour, such as territorialism and group identity, are only too obviously behind much that occurs in war, and their influence needs to be brought more fully into awareness. But we must be careful in accepting Jung's description of the archetypes. In more recent years, through the tremendously amplified access to the unconscious made possible in psychiatry through such drugs as LSD, a lot more information about unconscious imagery has been made available. It is possible that certain synthesising aspects of the mind produce images to represent huge areas of collected experience, i.e. the Mystic Mother or Madonna representing our collected experience of our mother.

Whatever may be the explanation of these archetypal themes, they are important because they illustrate how we as individuals, and as human beings collectively, have been able to develop our sense of conscious identity amidst enormous forces of unconsciousness, collectivity and external stresses. Below are some common archetypal symbols and their associated images.

anima   The female within the male, shown as a woman in a man's dream. Physically a man is predominantly male, but also has nipples and produces some female hormones. Psychologically, we may only express part of our potential in everyday life. In a man, the more feeling and caring side may be given little expression. Apart from this, some functions, such as intuition and unconscious creativity, may also be held in latency. These secondary or latent characteristics are depicted by the female in male dreams. In general we can say the woman represents the man's emotions, his nurturing and caring quality. It also holds in it an expression of his complex of feelings about women, gained as experience mostly from his mother—or lack of mother—but also from a synthesis of all his female contacts. So the whole realm of his experience of the female can be represented by the woman in his dream, and is accessible through the image.

<u>Good relationship with</u> or <u>marrying the woman</u>: shows the man integrating his own real emotions, sensitivity and intuition. This makes him more whole, balancing his exterior male qualities. It also shows the man meeting his experience of his mother in a healing way. This enables the man to have a realistic relationship with an actual woman. It also brings a sense of connectedness between his conscious self and what he senses as Life or, as Buckminster Fuller calls it, Universe. See *Great Mother* in this entry.

To be <u>in conflict with the woman</u>, or <u>unable to make real physical and pleasurable contact with her</u>: suggests difficulty in meeting what may have been a painful or threatening experience of mother. This can lead to becoming an intellectual but emotionally barren man. Or being possessed in a negative way by the female traits, becoming emotionally unstable, opinionated and illogical. Actual relations with women will be difficult. Actual emotional or intimate merging with a woman is threatening because it brings the man close to the pain or fear connected with mother. Sex may be possible but not close feeling union. See **woman**.

animus The male within the female, shown as a man in a woman's dreams. Physically a woman is predominantly female, but also has a clitoris and produces some male hormones. Psychologically, we may only express part of our potential in everyday life. In a woman, the more physically dynamic, intellectual and socially challenging side of herself may be given less expression. Apart from this, some features, such as innovation and creative rational thought, may be held in latency. These secondary or latent characteristics are depicted by the male in female dreams. In general we can say the man represents the woman's mental and social power, her ability to act creatively in 'the world'. It also holds in it an expression of her complex of feelings about men, gained as experience mostly from her relationship with—or lack of—father, but also from a synthesis of all her male contacts. So the whole realm of her experience of the male can be represented by the man in her dream, and is accessible through the image.

Good relationship with or marrying the man: shows the woman integrating her own ability to be independent and capable in outwardly active terms. This makes her more whole, balancing her 'female' qualities. It also shows the woman meeting her experience of her father in a healing way. This enables the woman to have a realistic relationship with an actual man. It also brings a sense of connectedness between her conscious self and what she senses as the 'commercial' world. See *father* in this entry.

To be in conflict with the man, or unable to make real physical and pleasurable contact with him: suggests difficulty in meeting what may have been a painful or threatening experience of father. This can lead to lack of ability to make clear judgments, and lack of decisiveness in areas outside feeling values. She is prone to acceptance of collective or long held social norms without question; family or national attitudes not applicable to present situations; and 'reasoning' which actually arises out of emotions connected to such family or social norms. Actual relations with men will be difficult, or entered into simply as a duty. Emotional or intimate merging with a man is threatening because it brings the woman close to the conflicts and pain connected with father. Sex may be possible but not a close feeling union. See **man**.

Christ Although people generally think of Christ as a historical figure, in dreams Christ is not this at all. He is a powerful process in the human unconscious. In the west we give this process the name of Christ, but the process or archetype is universal and has various names in different cultures. Sometimes represented in dreams as a fish or a big man, in general the Christ is an expression of the dreamer's own potential— what they can become in their life. But it also depicts what might be called a sense of the forces of symbiosis or co-operative activity operative in human life and the cosmos. There are at least four aspects to Christ as depicted in dreams.

The Sunday school or Church Christ: depicts social norms, the generally accepted morals and social rules. This 'Christ' comes about because the Church tends to represent traditional values, and also the attempt to press people to live these values. The dreamer may have a childlike relationship with this Christ or, if attempting to be self responsible, be in conflict with it. Some people find this Christ has a castrating role in their life, and flee in horror. In fact this aspect of social indoctrination may lead to such a burden of guilt and suppression that it can create psychic cripples. Trying to do all the 'right' things may lead us to the point where 'we can't say no to a glass of water without a pang of guilt'. Two of the great forces which push at the human soul or psyche are social pressure, such as the moral norm, and biological pressures, such as the sex drive; individuals may fight a lifelong battle with one or the other of these. The social criminal typifies battle with the first; the ascetic, battle with the second.

The ideal Christ: the psychological process which causes us not to take responsibility for our own highest ideals; our own yearnings for the good; our own most powerful urges arising against what we see as evils in the world. This influences us to wait for a sign from Christ in our dream in order to gain authority, or to overcome the anxiety associated with the drive. We want God to say we should act in a certain way because we are not willing to be self responsible. Example: 'I stood outside a castle. It was closed and guarded by soldiers in armour. Wondering how to get in I thought that if I dressed and acted as a soldier I would be allowed entrance. It worked and inside Christ met me and said he had important work for me to do' (Sonia). The closely guarded secret is Sonia's own impulse to do some sort of socially creative work. She doesn't want to acknowledge the impulse as her own; it is much easier if she can say 'Christ told me to do this'. In this way she avoids direct encounter with opposition.

The <u>unofficial Christ</u>. Example: 'A fierce battle was raging with bullets flying. I immediately fell down and played "dead". It wasn't that I was hurt in any way, but I didn't want to be at any risk in the fight. As I lay there, I saw a tall well built man in soldier's uniform walk to me. He gave no sign of any fear concerning the bullets, and quietly knelt beside me. I felt he was Christ, but was confused by him being a soldier. He placed a hand on my back and gradually worked his fingers under the shell of a large limpet type creature that I had never before known was parasitically attached to my back. I could feel him pull it away, but knew its tentacles still ran right into my chest. He then sat me up and told me how I could rid myself of the tentacles and so be healed' (Peter Y).

Peter had a debilitating psychosomatic illness at the time of the dream, causing pain where the tentacles ran. The shell is his defence against feeling his own hurts and inner conflicts. The dream shows him contacting a strength which is not afraid of his internal battlefield of conflicts, and can show ways of healing real human problems. The healing rests upon the dreamer's conscious action, not Christ's, suggesting the dreamer taking responsibility for his own situation. Peter realised he had been avoiding his own internal battlefield, but felt he had met a strength which would support his efforts to find healing. In fact he met his conflicts and grew beyond his ailments. Peter's conflicts were between his love for his children and his sexuality. This Christ is our undammed life; the flood of loving sexuality; the strength to burst through social rules and regulations because love of life pushes us. It doesn't give a hang about bullets, death, right or wrong, because it has a sense of its own integral existence within life, and its own rightness and place in eternity.

The <u>integral</u> or <u>cosmic Christ</u>. Example: 'I am a journalist reporting on the return of Christ. He is expected on a paddle steamer going upstream on a large river. I am very sceptical and watch disciples and followers gather on the rear deck. The guru arrives, dressed in simple white robes. He has long, beautiful auburn hair and beard, and a gentle wise face. He begins to tap a simple rhythm on a tabla or Indian drum. It develops into complex intermingling of orchestral rhythms as everyone joins in. I now realise he *is* Christ, and feel overwhelmed with awe as I try to play my part in the music. I'm tapping with a pen and find myself fumbling. A bottle or can opener comes to me from the direction of Christ. I try to beat a complementary rhythm, a small part of a greater, universal music' (Lester S).

Each of us has a sense of connectedness with the whole, with the cosmos. We may be little aware of this sense, our scepticism may deny it, as Lester's was doing. But finding it can enrich the rest of our nature. The sense brings with it a realisation of taking part in the unimaginably grand drama called life. It gives a feeling, no matter what the state of our body, crippled or healthy, that we have something that makes any faults in body or achievement insignificant. It doesn't take all the difficulties out of life, but it is a good companion on the way. In dreams and religion Christ is also represented as the son of the Cosmos or God. This aspect of Christ is cosmic, from beyond the Earth. This is a process in the cosmos which the unconscious senses and presents under the image of Christ, or other figures in different religions. It is possible that there is an innate process in human beings to do with love and symbiosis which humanity became aware of at a particular stage in the development of consciousness. This becoming aware was expressed in what we know as the historical Jesus. See **religion and dreams**; *the self* within this entry.

death and rebirth The symbols of death or the fear of death can be: sunset; evening; a crossed river or falling in a river; a skeleton; snarling dogs; sleep; anaesthetic; gravestones; cemetery; blackness, or something black; ace of spades; a fallen mirror; stopped clock; a pulled tooth; an empty abyss; the chill wind; falling leaves; a withering plant; an empty house; a lightning-struck tree; coffin; struggling breaths; the dead animal in the gutter; the rotting carcass; underground; the depths of the sea; the Void.

What lies beyond death is conjecture, but the archetype of death we are considering is not completely about physical death. It is about our observation of it in others; our conceptions of it gained from our culture and our impressions; the feelings which generate around our experiences and thoughts; our attempts to deal with our own aging and approach to death, plus what material the deeper strata of our unconscious release regarding it. It is about how our sense of conscious personal existence meets the prospect of its disintegration.

Unless we can come to terms with what is behind the haunting images of death we meet in our dreams, we fail to live fully and daringly; we are too haunted by death lurking in the shadows of injury and the unknown. Images of death and the associated emotions, carried within for years, can have a negative influence on our health. Coming to terms means the courage to feel the emotions of fear or chill and discover them for what they are—emotions. They are certainly not death, only our feelings about it. The differences shown in the two following examples illustrate the avoiding and the meeting. Example: 'So to get to the bedroom I had to jump across this gap. I tried to jump but missed and I fell and hit the bottom. The next thing I remember was I was floating up. I looked down and saw myself lying face down with arms spread out and I suddenly realised I was dead. I was so frightened that I woke up. I had the feelings of fear of dying, but I felt no pain' (Cath). Example: 'Suddenly I was in a huge underground cavern. It was hundreds of feet high and as wide. It had two great statues in it, both to do with death. The whole place overpowered me with a sense of decay and skeletal death, darkness, underground, earth, the end. I cried out in the dismal cave, "Death, where is your sting! Grave, where is your victory!" I immediately had the sense of being a bodiless awareness. I knew this was what occurred at death. Fear and the sense of decay left me' (Andrew).

Summarising these and many other dreams, it is not only the accumulated images of death, but also bodilessness and loss of power and identity which bring so much fear. There are two antipodes of human experience. At the tip of one is focused self-determining self consciousness. At the tip of the other is unfocused void without identity. Strangely enough we experience both each day in some degree—the first while awake, the second when we sleep. Yet to face the second with consciousness feels like all the horrors of death and loss. Yet facing it is important, especially to the second half of life.

The symbols of rebirth are: the cave; an egg; spring; the tree; the cross; dawn; emerging out of the sea; the snake; the bird; a seed; arising from the earth or faeces; green shoot from a dead branch; phoenix; flame; a pearl; the womb. Rebirth is as difficult to face as death. It holds within it not just the memories of the struggles and difficulties of our own physical birth and growth, but also the challenge of becoming the unknown future, the dark possibility, the new. The dream of Andrew in the underground cavern is an example of positive rebirth. After realising himself as bodiless awareness he emerges from the cave and finds himself near a tree. Example: 'A tremendous jolt of power poured into me from the tree. I saw that we had arrived at a place where a line of trees, about a 100 yards in length, stood very close together in a slight semicircle on the top of a bank. The trees had great spiritual power and the place was a holy temple. Two spiritual beings were there—an ancient Earth Being, and Christ' (Andrew).

The next example is of a dream typical of meeting memories of physical birth. As can be seen, the experience is powerful enough to cause physical shaking. Example: 'All I can see of what I enter is a very narrow space with a light showing through. But immediately I enter I realise I have made a mistake for I am being forced swiftly through a dark, very narrow tunnel. I feel pain as I am dragged along and I hear loud banging noises which frighten me, but although they are loud they seem to come from inside my head. I feel terrified and breathless and very relieved when I wake before reaching the end of the tunnel. In fact as I write this account I am shivering' (female, anon).

devil Usually repressed natural drives, particularly sexual feeling—one can express physical sex, yet still repress sexual longing and connected emotions of tenderness. It is what is unlived in us, and devil is lived spelt backwards. Any code of conduct, whether accepted from parents or peers, leaves aspects of our total self unlived. The struggle with paternal authority or power within oneself is often represented as the devil. If we change our code of conduct, we may meet the devil because we release the previously unlived area of self. As Pan: the same, except that Pan represents losing oneself to the natural urges.

father The dream images representing father are many: God, a god, a giant, a tyrant, executioner, devil, Pan—and of course father. A child is, figuratively, like a growing plant. It takes in lumps of external material and transforms them into its own being. A child unconsciously either takes father or mother as its main model for structuring its behaviour and aims. But also, huge areas of our basic self revolve around mother and father. Even not having an available father leaves an enormous imprint in this archetypal area. Our father in our dreams therefore is most often the overall effect, habits, traits, which arise from our experience—or lack of it—of our father. Father is also the great figure of original authority and strength in our life. He therefore depicts our relationship with outside authority or power. <u>Struggle or seeking to placate father</u>: may show how we deal with authority.

Our baby or child self has no restraints and, in its relationship with father, at times felt urges which as an adult we might find hard to believe or accept. In our dreams we frequently release these urges. <u>Killing father</u>: expressing anger, getting rid of him so there is no competition for mother, gaining your own ability to make decisions and be independent. At some point we need to kill him inside us to claim whatever strength we can from our experience of him and become independent. <u>Sex with father</u>: for the woman fulfilment of childhood desires to possess; for a man desire to receive his love. The father may not easily have shown his love, so the child becomes desperate to receive. <u>Burying father</u>: most likely same as killing; or facing his death and one's own independence.

hero/ine   The archetype of the hero has fascinated, taught, even ennobled human beings for thousands of years. Appears as Christ, Athena, Krishna, Mohammed, Mary, Ulysses, Superman, Florence Nightingale, a great game hunter, Hercules, or any film or TV hero such as Captain Kirk or Dr Who. We are the hero/ine of our own life. We brave great dangers, face monsters, pass through difficult initiations. Fundamental to the whole drama of the hero/ine is the evolution of our own identity from the depths of unconscious in the physical process of conception, through to developing self awareness as an adult. It is such an incredible journey, so heroic, so impossible of achievement, so fraught with dangers and triumphs, that it is the greatest story in the world.

We find it told over and over symbolically in all the 'holy' books as the birth of the holy child; the journey of the hero/ine; the creation of the world—our consciousness; the journeys of Moses. All pertain to the difficulties and means we use to be; to the art of keeping balance amidst the multitude of forces acting on our human psyche. The hero/ine is the one who dares, even though they feel afraid and in pain. The avoidance of fear and pain in our society, where chemical anodynes or tranquillisers are sought to remove any tiny discomfort, is a great tragedy. Not that we need to become masochists, but we miss our own wholeness through fear of our own power of experiencing. In other cultures the ability to meet pain and fear were considered spiritual strengths. They still are.

The following example shows one dreamer meeting his own fear and uncertainty. Example: 'I was in an ancient room. It had the feeling of being an old church. Then my wife and I were in bed in the room. A middle aged woman was in the room. She was a ghost. I felt afraid of her, but to meet the fear I tried to confront her. I reached out my hand to her. I was crying out in my sleep from fear. As she took my hand I was amazed and shocked to feel it was physically real' (see *Christ* within this entry, above).

the Great Mother   The symbols are Virgin Mary, sometimes one's own mother, a divine female, an old or ageless woman, the Earth, a blue grotto, the sea, a whale, a cave. Whatever the image, it often contains great religious feeling or spiritual uplift. After all, our mother was the most powerful being in our early world. Did she admire hunters? Then we would kill dragons and cleanse the world. Did she feel the weight of the world? Then we would be the peacemaker and bring her joy.

The symbols of mother represent not simply our relationship with her, but also how it influences our own growth towards independence. As a baby our consciousness of self does not feel separate from mother. The gradual separation of *the sense of self* is difficult. In some people it is never managed, even though they separate physically. Their mother, or their sense of their mother within them, still directs their decisions. The old joke about 'My mother wouldn't like this' is true. In many older cultures this break was worked out in ritual tribal custom. Today we have to manage these subtleties of our psyche alone. A woman must find a way of transforming the pleasure—or absence of it—of her mother's breast into a love for a male. If she cannot she may wish to return to the breast of another female, or be the man her father never was for her. A man must find a way of transforming his unconscious desire for his mother into love of a woman which is more than a dependent or demanding baby or youth. If he cannot he may seek his mother in a likely woman, ignoring who that woman is as a real person. And the acceptance of our mother as she really is—a human being—precedes the acceptance of ourself as we really are.

The symbols of the Great Mother hold in them our awareness, unconscious as it may be, of the forces of nature active in us. These forces, in the guise often of a beautiful woman dancing or beckoning, are both wonderful and dangerous. The dance of nature is unconscious. If we get in its way we will be ground under its heel as it dances on its beautiful way. To meet this aspect of ourself we must be both admiring and resourceful. The danger for a man might be that he loses himself in desire for all women or one woman; for a woman, that she becomes a spiritual whore, thinking she can uplift all through her womb.

the self   Our conscious self or ego is only a tiny part of our totality, as is obvious when we consider how much of our memory or experience we can hold in mind at any one time. The self, as defined by Jung, is both what we are consciously aware of, and the massive potential remaining unconscious. The self has no known boundaries, for we do not yet know the end of what the mind is capable of, or what consciousness touches out of sight of waking. The mass of experience and awareness which lies in the background of our waking awareness is like an inner guiding factor which, apart from expressing precise pieces in the form of remembered facts and events, guides us, if we listen, through intuition, feeling states, dreams or illumination. Its symbols are: a ring, a square area, a great tree, Christ, a shining being or animal, a talking animal, a strange stone or rock, symbols like the cross or mandala, a round table, God, a guru, an elephant, a crowned or shining snake. Here are some examples of the self in dreams.

Example: 'I am climbing a tree to get a stone. This stone has special powers that flower. I'm nearly there when I look down and notice that there aren't any branches on the left side of the tree. This causes me to consider the possibility of falling and that in turn leads to a fear of climbing any higher. I wake with my heart beating strongly, but little feeling of fear.' Example: 'I look into the third square, it was filled with an iridescent blue colour, shining and beautiful to look at, a beautiful substance. I felt it had to do with religion, but I couldn't quite grasp it.' Example: 'I was in a small town with a group of men. We were standing in a small square praying. As I prayed I realised I could fly.'

Awareness of what the self holds is important. It contains what is our own personal wisdom and insight regarding life in general and particular. It is not full of creeds and dogmas and conflict as are organised attempts to express the spiritual. But it does have its dark side. To grasp the stone with special powers, understand the significance of the iridescent blue square, or find real uplift in prayer as these dreams depict, we need a clear rational mind which allows intuition and feeling but is not relinquished or lost in the immensity of the self. Touching the vastness of our being we may feel ourself to be vast, all knowing, a guru. In this state, Jung says, a person loses all sense of humour and drops ordinary human contacts. Functionally what happens is that as a defence against meeting our pain and childhood trauma as we enter this vast storehouse of our being, as a way of escaping the self responsibility for our condition, one might fly off into feelings of loving all things, of knowing the mystery of it all, of being the Buddha. The problem is that while it might be true we are in essence the Christ, or have wisdom, these realisations are distorted by the undealt-with childhood traumas and longings. See **aura**; mandala.

the Shadow Depicted as: a shadowy figure, often the same sex as the dreamer; a zombie or walking dead; a dark shape; an unseen 'Thing'; someone or something we feel uneasy about or in some measure repelled by; what is behind one in a dream; anything dark or threatening.

The Shadow is any part of ourselves which we reject, and so do not allow expression in our life. We may so dislike aspects of our nature we fail to see them altogether and instead see them in other people and criticise them. Nations as well as individuals do this. The Nazis projected all problems on to the Jews; the Americans have not wished to see their own social sickness, and have looked instead at the Russians, no doubt the Irish blame the English, and the English use the class system, with its projections between employee and employer. It is easier than looking at one's own Shadow.

If you can think of the characteristics you loathe in others, that is a fair picture of what you repress in yourself. The great 'ladies' man' may hide a Shadow which feels inadequate sexually; the loving Christian mother might meet a Shadow full of resentment and anger at how she has been taken for granted. Meeting the Shadow through our dreams is a meeting with our own reality, which in turn enables us to look at the world realistically. The Shadow can be met.

Fraser Boa tells the story of a man who told his analyst he had dreamt of Red Rooster—a cartoon character used in American national parks. Red Rooster is bossy and tells people to keep their litter and cigarettes. The analyst asked the man if he recognised Red Rooster in himself. After some thought he said no, he couldn't see he was like that. The analyst suggested he go and ask his wife if she could see Red Rooster in him. He did this and was astonished when she said she could. After a few minutes of his attempts to suggest she was mistaken, she suggested he ask each of his three children. He took each one aside and was amazed when each said that of course they could see Red Rooster in him. He was always bossing people around and being authoritative. Red Rooster was his Shadow.

arena, amphitheatre   Focus of attention; mental capability to bring an unimaginable amount of associated information and experience together in considering something; area of conflict.

armour   The emotional and intellectual rigidity we use to protect ourself from hurt. Can depict muscular tension which blocks free flowing sexuality and feelings.

army   See **soldier; war**.

arrested   Suggests a restraint of one's easy expression by moral judgments or questions of right and wrong, guilt. See **police**.

art   See **painting**.

artist   The aspect of oneself which is in contact with the irrational, creative side of the unconscious; the desire or ability to be creative.

ascending   The rising feelings of passion or sexual pleasure; the transition from expressing our energy genitally to expressing it in self awareness is often shown as ascending. See **flying**, *stairs* and *lift* under **house and buildings**. Movement towards waking or becoming more aware; the mental; or an escape from anxiety or being 'down to earth'; sexual pleasure. If the lift goes out of the top of the roof, or the connection with base is missing: can show a critical situation of the mind being split from body awareness (schizoid). Ascending a hill or mountain or tree: often shows having a more inclusive view or understanding of one's activities and place in the scheme of things.

53

ascetic   Conflict with natural drives; desire to be less dominated by them, avoidance of sex; attempt to find the spiritual, which may be an inverted fear of one's unconscious or a bid for power to control; development of will. See **religion and dreams**.

Asclepius   A Greek god of healing, especially in relation to dreams. The people of Epidaurus claimed their city was the birthplace of Asclepius. L.R. Farnell suggests he was a hero who was elevated to a godlike status. See **dreams and ancient Greece**.

Aserinsky, E. and Kleitman, N.   Aserinsky, while working under Kleitman in a sleep study laboratory, was the first to observe the rapid eye movements (REM) now known to occur during dreaming. As Aserinsky had observed this in the sleep of babies, it was first assumed only to occur with infants. Later investigation proved it to occur with all people observed. See **science and dreams**.

ashes   What remains in our experience, perhaps as memory or wisdom, after the event or person has gone; death. Idioms: rake over the ashes.

astral travel   See **out of body experience**.

atom bomb   Anxiety regarding external world, political forces, etc., that the dreamer feels at the mercy of. Often coupled with dreamer's survival strategies. The end of a particular world for the dreamer, i.e. the end of school life, divorce, loss of spouse. Also: fear of the irrational forces of life and the unconscious which may destroy all we have built—our conscious self.

attack   Being attacked: feeling under threat from external events or internal emotions, impulses or ideas; feeling a victim in relation to others and self; taking a defensive attitude. Attacked by animal: one's own aggression or sexuality. Bird attacking: fear of ideas or opinions, verbal attack by others. Being the attacker: positive self expression; defending oneself against something one feels threatened by; attempt to destroy some urge or feeling in oneself. The word attack is also used in many ways, so might refer to an 'attack' of an illness, or 'heart attack'. Can express the difference between feeling threatened by a work/relationship/sex problem, or feeling challenged by it in a way to stimulate creativity or research. Someone else being attacked: anger or aggression towards another. See **fight; war.**

audience   Standing in front of: you might be dealing with an important issue in your life which attracts the attention of many associated ideas and feelings. Desire for attention; baring one's soul. In the audience: witnessing some emotion or process in yourself; considering some aspect of your life.

aura   An expression of the Self. What this means is that some part of our consciousness, such as the memory of our address, or emotion about our dog, will have many interconnections with other ideas and related feelings. We can associate the idea of address with home, room, family, food, rent, bed, and each of those with other connected ideas and feelings. Sometimes we touch a concept or feeling which has massive connections, so vast they begin to build up beyond usual levels of realisation. We might call it a mega-concept, which goes on building and generating realisations we have never made before—that is, we have never *made those connections* before. An aura around an object, person or animal depicts this mental function. See *the self* under **archetypes.**

automobile   See **car.**

autonomous complex   Many of the characters or elements of our dreams act quite contrary to what we wish ourself. This is why we often find it so difficult to believe all aspects of a dream are part of our own psyche. Some drives or areas of self do act or express, despite our attempts to contain them. These are named autonomous complexes. Recent research into brain activity shows that in fact the brain has different layers or strata of activity. These strata often act independently of each other or of conscious will. Sensing them, as one might in a dream, might feel like meeting an opposing will. Integration with these aspects of self can be gained.

autumn   Example: 'My husband was in a wheelchair, I was pushing him along a promenade. At the end of the promenade was a path which we took. The path went along the top of a cliff. The sea below was pretty rough, a typical autumn day at the seaside. All of a sudden the path came to an end' (Mrs C). Mrs C had this dream at a time when she started her own business, against her husband's wishes, and one week before he walked out on her. Autumn here depicts her sense of something ending. Can also be: 'the autumn of one's life'; mellow feelings.

avalanche   The power of frozen emotions. We can freeze sexuality by anger or jealousy, etc., and the buildup of tension might then release in a dangerous way.

awake   See **wake up**.

axe   See **weapons**. Idioms: axe to grind; to be axed (lose one's job).

B

baby General: one's own feelings and urges at that level of development—such as possessiveness, joy, curiosity, innocent love, infant trauma; feelings of helplessness; vulnerability; lack of responsibility; being cared for. Also a new phase of life; a new idea; new activity—as when we say someone has a new baby, meaning a new project or business. When <u>with a couple</u>: the marriage—what is created in a relationship; the life process in us, based on reproduction. In a <u>woman's dream</u>: desire for baby; responsibility of caring for baby; worries about having healthy baby. In a <u>man's dream</u>: desire for parenthood; weight of responsibility; fear of inability to produce. In <u>child's dream</u>: themselves at that age; feelings about a baby sibling.

Example: 'I have my own baby who is lying in a cot in a bedroom looking very weak and pathetic with eyes closed. I know that he or she is getting weaker and weaker through lack of food and care. In fact the baby seems to be dying. The feelings of guilt are terrible because I know it is my responsibility to do something to make it well. I keep saying to myself I must go and feed that baby—but I don't. I just keep worrying and feeling guilty' (JC). Because of circumstances we may not have been able to satisfy all our babyhood needs—we may have been weaned earlier than we wanted, our need for attention may have been unsatisfied—and these are shown as a baby in our dreams, as with JC. Dreams such as the above show how we sense the need of this part of us to be cared for and nourished. If some of these earliest needs are not met in some way, the development of our enthusiasm, our pleasure and ability to be involved and self-giving, may be curtailed.

Example: 'I am 48, have two children in their late teens

and definitely *DO NOT* want another baby. Nevertheless I have a recurring dream in which I am always in labour, experiencing no pain, and although there are nursing staff I am in some sort of laboratory, although everything is very pleasant. I never actually give birth and when I wake I always have a vague feeling of disappointment' (VI). This dreamer's conscious decision to have no more children is in conflict with her biological urge for another baby.

Example: 'My mouth was full of what looked like liver. It was also coming out of my left ear. When I turned away from the mirror I saw medical people in caps and gowns who kept telling me to bear down. I then gave birth to a baby out of my mouth. I am an invalid and very sick at present' (Mr MS). This man's dream is about preparation for death. The baby is the extraction of all that can live on after his present life is left behind in death.

bachelor Man's dream: oneself if unmarried; desire for freedom, or comparison with present if married. Woman's dream: possible sexual partner; husband prior to marriage.

back Back of house, etc.: more private; intimate; less formal; surreptitious; out of sight. Behind: repressed urges; one's past and memories; one's inner feelings; inferior. Idioms: at the back of; at the back of one's mind; backroom boys; by the backstairs/door; behind one's back; take a back seat. See **front; left behind.**

bag Example: 'I am in a strange town—usually where there are shops and lots of people. I don't know where I am or how I got there, but I suddenly realise I have lost my handbag. I know no one and do not know what to do. When I panic I wake' (Mrs R). Sometimes it represents the vagina, female sexuality; more often, as in example, it depicts the dreamer's identity. Our sense of identity is often dependent largely on social contacts and recognition. The bag, with all one's personal belongings and money, represents this social ability to get places and cope. Occasionally loss of childbearing function. Idioms: bag and baggage; in the bag; pack one's bag. See examples in **clothes**; **luggage**; **knapsack**; **suitcase**.

baker Creative ability.

ball See *sphere or ball* under **shapes and symbols**.

balloon Party mood; breasts; desire for sex (similarity to condom); the womb.

banana Male penis. Taking one or handing one to someone: desire to receive or have sexual relation. Man eating one: may be homosexual tendency.

band Teamwork; sense of different aspects of the personality working harmoniously; work for a musician.

bandage Hurt feelings; past emotional injury; healing process; death.

bank Resources—financial, mental and spiritual; one's internal sense of security; emotional resources such as confidence and sexual certainty; social power. River, field or canal bank: minor difficulty or obstruction; a boundary, such as the border of what you might permit sexually. Idioms: bank on; break the bank.

baptism New force entering your life, cleansing away old attitudes; opening to one's inner possibilities; life pervading and healing; an influx of what had been latent or potential in the self; birth. See **religion and dreams**; *Christ* under **archetypes**.

bar Strength; male sexuality; rigidness; energy; symbol of power. What we do with the bar: how we are expressing energy or power at that time. Barring of the way: obstacle; block against our self expression. Idioms: prop up the bar; colour bar.

barber Change of attitudes, thoughts or opinions about ourself. Because we can change our social appearance by a haircut or style, it depicts changes of mind, change of image. Also being in someone else's hands or influence.

bar room Often indicates how we relate to groups; our feelings about society; can be difficulties regarding alcohol; one's technique for avoiding confrontation with loneliness, anxiety, sense of failure, etc.

basement See *basement and cellar* under **house and buildings**.

bat Thoughts or influences emerging from the unconscious; fear of the unconscious. Cricket or baseball bat: male sexuality; aggression; defensiveness.

bath Relaxation; cleansing; wanting to 'come clean' or be rid of guilt. Such cleansing could depict a change of heart or forgiveness where old feelings are washed away. Also need to cleanse the body internally.

bay Similar to **beach**, but the crescent shape sometimes depicts a woman's sexuality and openness to mating. Idioms: at bay; keep at bay.

beach Family gatherings or relaxation and intimacy. Also a boundary, or threshold—to go further we would have to swim or take a boat, so a change is needed, new qualities must be developed. The threshold is a great tester of confidence and daring. It also confronts us with the vastness of life processes, space, eternity, which we stand on the brink of. How we deal with changing from one environment—school, work—to another such as parenthood or retirement. The beach might be the place where aspects of the unconscious meet us, out of the sea. See **sea**.

bed   See *bed* under **furniture**.

beer   See **alcohol**.

beggar   The emotions, drives and thoughts you seldom allow into expression. Feelings of failure. Desire to drop out.

behind   See **back**.

bell   Warning; signal calling for attention.

Bible   Traditional moral standards; religion; one's most inclusive realisations, in which case like **aura**. See **dream as spiritual guide; religion and dreams**.

bicycle   Personal effort or motivation which gets you somewhere. For many people a bicycle was their first experience of mastering a body skill and gaining greater freedom. Might be youthful freedom without responsibilities.

big   See **size**.

biological dream theory   J.A. Hadfield, in his book *Dreams and Nightmares* (Pelican 1954), puts forward what he calls a biological theory of dreams. He says the function of dreams is that, by reproducing difficult or unsolved situations or experiences, the dream aids a solving or resolution of the problems. He gives the example of a man climbing a cliff who slips fractionally. He then may dream of actually falling and waking terrified. Subsequently the dream recurs, but in each he tries out a different behaviour, such as clasping for a branch, until he manages to act appropriately to avert the disaster. He sums up by saying dreams *stand in the place of experience.* They make us relive areas of anxious or difficult experience. They thus help problem solving. But they not only look back at past behaviour, they act just like thinking in considering future plans and needs.

birds   Example: 'I was standing outside the house of my teens, with my mother. She had a very young bird on a long ribbon and the bird was flying very high in the sky' (Pauline). The life cycle of a bird has so many similarities with important human stages of maturity we frequently use it to represent oneself, as in the example. Pauline uses the bird to depict her own urge to be independent of her mother's influence, opinions, likes, dislikes and decisions. Later in the dream her mother hands Pauline the ribbon to hold, suggesting an offer of independence. As soon as she lets go of the ribbon, a huge black bird attacks the ribboned one. The ribbons are a reference to Pauline's own girlhood. When she lets go of her girlhood, moving towards independent womanhood, she feels threatened by the internalised negative side of her mother, such as her possessiveness—the black bird. Internalised means all the standards, self controls she learned from her life with her mother, which she now carries within her even if absent from her mother.

General: Imagination; intuition; the mind; thoughts; our spiritual longings; expanded awareness—in this form, perhaps a large bird which can fly high. Because wider—or spiritual—awareness means looking beyond the usual boundaries of what we see, this may be painful. Hatching from the egg: our birth and infancy. The nest: home; family environment; security; even the womb. Leaving the nest: gaining independence. Making a nest : home building; parental urges. Flying:

rising above something; independence; freedom; self expression.

Freud said the bird represents the male phallus, and flying means the sexual act. Many languages use the word 'bird' to mean woman. In Italy it alludes to penis. The bird is also used to denote the sense of death and survival. Bluebird: especially represents the spirit or soul after death. Baby bird: our own childhood, as in the following example. The old lady is once more reference to the mother, to whom the bird is first connected before moving on to the difficulty of independence. Example: 'An old lady made room for me to sit at the end of one of the three seats of a bus. As we drove away a very large chicken-size baby bird flew in. It had short stubby wings and yellow down, but flew expertly. I believe it first landed on the lady and chirped squeakily. But in its squeaks it actually spoke, saying it had lost its mother. It sounded as if it were crying' (Andrew). Idioms: charm the birds from the trees; a bird told me; bird has flown; bird in the hand; bird of ill omen; free as a bird; odd bird.

black bird Unconscious drives; death; the negative aspect of mother.

chicken Nourishment; the female in a male; being 'chicken'. Cock: a male or the male sexual characteristics; confidence. Hen: mother. Idioms: chickenfeed; chickenhearted; she's no chicken; cock of the walk.

crow, rook, raven Being carrion birds, and so often seen near corpses, they are linked with death; bad news; fear; unconscious feelings. The negative aspect of father.

dove Peace; awareness of one's potential; religious experience. See **religion and dreams**.

eagle, buzzard, hawk Sometimes the hunting providing parent; dominance. Often the ability to develop an integrated vision or perception out of a wide range of experience. This is because the height the bird flies at and its steady gaze give it unusual perception and wide awareness. See **aura** as it relates to mega concept.

owl Because the owl sees in the dark, it represents our intuitive sense which 'sees' into our unconscious. This sense 'feeds' by watching (or acting as an integrating function for) the many dark or hidden aspects of our experience and behaviour. Because this part of our mental process is aware of the hidden activities in the depths of our body and mind, it can initiate our conscious self into the mysteries of life and death. If one can imagine having a council of all living things, we would all have in common the drive to reproduce, and there would be huge links of understanding regarding care and rearing of young and perhaps of mate. The unconscious seems to have a sense of this synthesis of all life, and the owl, representing it, speaks with this sort of collective wisdom. See second example in *wife* under **family; aura; dream as spiritual guide**.

peacock Pride; self display; sometimes the same as phoenix.

phoenix The ability to find a new impulse, new strength, new growth even in death.

vulture A relative waiting for you to die, or vice versa; people around you trying to live on you, or vice versa; difficult feelings about dependents.

birth Woman's dream: desire to have a baby. Man's dream: envy of the creative ability of women. When we were born, one world of experience ended for us and another began. Birth in a dream has the same meaning. The beginning of a new way of life; new attitude; new ability; new project. But also the death of the old. Can be about our own physical birth, its difficulties and trauma. But most difficult birth dreams are about coming to terms with our existence. Many of us are still wondering whether we wanted to be, or want to be, born. Lots of us live at a remove from life because of this.

Birth of a <u>shining, talking or holy child</u>: the beginning of awareness (not intellectual knowledge) of how the conscious self is interwoven with the forces and beings of the cosmos. <u>Birth pains</u>: the creative process; pain of arriving at a wider vision. Giving birth to a more mature self is a struggle; the new in our life is born out of such pains. See **baby**.

bite Aggression; the desire to suckle the breast hidden under aggression—this applies to women as equally as men.

The following example shows another aspect of bite: 'I had to get a large spider into a small dwelling. At one point it was like trying to get the spider into a narrow necked bottle, the spider was unwilling, and bit my finger. I was worried the bite might be poisonous, but it seemed all right' (Alan P). The large spider, small dwelling and finger refer to sexual intercourse. Alan feels fear of introducing his finger into the bottle because he might be bitten. So here the bite refers to the injection of fearful emotions, unwillingness, into his sexual impulse. The spider often refers to the mother, and in fact Alan's mother made him fearful of sex. So the bite is clearly to do with feeling attacked by anxieties or one's urges.

black person Depends which skin colour one has. <u>If white</u>: one's natural drives; feelings about coloured people; or if person is known, what you feel about them. <u>If black or brown</u>: one's own cultural feelings; same as any 'person' dream.

Example: 'I was in a cubicle or small toilet with a very black coloured woman. She told me there was something wrong with her vagina. She was undressed. I rubbed her vagina and we both felt enormous passion. I then awoke but couldn't at first remember the dream. I have refrained from sexual intercourse for some weeks, as I always feel shattered/ tired afterwards. Anyway I woke very wet, yet couldn't remember any orgasm. I could remember some question of sex as I awoke. Then I remembered the dream and continued it in fantasy. I experienced powerful urges to find a woman to have a non-committed sexual relationship with. But in the end I wanted to share my feelings with my wife, but she seemed deep asleep and unresponsive. When I slept again I dreamt I was in London, had got off one bus, but was not at any destination. I was standing about not making a move to find my direction. Then I began to look' (Alfred C). To understand this dream in some depth it is helpful to think of a sexual drive as a flow, like a river. As such it can be blocked, in which case it will seek an alternative route. Sexual energy or flow is not simply a mechanical thing, though; it is also deeply feeling in its connection with the most profound sides of human life such as parenthood and the caring and providing for young. In the history of white people a great deal of sexual frustration has arisen out of the ideas of sin and guilt in their religion. A view arose for the white race that the black races had an easier and less frustrating relationship with the natural —which includes not only sexuality but the body as a whole, and nature also. So when Alfred dreams of the black woman, he is meeting what is natural and flowing in himself, but which he has blocked by his will because he felt shattered after sex. The part about the bus shows him trying to find a direction in which his sexual feelings could move satisfyingly in connection with other people.

Unfortunately, as Jung points out in *Man and His Symbols,* people in modern society, whether black, yellow, brown or white, have lost their sense of nature and the cosmos as being anything other than processes without consciousness or living feeling. Jung says, 'No river contains a spirit, no tree is the life principle of a man, no snake the embodiment of wisdom. No voice now speaks to man from stones, plants, and animals, nor does he speak to them believing they can hear.' The importance of such dreams as Arthur's is that it shows the passionate relationship between our personality and the primitive and natural. A black person, born and bred in a modern setting, would most likely dream of a black bushman to depict their own natural drives. See **identity and dreams; Africa; sex in dreams**.

blindness   Unwillingness to 'see' something; losing sight of something; not seeing traits which we don't like about ourself. Idioms: blind impulse; none so blind; turn a blind eye; blind leading the blind. See *eye* under **body**.

boat, ship   Our journey through the seas of life and how we meet the rough and smooth experiences, as with following example. The dream occurred a few weeks before a breakdown centering on the dreamer's wife leaving him. 'I am in a large glass boat with my wife. The sea is very rough and I am afraid the boat will sink' (Ron D).

Many boat/ship dreams depict something else: a situation we are involved in with other people which is difficult to get out of, such as marriage, business partnership, armed forces. Keel: basic personal strengths. Bows: one's strength to meet life's changes. Rudder: sureness about direction in life. The ship sinking : fear of relationship ending—could be children leaving mother, so the collective 'boat journey' has finished; illness; death. Leaving boat but leaving bag on it: lack of identity, alone—perhaps when children have gone or job ended. Lots of small boats: other people's relationships. Small boat with one other person: one's relationship with that person. Going on a cruise: desiring relationship with others, or to be a part of other people's lives. Boat journey by night: classic archetype of searching for one's roots in life; the journey into the unconscious. Anchored boat: security; stable relationship; opposite of drifting. Motorboat: similar to **car**, but more sense of isolation or aloneness. Ferryboat: if across a river, death; end of a relationship; transition from one phase of life to another. Disembarking: leaving a phase of life, such as motherhood or marriage. Embarking alone: independence or loneliness. Idioms: burn one's boats; in the same boat; miss the boat; rock the boat; ships that pass in the night; ship comes in; a tight ship. See **submarine**.

body   It refers to oneself, as in the word some*body*. Although it includes the totality of our experience, it seems to be most pointedly referring to our sense of **identity**. From this sense of ourself we project meaning on to the rest of the world in some degree. Thus many symbols are stylised body forms. The cross is a standing figure with arms outstretched; a church's structure a representation of the body, and the miracle of sexual reproduction—the mystery enacted within it; a maypole, the penis. Therefore various things can represent our body or aspects of ourself. Seeds, swallowed teeth can be sperm; anything long and pointed, even a finger, can be the penis; anything hairy, a male; anything receptive like a bottle, bowl or cave, a woman or vagina.

A body, or our body, also represents physical life; material existence; the process which causes growth and aging. This includes all the processes of nature in us. A dead body: our skin or shape is felt as our boundary, the edge of our universe. The dead body depicts a whole set of personality traits or attitudes, very often potentials, which have been denied life by us. We have not allowed them expression. A person hurt in love might kill out any feelings towards the opposite sex. This 'dead' part of them can be shown as a body. May also be the way we meet feelings about death. Sickness in body: can refer to an awareness of illness in part of body shown. Most often depicts psychological problem symbolised by part of body— see body parts below. Maggots in body: possible need to cleanse body of toxins or infection; sense of dis-ease emotionally in that area of self. Injuries: hurts or events that may lead to emotional scars—see body areas below. See **dead people dreams; hiding**.

Bodiless: Example: 'I felt as if I was going very deep inside myself. It was dark but at first there were noises of the world around me. I seemed to go in much deeper and it was very dark, but with the feeling of great space. Everything was all right until I didn't hear any noise at all, all that space and no noise was too much and my whole body freaked out and then pulled out very fast before I could stop it' (Kate P). The 'noises' around us, sensory impressions, other people's expressed feelings and actions, are building bricks for our sense of self. In a real sense we create each other by believing in each other. With prolonged absence of other people and events, and especially if we lose our 'noises' and body awareness, we feel we—our sense of identity—is dying. Bodilessness may therefore show us feeling unrecognised, unnoticed. May also be feelings of loneliness; being cut off from sexuality and body drives. In its positive side it is exploration of the unconscious and void. See **identity and dreams**.

If you are right handed, the left of the body: represents inner feelings which support outer action, such as confidence; our less used or supportive functions. If we are an intellectual, the left might depict one's feelings, and vice versa. The left may represent our mother's influence in our life and body. The right of the body: our outer activity and dominant functions; expressed abilities; our father's influence in life and body. If father is an anxious man there might be a lot more signs of stress on this side of the body. Top half of body: thinking, feeling. Bottom half: sexuality and instincts. Half a body: if top missing, lack of thinking and higher emotion; if bottom, trauma to, loss or denial of, sexuality and sensuality. Old head on baby body: immature sexuality and emotions; vice versa: immature personality. Dismembered body: emotional or mental stress and breakdown; may be followed by emergence of new self.

The areas of our body are sometimes thought of as sense organs. This may seem strange but is very simple. Without language, communication would be difficult. So language enables us to sense what another being is communicating. If we had been castrated or had a hysterectomy prior to adolescence, we would never develop sexually. Without that development we would not understand two kissing people; or what a mother was feeling when she held her baby. Out of the sex drive develops a whole world of feelings and tenderness which enables us to understand many things we see in the world. *It is therefore important when reading the particular descriptions below to remember that each psychological area of our body gives us some insight into ourself and life around us, which is missing if the area is injured or traumatised.*

abdomen Example: 'The people watching are saying "Kill her! Kill her! Kill her!" Then someone finds an extra bullet, puts it in the gun and shoots me in the stomach. I wake with my body completely straight with my hands on my stomach. I feel my whole body cracking up inside' (Vanessa). Almost half the dreams on file which mention abdomen, belly or stomach show the dreamer being shot, as in the example. This is obviously to do with a particular type of hurt. When human beings learned to stand up, they exposed their vulnerable underbelly. If we are hurt or threatened we tense the pelvic and abdominal area. Vanessa wakes to just such tension, with a sense of her body being fragmented. The opposite is to dream of <u>waves of pleasure</u> moving within us, which gives us a sense of integration within ourself and with the world.

In general the abdomen represents the potential of our fully active natural drives—hunger; longing to be held; desire to give of ourself. If these are hurt, we tend to hold ourself back from active social expression or intimacy of feelings in relationships. Our abdomen is also our digestive ability, both physical and psychological. Stomach or abdominal dreams may refer to some dis-ease in the actual organs. We might not *be able to stomach* something we have met in the everyday world. To <u>vomit</u>: a discharging of unpleasant feelings resulting from ingesting (hearing, reading, being told, experiencing) something unpleasant.

In her dream Vanessa was re-enacting the Hungerford disaster, and feeling the fear it engendered. <u>Shot in the belly</u>: sex; painful response to relationship. <u>Idioms</u>: bellyaching; have a bellyful; eyes bigger than one's belly; have a strong stomach; turn one's stomach; butterflies in stomach.

abscess Example: 'Was looking at my knuckle and saw that I had a nasty boil which had come away as I did the washing up and all that was left was a big hole, pink and healthy looking skin around. It felt very close to my knuckle bone. (My lover had told me he was leaving me for good, and going back to his children. That evening, I cried most of the night.)' (Hilary K). In Hilary's case the abscess has released its pus, or painful feelings, perhaps through her prolonged crying. <u>Abscess still swollen and unrelieved</u>: emotions still repressed and may be causing psychological infection, influencing views and decisions negatively. The emotions are, with Hilary, affecting her 'grasp'. She also uses other imaged word play in 'near the knuckle'. Washed up shows her clearing away the influence of her 'evening meal' of experience. The dream abscess may also represent a site of physical illness which may or may not be obvious while awake. See **individuation**.

ache Indicates where we may be holding back on expressing the energy relevant to that part of the body. A man who dreamt of an ache in his throat later discovered in therapy that he had been holding back emotions about his father who had died suddenly. On release he was able to say how much he loved his father. <u>In chest</u>: withheld emotions. <u>Lower back</u>: sexual energy blocked. <u>Idioms</u>: my heart aches; a pain in the arse.

anus In general, babyhood self expression and pleasure. Basic and perhaps rejected feelings. Also our will. <u>If relaxed</u>: easy self-expression. <u>If tense</u>: holding back feelings you might be judging as 'shitty'. <u>If playing with or being entered by penis or finger</u>: introverted sexuality; self pleasure, narcissism. <u>Excrement</u>: the negative emotions and ideas we might not want to let go of; sometimes money. <u>Holding or letting go</u>: how we give of ourself; whether we can 'let go'; our generosity or lack of it. <u>Idioms</u>: talking out of your arse; pain in the arse; an arsehole; head up the arse; disappears up the arse; all tits and arsehole—no ability to reason. See **excrement**.

arms Our ability to love, give, take, create, defend, reach out. <u>Injury to</u>: loss of confidence; loss of or psychological trauma regarding abilities. <u>Left arm</u> is the supportive feelings. <u>Right arm</u> is extroverted activity. <u>Tied up</u>: sense of restriction to activities. <u>Bicep</u>: strength; sense of being capable. <u>Idioms</u>: chance one's arm; give one's right arm; arm twisting; keep at arm's length; with open arms; one arm tied behind back; babe in arms; strong arm tactics.

back Strength, but particularly moral fibre. A psychiatrist once told me that many men in a tramp's home were diagnosed CWB; it meant 'congenitally without backbone'. Example: 'I was looking across a hedge at a bull. I seemed to be just looking at its back' (Andy). Andy was a teenager, uncertain of himself. In this dream he was looking at his strength.

<u>Someone on one's back</u>: feeling dominated by someone else; carrying one's parents' wants and decisions instead of one's own. <u>Idioms</u>: backbreaking; back to the wall; behind one's back; get off my back; put somebody's back up; rod for one's back; pat on the back; stab in the back; turn one's back on; scratch my back.

blood One's energy and sense of existence. Being hurt—such as hurtful remarks, being told we are not loved—can sap our motive to live and may be depicted as blood; injury, often from past trauma, which is causing us to lose energy or motivation; our fundamental biological, evolutionary life, and thus a link with all life, so seen as a sacrament. This is portrayed not as injury but <u>nourishment</u>, <u>wine</u> or <u>bloody meat</u>. <u>In sexual dreams</u>: may refer to loss of virginity, menstruation or fertility; or hurt to sexual drive.

chest   Like a wooden chest, a place to store emotions. Generally it represents our emotions; pride. Man's dream: sense of social confidence; if healthy: positive sense of social recognition. Woman's dream: ability to give of oneself; good feelings about womanhood. See **breath**.

Breasts in woman's dream: Example: 'I was about to lie down naked near my grandmother as I was caring for her, when she started to suckle my breast. For a short time I was very frightened that she would hurt me or even suck my breast right off, but she didn't and it felt very good as I fed her. It felt as if we were one, our bodies forming a circle' (Kate). Here Kate gives of herself, even though frightened, and feels whole —the circle. In many women's dreams the breasts figure prominently in a generally sexual dream. Breasts in a man's dream: return to infant dependence; sexual desire.

hair   Thoughts; self image; attitudes. Changing hairstyle: changing attitudes; a change of mind. Cutting hair right off: less thinking; denial of sensual and physical drives, as monk. Tight hairstyle: discipline; self restraint. Plaited or ponytail: girlhood; socialised thoughts and feelings. Long hair: freedom; permissiveness; girlhood with woman. Long matted hair: not caring about social image or self; dropout. Wig: false attitudes or thoughts. Fair hair: awareness; 'light headed'. Dark hair: unconscious area of thoughts and attitudes; 'dark' thoughts or attitudes. Genital or armpit hair: sexuality.

Woman's dreams—Armpit or leg hair: social expression of sexuality or physicality. Head hair: may be expression of female sexuality, as Paul's suggestion women should cover hair in church. Hair on chest of female, even child: the male side of the woman; might be parents' desire for a boy generating male characteristics.

Man's dreams—Beard: might represent uncertainty, so hiding behind the beard; male sexuality. White beard: wisdom or experience. Very long beard: sense of eternal. Baldness ageing; feeling obsolete. Chest hair: masculinity, virility.

73

Idioms: keep your hair on; hair raising; have us by the short hairs; let one's hair down; make your hair curl/stand on end; didn't turn a hair; put hairs on your chest; tear one's hair out; split hairs. See **shampoo**.

hand Most frequently dreamt of part of body. In general it represents self expression, grasp of life, of ideas, of opportunities; our hold on people, our children, situations, extensions of our power to give, take, wound, heal, support or do. fingers: manipulation; penis, dexterity. Handshake: contacting an aspect of self. Idioms: secondhand; in the hands of; bite the hand that feeds; hands are tied; soil one's hands; hand to hand; hand to mouth; upper hand; burnt fingers; at one's fingertips; snap one's fingers; green fingers; have a finger in; itchy fingers; sticky fingers; fingers crossed; lay a finger on; point the finger at; get one's finger out; work fingers to bone. See also example in *sweets* under **food**.

head Thoughts; opinions; intellect; decisions; intentions; self image. Fairly understandable from the huge number of idioms about head and face, such as 'lose one's head/face', so one might literally dream of a headless figure.

Face: self image; concerns about how others see you; expression of or hiding of inner feelings and attitudes. Idioms: above one's head; over one's head; enter one's head; get something into one's head; go off one's head; swollen or big head; head above water; head in sand; face the facts; face the music; face value; flat on one's face; facelift; long face; poker face; blue in the face.

Ears: subtle information; rumours. Idioms: an ear for; all ears; reach one's ears; flea in the ear; gain the ear of; ears burning; long ears; lend an ear; hear from; will not hear of; hearing things.

Eyes: how we **see** the world and ourself. Although eyes are not mentioned much in the collection of dreams used for data in this book, saw, see, seeing, look and looking, constitute the highest number of mentions. In a computer word count of

1,000 dreams, these words were mentioned 1,077 times. Feel, feeling, felt, came second, with 855 hits. So dreams are predominantly a looking at and seeing activity, in the sense of insight and awareness.

Eyes are used in many ways in dreams. As these quotes show, eyes can represent the soul or psyche in its many moods—dark deep eyes; desperation in its eyes; shining eyes; impersonal eyes; staring eyes; eye to eye. Example: 'I saw a young soldier with a gun, but as our eyes met we were attracted to each other, and he put his arm round me' (Pauline B). As the example shows, eyes can represent the state of a relationship. Lack of eye contact: avoidance of intimacy. Closed eyes: introversion or avoidance of contact; not wanting to see. Example: 'I was dimly aware of a biggish black bird that came down close beside us on the step and pecked at the baby's eye, then it flew off. The eye was gone completely' (Heather C). Heather's dream shows the eye depicting the 'I' or identity. In fact her sense of self was damaged in infancy.

In many dreams the eyes represent our understanding, or how we 'see' the world, our view of things or other people; also intelligence; our attention; our boundaries of awareness. Blindness: not being aware, not wanting to see something— usually about oneself. Loss of sight in right eye : not seeing what is going on in the outside world. Loss of sight in left eye: not seeing what you are really thinking or feeling; not aware of self, motives, behaviour; no 'in-sight'. Idioms: I see; can't you see; you must be blind; I saw it with my own eyes; all eyes; eye opener; evil eye; sheep eyes; one in the eye; turn a blind eye.

Mouth: pleasure area; our hungers, sexual pleasure. Also, because we speak with our mouth and tongue, they can represent what we say; a dream of our mouth being buttoned— button your lip—or sewed up could suggest that inwardly we regret having said certain things and need to hold our tongue. Chewing: considering; mulling over something. Idioms: all mouth; a big mouth; nasty taste in the mouth; mouthwatering.

Nose: curiosity; intuition, as with 'smell a rat'; penis. Idioms: have a nose for; nose out of joint; rub nose in it; up one's nose.

Teeth: the ageing process as it relates to maturity. This is because we lose our first teeth as we leave childhood behind, and lose our adult teeth as we leave youthfulness behind. Also aggression; ability to 'chew things over'. Bad tooth: a painful or rotten part of one's feelings, life or relationships; angry or regretful words. Teeth falling out: example: 'I felt a tooth was loose and started pushing it with my tongue. Then I took hold of it between thumb and forefinger and pulled it out. I felt okay about this, but then another tooth was loose, and another, and I pulled them out. Running to the bathroom I looked into the mirror, horrified and frightened. All my teeth were coming out. Not knowing how to deal with this I ran to my mother, showing her my mouth, empty now except for two teeth. My mother appeared not to see my lack of teeth, or notice my fear' (Eve). Eve was 18 at the time of the dream. She explored it and found a fear of ageing and death. Also apprehension about maturing and facing independence and responsibility; loss of attractiveness. Im Tofeeq, a Palestinian woman, told me that among the Arabs it is believed that if you dream of losing teeth it means your brother or son is in trouble. She had a dream in which three of her teeth fell out. The next day she received a call from America to say her son had been shot in the head three times by a gunman.

A woman swallowing teeth: the throat and Eustachian tubes are like the uterus and Fallopian tubes, so can depict conception or fear of it. False teeth: lies told; false face; not keeping spoken promises. Idioms: show one's teeth; get one's teeth into; gnash one's teeth; grit one's teeth; teething troubles.

Tongue: speech, expression of what we feel; saying what is deep inside us, perhaps unknown to ourself; penis. Idioms: find one's tongue; tongue in cheek; lose one's tongue; sharp tongue; hold one's tongue; forked tongue.

internal organs   Often to do with concerns over health. Could be a sense of illness in that part of body, but mostly our anxiety about illness. Heart: emotions; pity; sympathy; likes and dislikes. Idioms: lost your heart; have a heart; have no heart; heart like stone; change one's heart; done one's heart good; from the bottom of one's heart (too many more to list). Brain: intellect; thinking; insight; creativity. Idioms: brainstorm; brainchild; pick someone's brains; harebrained; scatterbrained. Lungs: might relate to tension, feelings of being 'suffocated' in a relationship or situation, as one may have been with one's mother or home life. Often to do with smoking or related to such idioms as relate to breathing, such as: catch one's breath; bated breath; hold one's breath. Ovaries and uterus: for many women, represent their sense of validity or adequacy, just as testes do for men. See *vagina* within this entry; **individuation**.

legs   Support; motivation. To 'have one's legs knocked out from under one' means loss of confidence and urge to carry on with life. Although we may depend upon someone like a partner or parent for support, or work or position for self value, ultimately the legs represent our own emotional or conceptual support system. So we may be considering what sense we have of our own value when trying to understand leg(s) in our dream. See **left; right; lame.** Feet: foundation; to have 'one's feet on the ground'; to be well or badly 'grounded'; fundamental issue in our life. Idioms: put one's foot in it; feet of clay; let the grass grow under your feet.

muscles   One's strength, therefore confidence and sense of adequacy; sense of being outwardly forceful; masculinity in its physical side. Also may refer to physical muscle.

neck   Connection between body (feelings and sexuality) and head (thinking and willing); weak point. Often refers to attitudes, as in idioms: breaking one's neck; up to his neck; risk

body

one's neck; stick one's neck out; dead from the neck up/down.

pelvis The whole sphere of sexuality and sensuality, not just the sex act. Our unconscious often connects sex with giving oneself, a death of self, and making connections or bonds—obviously reproduction, also. <u>Penis</u> and <u>testicles</u>: see *penis* in this entry. <u>In a man's dream</u>: what he is doing with his sexual urge. <u>A woman's dream</u>: her feelings about sex with a male. What she is doing to a male or the male in herself. See *vagina* and *penis* in this entry.

penis For a man the penis represents more than simply his sexual appetite. It depicts the whole drive of life through his glandular system which develops the body type he has, predisposes his body towards male sexual characteristics; brings a certain creative explosiveness to his personality; creates urges towards fatherhood and loving his woman, with connected desires to supply the needs of family if he is emotionally healthy. The positive aspect of the penis/masculinity is for him to demand his woman meets his maleness, his caring aggression, his sexual desire, with her own fiery energy and strength. In general, direct reference to sexual feelings, fears, or problems. As these can be quite complex several examples are given below.

Example: 'So for the third time I held the woman and made love. The woman's vagina was like a flower; I don't mean to look at, but in physical sensation. My penis felt like it was penetrating petals of flesh and touching with great pleasure a central receptive area. I was left with the feeling of being able to make love again and again without any negative effects. It was a very positive and healthy feeling' (John T). John is feeling confident about his sexual drive. Although a powerful drive, subtle feelings and fears have an intense influence not only on the pleasure of sex, but also the response of the physical organs. The relationship with the penis and sex act in one's dream shows what fears, hurts or attitudes are influencing the sexual flow. See **castration**.

<u>In a woman's dream</u>: one's relationship with, desire for, a mate; relationship with one's own male self—ambition, work capability, aggression, intellect; depicts the relationship with, genital sexuality with, one's partner. As with Sally in the next example, the events in the dream define the problem or relationship. Example: 'My lover Terry, myself and another woman are all on our bed. The other woman seemed very sure of herself and kissed Terry in a very intimate way, he doing the same to her as I lay very near to both of them. Then Terry stuck his bottom in the air and started to lick my chest and breast. I found myself licking around the penis, felt I was under some kind of pressure from both the other two to do so but didn't feel too shattered as I did it with love for Terry, but I had a bitter taste in my mouth' (Sally P). In talking about this dream Sally said she often struggled with what she wanted and what her partner wanted in sex. She might go along with his needs, but not find it palatable. Even if she did do it with some love, it might have a 'bad taste in her mouth'.

Example: 'I felt as if I were as one with Terry and I realised he was trying to make a journey into his mother's vagina, as his penis. Her vagina looked like a long dark tunnel and was threatening to him. I said, "You haven't given your mother satisfaction and you say you will not." Then he was really smashed up in body. Withdrawing into a garden with a high green hedge. I took a leaf from the hedge and began to pull it apart with my hands. Terry said, "Look what you are doing, teasing me." I felt withdrawal wasn't the way and started to follow him, walking alongside the hedge. I said, "It feels like you are strangling me, so why don't you do it and kill me?" (We have been going through a lot of sexual withdrawal, Terry saying his sexuality was his to do with as he wanted.)' (Sally P). This second dream of Sally's is a shrewd summing up of Terry's sexual fears. In fact Terry suffered a great deal of anxiety about sex, and later uncovered the sort of fear and desire to avoid giving his mother satisfaction in becoming a full blooded man shown in the dream. Our unconscious is a very capable psychologist, and while Terry in Sally's dream represents her insights regarding him—and must not be seen as a statement of fact about Terry—such insights are often enormously useful in dealing with relationship difficulties.

Example: 'Was in a house with my wife. Outside the door was *something* which wanted to come into her—an invisible being. We were frightened and it said "Do not be afraid, I want you to put your penis in your wife and wait for me to activate you. In that way you will form a body for me." I woke and realised the dream was moving me to parenthood. Already having three children I realised this would mean another 20 years of responsibility. Nevertheless my wife and I made love. Two weeks later I dreamt my wife was pregnant with a son. In fact nine months later she bore a son' (Nigel I). In this interesting dream sequence the penis is Nigel's drive to be a father. See **castrate**; **bed**; **knob**; **pole**; **reptiles**; **sausage**; examples in **flower** and **tunnel**.

shoulders   Ability to bear or to carry what life brings. Idioms: have broad shoulders; put one's shoulder to the wheel; a shoulder to cry on; rubs shoulder with; chip on the shoulder.

skin   One's contact with the world; what tactics we use to deal with others. Rough skin: rough exterior. Burnt skin: hurt in relationship with outside world or people. Shed skin: like a snake, changing one's old way of life; old attitudes. Idioms: under one's skin; a thick skin; skin deep; skin alive.

vagina   The vagina refers to much more than a woman's sexual feelings and drives. It depicts the urges and processes of her being which are the foundations of her waking personality. The ability to procreate; the glandular bias which connects with what the conscious personality faces in emotional, mental and physical disposition; the caring, nurturing feelings which emerge out of sexual mating when healthy; the desire for a mate; the sense of connection and identity with other women, other female creatures and female aspects of nature. In its positive aspect it may represent the sure confidence with which a woman may demand from her man that he treat her womanhood with the respect it deserves. This means meeting the full flood of her sexual need with its desire for a child, a caring and supportive nest to rear that child in, and her female creativity which may rise from that basic reproductive drive into other social creativity and personal demand for respect.

Example: 'He was very brown, could have been a native but he didn't feel strange to me. We were making love, I was very aware of the pleasure in my lower body. It was very slippy slidy and wet, there was enjoyment for both of us. Very intense body feelings with a childlike quality, not passion— but pleasure and joy in my vagina' (Susy I). Susy is feeling happy and joyful about her 'native' or natural sexual feelings —particularly the sensual side of sex. Sensual pleasure, as with emotional pleasure, is as much a food for our physical and emotional self as bread is for our physical body.

In a woman's dream: generally how one feels about one's own sexual needs, but this includes procreation as well; the health or feeling state of the sexual self and physical vagina; her central femininity; sexual urge; ability to have a child; concept of her physical attraction; temple or church of life, one's experience of motherhood or experience of the procreative relationship with one's mother. Example: 'I had very little pubic hair and thought it must be because I had just had a shower, but, no, on looking again I had very little hair. I was hugging Mary (a friend), my arms around her back and one hand holding her vagina. It was then I noticed she was the shape of a man there. I drew away for a second at the discovery then felt OK as it meant I was hugging a male/female person. We were very warm together. (Two days before this dream my husband had said his mother called a vagina a Mary.)' (Lucy R). Lucy is 'touching' or becoming aware of

81

what could be seen as her own wholeness, which includes her male nature.

In male dreams: the vagina represents one's feelings or fears about meeting a woman's full sexuality; the deep experience of the relationship with one's mother; birth and how mother met one's emerging male sexuality; one's desire for sexual expression. Bleeding vagina: his trauma, fears about a woman and sex. Example: 'She was now quite naked, dead and stiff, but still bleeding from the vagina. I walked along, the dead body walked like a clockwork soldier. It was quite horrible to see its semblance to life' (Derek A). Derek's relationship with a woman, and with his own emotions and sexuality, is 'dead' and deeply hurt—the blood. He can mechanically have sex—the clockwork soldier—but not with deep feeling bonds or satisfaction.

bomb   Explosive situation; sudden anxiety-producing events—as when we say something occurred out of the blue; one's own aggression; fear of death; remembered anxieties of war; social bombshells, such as being criticised in the press.

book   Memories; things you have learnt from experience; attitudes toward learning; other people's opinions. Old books: inherited wisdom; spiritual awareness.

bottle   Vagina. Of wine, spirits or beer: sometimes an influence entering your life to change it; relaxation. Of red wine: you may have felt there is more in life than your own ego, its worries and desires; sense of sharing life.

boy   If known: what you feel about that boy, but referring to oneself, i.e. one might think the child cautious and anxious, so it depicts one's own childhood feelings of caution and anxiety. Male dream: oneself at that age; the difficulties faced, habits acquired, attitudes imprinted on one by experiences at that age. Circumstances may not have permitted parts of us to mature, as when a child loses its mother, so does not develop a relationship with a woman. So could be part we need to 'father' towards maturity. Also the eternal potential for growth, openness to the new and enthusiasm about tomorrow. <u>If older than yourself</u>: your potential, or how you feel about maturing. <u>Female dream</u>: your own developing ability to express in outer action. Feelings about a son. See *son* under **family**.

bread   Fundamental nourishment; our basic emotional and biological needs. In a spiritual sense it represents our universal experience of physical or bodily life.

break   Broken promise; shattered idealism, hope or faith; feeling broken in spirit; changes as we 'break' with the past. <u>Idioms</u>: lucky/bad break; break a habit; break down/up; break new ground; broken heart; break the ice; break the news; breakthrough; break with.

breath   <u>Holding the breath</u>: expression of will. We hold the breath when repressing emotions and anxiety. <u>Fast breathing</u>: excitement; emotional release; experience of fear. <u>Under water and not breathing</u> : womblike state; experience of level of awareness without sexual, biological drives, and without opposites; return to deep relaxation. Healthy if you can easily emerge; might be an escape from waking reality if you cannot. See *lungs* under **body**.

bride   Feelings about or desire for marriage. <u>Female dream</u>: your marriage and what it means to you; feelings or hopes about marriage; feelings about daughter. <u>Male dream</u>: frequently depicts one's relationship with your own feelings and nonrational nature. <u>If getting married</u>: integration of inner feelings and unconscious, especially if bride is oriental or coloured.

83

bridegroom Desire to be married or find a partner. <u>Female dream</u>: feelings about marriage or getting married; integration with intellect and exterior capability. <u>Male dream</u>: feelings about marriage; attempt to integrate conscious and unconscious.

bridge Example: 'Having been enjoying ourselves with some work mates at a social club, my husband and I are travelling down a country lane in an open horsedrawn carriage. It is dark. We come to a humpbacked bridge. As we arrive at the brow of the bridge a voice says, "Fair lady come to me". I float and everything is black and peaceful. Then great fear overcomes me. I wake with terror and feelings of horror' (Evelyn K). Evelyn's dream paints a vivid picture of her journey through life, drawn by the natural forces within her, shown as a horse. She has enjoyed life, but comes to the 'brow' of her life, her 40th year, and feels it is all downhill now into old age, which horrifies her.

The bridge generally has this significance of crossing from one phase of life, activity or emphasis, to another. It depicts connection between yourself and a relationship; self and opportunity; self and change in life. <u>Fallen bridge</u>: lost opportunity; broken bonds and connections. <u>Idioms</u>: burn one's bridges; cross that bridge when I come to it; water under the bridge.

brother See **family**.

bubble Illusion; delicate and easily lost; daydreams, sometimes the transitory human existence.

bud Vagina; the penis; the unfolding of the world of sexuality, full of emotional and physical levels of experience and richness.

Buddha, Buddhist   Often in western dreams associated with the denial of our ego; liberation from thinking and desiring; in a Christian person's dream may be a threat to their belief system.

bullet   Sexual impregnation; aggression; penis; desire to hurt; pain.

burglar, intruder   Fears or difficult emotions arising from the unconscious, neglected parts of oneself which if met could change one's viewpoint to a more mature or inclusive one. Female dream: repressed desire for male partner or sex; or desire for a better sexual relationship. See second example in *door* under **house and buildings**.

burial   Letting go of the past as we knew it, and opening the way to a meeting with what we gained from it; repressing experience which may be painful or we do not wish to meet. Buried alive: memories of birth and its fears.

burning   Burning emotions; release of emotions or energy. See **fire**.

bus   Experience, undertaking or relationship with a group of people; direction taken in company with others. Idioms: miss the bus.

business and dreaming   Although the world of business and the world of dreams are often considered to be incompatible, this is not so. Once one realises that dreams may be the 'printout' of the most shrewd and capable computer we have access to, we can see them as a source of useful information. If one is in business, there is information in one's own memory, along with considered projects, questions about problem areas, which have never been put on an electronic computer. And there is no computer program outside our own mind which can handle and manipulate all the variables, the integrating of different information sources—written words, feeling hunches, spoken information, personal observation and experience—and then sift, explore different combinations, and reach into pure creativity by leaping into the new.

Dreams should not be seen as oracles, but if we take their information into account along with our other sources, we find them a real addition to our business equipment. See **creativity and problem solving in dreams**.

C

cage, cell   If the <u>dreamer is in the cage</u>: frustration arising from a sense of social pressure restraining expression, or from one's moral restraints imprisoning one; feeling caged by lack of opportunity or lack of developed abilities. The cell often depicts how we imprison ourself within our own anger, resentment or depressed feelings; or we may be trapped by childhood trauma. <u>Something or somebody else caged</u>: desire to restrain whatever is represented by the thing, person, that is caged.

calendar   Passage of time; reminder or suggestion of something important arising.

camera   Taking notice; memory; sometimes what we may have noticed out of the corner of our eye but not processed into waking awareness. See **photo**.

canal   Most often the way we direct or control our emotions —therefore relates to relationships and goals.

cancer   Fear of this illness; a part of our personality or being which is out of harmony with our wholeness; expression of how we feel about other people's—especially our mother's— emotional influence. This influence might be eating away at our own sense of well-being. Occasionally awareness of illness in part of body suggested.

candle   Male sex organ. <u>Lighting a candle</u>: a birth; prayer. <u>If lit amid darkness</u>: finding understanding or courage amid doubts, fears, depression. <u>Candle burning out</u>: awareness of

candle

death. Occasionally measure of how much time we have left in life. <u>Idioms</u>: burn the candle at both ends; not fit to hold a candle.

cane   Aggression; sadistic or masochistic sexuality.

canyon   See **valley.**

cap   See *hat* under **clothes.** <u>Idioms</u>: cap in hand; thinking cap.

capital city   such as London, Tokyo, Moscow, unless the home of the dreamer, depict material opportunity; central issues in dreamer's life; the central sense of self, around which other issues revolve. If somewhere like Jerusalem or Mecca then one's central religious drives and ideas.

captain   See **roles.**

car   Our motivating drives—sex drive, ambition, sense of failure, whatever is driving us in life; desire to 'get somewhere' in life; independence; feelings about the particular car in dream. If <u>dreamer driving</u>: being independent; self confidence; being responsible for one's own life direction. <u>With one other person</u>: relationship with that person. <u>Alone in vehicle</u>: independence; making decisions alone; feeling alone. <u>Crashing vehicle</u>: self-desired failure, perhaps to avoid stress of responsibility and change; fear of failure; failure in relationship; argument—you may be on collision course with boss or partner; occasionally psychological breakdown threatened. <u>Another driver</u>: being passive; being influenced by the opinions or emotions of someone else, or one's own secondary characteristics, i.e. anxiety or emotional pain may lead us to make many decisions and so may be the driving force in our life, rather than what might be more satisfying. <u>Driving carelessly</u>: lack of responsibility, socially or sexually; need for more awareness. Reversing: sense of not getting anywhere; feeling that one is slipping backward; reversing a decision; change of direction. Overtaking: getting ahead. Overtaken: feeling of being left behind or not competing. Car body: dreamer's body. Car torn apart, dismantled: stress; failure to care for one's body; self destructive attitudes. Fuel: feeling drives; motivation; whatever has 'fuelled one's drive'. Old car, scrapped car: sense of old age; feelings about death. Car engine: energy; heart; central drive. Running over someone: 'killing' some part of self through misplaced drive or ambition; aggression.

cards, playing   Opportunity; sense of fate. The different suits depict different things. Hearts: emotions; relationships. Diamonds: riches; intellectual. Spades: one's body; movement; sensuality. Clubs: instinctive drives such as fear, sex, hunger. Business card: identity or opportunity. Greetings card: hoping for news; thoughts about sender. See **games**.

carpet   See *carpet* under **furniture**; **colour**; **shapes and symbols**.

carriage   Similar to **car** but, because drawn by an animal, more suggestive of a direction brought about by biological drives such as sex and ageing. Can depict how you are dealing with such drives. See example in **bridge**.

carried   An ability being used; what one is 'carrying' in life, such as carrying a grudge. Being carried: a desire to drop responsibility; a return to childhood relationship. Carrying a person: treating someone else, or some part of yourself, as a child or invalid; feeling you are 'carrying the load' in life, work or a relationship; over zealous, as depicted by idiom

carried

'carrying things too far'. <u>Idioms</u>: carried away; carry a torch; carry the can.

case   See **bag**; example in **clothes**.

castle   See **house and buildings**.

castrate   Example: 'On looking at my son I see his penis has been completely cut off. I feel terribly upset, but notice that on each side of the remaining hole, special pieces of tissue have been implanted. These are budding, just like a plant, and I know, or am told, that a whole penis will grow' (Edmond U). Edmond did in fact frequently 'cut off' his sexuality by abstinence. The dream graphically shows that sexual drives are like a living process.

Trauma and/or fear regarding sexual drive, possibly leading to 'cutting off' full sexual flow; fear of the responsibility which develops with sexual maturity; the difficulty in facing the pains and adjustments which come with rejection by the opposite sex, competition for work and wealth, standing without parental support, making decisions, discriminating in the world of ideas and exercise of will.

<u>Doing it to oneself</u>: denying one's own sexual drive; introverted anger at sexual drive; the conflict of choice between feminine and masculine. <u>Done to one</u>: trauma in sexual nature. <u>Doing it to another</u>: one's own sexual pains or trauma may lead to the unconscious killing out of sexuality in one's children or others.

cataclysm   See **end of the world; atom bomb**.

catacomb, crypt   Example: 'I was in some kind of cave or crypt. My father told me and my family of his coming death. He was calm and caring but my mother, sister and myself were grief stricken and for some reason went to buy him gifts' (Clare M). Usually refers to feelings connected with death, as in the example. It suggests, even in this, a womblike condition, and birth or a child may also figure in the same dream. Also a place of power or hidden forces, where a connection may be made with our unconscious, our inner link with other people and the energies of our body.

categories of dreams Griffith, Miyago and Tago give 34 types of dream themes, from falling to being hung by the neck. For the lay dreamer it is more useful to put dreams into much broader categories such as psychological, ESP, body, sexual, spiritual and problem solving. In researching the data for this book, some special cluster of dream themes were noticed. For instance a cluster was noted in women past middle age; they dreamt of walking in a town and losing their husband. Description of these clusters can be seen in *son* and *husband* under **family**; *losing teeth* under **body**; **flying**; *secret room* under **house**; **dead people**; **individuation**. See also **dream as meeting place; dream as spiritual guide; dream as therapist and healer; sex in dreams; ESP in dreams.**

caterpillar Male sexuality; prenatal forces of growth; bacteria.

cave Example: 'I am in a large, airy cave-like room. I am pregnant and wearing a white gown. I am lying on my back on a flat slablike surface with my legs drawn up' (Joan D). Prenatal life; the vagina; the process of reproduction and birth. Also an entrance to our unconscious; in some dreams a real contact with the forces of our evolutionary journey. We may find in the cave a fear of madness or being lost; a sense of meeting the divine; our own traumas or destiny; a meeting with death and rebirth. See **catacomb, crypt; unconscious.**

Cayce, Edgar Born in Hopkinsville, Kentucky on 18 March 1877, died Virginia Beach, January 1945. Cayce was an uneducated man who found he could put himself into a sleep state in which he had access to a collective mind or universal consciousness. Cayce was a very Christian man and couched his statements in a Biblical manner. In his sleep state, however, he could verbally respond to people's questions and, using medical terms he did not know consciously, diagnose illness in people, even at a distance; speak foreign languages he had never learnt; get information he had no conscious access to. Because of this he was asked to the White House twice. At one period a hospital was built in which he worked with six doctors, diagnosing from his sleep condition. In this state, when asked how he could get information about the past, about people at a distance, etc., he replied that every person has access to what he called the cosmic mind while they sleep, but few people can bring this contact through to conscious expression. He also maintained that prolonged working with one's dreams gradually made conscious this contact with our cosmic life. For Cayce, humans are cosmic beings. A lifetime was a brief interlude of learning in an eternal pilgrimage through time and space. The conscious personality we so often raise so high is but a temporary experience assumed by an older larger being, the Individuality, or Self as Jung called it. The ego dies at death, but the Individuality absorbs its experience. Dreams are the meeting point between this older self and the personality it assumes but briefly. (Cayce's biography is *There Is A River* by Thomas Sugrue. Cayce dictated 14 million words from his sleep state; a record of these is kept at the Association for Research and Enlightenment, Virginia Beach, Va.)

cellar   See *basement and cellar* under **house and buildings**.

cemetery   Depicts our thoughts and feelings regarding death; our family heritage of attitudes or traditions; contact with the dead; things in our life we have 'buried'; being melancholy about life or feeling 'different' to other people; a relationship which we think is 'dead and buried'.

centre, middle   See **shapes and symbols**.

ceremony, ritual   Example: 'A ritual began whereby a large knife was drawn and a few deep cuts were made to both our faces. I put my hands to my face and saw them covered with blood, crying and crying' (OS). Similar to initiation. In the example the girl is with her boyfriend; she may thus have been 'initiated' into sexual activity; sex with her boyfriend has changed her image of herself.

A ritual depicts important change, such as entrance into puberty; deeper levels of oneself; new attitudes or skills; just as marriage is an entrance into a new type of life and social situation. From the wider sense of self our unconscious has, things are seen as important which consciously we feel are trivial. A ceremony in a dream brings such things to our attention.

chain   Restriction; strength; dependence. We might feel 'chained' to our marriage partner or work. See example in **abandoned**.

champagne   See **alcohol**.

chased   Example: 'Three men with clubs were chasing me, but never actually caught me as I woke in terror. I was determined to tell myself it was only a dream, and the next night as they were chasing me I remembered it was only a dream and lost all fear—stopped running—turned to face them and said "This is only a dream, you can't hurt me." As they came closer they faded into nothing and I never saw them again' (Account of dreams when six years old, Mr C). The example shows how we can be pursued by fears or emotions, and can either continue to avoid them or face them. We are, in a real sense, pursued by what we have created with our thoughts, emotions, action and inaction. What we are avoiding might be sexual feelings; responsibility; expressing what we really feel in public; our fear of death; sense of failure; guilt; emotional pain; grief, etc. We can never escape from ourself, so such feelings may pursue us through life unless we meet them.

Chased by opposite sex: afraid of love or sex; haunted by a past relationship. By animal: one's passions; anger; natural feelings. By Thing or shadowy creature: usually past experience or trauma; a hurt from childhood. Chasing: something you are pursuing in life; something or someone you want; aggression. See **follow**.

chasm   Feelings about death, sex, the unconscious or the unknown. See **abyss; valley**. See also **falling**.

chemist   Usually health concerns; healing; can be similar to doctor—wisdom about self, insight into self.

chest, box   May refer to one's physical chest; more often the way we hide in ourselves, or keep hidden, our own feelings; our most valued ideals and hopes; our best insights; the best in us.

child   See: **boy; girl;** *daughter* and *son* under **family**.

childbirth   See **baby; birth**.

choke   Conflict; indecision—as when we choke on our words; repression of emotion.

church   Religious feeling or beliefs, including moral code, or our feelings about organised religion. Each of us has a sense of our relationship with the forces of life within us, and the world outside us. A church may depict this sense and what we do with it; our sense of what is holy or fundamental to all life, and therefore eternal, such as the urge to exist; the cycles of life and growth; reproduction and interdependence. See *Christ* and **archetypes; religion and dreams**.

cigar, cigarette   Masculinity; penis. Cigarette: anxiety or release from it; dependence; feeling of having a support or help to meet stress; may associate with feelings about cancer.

cinema   Our image of self. See **theatre**.

city, town   One's relationship with society; one's sense of community; the mental and emotional environment in which one lives; in some dreams work and opportunity. Home town, town of birth: the familiar way of life; the way you usually go about things. Strange town: the new; different attitudes or way of life. Alone in a town: feeling isolated and out of touch. In a deserted town: outmoded social attitudes or way of life. Lost in a town: feeling uncertain regarding your place or direction in society. Idioms: go to town; ghost town; man about town; paint the town.

cliff   Example: 'I was standing on a clifftop overlooking the ocean. By my side was a man. He had short cropped silver hair, gleaming, and piercing blue eyes. He seemed old, but was broad, muscular and gave me the impression of having lived many lifetimes, or being very wise. He indicated the sea and I understood I should plunge into it. I did so, leaving my body behind, and became a part of the sea. At the same time it seemed I could at any time stand beside the man on the cliff again' (Debbie). On edge; danger; decision; taking a risk; a barrier; or the unknown, depending on dream content. In the example we see the cliff presented as a wider view of life, one which includes death. It is shown as the uphill struggle in life, looking back or down from which one has wisdom. It is also the test of self trust, facing fear.

climb   Example: 'We climbed this tree, the baby as well, to see what was at the top. The baby fell out of the tree. We climbed down and took the baby to a room and lay it on a bed. It seemed to be asleep and didn't wake up. Later we went back to the room to see the baby but it had gone. In its place was a bluebird. As we looked the bluebird flew away' (dream of a nine-year-old girl). The example shows a common use of climb—to see what is there, beyond, above, out of sight. The child is exploring growth, to see what maturity and death have in store. We also climb to avoid something; to get away; to climb out of some mess we are in, in which case it expressed effort on our part; we climb to get something, to reach it, so this can be ambition or motivation. Climbing has risks though. Attaining new heights in work or a relationship we reach the new and face anxiety, so may have a fear of failing/falling. Climbing may also depict the first half of life, and going downhill middle or old age. Idioms: climb down; social climber. See **hill**; **mountain**.

clock, watch   The restrictions we place upon ourself; our sense of duty and timing; realisation of urgency or having 'lots of time'. Ticking clock: might be the heart. Big clock: one's life, how much time one has left. Clock watching: tension; being bored or lacking satisfaction; feelings about ageing. See **time of day**.

close   Close a door, etc.: to be closed emotionally; decision; protectiveness. For close as in *near* see **positions**. See *door* under **house and buildings**.

clothes   Example: 'I am packing for a holiday, surrounded by a lovely selection of all sorts of clothes. I am matching outfits, shoes, scarves, handbags. It gives me great pleasure. I am wearing an old navy blue dress which is too short for me. So short I feel panic because there will not be enough time to change. I am now on the top deck of a bus. I have one battered suitcase and am wearing the same dress, trying vainly to pull it down over my knees. Suitcase bursts open and it is full of old clothes fit for a jumble sale' (Valerie H). Clothes can mean many things, depending upon dream context. In the example the clothes are feelings of pleasure and confidence, and also discomfort and lack of confidence.

In general they indicate the stance or attitudes we use to meet other people or special situations such as work or danger; protection, such as might be given by our feelings of reserve, shyness, anxiety or aggressiveness in fending off sexual or other advances; clothes depict self respect and how we see ourselves in society—the difference between what we want and what we feel others want of us; our clothes, especially when we consider their colour, can also express our emotional condition and moods. Constance Newland gives the example of dressing in violet symbolising being inviolate sexually. Overdressed , unable to get clothes off: too cautious in relationships; difficulty in changing attitudes or self image; self protectiveness; avoiding intimacy.

Naked or see-through clothes: example: 'I am at the doctor's being examined. It is always the same. I have all my clothes off and he examines me from the roots of my hair down to my toenails. I am just at the point where I am going to ask him for his diagnosis when he fades away' (Miss L). Desire to be attractive and noticed, as in the example, where Miss L is enjoying an acceptable form of intimacy; being open about what you really feel; fear of other people seeing what you really feel, think and desire; anxiety about not being adequate socially; lacking ability to conform to social norm. See **nude**. Ragged or inappropriate clothes: feelings of inadequacy. depressed feelings; rebellion against authority or society. Armour, protective clothing : defences against internal anxieties, past hurts and external intimacy. Other people's clothes: the social attitudes and responses we have adopted from others. Children's, teenage clothes in adult's dream: youthful or immature attitudes or behaviour. Undressing: revealing one's real character; move towards intimacy. <u>Dirty</u>, <u>untidy clothes</u>: difficult or grubby feelings; one's inner condition, such as an untidy mind, or grubby feeling values. <u>Worn out or old clothes</u>: attitudes ready to be left behind; old habits no longer useful; feeling worn out, old or tired. <u>Tight clothes</u>: being too restricted in attitude; being tight emotionally. <u>New clothes</u>: change in attitudes; new feeling about self. <u>Someone else's clothes</u>: could be feelings from that person; their attitudes; memories. <u>Man in woman's clothes</u>: unacceptability of male role, with its connection with breadwinning, aggression, being cannon fodder in war; homosexual tendency; desire for mother. <u>Woman in male clothes</u>: unacceptability of female role, motherhood, housewife; lesbian tendency; desire for father figure. <u>Clothing inappropriate to dream surroundings</u>: attitudes or behaviour inappropriate to one's situation. <u>Changing clothes</u>: altering one's mode of behaviour, role or mood. <u>Idioms</u>: dress to kill; dress up.

apron Mother role; household world; getting to work on a family situation.

belt Often tightly restrained sexuality or emotions; protectiveness. <u>Idioms</u>: belt up; tighten one's belt.

blouse and shirt Feelings and emotions. <u>Idioms</u>: stuffed shirt; shirt sleeves, informal.

coat The general 'self' we use in public; we might be shy in public but very warm with a single friend. <u>Overcoat</u>: usually protectiveness; not giving any secrets away; not showing intimacy or vulnerability. Can also depict our belief system, political or religious, we use to meet the world. Such systems may be a way of allaying anxiety about decisions and self responsibility, and without them we may feel vulnerable and exposed.

<u>Idioms</u>: dragged by one's coat tails; up one's sleeve; coat of many colours.

dress Femininity; exteriorisation of feelings.

gloves Protection, as in wearing rubber gloves; keeping 'one's hands clean', as in the sense of avoiding 'dirty business'; being out of touch. Can also represent someone's hand —holding their glove would be holding their hand. <u>Picking up a dropped glove</u>: similar to picking up a handkerchief dropped by a woman—an invitation to a relationship. <u>Idioms</u>: hand in glove; iron fist in velvet glove; with kid gloves; with the gloves off.

hat Opinions, beliefs, mental attitudes—for instance a Jewish skull cap would represent the religious beliefs of the wearer. <u>Idioms</u>: at the drop of a hat; brass hat; eat one's hat; hang on to one's hat; under one's hat; old hat.

raincoat The attitudes we use to meet difficult emotions or events; often appears in dreams of dead spouse, suggesting tears or the release of emotions. See **rain**.

shoes Position in life; life situation; the condition of one's chosen direction, i.e. formal dancing shoes in a discotheque would suggest outmoded approach. <u>Idioms</u>: be in someone else's shoes.

skirt More particularly sexual than dress. Colours and length say a lot about what is being done with sexuality in a social sense.

trousers Maleness; protection; socialised sexuality. <u>Idioms</u>: wears the trousers; with their trousers down.

underclothes, knickers, underpants, briefs Intimate sexual feelings. <u>If black</u>: restraint or unconscious sex drives. <u>Dirty or grubby</u>: sex attitudes we are not proud of; difficult feelings about biological side of self.

work clothes Working at something; attitudes concerning work.

clouds If bright: usually feelings of uplift or religious feelings. If dull: depression, feeling overshadowed by something.

coffee Mostly social ritual; something stimulating. Offering, being offered coffee: friendship, intimacy; what we thirst for or desire.

coffin Nearly always a reminder of one's own mortality. Also death of a relationship and the feelings of loss; one's feelings about the death of someone such as a husband. See **funeral**.

cold Held back emotions, especially fear; feeling neglected or 'left out in the cold'; sometimes connected with feelings about death. Idioms: cold shoulder; cold storage; cold feet.

collective unconscious Jung describes this as the 'inherited potentialities of human imagination. It is the all controlling deposit of ancestral experiences from untold millions of years, the echo of prehistoric world events to which each century adds an infinitesimal small amount of variation and differentiation. These primordial images are the most ancient, universal, and deep thoughts of mankind.'

Jung tried to explain his observation of a strata of being in which individual minds have their collective origin in a genetic way. This seems unlikely, and Rupert Sheldrake sees it as a mental phenomena. Dr Maurice Bucke called it cosmic consciousness. J.B. Priestley saw it as 'the flame of life' which synthesised the experience of all living things and held within itself the essentials of all lives. If we think of it as a vast collective memory of all that has existed, then we can say the life of Edgar Cayce exhibited a working relationship with it.

Such a collective level of mind would explain many things,

such as telepathy, out of body experiences, life after death, which have always been puzzling because they are difficult to explain using presently known principles.

colours   Example: 'I was standing in a very beautifully carved chapel or religious place. There seemed to be shadowy nun or monk-like figures around. But it was the exquisite colouring of the place which filled me with a sort of ecstasy. Everything was in the most delicate shell pink' (SC). In many dreams where colour predominates there are usually strong feelings, as in the example. This suggests colours depict our emotions and feeling tones. Where a dreamer is largely intellectual or out of touch with their feelings, the colour would stand in the place of the emotion instead of alongside it, as with SC.

White is the most frequently mentioned colour in the collection of dreams used for this book, black next, then blue.

black   The unconscious; unknown; hidden or avoided; the unaccepted side of self; not being aware; depression; fear; death. Also the earthy, or source of life and growth. What is hidden in the unconscious or body can be powerfully transformative. Black clothes or undergarments: hidden or unconscious feelings or sexuality. Black animals: unconscious drives and urges. See **dark**.

blue   Light blues: our sense of intuition; having a wide awareness of life; religious feelings. Also coolness of nature. Often seen in visions of the womb as a blue grotto or woman with halo of blue, so connects with prenatal and infant relationship with mother. Dark blues: in many women's dreams, threatening men appear dressed in dark blue or navy blue overalls; depression; negative thoughts or intuition. Idioms: blue film; blue funk; blue pencil; blue stocking; feel blue; out of the blue.

brown   Depression; dullness; earthiness; excrement; conceal-ment. Idioms: brown study; browned off.

green   Potential for growth; healing or positive change. Often found in dreams about heaven. Dark greens: evil intentions; growth of negative attitudes; sickness; envy; jealousy. Idioms: green fingers; green light; green, meaning naive.

indigo, violet   Mostly religious feelings; intuition.

orange   Blending or balance of emotions and intellect. Some-times warmth; religious feelings or insight.

red   Example: 'An old woman with a very pink, lined face, and wearing a clashing red hat, knelt close to my face. The woman leaned forward to poke my hand, and I recoiled, screaming myself awake' (Joy S). Even where red appears quite casually in a dream, as with the hat in the example, there is frequently fear, screaming, horror or a sense of danger in the same dream. Less frequently, red represents blood; menstruation; the biological life force; conception; death. Red face: anger; high emotion. Red brick building : homeliness; warmth. Red furniture or decor: plush; richness. Red flowers: love; passion; dangers of passion. Red clothes or motif: sexu-ality; passion; strong emotions. Red and grey together : emo-tions connected with depression. Rose pink: love. Pale pink: baby feelings; weakness. Idioms: see red; in the red; red car-pet; red light district; red faced.

white   Awareness; clearness of mind; purity; cleanness; light feelings. In certain dreams white is very threatening; perhaps we have connections with hospitals in these dreams. Exam-ple: 'There was a huge white kitchen. I was scared when I entered it and there was a door leading out of it into a white corridor with a turquoise carpet which scared me even more' (HH). Maggots, mould, dead or sick people and shrouds can also be white, so white can depict death or sickness. White clothes: a sense of wholeness; purity or marriage. White animals: urges and sexuality which has been accepted or integrated with conscious activities.

yellow   Lightness of feeling; intellect; extroversion; cowardice.

comb   Something you are doing or thinking about doing to tidy up your thoughts or self presentation. Idioms: fine tooth comb.

compass   Your attempt to find a direction or activity you feel confident about.

compensatory theory   Jung, Hadfield and several other dream researchers believe the dream process is linked with homoeostasis or self regulation (see *Man and His Symbols,* Jung; *Dreams and Nightmares,* Hadfield; *Mind and Movement,* Crisp). This means that the process underlying dream production helps keep psychological balance, just as homoeostasis keeps body functions balanced. Put bluntly, dreams are said to compensate for conscious attitudes and personality traits. So the coldly intellectual man would have dreams expressive of feelings and the irrational, as part of a compensatory process; the ascetic might dream of sensuous pleasures, and the lonely unloved child dreams of affection and comfort. Although dreams can be seen as self regulatory, this narrower view of compensation is only seen in a few dreams. See **computers and dreams; sleep movements; science and dreams; sleep walking**.

computers and dreams   Because of the ease with which computers can file, sort, cross reference and present information, a great deal of work has been done in analysing the content of thousands of dreams *(The Content Analysis of Dreams,* Hall and Van De Castle). As computers are an everyday part of many homes, we can easily use them to gain insight into our own dreams. Two areas of help are as follows.

We can enter many dreams, then with a program such as Seeker or Masterfile, easily scan through them to see the frequency of dream themes. This approach to dreams—self insight through a series of dreams—is explained by Hall in *The Meaning of Dreams*. Important issues in our life and development occur as frequent dream themes, and are easily seen using a computer.

The program Brainstorm (Brainstorm Software Ltd) makes cross referencing dream symbols and associated comments easy. Using this program, if one dreamt of a tree and wrote one's associations, then six months later dreamt of a tree and entered this, the program instantly reminds you of the past reference to tree and can display it. Gradually a reference base of your own dreams and comments can be built up and quickly scanned. Such comparisons help to form a personality profile of yourself or others.

contraceptive   Example: 'I was in my mother's bedroom with my teenage boyfriend. We were laying in my parents' double bed and he was kissing my breasts. I realised we were near to making love and told him I was not on the pill. Seeing him taken aback, I told him my father has contraceptives in a nearby drawer. The dream fades as he is trying to put one on' (Julia). Julia, a teenager, is obviously approaching her readiness for lovemaking. She has accepted the sexual standards of her parents—their bed. The contraceptive represents anxiety about pregnancy; sexual responsibility; sexual standards; sexually transmitted diseases.

cooking   Example: 'I saw piles of French loaves. On picking one up I saw that although the crust was crisp, the inside was runny wet dough. I wondered if cooking would make them usable' (Derek L). As in the example, ways we transform 'inedible' or 'unpalatable' aspects of our life. Also nourishing ourself; creativity; our ability to make something new of the varied opportunities or experiences we have; giving of ourself. See *cook* under **roles**; **food**; *kitchen* under **house and buildings**.

cord   May be similar to chain or rope—a restriction. But often depicts the feeling bonds we have with another person or situation; the umbilical, in the sense of a dependency that holds us. <u>Breaking the cord</u>: becoming independent of parents or authority figures—often anger or resentment is directed at the person we are dependent upon.

core   See **centre**.

corner   Example: 'I was afraid the thugs would corner and attack me' (Pauline B). Example: 'I went into an obscure corner of the cloakroom and hung up the coat—then I went through the pockets' (Mrs RE). Feeling trapped or restricted; or, as in the second example, a hidden or little admitted aspect of oneself. Occasionally such boundaries or restrictions might produce a sense of snugness or security. <u>Street or projected room corner</u>: the unexpected or unseen; new experience; public gaze; indecision or the act of making a decision. <u>Idioms</u>: drive somebody into a corner; in a tight corner; knock the corners off someone; turn the corner; hole in the corner affair.

corpse   See *dead body* under **body**.

corridor   Example: 'I'm trapped in a long passageway or corridor. I can't get out. I'm feeling my way along the wall—there is a small light at the end of the tunnel, I can't get to it. I'm very frightened. I wake up before I get to the end. Then I feel afraid to go back to sleep' (Margaret). The example may refer to the experience of birth in the birth canal. Such a corridor can also depict our sense of not being able to get out

corridor

of an unsatisfactory situation. No man's land; limbo; in-between state; the process of going from one thing to another. See *white* under **colour**.

cosmetic Desire to attract attention; our public traits; cover up.

countryside One's natural feelings; a relaxed state; the forces of 'nature' in us; our moods—a rainy countryside would be a more introverted mood than a lively sunny scene. Country lanes: meeting what is natural in us—this may disturb the dreamer, perhaps being in the form of a wolf or animal. See **lane; landscapes;** *farmer* under **roles; settings**.

crab The shell of brittle emotions we guard ourself with; grasping or hurtful attitudes. Being nipped by crab: physical or psychosomatic pain or even illness caused by being too tight or self protective. See *shellfish* under **fish**.

crack A flaw in one's thinking; a weakness in the attitudes or defences we use in meeting life; the unexpected; the irrational breaking through into consciousness; the vagina. Idioms: cracking up; crack of doom; paper over the cracks.

crater Past trauma.

creativity and problem solving in dreams Few dreams are, by themselves, problem solving or creative. The few exceptions are usually very clear. Example: 'My mother-in-law died of cancer. I had watched the whole progression of her illness, and was very upset by her death. Shortly after she died the relatives gathered and began to sort through her belongings to share them out. That was the climax of my upset and distress, and I didn't want any part of this sorting and taking her things. That night I dreamt I was in a room with all the relatives. They were sorting her things, and I felt my waking distress. Then my mother-in-law came into the room. She was very real and seemed happy. She said for me not to be upset as she didn't at all mind her relatives taking her things. When I woke from the dream all the anxiety and upset had disappeared. It never returned' (told to author during a talk given to the Housewives Register in Ilfracombe).

Although in any collection of dreams such clearcut problem solving is fairly rare, nevertheless the basic function in dreams appears to be problem solving. The proof of this lies in research done in dream withdrawal. As explained in the entry **science, sleep and dreams**, subjects are woken up as they begin to dream, therefore denying them dreams. This quickly leads to disorientation and breakdown of normal functioning, showing that a lot of problem solving occurs in dreams, even though it may not be as obvious as in the example. This feature of dreaming can be enhanced to a marked degree by processing dreams and arriving at insights into the information they contain. This enables old problems to be cleared up and new information and attitudes to be brought into use more quickly. Through such active work one becomes aware of the self, which Carl Jung describes as a centre, but which we might think of as a synthesis of all our experience and being. Gaining insight and allowing the self entrance into our waking affairs, as M.L. Von Franz says in *Man and His Symbols,* gradually produces 'a wider and more mature personality' which 'emerges, and by degrees becomes effective and even visible to others'.

The function of dreams may well be described as an effort on the part of our life process to support, augment and help mature waking consciousness. A study of dreams suggests that the creative forces which are behind the growth of our body are also inextricably connected with psychological development. In fact, when the process of physical growth stops, the psychological growth continues. If this is thwarted in any way, it leads to frustration, physical tension and psychosomatic and eventually physical illness. The integration of experience, which dreams are always attempting, if successful cannot help but lead to personal growth. But it is often frozen by the individual avoiding the 'growing pains', or the discomfort of breaking through old concepts and beliefs.

Where there is any attempt on the part of our conscious personality to co-operate with this, the creative aspect of dreaming emerges. In fact anything we are deeply involved in, challenged by or attempting, we will dream about in a creative way. Not only have communities like the American Indians used dreams in this manner—to find better hunting, solve community problems, find a sense of personal life direction—but scientists, writers, designers and thousands of lay people have found very real information in dreams. After all, through dreams we have personal use of the greatest computer ever produced in the history of the world—the human brain.

1 In Genesis 41, the story of Pharaoh's dream is told—the seven fat cows and the seven thin cows. This dream was creative in that, with Joseph's interpretation, it resolved a national problem where famine followed years of plenty. It may very well be an example of gathered information on the history of Egypt being in the mind of Pharaoh, and the dream putting it together in a problem solving way. See **dream process as computer**.

2 William Blake dreamt his dead brother showed him a new way of engraving copper. Blake used the method successfully.

3 Otto Leowi dreamt of how to prove that nervous impulses were chemical rather than electrical. This led to his Nobel prize.

4 Friedrich Kekulé tried for years to define the structure of benzene. He dreamt of a snake with its tail in its mouth, and woke to realise this explained the molecular formation of the benzene ring. He was so impressed he urged colleagues, 'Gentlemen, learn to dream.'

5 Hilprecht had an amazing dream of the connection be-

tween two pieces of agate which enabled him to translate an ancient Babylonian inscription.

6 Elias Howe faced the problem of how to produce an effective sewing machine. The major difficulty was the needle. He dreamt of natives shaking spears with holes in their points. This led to the invention of the Singer sewing machine.

7 Robert Louis Stevenson claims to have dreamt the plot of many of his stories.

8 Albert Einstein said that during adolescence he dreamt he was riding a sledge. It went faster and faster until it reached the speed of light. The stars began to change into amazing patterns and colours, dazzling and beautiful. His meditation on that dream throughout the years led to the theory of relativity.

To approach our dreams in order to discover their creativity, first decide what problematic or creative aspect of your life needs 'dream power'. Define what you have already learnt or know about the problem. Write it down, and from this clarify what it is you want more insight into. If this breaks down into several issues, choose one at a time. Think about the issue and pursue it as much as you can while awake. Read about it, ask people's opinions, gather information. This is all data for the dream process. If the question still needs further insight, before going to sleep imagine you are putting the question to your internal store of wisdom, computer, power centre, or whatever image feels right. For some people an old being who is neither exclusively man nor woman is a working image.

In the morning note down whatever dream you remember. It does not matter if the dream does not appear to deal with the question; Elias Howe's native spears were an outlandish image, but nevertheless contained the information he needed. Investigate the dream using the techniques given in the entry **dream processing**. Some problems take time to define, so use the process until there is a resolution. If it is a major problem, it may take a year or so; after all, some resolutions need re-structuring of the personality, because the problem cannot disappear while we still have the same attitudes and fears. See **secret of the universe dreams; dream processing**.

cricket · See **games**.

crossing   A change, but often with much vulnerability; an obstacle, usually of a feeling nature, to overcome. Maybe fear or uncertainty causes us to be unable to make the change, so we dream of a bridge giving way. Such changes often are to do with major life junctures, such as from youth to adulthood, prepuberty to adolescence, single to married, young to middle age. Sometimes it can be a trial or test such as initiation. Crossing a river or chasm: feelings about death. See **bridge; river; road; individuation**.

crossroad   Example: 'I keep in touch with an old boyfriend who I have not seen since I was 18, which is 14 years ago. In my dream I was on holiday on a coach which stopped at the crossroads. I met my old boyfriend who had come from the other direction and we walked together. I felt enormous plea-sure being in his company again. A hearse passed us slowly with a child's coffin' (Mrs R). Crossroads represent decisions, as in the example. In trying to decide what direction to take, Mrs R still finds emotions tie her to the past, but the dead child shows she really knows the relationship has ended. Crossroads also have a certain amount of anxiety involved, as with crossing.

crowd   Feeling crowded out; public opinion; one's feelings about people in general. Lost in a crowd: feeling without per-sonal direction; confusion on meeting many opinions; desire not to stand out. Attacked by crowd: fear of public opinion; feeling one's own angry urges as threatening. Talking to, lead-ing, or part of crowd at a central event: an impulse or idea which unifies many parts of one's own nature—as the many aspects of our own being, such as visual impressions, sensuality, thoughts, musical sense, religious feelings, sexual drive, intuition, fear, ambition, hunger, our desire for acclaim, the sadist in us and so on, constitute a crowd. How we relate to the crowd: suggests our relationship with our own inner community and the external public. Being unable to tolerate parts of ourselves leads to intolerance towards other people with those traits.

crown   Success, either desired or achieved; realisation of expanded awareness. See **dream as spiritual guide**.

crucifixion   Masochism; guilt; feelings of being a scapegoat; frequently connected with the pains of being born. Also parts of us may have been 'killed' and if they are coming alive again —being felt once more—the pain of their emergence is shown as crucifixion. In some cases the dying of an egocentric self as it gives way to a wider awareness emerging from unity of unconscious and waking self. See **religion and dreams**.

crystal   The human sense of the eternal; the self; rigid views or emotions. Crystal ball: intuition; introversion.

cuckoo   Wanting to, or feeling your partner is, having sex outside your relationship. See **birds**.

cul de sac   Sense of efforts leading nowhere; a woman's legs, with the vagina at the end.

cup   Offering oneself; a woman offering herself and sexuality; a receptive state of being which can receive intuitively from the unconscious.

D

dam The way we attempt to 'bottle up' our emotions and drives such as ambition or sexuality. There is often tremendous power or energy waiting to be used or directed.

dancing Example: 'We were both shy of each other but as the dance went on I found I could move so well to his steps that we felt like one, it was so effortless that it felt like floating' (Heather). The example shows the general meaning of dancing, feeling at one with someone or aspects of yourself. It shows unity, as seen in the cells working as a harmonious whole. It can also mean happiness; sexual mating dance; getting closer or more intimate. If the <u>dance is awkward</u>: lack of harmony connected with what is depicted. <u>Animals dancing</u>: harmony with unconscious drives and sexuality. <u>Skeletons or dark 'things' dancing</u>: developing a relationship with what we fear—meeting it; dancing with death. In life we always dance with death, meaning we have an intimate relationship with it, but might not be ready to recognise who our partner is.

danger Most often anxiety. We may fear the danger of allowing our sexual urges—the danger of falling in love with its possible pain—the danger of failing if we take a risk. These may be depicted as impending danger in a dream. In such cases the real danger is of taking our **anxieties** as reality, instead of seeing them for what they are, a reaction to a situation. A <u>relative</u>, <u>loved one in danger</u>: the temptation is to believe the dream is presaging a real event. Our concern for children and loved ones, but more often our **fears** regarding them, create most of such dreams. A woman told me a dream in which her daughter was strangled while at university. In processing her dream the woman wept strongly as she met feelings of fear about her daughter leaving home and living independently at university. See **attack; predictive dreams**.

dark   Example: 'I ran down very dark streets, like a maze, and could not find a way out of them' (Mrs N). Darkness has many meanings, depending on what else appears in the dream. In the example the feeling is of being lost and trapped in depressing feelings.

What is unknown; not defined by the intellect or conscious self; unconscious; depression; confusing; terrifying; secrets we hide from self or others; things we do 'under cover of darkness'; age; the womb; death. The following dream depicts particular aspects of darkness. Example: 'It was a festival in this strange world, in which everything had a rather dark, dilapidated look' (Tom). Dark here is ancient, things dating from times past. This may refer to our sense of our own childhood which feels like the ancient past, or to our unconscious knowledge of family and cultural attitudes and experience. In general the 'strange' world of the unconscious or sleep.

Example: 'I was overwhelmed by terror, as if the very darkness of the tunnel was a living force of fear which entered and consumed me. I screamed and screamed, writhing in uncontrollable fit-like contractions. Nevertheless a part of me was observing what was happening and was amazed, realising I had found something of great importance' (Andrew P). Because the dreamer explored this dream with me, I know the darkness was depicting fear Andrew experienced while a nine year old in hospital. He was given a rectal anaesthetic because he was about to have a nose operation. He fought and begged for the nurses to stop, but to no avail. This led to a very real feeling that humans were terrifyingly dangerous animals who would not respond even if you were on your knees begging. So trauma was the fear in the darkness. Darkness here is the unconscious area of experience.

Example: 'I am back in time looking at an old cottage. I see the windows, walls and doors, everything about the place. It is dark and old and warm. I see the curtains and bedrooms, all the ornaments and I feel safe and comfortable' (Mrs R). Here dark is comfortable, perhaps because it is undemanding; one is not in any glare of attention or activity. It is the relaxed quiet of evening. This woman has a relaxed relationship with her unconscious.

Example: 'I met a woman I know in a long, dark underground tunnel. She was waiting for me. We had sexual intercourse. She had a very formed vagina mouth, and a very large clitoris, like a small penis. I masturbated this' (Norman). Norman has no fear of the tunnel. It is his secret desire and pleasure which he admits to no one, often not even to himself. Dark here is one's secret self.

Dark water: emotions which are felt and powerful but have not been defined or their source understood. Dark colours: feelings emanating from unconscious sources; depressed or unhappy feelings. Idioms: a dark horse; in the dark; keep it dark. See *night* under **day and night**.

daughter   See *daughter* under **family**.

day and night

day   Example: 'It was a beautiful hot sunny day, and I was in a children's playground talking to a woman I knew vaguely' (Kim B). Mostly our mood. In the example Kim feels bright and cheerful. An overcast day would be the reverse. Also being conscious; 'seeing' what we are doing; our waking experience. See **light; time of day**.

night   Example: 'I was creeping through a field at night. In darkness I and others were trying to accomplish some secret act, rather as spies or underground agents might' (Tom). Similar to dark. Usually the unconscious, dark or little-sensed areas of oneself. In the example the secrecy occurs because parts of Tom's childhood experience were 'hidden' behind the forgetfulness or unconsciousness of emotional hurt. Also loneliness; areas of subtly felt urges or feelings. And sometimes freedom; we may be constrained by the social or moral rules we apply to ourself during the 'day' or waking consciousness, but on the edge of consciousness, or in sleep, we find a wonderful freedom which allows us escape. Sometimes shown by <u>escaping from a house at night</u> and running away. See **dark**.

dead end   See **cul de sac**.

dead people dreams   Example: 'My husband's mother, no longer alive, came and slid her arms carefully under me and lifted me up. I shouted "Put me down! Put me down! I don't want to go yet." She carefully lowered me on to the bed and disappeared' (EH). Most dreams in which dead people appear are expressive of our attempts to deal with our feelings, guilt or anger in connection with the person who died; or our own feelings about death. In the example the dreamer is feeling fear about being carried off by death.

When someone close to us dies we go through a period of change from relating to them as an external reality, to meeting and accepting them as alive in our memories and inner life. In the next example the man has not only come to terms with his mother's and his own death, but also found this inner reality. Example: 'A dark grey sugar loaf form materialised. This pillar lightened in shade as I watched. It didn't move. I began to think it was Mrs Molten who died in 1956. The feeling grew stronger but still the colour lightened. Then it bent over and kissed my head. In that instant I knew it was my mother. An ecstatic joy and happiness such as I have never known on earth suffused me. That happiness remained constantly in mind for the next few days' (Mr M).

dead husband or wife   Many dreams of dead people come from women who have lost their husband. It is common to have disturbing dreams for some period afterwards; or not be able to dream about the husband (or wife) at all; or to see the partner in the distance but not get near. In accepting the death, meeting any feelings of loss, grief, anger and continuing love, the dream may become as below. The example both shows the resolution of the loss, but also the paradox felt at realising the meeting was an inner reality. Example: 'A couple of months ago as I was waking I felt my husband's arm across me and most realistically experienced my hand wrapping around his arm and turning towards him (which I had done so often in his lifetime) and saying "I thought you had died. Thank God you have not." Then I awoke alone and terribly shaken' (Mrs I). A critic might say this is only a dream in which a lonely woman is replaying memories of her dead husband's presence for her own comfort—thus her disappointment on being disillusioned. Whatever our opinion, the woman has within her such memories to replay. These are reality. The inner reality is of what experience was left within her from the relationship. Her challenge is whether she can meet this treasure with its share of pain, and draw out of it the essence which enriches her own being. That is the spiritual life of her husband. The 'aliveness' of her husband in that sense is also social, because many other people share memories of him. What arises in their own lives from such memories is the observable influence of the now dead person.

But the dead also touch us more mysteriously, as in the next example. Example: In a recent news programme on television, a man who survived a Japanese prisoner of war camp in Singapore had been given a photograph of children by a dying soldier he did not know. The man had asked him to tell his family of his death, but did not give his name. The photograph was kept for 40 odd years, the man still wanting to complete his promise but not knowing how. One night he dreamt he was told the man's name. Enquiries soon found the family of the man, who had an identical photograph. See *husband* under **family**.

death   Example: 'My son comes in and I see he is unwashed and seems preoccupied and as if he has not cared for himself for some days. I ask him what is wrong. He tells me his mother is dead. I then seem to know she has been dead for days, and my two sons have not told anyone. In fact my other son has not even accepted the fact' (Anthony). Anthony is a divorcée. Processing the dream he realised the two sons are ways he is relating to the death of his marriage to the children's mother. A dead body, death of someone we know: very often, as in the example, the death of some aspect of our outer or inner life. Our drive to achieve something might die, and be shown as a death in our dreams. Lost opportunities or unexpressed potentials in ourselves are frequently shown as dead bodies. All of us unconsciously learn attitudes or survival skills from parents and others. Often these are unrecognised and may be shown as dead.

Example: 'During my teens I was engaged to be married, when I found a more attractive partner and was in considerable conflict. Consistently I dreamt I was at my fiancé's funeral until it dawned on me the dream was telling me I wanted to be free of him. When I gave him up the dreams ceased' (Mrs D). If the death is of someone we know: frequently, as in the example, desire to be free of the person; or unexpressed aggression; perhaps one's love for that person has 'died'. We often 'kill' our partners in dreams as we move towards independence. Or we may want someone 'out of the way' so we do not have to compete for attention and love.

Death of oneself: exploration of feelings about death; retreat from the challenge of life; split between mind and body. The experience of leaving the body is frequently an expression of this schism between the ego and life processes. Also death of old patterns of living—one's 'old self'. The walking dead, rigor mortis: aspects of the dreamer which are denied, perhaps through fear. Dancing with, meeting death or dark figure: facing up to death.

Example: 'I dream I have a weak heart which will be fatal.

death

It is the practice of doctors in such cases to administer a tablet causing one painlessly to go to sleep—die. I am completely calm and accepting of my fate. I suddenly realise I must leave notes for my parents and children. I must let them know how much I love them, must do this quickly before my time runs out' (Mrs M). This is a frequent type of 'death' dream. It is a way of reminding ourselves to do now what we want to, especially regarding love. Although the unconscious has a very real sense of its eternal nature and continuance after physical death, the ego seldom shares this. We have an unconscious realisation that collective humanity carries the living experience from the life of the dead. The farmer today unconsciously uses the collective experience of humanity in farming. What innovation he does today his children or others will learn and carry into the future. Idioms: dead and buried; dead from the neck up/down; dead to the world; play dead. See *death and rebirth* under **archetypes**.

deep   Usually we live on the surface of our mind. In sleep we dive down deeper but lose our sense of self. If we maintain some awareness in these 'deeps' of the mind, it is somewhat like snorkelling in deep sea; we realise what immense and unbelievable depths lie beneath us. Dreams often portray this as depth—a hole; deep water; a chasm; space; our non-verbal life in the womb, or early childhood, which is remembered as patterns of feeling reaction rather than verbal utterance. In the depths we may find gems, skeletons, archaeological objects, and these relate to the memory of our evolutionary past, family influences we carry within us unknown. Deep cuts: suggests a hurt which penetrates us; or emotions which affect us powerfully. Idioms: in deep water; in the deep end; deeply troubled; deeply hurt.

defaecate   Self expression; release of tension; getting rid of negative experience or emotions; creative expression; permitting the natural in oneself. See **excrement**.

defence mechanisms   Although the dream process attempts to release difficult emotions, trauma and past experience, most people have inbuilt mechanisms which prevent this spontaneous healing activity. It is natural to pull our hand away from a hot surface because of the pain. We do this 'without thinking'. Similarly we unconsciously pull away from any painful or frightening emotions, even though it may be in our best interests to release or integrate them. The non-release leads to physical tension; a massive use of energy to contain such emotions; and even development of physical illness. Resistance may also be in the form of not wanting to change; fear of the new; feeling threatened by fresh views of life or any questioning of the values one has long lived by. To free oneself from such resistances needs a positive motivation and the learning of new psychological and even physical skills, as presented in forms of psychotherapy.

déjà vu   Many dreamers say they find a connection between a place they dream of—especially a house—and a place they later see while awake. Most of these descriptions appear to be attempts to find connections obvious to no one but the dreamer. A strong desire to have the inner world connect with the real world seems to be the motivation. This may be through a need for human life to have meaning and connection with a wider, invisible, life. The evidence of thousands of dreams suggests that searching for meaning in this direction is misplaced. Meaning arises from a love or acceptance of the many aspects of oneself, and thus the expansion of awareness into what was unconscious. While there may be valid cases of *déjà vu,* they are rare.

demolition   Major changes in dreamer's inner or outer life have been, or are being, undertaken; breakdown of old attitudes and approaches.

departing Example: 'I was leaving some people, like at a junior school. Some of the children tried to detain me, with the attitude that I was defying teacher's authority, and they restrained me with the rules they restrained themselves with. I broke free and walked off' (Timothy). As in the example, a breaking away from old or habitual patterns of behaviour; leaving a situation, such as a relationship, a financial set-up or work; the struggle to become independent as in leaving home. Sometimes desire to get away from responsibility or difficulties. Can also refer to death, perhaps when we see a spouse walking away from us, or departing on a journey. This is not necessarily a prediction, but confronting the situation. Idioms: new departure; the departed (dead); leave in the lurch; leave someone to it; left holding the baby.

depression and dreams One hundred and forty dreams were collected from a group of patients suffering depression. The same number of dreams were collected from people similar in age and social background, but not suffering depression. The dreams were given code numbers, mixed and given to an independent judge. He was asked to look for any evident themes of self punishment, such as 'I was waiting for my friends all night but they never turned up', 'my fiancé married somebody else'. Such self punishing themes were found to occur with greater frequency in the depressives' dreams.

descending, down Example: 'I look down and the stairs and bannister rail are swarming alive with a black moving wave of crawling things, like some awful insects; and in the hallway is a swamp with crocodiles and other hideous things. My terror is terrible and I cry out to stop dreaming this nightmare. The person who actually lived in this part of the house was the owner's mother. She treated me badly but no one knew as she was artful in her abuse. She pulled me along by my hair, locked me in a cupboard, and once locked me in the orchard—four high walls and a hidden door' (Rita). Something below us: as in Rita's dream, where there is fear, it can depict past trauma which is not being faced (literally run away from); something we have left behind or we feel 'above'.

Descent, going down stairs or in a lift: getting more down to earth or practical; a return to difficulties after living in our fantasies or escapism; depression; sexual restraint; a return from meta conception (see **aura**). Descending into cave, cellar, hole: awareness of unconscious content; experience of womb existence. Example: 'Then I was climbing down a steep hill. Arriving at the foot I found rippling sparkling water. I stopped and looked around and found everything incredibly beautiful—the green fields and the pebbles in the water, the soft fresh air; then I looked up and the sky was a glorious picture, the sun so warm and the clouds fluffy and soft and pretty. I felt at peace and so happy, and thanked God with all my heart for giving us so much beauty' (Mrs RE). Going down a hill: can mean loss of status, ageing, failure or death, but is also, as shown in the example, a positive sense of life after death. Idioms: feel down; down and out; down in the dumps; down to earth.

desert or wilderness   Loneliness, literally being deserted; lack of emotion or satisfaction; no creativity or growth in one's life; dry intellectualism; death; sexual barrenness. Occasionally as the symbol in the Bible of wandering in the wilderness, which depicts the human sense of having no real meaning or direction, of being a wanderer in the infinity of time and decision; it shows the difficulty of being self responsible and making decisions in the infinity of choices, and of honouring the self in such decisions.

desk   Work; authority; discipline.

destination   Because the unconscious has a powerful faculty for synthesising our experience, it frequently arrives at a sense of what we most wish for or want to create through our life.

Yet we may not have become aware of what has been realised unconsciously; it may be depicted by a place we are heading towards, or a goal; a destination we do not remember. Also our conscious ambition and desire; our hopes; what we have struggled long for.

devil   See **evil**; **aboriginal**. See also **active/passive**.

devour   Being eaten by dogs or creatures: losing our sense of identity, or what we think or want, in meeting other people's will, anger or ideas; being 'consumed' by fear, emotion or a drive; fear of death. Swallowed by large creature or fish: opening to awareness of unconscious content. Devouring: being possessive; hungering for something.-

diamond   See **jewels**.

digging, excavation   Example: 'I entered a neglected garden adjoining a house I had formerly lived in. I was astonished that I had never noticed this garden before. I took a spade and hoe and began to work vigorously in order to put things right, digging like a navvy. But wherever I put my spade I turned up live shells and hand grenades—highly explosive and very dangerous. I was terrified I would be blown to pieces and hurried away' (from *Organism of the Mind*, G.R. Heyer, Kegan Paul, 1933). The dreamer in the example was a man in his 40s who had taken up meditation on the suggestion of a friend. It shows him discovering and uncovering a part of himself he had not known before. In doing so he meets explosive emotions and conflicts he is not used to dealing with. Digging usually depicts delving into hidden or buried areas of ourself. We may uncover feelings from our childhood—creative realisations, features of the unconscious, even dead bodies or ancient creatures. Digging can also represent our work on renovating our attitudes, personality structure or habits. See **garden**.

dinosaur Our personality is a young new thing. It grows throughout our life, but its roots reach into the processes of life and consciousness active in our own being which are as ancient as life on this planet. Life on the planet is also only an extension of processes active in the cosmos. So in dreams we often sense this primordial past out of which our present self has grown, and frequently depict this meeting as a prehistoric animal.

dirty Actions or feelings which we feel are grubby or immoral. The unconscious has a natural morality based on its sense of connection with the universal principles of mating, birth, growth and death. Where our social or sexual life does not align with this or our own consciously accepted principles, we may dream of being dirty.

disappearance Depicts the way our conscious self relates to the unconscious. Memories, emotions or ideas suddenly appear in awareness, but can disappear just as rapidly, sometimes never to be seen again. See **vanish**.

displacement Displacement of aggression from a threatening target to a less threatening one is a common human and animal practice. If we are angry at our partner we may kick the cat or nag at the children instead of confronting the real target. Freud stated that in dreams we express what we usually censor, or would be censored socially, in terms of behaviour or sexuality, but often in a displaced way. What appears to be most important and full of emotion in the dream may, according to this statement, be really of least significance.

diving Taking a chance; facing anxiety. Diving underwater: delving into one's mind or unconscious. Exploring the meaning of a dream, or an eventful meditation, might be depicted as diving underwater in dreams.

divorce   May be an expression of anger towards one's spouse; fear of or hope for breakup of marriage. <u>Male dream</u>: difficulty with one's feelings. <u>Female dream</u>: difficulty with social extroversion and intellect.

doll   Example: 'She continues to attack him and, to my horror and feeling of helplessness, his head comes off. But the neck is made of some sort of material with a string hanging off it, and I realise it is a doll's head' (Mr RH). Many 'doll' dreams are, as the example, using the doll as a target for violence. This may refer to how the dreamer felt as a child when smacked or attacked emotionally—like a helpless doll. Also, in general, childhood states of feeling about ourself; a means of displacement for anger or feelings the dreamer would like to discharge on another; a feeling of wanting to be a precious 'doll' to someone; wanting to be loved. See also **toy**.

door   See *door* under **house and buildings**.

dragon   Because the part of our mind we name 'the unconscious' is so ancient and huge, we sometimes depict contact with it as a dragon or monster. Also the untamed or unsocialised sexual drive which can overpower or trap a girl emerging into womanhood, or threatens a youth facing manhood. The overcoming of it means facing one's fears of the vast power of such natural drives, and finding satisfying expression.

drama   See **film; theatre**.

dream analysis   Sigmund Freud was the founder of modern therapeutic analysis of dreams. Freud encouraged clients to relax on a couch and allow free associations to arise in connection with aspects of their dream. In this way he helped the person move from the surface images (manifest content) of the dream to the underlying emotions, fantasies and wishes (latent content), often connected with early childhood. Because dreams use condensation—a mass of different ideas or experiences all represented by one dream image or event—Freud stated that the manifest content was 'meagre' compared with the 'richness and variety' of latent content. If one succeeds in touching the feelings and memories usually connected with a dream image, this becomes apparent because of the depth of insight and experience which arises. Although ideally the Freudian analyst helps the client discover their own experience of their dream, it can occur that the analyst puts to the client readymade views of the dream. Out of this has occurred the idea of someone else 'analysing' or telling us about our dream.

Carl Jung used a different approach. He applied amplification (see entry), helped the client explore their associations, used active imagination (see entry) and stuck to the structure of the dream. Because amplification also put to the client the information and experience of the therapist, again the dreamwork can be largely verbal and intellectual, rather than experiential.

In the approach of Fritz Perls (gestalt therapy) and Moreno (psychodrama), dream analysis is almost entirely experiential. The person exploring the dream acts out or verbalises each role or aspect of the dream. If one dreamt of a house, in gestalt one might start by saying 'I am a house' and then go on to describe oneself just as one is as the particular house in the dream. It is important, even if the house were one existing externally, not to attempt a description of the external house, but to stay with the house as it was in the dream. This is like amplification, except the client gives all the information. This can be a very dramatic and emotional experience because we begin consciously to touch the immense realms of experience usually hidden behind the image. When successful this leads to personal insights into behaviour and creativity. See **dream processing**; **amplification**; **gestalt dream work**.

dream as a meeting place   Any two people, or group of people who share their dreams, particularly if they explore the associated feelings and thoughts connected with the dream images, achieve social intimacy quickly. Whether it is a family sharing their dreams, or two friends, an environment can be created in which the most profound feelings, painful and wonderful, can be allowed. Such exposure of the usually private areas of one's feelings and fears often presents new information to the dreamer, and also allows ventilation of what may never have been consciously expressed before. In doing so a healing release is reached, but also greater self understanding and the opportunity to think over or reconsider what is discovered.

Herbert Reed, editor of the dream magazine *Sundance,* and resident in Virginia Beach, Va., initiated group dreaming experiments. It started because Reed noticed that in the dream groups he was running, when one of the group aired a problem, other members would subsequently dream about that person's problem. He went on to suggest the group should attempt this purposely and the resulting dreams shared to see if they helped the person with the problem. The reported dreams often formed a more detailed view of the person's situation. In one instance the group experienced many dream images of water. It aided the woman who was seeking help to admit she had a phobia of water and to begin thinking about learning to swim. In another experiment, a woman presented the problem of indecision about what college to transfer to and what to study. Her group subsequently said they were confused because they had not dreamt about school. Several had dreams about illicit sex, though, which led the woman to admit she was having an affair with a married man. She went on to realise that it was the affair which was underlying her indecision. She chose to end the affair and further her career.

Whatever may be underlying the results of Reed's experiments, it is noticeably helpful to use the basic principles he is working with. They can be used by two people equally as well as a group—by a parent and child, wife and husband, businessman and employee. One sets out to dream about each other through mutual agreement. Like any undertaking, the involvement, and therefore the results, are much more pronounced if there is an issue of reasonable importance behind the experiment. It helps if one imagines that during sleep you are going to meet each other to consider what is happening between you. Then sleep, and on waking take time to recall any dream. Note it down, even if it seems far removed from what you expected. Then explore its content using the techniques in **dream processing**.

Example: 'My wife and I decided to attempt to meet in our dreams. I dreamt I was in a room similar to the back bedroom of my previous marriage. My present wife was with me. She asked me to help her move the wardrobe. It reminded me of, but did not look like, the one which had been in that bedroom. I stood with my back to it, and reached my hands up to press on the top, inside. In this way I carried it to another wall. As I put it down the wood broke. I felt it ought to be thrown away' (Thomas B). Thomas explored the dream and found he connected feelings about his first marriage with the wardrobe and bedroom. In fact the shabby wardrobe was Tom's feelings of shabbiness at having divorced his first wife. In his first marriage, represented by the bedroom, he always felt he was married for life. In divorcing, he had done something he didn't like and was carrying it about with him. He says 'I am carrying this feeling of shabbiness and second best into my present relationship, and I need to get rid of it.'

dream as a spiritual guide   Dreams have always been connected with the spiritual side of human experience, even though today many spiritual leaders disagree with consideration of dreams. Because dreams put the dreamer in touch with the source of their own internal wisdom and certainty, some conflict has existed between authoritative priesthood and public dreaming. A lay person finding their own approach to God in a dream might question the authority of the priests. No doubt people frequently made up dreams about God in order to be listened to. Nevertheless, despite opposition, Matthew still dreamt of an angel appearing to him; Joseph was still warned by God to move Jesus; Peter still dreamt his dream of the unclean animals.

The modern scientific approach has placed large question marks against the concept of the human spirit. Study of the brain's functions and biochemical activities have led to a sense of human personality being wholly a series of biological and biochemical events. The results of this in the relationship between doctor and patient, psychiatrist and client, sometimes results in the communication of human personality being of little consequence. It may not be put into words, but the intimation is that if one is depressed it is a biochemical problem or a brain malfunction. If one is withdrawn or autistic, it is not that there is a vital centre of personality which has for some reason chosen to avoid contact, but that a biochemical or physiological problem is the cause—it's nothing personal, take this pill (to change the biochemistry, because you are not really a person). Of course we have to accept that human personality must sometimes face the tragedy of biochemical malfunction, but we also need to accept that biochemical and physiological process can be changed by human will and courage.

In attempting to find what the human spirit is by looking at dreams, creativity stands out. The spiritual nature may not be what we have traditionally considered it to be. An overview of dreams and how dreamers relate to them suggests one amazing fact. Let us call it the 'seashell effect'. When we hear sounds in a shell that we hold to our ear, the noises heard seem exterior to oneself, yet they are most likely amplification of sounds created in our own ear, perhaps by the passage of blood. Imagine an electronic arcade machine which the player could sit in and, when running, the player could be engulfed in images, sounds, smell and sensation. At first there is shimmering darkness, then a sound, and lights move. Is it a face seen, or a creature. Like Rorschach's ink blots, the person creates figures and scenes out of the shapeless light and sound. A devil appears which terrifies the player. People, demons, animals, God and angels appear and fade. Scenes are clearcut or a maelstrom of movement and ill-defined activity. Events arise showing every and any aspect of human experience. Nothing is impossible.

If, on stepping out, we told the player that what occurred was all their own creation due to unconscious feelings, fears, habits, thoughts and physiological processes occurring within them, like the seashell effect, they might say 'Good God, is that all it was, and I thought it was real. What a waste of time.'

Whether we can accept it or not, as a species we have created out of our own longings, fears, pain and perhaps vision, God, with many different names—politics, money, devils, nationalism, angels, art, and so on and on. All of it has flowed out of us. Perhaps we even deny we are the authors of the Bible, wars, social environments. Responsibility is difficult. It is easier to believe the source is outside oneself. And if we do take responsibility for our amazing creativity, we may feel 'is that all it is—me?' Yet out of such things, such fears, such drives, such unconscious patterns as we shape our dreams with, we shape our life and fortune, we shape our children, we shape the world and our future. The shadow of fear we create in our dream, the situation of aloneness and anger, becomes a pattern of feelings, real in its world of mind. We create a monster, a Djinn, a devil, which then haunts and influences us. Or with feelings of hope, of purposiveness and love, create other forces in us and the world. But we are the creator. We are in no way separate from the forces which create our existence. We are those creative forces. In the deepest sense, not just as an ego, we create ourselves, and we go on creating ourselves. We are the God humanity has looked so long for.

The second aspect of the human spirit demonstrated by dreams is consciousness. The unconscious mind, if its function is not clogged with a backlog of undealt with painful childhood experience and nonfunctional premises, has a propensity to form gestalts. It takes pieces of experience and fits them together to form a whole. This is illustrated by how we form gestalts when viewing newsprint photographs, which are made up of many small dots. Our mind fits them together and sees them as a whole, giving meaning where there are only dots. When the human mind is working well, when the individual can face a wide range of emotions, from fear and pain to ecstasy, this process of forming gestalts can operate very creatively. This is because it needs conscious involvement, and if the personality is frightened of deep feeling, the uniting of deeply infantile and often disturbing experience is cut out. Yet these areas are very rich mines of information, containing our most fundamental learning.

If the process is working well, then one's experience is gradually transformed into insights which transcend and thereby transform one's personal life. For instance, we have witnessed our own birth in some manner; we also see many others appearing as babies. We see people ageing, dying. We see millions of events in our life and in others. The unconscious, deeply versed in imagery, ritual and body language, out of which it creates its dreams, picks up information from music, architecture, traditional rituals, people walking in the street, the unspoken world of parental influence. The sources are massive, unbelievable. And out of it all our mind creates meaning. Like a process of placing face over face over face until a composite face is formed, a synthesis of all the faces; so the unconscious scans all this information and creates a world view, a concept of life and death. The archetypes Jung talks of are perhaps the resulting synthesis of our own experience, reaching points others have met also. If so, then Christ might be our impression of humanity as a whole. If we dare to touch such a synthesis of experience it may be searing, breathtaking.

It breaks the boundaries of our present personality and concepts because it transcends. It shatters us to let the new vision emerge. It reaches, it soars, like an eagle flying above the single events of life. Perhaps because of this the great hawk of ancient Egypt represented the human spirit.

Lastly, humans have always been faced by the impossible. To a baby, walking and not wetting its pants is impossible, but with many a fall and accident it does the impossible. It is a god in its achievement. To talk, to fly heavier-than-air planes, to walk on the Moon, were all impossible. Humans challenge the impossible every day. Over and over they fall, back into defeat. Many lie there broken. Yet with the next moment along come youngsters with no more sense than grasshoppers, and because they don't know what the difference is between right and left, do the impossible. Out of the infinite potential, the great unknown, they draw something new. With hope, with folly, with a wisdom they gain from who knows where, they demand more. And it's a common everyday sort of miracle. Mothers do it constantly for their children—transcending themselves. Lovers go through hell and heaven for each other and flower beyond who they were. You and I grow old on it as our daily bread, yet fail to see how holy it is. And if we turn away from it, it is because it offers no certainties, gives no authority, claims no reward. It is the spiritual life of people on the street. And our dreams remember, even if we fail. For this is the body and blood of the human spirit.

dream as a therapist and healer   There is a long tradition of using dreams as a base for both physical and psychological healing. One of the earliest recorded incidents of such healing is when Pharaoh's 'spirit was troubled; and he sent for all the magicians of Egypt and all its wise men; and Pharaoh told them his dream, but there was none who could interpret it'. Then Joseph revealed the meaning of the dream and so the healing of Pharaoh's troubled mind took place (Genesis 41).

dream as a therapist and healer

The Greek Temples of Asclepius were devoted to using dreams as a base for healing of body and mind (see **dreams and ancient Greece**). The Iroquois Amerindians used a social form of dream therapy also (see **Iroquoian dream cult**). The dream process was used much more widely throughout history in such practices as Pentecostal Christianity, shaktipat yoga in India, and Anton Mesmer's groups (see **sleep movements**).

Sigmund Freud pioneered the modern approach to the use of dreams in therapy, but many different approaches have developed since his work. Examples of the therapeutic action of gaining insight into dreams are to be found in the entries on **abreaction, recurring dreams, reptiles**. The entry on **dream processing** gives information about using a dream to gain insight and healing. See also **dream as meeting place**.

A feature which people who use their dreams as a therapeutic tool mention again and again is how dreams empower them. Many of us have an unconscious feeling that any important healing work regarding our body and mind can only be undertaken and directed by an expert; the expert might be a doctor, a psychiatrist, psychotherapist, or osteopath. Witnessing the result of their own dream process, even if helped by an expert, people feel in touch with a wonderful internal process which is working actively for their own good. One woman, who had worked on her dream with the help of a friend (non expert), said 'It gave me great confidence in my own internal process. I realised there was something powerful in myself working for my own good. It was a feeling of cooperating with life.' One is frequently amazed by one's own resources of wisdom, penetrating insight and sense of connection with life, as met in dreamwork. This is how dreams play a part in helping one towards wholeness and balance. The growing awareness of one's central view of things, which is so wide, piercing and often humorous, brings developing self respect as the saga of one's dreams unfolds.

There may be no hint of this, however, if a person simply

records their dreams without attempting to find a deeply felt contact with their contents. It is in the searching for associated feelings and ideas that the work of integrating the many strands of one's life begins. Gradually one weaves, through a co-operative action with the dream process, a greater unification of the dark and the light, the painful and transcendent in one's nature. The result is an extraordinary process of education.

dream deprivation   See **science, sleep and dreams**.

dreamer   Our current 'self image' is displayed by what we do in our dreams. If we are the active and central character in our dreams, then we have a positive, confident image of ourself. The role we place ourself in is also the one we feel at home with, or one which is habitual to us. If we are constantly a victim in our dreams, we need to consider whether we are living such a role in everyday life. Dreams may help us look at our self image from a more detached viewpoint. We can look back on what we do in a dream more easily than we can on our everyday waking behaviour. This helps us understand our attitudes or stance, a very growth-promoting experience. It is important to understand the viewpoint of the other dream characters also; although they depict secondary views, they enlarge us through acquaintance. See **identity and dreams**.

What we ourself are doing in our dreams is an expression of how we see ourselves at the time of the dream, our stance or attitude to life, or what could be generalised as our self image. It typifies what aspects of our nature we identify with most strongly.

Example: 'My husband and I are at some sort of social club. The people there are ex-workmates of mine and I am having a wonderful time and am very popular. My husband is enjoying my enjoyment' (quoted from article by the author in *She* magazine). The dreamer describes herself as 'a mature 41-

year old'. The dream, and her description of it, sum up her image of herself in just a few words. She sees herself as attractive, sociable, liked, happily married. She is probably good looking and healthy. But the dream carries on. She and her husband 'are travelling down a country lane in an open horse drawn carriage. It is very dark and is in the areas we used to live. We come to a hump-backed bridge, and as we arrive at the brow of the bridge a voice says, "Fair lady, come to me." My body is suddenly lying flat and starts to rise. I float and everything is black, warm and peaceful. Then great fear comes over me and I cry out my husband's name over and over. I get colder and slip in and out of the blackness. I wake. Even with the light on I feel the presence of great evil.' From a very positive sense of self, she has moved to a feeling which horrifies her. How can such a confident, socially capable woman, one who has succeeded professionally as well as in her marriage, have such feelings? The answer probably lies in the statement of her age. At 41 she is facing the menopause and great physical change. The image of herself she has lived with depended, or developed out of, having a firm sexually attractive body, and being capable of having children. Losing whatever it is that makes one sexually desirable must change the image others have of one, and that one has of oneself. The hump of the bridge represents this peak of her life, from whence she will start to go downhill towards death, certainly towards retirement. So she is facing midlife crisis in which a new image of herself will need to be forged.

To define what self image is portrayed in your dreams, consider just what situation you have created for yourself in the dream, and what environment and people you are with. Example: 'I am a shy 16 year old and am worried about my dream. In it I am walking along the school's main corridor. I try to cover myself with my hands as a few people go by, not noticing me. Then a group of boys pass, pointing and laughing at me—one boy I used to fancy. A teacher then gives me clothes. They are too big but I wear them because I have nothing else' (HM). Adolescence is a time of great change anyway, when a lot is developing as far as self image is concerned. Her nakedness shows how vulnerable she feels, and how she has a fear that other people must be able to see her developing sexuality and womanhood. It is new to her and still embarrassing, particularly with boys she feels something for. She tries to cover up her feelings, and uses attitudes she has learnt from parents and teachers, but these are not suitable. So we might summarise by saying that the situation she places herself in within the dream shows her present uncertainty and sense of needing clothes—attitudes or confidence —of her own. See **identity in dreams; individuation**.

dream process as computer   The brain is not a computer, but it has the power to compute. The word *computare* is Latin, and comes from *putare,* to think. Neither is a computer anything like a human brain. But there are parallels. Christopher Evans, a psychologist, computer scientist and world authority on microprocessors, says the brain and computers are both information handling devices, taking impulses which in themselves mean nothing, like sound waves, and processing them. It is also his theory that both computers and the waking-brain function are taken off-line to re-program. Our behaviour responses and information bases need bringing up to date with any new experience and information that is relevant. In the case of the computer, off-line means having modifications made to programs; in the human it means sleeping and dreaming, the dream being the powerful activity of review, sifting and reprogramming. Thirdly, the brain and computer use programs. In humans, a program means a learnt set of responses, values or activities, such as walking or talking, but including more subtle activities such as judging social or business situations.

If, as Christopher Evans believes, dreaming is partly a period of revising and updating responses, insights and skills, then by working with the process one can make it more efficient. The background for this statement is that many people have recurring dreams which change very little. Looking at this from the 'programming' view, the attempt to revise is thwarted. But individuals can free such 'stuck' dreams by using dream processing.

Also, as some dreams are obviously a synthesis of experience and information gathered over a lifetime, the dream process is much more than a computing function which sorts new information and updates. It is also capable of creative leaps through synthesis and conjecture. J.B. Priestley's dream of the birds (see **religion and dreams**) appears to be a massive synthesis of things observed over a lifetime. It also depicts a brain function like computer simulation, which takes information and forms it into an experimental view of possibilities arising from the thousands of millions of separate bits of gathered data. See **ESP in dreams; creative and problem solving dreams.**

dream processing   Below are described simple techniques which make it possible to gain information quickly from dreams. They have been put as a series of questions.

What is the background to the dream?   The most important aspects of your everyday life may have influenced the dream or feature in it. Briefly consider any aspects of your life which connect with what appears in the dream. Example: 'I have a plane to catch. I get to the plane but the suitcase is never big enough for my clothing which I have left behind. I am always anxious about stuff left behind. I wake still with the feeling of anxiety' (Jane). When asked, Jane said plane flights had been a big feature of her life. She had moved home often, travelling to different parts of the world, leaving friends and loved ones behind.

What is the main action in the dream?   There is often an overall activity such as walking, looking, worrying, building something, or trying to escape. Define what it is and consider if it is expressive of something you are doing in waking life. Activities such as walking or building a house need to be seen as generalisations; walking can simply represent taking a direction in life. When you have defined the action, look for further information under the other headings in this book, such as **swimming** or **sitting**.

What is your role in the dream?   Are you a friend, lover, soldier, dictator, watcher or participant in the dream? Consider this in relationship with your everyday life, especially in connection with how the dream presents it. Where possible, look for the entry on the role in this book. See **dreamer**.

Are you active or passive in the dream?   By passive is meant not taking the leading role, being only an observer, being directed by other people and events. If you are passive, consider if you live in a similar attitude in your life. See **active/passive**.

What do you feel in the dream?   Define what is felt emotionally and physically. In the physical sense are you tired, cold, relaxed or hungry? In the emotional sense do you feel sad, angry, lost, tender or frightened anywhere in the dream? This helps clarify what feeling area the dream is dealing with. It is important also to define whether the feelings in the dream were satisfyingly expressed or whether held back. If held back they need fuller expression. See **emotions and mood**.

Is there a 'because' factor in the dream?   In many dreams something happens, fails to happen, or appears . . . because! For instance, trapped in a room you find a door to escape through. All is dark beyond and you do not go through the door 'because' you are frightened of the dark. In this case the 'because' factor is fear. The dream also suggests you are trapped in an unsatisfying life through fear of opportunity or the unknown.

Am I meeting the things I fear in my dream?   Because a dream is an entirely inward thing, we create it completely out of our own internal feelings, images, creativity, habits and insights. So even the monsters of our dream are a part of ourself. If we run from them it is only aspects of ourself we are avoiding. Through defining what feelings occur in the dream you may be able to clarify what it is you are avoiding. See **nightmares**; **dream as spiritual guide**.

What does the dream mean?   We alone create the dream while asleep. Therefore, by looking at each symbol or aspect of the dream, we can discover from what feelings, thoughts or experience, what drive or what insight we have created the drama of the dream. In a playful relaxed way, express whatever you think, feel, remember or fantasise when you hold each symbol in mind. Say or write it all, even the seemingly trivial or 'dangerous' bits. It helps to act the part of each thing if you can; for instance as a house you might describe yourself as 'a bit old, but with open doors for family and friends to come in and out. I feel solid and dependable, but I sense there is something hidden in my cellar'. Such statements portray oneself graphically. Consider whatever information you gather as descriptive of your waking life. Try to summarise it, as this will aid the gaining of insight.

Try amplifying your dream   You will need the help of one or two friends to use this method. The basis is to take the role of each part of the dream, as described above. This may seem strange at first, but persist. Supposing your name is Julia and you dreamt you were carrying an umbrella, but failed to use it even though it was raining, you would talk in the first person present—'I am an umbrella. Julia is carrying me but for some reason doesn't use me.' Having finished saying what you could about yourself, your friend(s) then ask you questions about yourself as the dream figure or object. These questions need to be simple and directly about the dream symbol. So they could ask 'Are you an old umbrella?' 'Does Julia know she is carrying you?' 'What is your function as an umbrella?' 'Are you big enough to shelter Julia and someone else?' And so on. The aim of the questions is to draw out information about the symbol being explored. If it is a known person or object you are in the role of—your father for instance—the replies to the questions need to be answered from the point of view of what happened in the dream, rather than as in real life. Listen to what you are saying about yourself as the dream symbol, and when your questioner(s) has finished, review your statements to see if you can see how they refer to your life and yourself.

If you are asking the questions, even if you have ideas regarding the dream, do not attempt to interpret. Put your ideas into simple questions the dreamer can respond to. Maintain a sense of curiosity and attempt to understand, to make the dream plain in an everyday language sense. Lead the dreamer towards seeing what the dream means through the questions. When you have exhausted your questions ask the dreamer to summarise what they have gathered from their replies. See **postures, movements and body language** for an example of how to work with body movement to explore a dream meaning.

Can I alter the dream to find greater satisfaction? Imagine yourself in the dream and continue it as a fantasy or daydream. Alter the dream in any way that satisfies. Experiment with it, play with it, until you find a fuller sense of self expression. It is very important to note whether any anger or hostility is in the dream but not fully expressed. If so, let yourself imagine a full expression of the anger. It may be that as this is practised more anger is openly expressed in subsequent dreams. This is healthy, allowing such feelings to be vented and redirected into satisfying ways, individually and socially. In doing this do not ignore any feelings of resistance, pleasure or anxiety. Satisfaction occurs only as we learn to acknowledge and integrate resistances and anxieties into what we express. This is a very important step. It gradually changes those of our habits which trap us in lack of satisfaction, poor creativity or inability to resolve problems.

Summary To summarise effectively gather the essence of what you have said about each symbol and the dream as a whole and express it in everyday language. Imagine you are explaining to someone who knows nothing about yourself or the dream. Bring the dream out of its symbols into everyday comments about yourself. A man dreamt about a grey, dull office. When he looked at what he said about the office he realised he was talking about the grey, unimaginative world he grew up in after the Second World War, and how it shaped him.

Further information on using these techniques can be found in Tony Crisp's work *The Instant Dream Book,* published by C.W. Daniel. See **amplification; plot of dream; adventure of the dream world; dreamer; postures, movement and body language; settings; symbols and dreaming; word analysis of dreams; wordplay and puns**.

dreams and ancient Greece   Antiphon, a Greek living in the fourth century BC, wrote the first known descriptive book of dreams. It was designed to be used for practical and professional interpretations. He maintained that dreams are not created by supernatural powers but natural conditions. In the second century AD a similar book was written by Artemidorus, a Greek physician who lived in Rome. He claimed to have gathered his information from ancient sources, possibly from the Egyptian dream book dating from the second millennium BC. He may have used works from the Assurbanipal library, later destroyed, which held one of the most complete collections of dream literature. Artemidorus classified dreams into dreams, visions, oracles, fantasies and apparitions. He identified two classes of dreams: the *somnium,* which forecast events; and the *insomnium,* which are concerned with present matters. For the *somnium* dreams Artemidorus gave a dream dictionary. For example, he said abyss meant an impending danger, a dream of warning, and to see a candle being lighted forecasts a birth, to exhibit a lighted candle augers contentment and prosperity, a dimly burning candle shows sickness, sadness and delay. This last interpretation is taken from folklore of the times and, because dreams tend to use commonly used verbal images, was probably true. He maintained that a person's name—that is their identity, and the family, national and social background from which they arose—has a bearing on what their dream means.

Plato (429–347 BC) said that even good men dream of uncontrolled and violent actions, including sexual aggression. These actions are not committed by good men while awake, but criminals act them out without guilt. Democritus said that dreams are not products of an ethereal soul, but of visual impressions which influence our imagination. Aristotle (383–322 BC) stated that dreams can predict future events. Earlier Hippocrates, the 'father of medicine', discovered that dreams can reveal the onset of organic illness. Such dreams, he said, can be seen as illogically representing external reality.

Hippocrates was born on the island of Kos. On the island was the famous temple dedicated to Aesculapius, the god of medicine. There were about 300 such temples in Greece alone, dedicated to healing through the use of dreams. Hippocrates was an Aesculapian, and learnt his form of dream interpretation from them. In such temples the patient would ritually have to cleanse themselves by washing, and abstain from sex, alcohol and even food. They would then be led into what was sometimes a subterranean room with harmless snakes in—these were the symbol of the god. In the morning the patients were asked their dream, and it was expected they would dream an answer to their illness or problem. There are many attestations to the efficacy of this technique from patients.

dream within dream A dream presents us with emotions or information we may be avoiding while awake. Usually a dream within a dream is a ploy one uses to explain away the impact of the feelings met—which is all the more reason to understand the dream.

drink To absorb or take something subtle into oneself. This may be taking in feelings such as pleasure; absorbing a mood; 'drinking in' our surroundings. When <u>connected with thirst</u>: suggests needs or longings being met. If in company <u>with someone of the opposite sex, or a group</u>: taking in the pleasure or otherwise of the relationship or group. Sometimes connected with childhood emotional need. See **alcohol**.

driving See **car.**.

drowning Example: 'I fell into a pond. My brother was frightened to be by himself so he jumped in. We were both drowning in the water and we shouted out for Mum. My brother drowned' (Poppy S). Poppy dreamt this while feeling insecure and anxious because her father was ill. Because of the water, drowning depicts fear of being overwhelmed by difficult emotions or anxieties. <u>Someone else drowning</u>: may occasionally show our apprehension about their health or well being, having the suggestion of death or breakdown.

drum May represent the heart, sexual tension, intercourse, masturbation, depending on context in dream. Can be our awareness of the natural rhythms of our own life processes, such as heartbeat, menstruation, circulation, and the feelings arising from our depths. See **music**.

drunk Loss of control; lack of reason; having no soul or self control; abandonment to the irrational or natural urges. Thus freedom from the burden of self awareness, responsibility and decision making. See **alcohol**.

dwarf, malformed figure   A part of our personality left un-developed or not integrated. For instance we may have musi-cal ability which was suppressed by the need to bring up children. Also a part of self malformed by painful childhood experience or lack of emotional nourishment. It may therefore be a link with our unconscious.

E

earth The things we take for granted which act as the supportive background to our life and activities, such as parental love, our own reality as a person, social order, the thousands of things which constitute 'reality' for us. Also the 'ground we stand on'; attitudes and relationships we have taken for granted; everyday life; the past. <u>Soft earth, fields</u>: mother; the fundamental processes of life out of which we have our being and which continually nurture us. <u>Under, swallowed by the earth</u>: the unconscious habits, drives and psychobiological processes which existed before our emergence as a conscious self, and in which we might lose self in death. <u>Idioms</u>: down to earth; go to earth; like nothing on earth. See also **unconscious**.

earthquake Insecurity; the breakdown of opinions, attitudes or relationships which seemed so dependable. May also show great inner change and growth which makes us feel uncertain of our 'ground'. The growth from youth to puberty may be felt as an earthquake, as also maturity to middle age. See **earth**.

east Personal connection with source of life; birth; the mysterious or religious aspect of self.

eating Satisfying one's needs or 'hunger'. This can be any area of need, such as emotional, mental, sexual, depending on dream context. Example: 'I am putting four of our puppies under the grill and cooking them' (Maureen). Although Maureen hasn't eaten her puppies yet, her dream illustrates how food is used to represent emotional needs. Maureen is childless, has a lot of mother love, planned the pregnancy of her bitch, and gets enormous satisfaction from rearing the puppies. She is literally hungry for the exchange of love and care she finds in dealing with her puppies.

Occasionally shows information about actual nutritional needs or physical allergies. Also, to eat is to continue involvement in the fundamental processes of life, a celebration of interdependence. To not eat: shows a conflict with the physical reality of one's body and its needs; an avoidance of growth or change; an attempt to be isolated from others, reality, the whole. Avoiding certain foods: expression of decision making in dealing with needs; food allergy. Giving food to others: giving of oneself to others, or nurturing some aspect of oneself. Eating objects or repulsive food: meeting objectionable experiences; trying to 'stomach' things which make you 'sick'.

Example: 'I ran into a house and came face to face with a huge stag. I noted the open back door, whereupon he started eating my leg. I was pushing against his horns and managed to stop him chewing me' (Jasmine C). Being eaten : the first part of Jasmine's dream (not quoted) is obviously sexual. Being eaten therefore suggests she is being consumed by her sexual drive. Being eaten, especially if it is the face, also shows how our identity, or our fragile sense of self, is feeling attacked by emotions or fears, other people, or internal drives. The classic story of Jonah illustrates this, and shows how the conscious personality needs to develop a working relationship with the unconscious. Eaten by dogs, maggots: feelings about death. See **food**. See also *dog* under **animals; individuation**. *Idioms:* eaten away; eat dirt; eat humble pie; eat like a horse; eat one's heart out; eat one's words; eat out of one's hand; eat you out of house and home; what's eating you?; proof of the pudding is in the eating; dog eat dog.

egg   Potential; parts of self as yet unrealised or not fertilised by our conscious action or quality; the female ovum; a sense of wonder regarding life; our prenatal life.

Egypt   Usually the hidden side of self; the riches of the unconscious. In the Biblical symbolism, life dominated by material values.

ejaculation, emission   Example: 'I was in a cubicle or small toilet with a very black coloured woman. She told me there was something wrong with her vagina. She was undressed. I rubbed her vagina and we both felt enormous passion. I then woke but couldn't at first remember the dream. I have refrained from sexual intercourse for some weeks, as I always feel shattered/tired afterwards. Anyway I awoke very wet, yet couldn't remember any ejaculation. Then I remembered the dream and continued it in fantasy. I experienced powerful urges to find a woman to have a non-committed sexual relationship with. But in the end I wanted to share my feelings with my wife, but she seemed deep asleep' (Alan P). The example shows how our sexual needs attempt to satisfy themselves even though we may make a conscious attempt to deny them. The ejaculation, male or female, shows the sexual nature of one's dream, even if the symbols seem to have no obvious connection. The attitudes in one's dream also show something of our relationship to sex. This may be mechanical, fearful, loving, etc. Alan sees sex as a problem to be solved, and has difficulties around commitment.

embryo   An extremely vulnerable aspect of us; our own prenatal experience; or our feelings connected with our prenatal life—for instance we may have been told our mother tried to abort us. Even if this is not so, the idea acts as a focus for our feelings of rejection and infantile pain. The embryo or foetus would therefore symbolise such feelings. See **baby**.

emotions, mood   There is a level of human experience which is typified by intense emotional and physical response to life. Such emotions and bodily drives may remain almost entirely unconscious until touched by exploring our dream content in the right setting. When such feelings and bodily movements arise, as they do in dreams, we may be amazed at their power and clarity. See **dream processing; sleep movements**.

If we take away the images and events occurring in a dream and simply look to see what feelings or emotions are evident, the dream is often more understandable than if we try to interpret the symbols. Feelings in dreams are nearly always undistorted. We therefore do not need to interpret them, simply to acknowledge them and see if we can recognise where they occur in waking life. The images in a dream may be the way we unconsciously pictorialise our flux of feelings and the play of internal energy flows. For instance love or sexual drive can give rise to physical movement—as in sexual intercourse. Repression of sex or love also represses such physical movements, leading to tension and conflict, which might be presented in the drama of a dream.

Example: 'I was with my wife, walking along a street, on holiday with her. But I felt awful tension. It was the sort of stress I feel when I have turned off my sexual flow—as I have at the moment' (Brian V). Brian can easily see the connection between the dream feelings and his everyday life, although sometimes we need to practise this. But the situation could as easily be expressed as a dream image of a blocked river. The underlying feelings would then be less easy to grasp.

Example: 'I was in a very ancient crumbling building, confronted by a large stone door, deeply engraved with many designs and creatures. I began to open the door and felt high feelings of anxiety. I realised this was an initiation and I must calm my feelings in order to pass beyond the door, i.e. if I were controlled by my feelings I would run away' (Derek F). How we meet the emotions in our dreams illustrates our habitual method of dealing with them. The feelings of anxiety in Derek's dream were met and moved beyond, but this is unusual. This is because most of us change our direction as soon as there is a hint of fear. The amount of nicotine and alcohol human beings consume suggests how poorly we meet anxiety. Going beyond fear or pain is an initiation which opens doors for us. We might now apply for the job, ask for the date, raise the issue, express the creativity, make the journey abroad, which anxiety previously kept us from. We see this in the next example: 'I had a ring on my marriage finger. It was a thin band of gold. I woke up frightened' (Angela). Angela is not married and feels anxiety about the commitment.

Dreams give us a safe area to express emotions which might be difficult or dangerous to release socially. Anger in a dream may be expressing what we failed to express in a waking encounter, or it might be our habitual response. It may also be directed against ourself. Dreams also contain many positive emotions. Sometimes they present a new aspect of feeling which is life enhancing. A person who habitually felt at odds with her father and relatives experienced a dream in which she felt forgiveness for the first time. This was entirely new for her and led to a reconciliation with her family.

Some feeling states in a dream are subtle, and may be more evident in terms of the symbols than the feelings. A grey drear environment suggests depression and lack of pleasure. A sunny light environment with flowers and colour shows pleasure and good feelings. A country landscape depicts quite a different feeling state to a smoky busy city street. We can define these for ourself using the techniques described under **dream processing**.

Whatever feelings or emotions we meet in our dreams, many of them are bound to be habitual responses we have to life. Where these habits are negative we can begin to change them by working with the dream images as described in the last question under **dream processing**. See **love**; **hostility**.

empty   Example: 'I was down in a low bit of a village, trying to get to a road high up on a hill where the sun was shining and was walking through dark, empty houses' (Heather). The use of empty in this dream can be understood by the comparison existing between the 'down low, empty houses' feeling, and the 'high up, sunny hill' feeling.

Generally lack of pleasure, enthusiasm, good feelings; loneliness; lack of relationship; sense of isolation. Or lack of one's potential, opportunity, space to be oneself. <u>Empty house</u>, <u>buildings</u>, <u>shell</u> : outgrown habits or ways of life; old attitudes; death; potential. See also **house**.

enclosed, enclosure   The defences we use, such as pride, beliefs, anger, to protect ourselves from deeply feeling the impact of the world, relationships, love, anxiety or pain. These are often felt as traps or restraints, even though they are parts of our own personality. For instance one may feel trapped by one's own feelings of dependence upon family.

Example: 'I am trapped in a bricked room with no way out and I shout for somebody to help me. Then either a big bird or a creature with long arms tries to catch me, and I scream' (Karen S). Karen had previously lost a baby, been divorced, had an unsatisfying relationship with a man. She feels trapped by the defences she has herself built 'brick by brick', but is frightened of the opportunity of change represented by the bird. What encloses or traps us in our dream gives a clue to what constrains us in waking.

Example: 'As I go through a tunnel it either gets smaller so I can't get through, or it goes on so far there is no end to it. I am trapped and terrified' (Don M). This sort of enclosed dream is typical of trauma relating to a difficult birth. In fact Don's mother was in labour for four days, and never had another child because of the pain.

end   Used in many different ways, depending on context. Generally it represents a goal; point of change; release; death. Example: 'I was due to be executed—what for I don't know. I was not especially afraid of this, but my most vivid feelings were of great sadness at the people I was leaving behind, and for all the things I wanted to do in life, but would not now be

able to. Then at the end I was watching myself being hanged'
(DK). Many people dream this 'end of life' theme. In virtually
every one of these dreams there is a highlighting of 'things to
do'. Such dreams are a way of deciding what is of most value
in the dreamer's life.

  End of path, road: the end of one's life; the boundary of
what one already knows or has done; end of a relationship
(especially if walking with person). End of tunnel, cave: finding the way out of a difficult or depressed stage of life. End of
table, queue: feeling left out, unconsidered, forgotten; putting
oneself last. End of garden, room, road: can be used to show
polarity or opposites, as in following. Example: 'I found myself alone in the garden at the far end of the house near the
stables' (MM). Here 'the end' relates to being alone, as opposed to being in the house with people. Idioms: at an end;
end of one's tether; wits' end; end of the day; be the end of; a
sticky end; dead end; the deep end; end it all; end of the line;
both ends meet; not the end of the world; loose ends; to no
end; light at the end of the tunnel. See **cul de sac.**

engine   One's motivating drive or energy; the body's energy
and mechanical or automatic functioning; the sexual or natural urges; sometimes the heart. See **machine.**

enter, entrance   New experience or new area of experience.
Secret entrance: an attitude or psychological 'stance' which
opens a new experience of self, or allows access to parts of
oneself usually inaccessible. See **door.**

erotic dreams   See **sex in dreams.**

escape   Example: 'I dreamt I was a prisoner with many
others. Myself and other men were outside the prison working. Then a tremendous explosion blew a hole in the prison
wall. I knew prisoners were trying to escape. I saw some
wardens and shouted or signalled to the prisoners to be care-

ful' (Terry D). Terry worked as a therapist without scholastic qualification. Terry represents his attitudes to authority as the prison, and sees more of his work potential escaping those attitudes.

Example: 'I often dreamed I was being chased by boys or men. I would suddenly take off like a helicopter and fly away. Sometimes narrowly escaping from my pursuer' (MC). As in the example, we often use 'escape' in a dream to avoid difficult feelings. This is like reading an exciting novel because it distracts our attention from problems in our marriage. The problems remain. <u>Something escaping from us</u>: a realisation, emotion or opportunity eluding awareness. See **enclosed**.

ESP in dreams   Many dreams appear to extend perception in different ways.

dreaming the future   Just before his title fight in 1947, Sugar Ray Robinson dreamt he was in the ring with Doyle. 'I hit him a few good punches and he was on his back, his blank eyes staring up at me.' Doyle never moved and the crowd were shouting 'He's dead! He's dead!' He was so upset by the dream Robinson asked Adkins, his trainer and promoter, to call off the fight. Adkins told him 'Dreams don't come true. If they did I'd be a millionaire.' In the eighth round Doyle went down from a left hook to the jaw. He never got up, and died the next day.

The problem is that many such dreams felt to be predictive never come true. Often dreamers want to believe they have precognitive dreams, perhaps to feel they will not be surprised by, and thereby anxious about, the future. When the baby son of Charles Lindbergh was kidnapped, and before it was known he was murdered, 1,300 people sent 'precognitive' dreams concerning his fate in response to newspaper headlines. Only seven of these dreams included the three vital factors—that he was dead, naked and in a ditch.

Out of 8,000 dreams in his Registry for Prophetic Dreams,

Robert Nelson, who was sent dreams prior to what was predicted, has found only 48 which bear detailed and recognisable connection with later events.

dreaming together   Example: 'I dreamt my sister was attacking me with a pair of scissors. She backed me against a wall and stabbed me. During the day after the dream my sister phoned me at work and said she'd had an awful dream in which she stabbed me with scissors' (D). The Poseidia Institute of Virginia Beach, Va., have run a number of group 'mutual dreaming' experiments. Although the Institute suggests very positive results, a critical survey of the dreams and reports reveals a lack of hard evidence. Like other areas of ESP dreaming, it can seldom ever be willed. But the dreams did show themes related to problems regarding intimate meeting. Also, some of the dreams were directly about the goal of dream meeting, as in the following example.

Example: 'I find the group of people I am looking for. There were maybe six or more people. They were asleep on mattresses except for two or three. These were awake and waiting for me, and wearing small pointed hats such as Tibetan Lamas wear. In the dream I realised this meant they had achieved sufficient inner growth to remain awake in sleep. We started to communicate and were going to wake the others' (Tom C). See **dream as a meeting place**.

the dream as extended perception   Even everyday mental functions such as thought and memory occur largely unconsciously. During sleep, perhaps because we surrender our volition, what is left of self awareness enters the realm where the nine-tenths of the iceberg of our mind is active. In this realm faculties can function which on waking seem unobtainable. For example:

1   Extending awareness to a point distant from the body, to witness events confirmed by other people. This is often called out of body experience (OBE), but some of these

experiences suggest the nature of consciousness and time may not be dualistic (having to be either here or there). See **out of body experience**.

2   Being aware of the death or danger of a member of family. Kinship and love seem to be major factors in the way the unconscious functions. See **dead people dreams**.

3   Seeing into the workings of the body and diagnosing an illness before it becomes apparent to waking observation. Dr Vasali Kasatkin and Professor Medard Boss have specialised in the study of such dreams. In a recent dream told to me, a man looked back into a bedroom and saw a piece of the wall fall away. Waves of water gushed from a main pipe. The dreamer struggled to hold back the piece of broken pipe. Within two weeks his colon burst and he had to have a major operation. See **meditation**.

4   Access to a computer-like ability to sort through a massive store of information and experience to solve problems. These dreams are often confused with precognitive ability. Prediction does occur from these dreams, but it arises, as with weather prediction, from a massive gathering of information, most of which we have forgotten consciously. Morton Schatzman, in a *New Scientist* article, showed how subjects can produce answers to complex mathematical problems in their dreams. See **dream process as computer; creativity and problem solving in dreams**.

5   Tapping a collective mind which stores all experience, and is sensed as godlike or holy. See **dream as spiritual guide**.

6   It seems likely that before the development of speech the human animal communicated largely through body language. Some dreams suggest we still have this ability to read a person's health, sexual situation, intentions and even their past, through body shape, posture and tiny movements. See **postures, movement and body language**.

See **Cayce, Edgar; collective unconscious;** *wife* under **family**. See also **hallucinations**.

Evans, Christopher   In his book *Landscapes of the Night,* Dr Evans puts forward a new theory of dreaming. He states that our brain has 'programs' for dealing with survival. We have basic behaviour programs for walking and talking, rather like a computer might have. We also have programs for social interaction and skills. In the different roles such as lover, parent, breadwinner, employer, we need different skills. But also, to deal with our own process of change, our internal urges, anger, drive to succeed, we need skill to handle them well. A person who doesn't handle anxiety or stress can easily fail in work or in relationships. Many people do not enter a relationship because of the problems it poses. Dr Evans suggests that dreams are the means by which we both practise and update our programs of survival. Our experience of the day may question or enhance our behaviour stratagems for success at work or in relationships. Without the reprogramming occurring in dreams we would be stuck at one level of behavioural maturity. 'As we gain in experience, as our input gets richer and more diverse, we modify our programs rather than replace them with a completely fresh set.'

evening   Relaxation; quiet peace; time for oneself; nearness to the 'shadows' of the unconscious, the parts of self we do not like. Sometimes the last years of life; old age. See also **autumn**.

evil   Example: 'At the top of the stairs is a small door, half opened as if inviting me to go up. I get an overpowering sense of something evil beyond the door just waiting for me' (Charles M). Usually refers to some of our own urges which we have judged as wrong because of moral values, and thus denied expression. Charles probably feels that what he identifies with as himself—his established values and beliefs—is threatened by what he senses beyond the door. Whatever threatens our 'I' or ego is often felt to be evil, even if it is natural urges. The unbalanced and real evils in the world, such as terrorising of individuals and minority groups, can of course be shown as the feeling of evil.

Example: 'I am lying on the floor in my bedroom with a towel over me. I am trying to hide and protect myself because I am terrified. There are four devils trying to get into my body and take over. My bedroom is going like a whirlpool around me, like evil all around me. I wake in a hot sweat and am terrified to go back to sleep' (Joanna). Joanna is most likely in conflict with her sexuality—the bedroom. When we fight with our own urges they often feel like external agencies—evil forces—attacking us. Sometimes refers to repressed emotional pain. See **aboriginal**; *devil* under **archetypes**. See also **active/passive**.

exams, being examined   Self criticism or attempts to live up to moral or intellectual standards; habits of concern over accomplishments; worry about some coming test of self value, such as a new job or new sexual partner. Examined by doctor: concern over health; desire for attention. See **test**.

excrement   Feelings of repulsion; emotions or parts of experience which need to be let go of; infant level of self expression and self giving; physical need to have a healthy bowel. Sometimes personal creativity; being able to let go of what you don't need—so can link with money and generosity; the primal level of our being; sensuality and infant sexuality. Shitting on someone or something: expressing desire to belittle them or to feel superiority; heaping unjust accusations on someone; bringing something which appeared powerful into perspective. <u>Idioms</u>: in the shit; feeling shitty; talking a lot of shit; being shat on. See **toilet**.

explosion   Anger; dramatic release of energy in making changes in self expression; social upheaval; fear; orgasm.

eyes   See *eyes* under **body**.

F

face See *head* under **body**.

faeces See **excrement**.

failure Example: 'I was in a race riding a horse but couldn't get to the starting gate in time. The others were way ahead of me jumping the fences. I couldn't catch up, and one fence I came to grew to a huge height and was like a steel barrier. I couldn't get over it and felt a failure' (Ron S). Ron had not done well at school, had not taken any particular training, had no steady relationship or children. In his late 20s, Ron looked at his friends, married with families and steady jobs, and felt a failure. From the dream he realised he was viewing life as a competitive race to succeed. This was stopping him from following his real interest, psychotherapy, which his family viewed as playing games. He could ride his horse into the fields and explore. He did, by going to America, training, raising a family.

In general, failure indicates comparison; competitiveness; it sometimes depicts alternatives—failure is the alternative to success. So the failure might be 'because'. See *Is there a 'because' factor in the dream?* in **dream processing**; **falling**.

fair See *hair* under **body**.

fairground One's public activity; the range of human fate—rich to poor, midgets to giants; 'swings and roundabouts' of life. Carnival, fiesta : dropping social or moral restraints; letting go; creativity; social connections. See also **marketplace**.

157

falling   Some dream researchers suggest falling is one of the main themes in dreams. In the sample used for this book, the words fall, falls, fell, falling occur 72 times in 1,000 dreams. The words find, finds, finding, found occur 297 times. And the words connected with looking and seeing occur 1,077 times.

During our development or growth we 'fall' from our mother's womb when ripe; being dropped by a parent must be our earliest sense of insecurity; we fall many times as we learn to stand and walk; as we explore our boundaries in running, climbing, jumping and riding, falling is a big danger; at times it could mean death. Out of this we create the ways falling is used in dreams.

Example: 'I am sitting in a high window box facing outwards, with my son and a friend of his on my left. I feel very scared of falling and ask my son and his friend to climb back into the building. I feel too scared to move until they shift' (Trevor N). At the time of the dream Trevor was working, for the first time in his life, as a full-time freelance journalist. His wife was out of work and his frequency of sales low enough to cause them to be running out of money. The building behind him in the dream felt like a place he had worked nine to five —security. Falling was failure, getting in debt, dropping into the feelings of self doubt and being incapable.

In general, then, falling represents loss of confidence; threat to usual sources of security such as relationship, source of money, social image, beliefs; tension. Sometimes it is loss of social grace; losing face; moral failure—falling into temptation; coming down to earth from a too lofty attitude; sexual surrender.

Example: 'I was on a road which led up to the hospital I was put in at three. I felt a sense of an awful past as I looked at the road. Then I was standing on the edge of a precipice or cliff. My wife was about four yards away near the road. I stepped in an area of soft earth. It gave beneath my weight and I sank up to my waist. I realised the cliff edge was unstable and the whole area would fall. I was sinking and shouting to my wife to help me. She was gaily walking about and made light of my call for help. I cried out again. Still she ignored me. I shouted again for her help. She took no notice and I sank deeper, the ground gave way and I fell to my death' (Barry I). Through being put in a hospital at three without his mother, Barry had a deep seated fear that any woman he loved could desert him. His fall is the loss of any sense of bonding between him and his wife out of this fear. His death is the dying of his feeling of love and relationship, and the pain it causes. Understanding these fears, Barry was able to leave them behind in later dreams and in life.

By learning to meet our insecurities (perhaps by using the last question in **dream processing**) we can dare more in life. This is in essence the same as meeting the fear of falling off our bike as we learn to ride. If we never master the fear we cannot ride. Therefore some dreams take falling into realms beyond fear. The following examples illustrate this.

Example: 'Near where I stood in the school gymnasium was a diving board, about 20 ft off the ground. Girls were learning to dive off the board and land flat on their back on the floor. If they landed flat they didn't hurt themselves—like falling backwards standing up' (Barry I). The school is where we learn. Once we learn to fall 'flat on our back', i.e. fail, without being devastated or 'hurt' by it, we can be more creative. Going fast to an edge and falling: could mean overwork and danger of breakdown of health.

Example: 'As I prayed I realised I could fly. I lifted off the ground about 3 feet and found I could completely relax while going higher or falling back down. So it was like free fall. I went into a wonderful surrendered relaxation. My whole body sagging, floating in space. It was a very deep meditative experience (Sarah D). Sarah has found an attitude which enables her to soar/dare or fall/fail without being so afraid of being hurt or dying emotionally. This gives a form of freedom many people never experience. This does not arise from denying or suppressing fears.

<u>Seeing things fall</u>: sense of danger or change in regard to what is represented. <u>Person falling</u>: wish to be rid of them, or anxiety in regard to what they represent; end of a relationship. <u>Child</u>, <u>son falling</u>: see **baby**; *son* and *daughter* under **family**. <u>House falling down</u>: personal stress; illness; personal change and growth due to letting old habits and attitudes crumble. Example: 'I was standing outside my mother's house to the right. The ground in front had fallen away. The house was about to cave in. I felt no fear or horror. Instead I was thinking about new beginnings and the possibility of a new house' (Helen B). Helen is here becoming more independent and leaving behind attitudes and dependency. See **house**; **abyss**; **chasm**. See also **flying**.

family   From our family we learn most of the positive and negative patterns of relationship and attitudes towards living, which we carry into daily events. Father's uncertainty in dealing with people, or his anxiety in meeting change, may be the roots of our own difficulties in those areas. If our mother is unable to develop a feeling contact with us, we may lack the confidence to meet our emotions.

Our maturation as a man or woman calls us in some way to meet and integrate our childhood desire, which includes sexual desire for our parent of the opposite sex, and rivalry with, mingled with dependence on, the parent of the same sex. Even a missing parent, the mother or father who died or left, is a potent figure internally. An absence of a father's or mother's love or presence can be as traumatic as any powerfully injuring event. Our parents in our dreams are the image (full of power and feeling) of the formative forces and experiences of our identity. They are the ground, the soil, the bloody carnage, out of which our sense of self emerged. But our identity cannot gain any real independence while still dominated by these internal forces of our creation. Heraclitus said we cannot swim in the same river twice; attempting to repeat or compete with the virtues of a parent is a misapprehension of the true nature of our own personality. See **individuation**.

Family group: The whole background of experience which makes up our values and views. This background is made up of thousands of different obvious and subtle things such as social status; amount of books in the home; how parents feel about themselves; how they relate to life outside the family; whether dominant roles are encouraged; what nationality parents are; what unconscious social attitudes surround the family (i.e. the master and servant, or dominating employer and subservient employee, roles which typified England at the turn of the century still colour many attitudes in the UK). Simply put, it is our internal 'family' of urges and values; the overall feeling tone of our family life—security, domination, whatever it was; the unconscious coping patterns of the family.

Parents together in dream: our general wisdom; background of information and experience from which we make important decisions or gain intuitive insights. Parents also depict the rules and often irrational disciplinary codes we learnt as a child which still speak to us from within, and perhaps pass on to our own children without reassessment. These include everything from 'Don't speak with your mouth full' to the unspoken 'Masturbation is unholy.'

Dead parent in dream: the beginning of independence from parent; repression of the emotions they engendered in us; our emotions regarding our parent's death; feelings about death. See **dead people dreams**.

Example: 'My father was giving me and another woman some medicine. Something was being forced on us. I started to hit and punch him in the genitals and, when he was facing the other way, in the backside. I seemed to be just the right height to do this and I had a very angry feeling that I wanted to hurt him as he had hurt me' (Audrey V). Hurting, burying , killing parent: in the example Audrey's height shows her as a child. She is releasing anger about the attitudes and situations her father forced 'down her throat'. To be free of the introverted restraints and ready made values gathered from our parents, at some time in our growth we may kill or bury them. Although some people are shocked by such dreams, they are healthy signs of emerging independence. Old myths of killing the chief so the tribe can have a new leader depict this process. When father or mother are 'dead' in our dream, we can inherit all the power gained from whatever was positive in the relationship. Seeing parent drunk, incapable, foolish: another means of gaining independence from internalised values or stultifying drives to 'honour' or admire father or mother.

father Generally positive: authority; ability in the external world; family or social conventions; how we relate to the 'doer' in us; physical strength and protectiveness; the will to be. Generally negative: introverted aggression; dominance by fear of other people's authority; uncaring sexual drive; feelings of not being loved. See *father* under **archetypes; man.**

mother Generally positive: feelings; ability in relationships; uniting spirit of family; how we relate to feelings in a relationship; strength to give of self and nurture; intuition. Generally negative: will based on irrational likes and dislikes; opinion generated by anxiety or jealousy; domination by emotions; lack of bonding. See *Great Mother* under **archetypes; woman.**

siblings and children Whether *brother, sister, daughter* or *son* (see below in this entry), the most general use in our dreams is to depict an aspect of ourself. However it is almost universal to believe with great conviction that our dream is about the person in our dream. A mother seeing a son die in her dream often goes through great anxiety because there lurks in her a sense of it being a precognitive dream. Virtually everyone at some time dreams about members of their close family dying or being killed—lots of mothers dream this, and their children live till 80. But occasionally children do die. Is the dream then precognitive, or is it coincidental?

Example: 'I was walking along a rather dusty track carrying my younger son who would be around 10 months old and I was feeling rather tired. Suddenly I met a man who stopped to talk to me and commented I looked rather weary carrying the baby. He said, come with me and look over this wall and you will see such a sight that will gladden your heart. By standing on tiptoe I could just see over the wall and the sight I beheld took my breath away, it was so beautiful' (Johan E). Here Johan's son depicts the weight of responsibility she feels. The beauty is her own resources of strength in motherhood.

Example: 'I have just given birth to twins and they lay on the floor. We started to care for them. My mother took them to the doctor for his advice while I went to see my married sister who has two children. I met them there with the twins so that my sister could give her opinion on the babies. She had recent experience of childbirth and could tell us if the babies were good specimens' (Miss E). Miss E has no children of her own, so she is uncertain of her own capacity to have and raise them. The mother depicts her own mothering abilities, which seek confidence from an authority figure. Her sister is her own nearest experience of childbirth. So out of what she has learnt from observing her sister, she is assessing her own qualities.

Most often the family member depicts the qualities in ourself which we feel are part of the character of the person dreamt of. So the passionate one in the family would depict our passions; the intellectual one our own mind; the anxious one our hesitations. Use the questions in **dream processing** to define this. Having done this, can you observe what the dream depicts? For Miss E it would be questions regarding motherhood.

Example: 'My daughter told me the only positive part of my work in a helping profession was with a woman who had turned from it to religion. There followed a long and powerful interchange in which I said she had as yet no mind of her own. She was dominated by her mother's anxiety, and the medical rationalism of her training. When she had dared to step beyond her own anxieties to integrate the lessons of her own life, then I would listen again' (Desmond S). Desmond was divorced and struggling with his own pain and guilt about leaving his daughter while still a teenager. His daughter depicts this conflict between his feelings and his rational self.

brother Oneself, or the denied part of self, meeting whatever is met in the dream; feelings of kinship; sense of rivalry; feelings about a brother. <u>Woman's dream</u>, <u>younger brother</u>: outgoing but vulnerable self; rivalry. <u>Woman's dream</u>, <u>older brother</u>: authority; one's capable outgoing self. <u>Man's dream</u>, <u>younger brother</u>: vulnerable feelings; oneself at that age. <u>Man's dream</u>, <u>older brother</u>: experience; authority; feelings of persecution. See **boy**; **man**. <u>Idioms</u>: big brother; brothers in arms; blood brother.

sister Feeling self, or the lesser expressed part of self; rival; feelings about a sister. <u>Man's dream</u>, <u>younger sister</u>: vulnerable emotions; rival for love of parents. <u>Man's dream</u>, <u>older sister</u>: capable feeling self; feelings of persecution. <u>Woman's dream</u> , <u>younger sister</u>: one's experiences at that age; vulnerable feelings, rival for parents' love. <u>Woman's dream</u>, <u>older sister</u>: capable feeling self. See **girl**; **woman**. <u>Idioms</u>: sisters under the skin.

daughter One's relationship with the daughter; the daughter, or son, can represent what happens in a marriage between husband and wife. The child is what has arisen from the bonding, however momentary, of two people. In dreams the child therefore is sometimes used to depict how the relationship is faring. So a <u>sick daughter</u> might show the feelings in the relationship being 'ill'.

In a <u>mother's dream</u>: often feelings of support or companionship; feelings of not being alone in the area of emotional bonds; or one's feeling area; responsibility; the ties of parenthood; oneself at that age; one's own urges, difficulties, hurts, which may still be operative. Also a comparison; the mother might see the daughter's youth, opportunity, and have feelings about that. So the daughter may represent her sense of lost opportunity and youth—even envy; competition in getting the desire of a man.

In a father's dream: one's feeling self; the feelings or difficulties about the relationship with daughter; the struggles one's own feeling self goes through to mature; how the sexual feelings are dealt with in a family—occurs especially when she starts courting; sister; parental responsibility; one's wife when younger. Someone else's daughter: feelings about one's own daughter; feelings about younger women.

Example: 'I am standing outside a supermarket with heavy bags wearing my mac, though the sun is warm. My daughter and two friends are playing music and everyone stops to listen. I start to write a song for them, but they pack up and go on a bus whilst I am still writing. I am left alone at the bus stop with my heavy burden of shopping, feeling incredibly unwanted' (Mrs F). Such dreams of the daughter becoming independent can occur as soon as the child starts school, persisting until the mother finds a new attitude. See **child; woman.**

son Extroverted self; desires connected with self expression; feelings connected with son; parental responsibility. Mother's dream: one's ambitions; potential; hopes; your marriage—see example.

Example: 'My wife and I were walking out in the countryside. I looked around suddenly and saw my four-year-old son near a hole. He fell in and I raced back. The hole was narrow but very deep. I could see water at the bottom but no sign of my son. I didn't know whether I could leap down and save him or whether it was too narrow. Then somehow he was out. His heart was just beating' (Richard H). Richard had argued with his wife in such a way he feared the stability of their marriage. The son represents what they had created together —a child, a marriage. The marriage survived, as his dream self-assessed it would. <u>Death of son</u>: a mother often kills off her son in her dreams as she sees him make moves towards independence. This can happen from the first day of school on. Example: 'I am on a very high bridge over an extremely wide and deep river with steep banks. My son does a double somersault over the railing, falls into the water. I think he is showing off. I am unable to save him. My son is 18 and has started a structural engineering course at university' (Joyce H). The showing-off suggests Joyce feels her son is doing daring things with his life, and the relationship in its old form dies.

<u>Father's dream</u>: yourself at that age; what qualities you see in your son; your own possibilities; envy of youth and opportunities; rivalry. <u>Someone else's son</u>: feelings about one's own son; feelings about younger men. <u>Dead son</u>: see **dead people dreams**. See **boy**. See also **man**; first example in **falling**.

wife Depicts how you see the relationship with your wife; your relationship with your sexuality; sexual and emotional desire and pleasure; how you relate to intimacy in body, mind and spirit; your feeling, intuitive nature; habits of relationship developed with one's mother. Example: 'My wife was trying to get me out of her life, and out of the house. It was as if she were attempting to push me into a feeling of tension and rejection which would make me leave' (David P). Out of childhood experience, in which his mother repeatedly threatened to give him away, David was finding it difficult to commit himself emotionally to his wife. In the dream his wife represents these feelings, so he sees her—his anxiety and pain —pushing him to break up the marriage.

Example: 'I was standing with my wife at the end of the garden of the house I lived in as a child. We were looking over the fence to the rising meadow beyond. She said, "Look at that bird in the tree there." On our right, in a small ash tree, an enormous owl perched. It was at least 4 feet high, the biggest bird I have ever seen. I recognised it in the dream as a greater hooded owl, which was not native to our country. I was so excited I ran into the house to telephone someone—zoo, police, newspapers?—to tell them about the bird. I cannot remember contacting anyone, but felt the bird was there in some way to meet me. Also it was hungry and looking at next door's bantams. So I wondered what I could give it to eat' (David P). This shows the positive side of David's relationship with his wife. The garden is the boundaries which arose from his childhood. But he is growing—the garden—and looking beyond them in connection with his marriage. The amazing bird is the deep feelings he touches because he has a mate, like any other natural creature. Out of his mating he becomes aware of drives to build a home—nest—and give himself to his mate. These are natural and are a part of his unconscious or spiritual nature. The bird is a hooded owl which can see in the dark—the unconscious—because David is realising things he had never 'seen' before. The bird is masked, meaning putting the ego aside, which is a necessity for touching the wider dimension of life or the unconscious. The hunger of the bird shows an intimate detail of what David has learnt from his wife. She had been working as a waitress and bringing home pieces of chicken for him, saved from her own meal. The spiritual side of David wants to develop this quality of selfgiving, which his wife's love had helped him see.

Example: 'I have been a widower since January 1979, having married in October 1941. I continually dream I am in London where my business was. I am walking the streets with my wife and suddenly I see her ahead of me in a yellow raincoat and hat. I call her and try to catch up, but suddenly she vanishes. In spite of calling and searching I cannot find her' (Douglas G). This is a common theme dreamt by widowers or widows, <u>disappearance of spouse</u>. Douglas has 'lost' his wife. His dream shows the paradox of love after death of partner. His love is still there, years after her death. He is possibly still trying to love his wife as an externally real person, so his feelings can make no connection. To meet what actually remains of his wife, **within himself**, he would need to face his own internal grieving, emotions, and all the feelings, memories, angers and beauty which make up the living remains of his wife within him.

husband Depicts how you see the relationship with your husband; your relationship with your sexuality; sexual and emotional desire and pleasure; how you relate to intimacy in body, mind and spirit; habits of relationship developed with one's father.

Example: 'My recurring dream—some disaster is happening. I try to contact the police or my husband. Can never contact either. I try ringing 999 again and again and can feel terror, and sometimes dreadful anger or complete panic. I cry, I scream and shout and never get through! Recently I have stopped trying to contact my husband. I managed once to reach him but he said he was too busy and I would have to deal with it myself. I woke in a furious temper with him and kicked him while he was still asleep' (Mrs GS). The husband here depicts Mrs S's feelings of not being able to 'get through' to her man. This is a common female dream theme, possibly arising from the husband not daring to express emotion or meet his partner with his own feelings. For Mrs S this is an emergency. Although the dream dramatises it, there is still real frustration, anger, and a break in marital communications.

Example: 'There were three of us. My husband, a male friend and I, all riding small white enamel bikes. My husband proceeded slowly, first, with his back to us. Then my friend followed. Suddenly my friend ahead of me turned and gazed fully at me. He gave a glorious smile which lit up the whole of his face. I felt a great sense of well-being surge through me' (Joan B). The triangle: the example shows typical flow of feeling towards another male. The other male here depicts

Joan's desire to be attractive to other men. This is a danger signal unless one fully acknowledges the impulse.

Example: 'I was with my husband and our three children. About 2 or 3 yards to our right stood my husband's first wife —she died about a year before I first met him. I remember feeling she no longer minded me being with him, so I put my arms around him from the back, and felt more secure and comfortable with him' (Mrs NS). The first wife: the dreamer is now feeling easier about her husband's first relationship. The first wife represents her sense of competing for her husband's affections, even though his 'first woman' was dead.

Example: 'My dead husband came into my bedroom and got into bed with me to make love to me. I was not afraid. But owing to his sexual appetites during my married life with him I was horrified, and resisted him with all my might. On waking I felt weak and exhausted. The last time he came to me I responded to him and he never came back again. This happened three times. The last time I don't think it was a dream. I was not asleep. I think it was his ghost' (GL). Dead husband: in any experience of an apparently psychic nature, we must always remember the unconscious is a great dramatist. It can create the drama of a dream in moments. In doing so it makes our inner feelings into apparently real people and objects outside us. While asleep we lightly dismiss this amazing process as 'a dream'. When it happens while our eyes are open or we are near waking, for some reason we call it a ghost or psychic event. Yet the dream process is obviously capable of creating total body sensations, emotions, full visual impressions, vocalisation—what else is a dream? On the other hand, the dream process is not dealing in pointless imaginations. Many women tend to believe they have little sexual drive, so it is easier for GL to see her drive in the form of her husband. But of course, her husband may also depict how she felt about sex in connection with his 'sexual appetites'. It is a general rule, however, that our dream process will dramatise into a past life, or a 'psychic' experience, emotions linked with trauma or sexual drive which we find difficult to meet in the present.

Example: 'I dreamt many times I lost my husband, such as not being able to find the car park where he was waiting, and seeing him go off in the distance. I wake in a panic to find him next to me in bed. These dreams persisted, and then he died quite suddenly. He was perfectly healthy at the time of the dreams and I wonder if it was a premonition of me really losing him' (Mrs AD). <u>Cannot find husband</u>: many middle aged women dream of 'losing' their husband while out with him, perhaps shopping, or walking in a town somewhere. Sometimes the dream portrays him actually killed. Mrs AD wonders if her dream was a premonition. It is more likely a form of practising the loss, so it does not come as such a shock. The greatest shocks occur when we have never even considered the event—such as a young child losing its mother, an event it has never practised, not even in fantasy, so has no inbuilt shock absorbers. As most of us know, men tend to die before women, and this information is in the mind of middle-aged married women. Mrs AD may have unconsciously observed slight changes in her husband's body and behaviour, and therefore readied herself.

<u>Other woman's husband</u>: one's own husband; feelings about that man; desire for a non-committed relationship with less responsibility.

grandparents   Personal feelings connected with the grandparent; family traditions, such as established values or unconscious attitudes; spiritual values; old age; death.

relatives   Including uncle, aunt, cousin, nephew, niece, etc. Usually an aspect of oneself relevant to the character of the person dreamt about. Sometimes represents one's family traditions—unconscious attitudes, conventions, or even talents, which are part of the unique psychological and social environment a family provides.

170

famous people   One's own potential, often unacknowledged, and projected on to dream character; a parent; depending on how you relate to the famous person, your own ability to accept yourself as respected. Sometimes the person may, because of their life or roles, represent a particular quality such as courage, love, 'ruling' drives in life, authority, etc. Actor/actress: one is acting a role. Queen: often one's mother; a feeling or drive ruling your life. King: father; thinking.

Example: 'A film star I admire came and lay beside me in the night. He told me he loved me and would stay with me. I knew he was living with a woman who had borne his child, but he told me he was going to tell her he was leaving her. In the morning we walked along the road where I live, to tell the woman' (Sharon). Sharon processed her dream and saw the film star as her own strength and determination to further her career as a dancer. Being 18 she was faced with the decision of whether to become a wife and mother—the other woman —or put those urges into her work. In her dream she chose to be fully involved in her dancing.

Famous people can be seen as social guinea pigs. Collectively we expose them to enormous amounts of money, sexual opportunity, drugs, alcohol, and tremendous social and commercial pressures. Then we examine every part of their life to see how well they cope. Millions then identify with the image they portray of how to deal with reality at its worst. The famous person in our dream might therefore represent our coping mechanism.

fare   The price one pays to achieve a goal; getting the right attitude or stance. See **ticket**.

farm, farmyard   Care or expression of our natural drives, such as sexuality, parenthood, love of fellowship; the down-to-earth side of self; area in which our animal propensities— territorial fighting, fighting over mate, etc.—are expressed. See *farmer* under **roles**.

fat person Defences used against anxiety or feelings of inadequacy; healthy, jolly feelings; sensuality. <u>Becoming fat</u>: pregnancy; carrying 'more weight'.

fear See **emotions and mood**.

fence Example: 'I saw that we had got into a fenced off area where the gentry landowners parked their cars while they went shooting. I could see the landowner in his car beyond the fence, looking angry that I was in his property. I thought I would break through the fence with the elephant, but then saw a low area which the elephant easily stepped over' (Arthur P). The fence often depicts our sense of social barriers; need for privacy; territorial feelings; also our boundaries in relationship which might prevent us daring to express ourselves or be creative. See **wall**. <u>Idioms</u>: rush one's fences; wrong side of the fence; sit on the fence.

ferry Movement towards change; often associated with ferry across Styx, and death. <u>Ferry you know</u>: consider why you use the ferry, what you associate with it.

field Fields often appear with animals, and suggest the dreamer's contact with what is natural in themselves. Also freedom from social pressure; one's sense of oneself when away from other people, with one's own natural inclinations; field of activity or study; feeling states—depending on condition of field, cloudy, bright, overgrown. <u>Field across river</u>, <u>very green fields</u>: death or the dreamer's conception of spiritual realm. See **landscapes**.

fight Example: 'Some three years ago I had constant dreams with my mother. We were nearly always in some sort of argument or fight' (Marjorie B). Usually, as in the example, the dreamer's anger or frustration; may express difficulties in re-

gard to independence or self confidence; desire to hurt another person, or damage their reputation.

Example: 'I realised a door had been left open that should
have been locked and I felt very vulnerable. Suddenly a sword
of light appeared in my hand and a voice told me that it was
my weapon to fight the evil' (Mrs DE). A fight also depicts, as
in the example, fighting for our space; our values or honour;
we may fight for survival, for our health, fight crime (resist
criminal impulses); we may also feel attacked by another person's opinions; assaulted by sexual desire; fight against depression; have a conflict over moral issues. See **attack; war.**
Idioms: fight it out; fight like cat and dog; look for a fight.

film   An aspect of our own past or character which we do
not wish to acknowledge. It is easier therefore to view as not
about oneself; an attempt to view oneself objectively; images
of self and behaviour projected from the unconscious; one of
our means of escaping from reality. See **cinema.**

film star   See **famous people.**

find, found   Example: 'I went into a cellar. It was rather
cavelike. I had to scramble to get into it. The entrance was
difficult to find, but I had discovered it many years before and
been in lots of times. I found objects in the cellar and was
looking for something' (Tony C). Usually, as in the example,
to discover, realise, become aware of some aspect of oneself
and gain access to or use of. One might be living with constant resentments about one's past or present situation, and
then 'find' release from this for a day, yet not be conscious
how it was achieved. The dream might attempt to define this.
Or it might be a new idea you realise unconsciously in sleep.

Example: 'Then I was with my father (dead) and was
showing him a handful of exotic banknotes I had found in the
building. They were £100 notes. I wasn't sure if the money
was legal tender or not. The notes had an unusual design'

(Andy). Andy has found a sense of his own value—the money —but is not sure if other people also value him. The dream illustrates the attempt to 'find a place' in society. The effort to search and find is frequently to do with one's own identity, and what one is searching through is one's experience, as in Tony's cellar above, or this example: 'I was looking into the crowd in the film to find me and it was like looking at a snapshot, it felt very important that I find me, I saw my green slacks just showing, right at the back of the crowd' (Trudy K). See **look; see**. <u>Idioms</u>: find oneself; find fault; find out; find one's bearings.

fire Passion; sexuality; anger; desire; burning feelings such as resentment or frustration; our desire to destroy. Also our life process, often described as a flame which burns forever through different generations but leaves only ash behind; our vital energy; occasionally refers to physical illness.

Example: 'I was in a small terraced house with a friend I had known years earlier. It was her house, there were two or three children in it. Suddenly it caught fire, I wanted to stay and put the fire out but she did not. She dragged me outside and down the street. We saw the house burn down. I had this dream the day I got home from hospital, after undergoing a hysterectomy' (Mrs G). Here the fire depicts the consuming feelings of loss regarding Mrs G's childbearing function. Also the loss of an area or era of life. <u>Underground flames</u>: unconscious emotions or desires which one may need to face for real growth. <u>Fire in the sky</u>: great changes in viewpoint; meeting the next step in maturity.

Example: 'I found quite a large old fireplace. I asked my husband if he would like a fire. I thought it would be cosy if we both enjoyed the fire together. Woke up with a warm feeling towards my husband; he reached out to me' (Dinah Y). Here fire is not only homemaking and human warmth, but also sexuality. <u>Fireplace</u>: homeliness; the womb. <u>Idioms</u>: baptism of fire; between two fires; fire up; go through fire and water; play with fire; under fire; the old illness/love flared up.

flames Life itself, our life as it moves through experience leaving only memories; passion or anger. See **candle**; *fireman* under **roles**. Idioms: add fuel to the flames; old flame.

fish, sea creatures When we will to speak or move, unconscious physical and psychological impulses and processes occur to produce the response. These deeply unconscious processes are often depicted by fish. Also the attitudes and urges we have in common with humanity—the collective unconscious, and the impulses or insights arising therefrom—can therefore represent the Self or Christ; sexual drive in connection with reproduction, the many little fishes being sperm. In this sense we are the fish which swam the incredible journey and grew into a human, but is still on the odyssey of life and death. The fish may be the wisdom we have not yet brought to consciousness, regarding our personal journey in time and eternity. Fishing: creating a receptive state of consciousness which allows the deep insights or processes to become known; trying to find spiritual nourishment. Eating fish: integrating our inner realisations; partaking of Christ. Eaten by fish: feeling threatened by the unconscious; threat of losing conscious or rational direction of life. Dead fish: non-expression of basic urges.

Many little fish in round container: could be sperm, or depict becoming, or wanting to become, pregnant. Example: 'Last week I suddenly started having a recurring dream. In it I woke, walked downstairs, went into the kitchen and looked in the kettle. It was full of little fish' (Karen). The fact that Karen goes 'downstairs', suggesting the lower part of her body, and the shape of the kettle, which is a round container, make it likely this dream is about pregnancy. See *Christ* under **archetypes; religion and dreams; sea**. Idioms: big fish; big fish in a small pond; cold fish; fishing for compliments; fish out of water; queer fish; smell something fishy.

jellyfish Feelings arising from the unconscious which might be painful/sting the dreamer, bring a sense of helplessness/spinelessness, or are from a non-verbal level of memory.

octopus Feeling trapped by one's mother; dependence upon mother; one's own possessiveness. Hadfield, in *Dreams and Nightmares,* says that a baby often seizes upon its mother's breast with this feeling. The octopus can also symbolise any unconscious fear which may drag us into its realm of irrational terror.

shellfish Often the defensive shell we use to avoid hurt or sexual or emotional involvement; the female sexual organs. Oyster: also defensive shell, but may link with sexuality through common association; tight lipped; secretive; frigidity. See **crab**; *pearl* under **jewels**. Lacking shell: our naked vulnerability.

whale The powerful evolutionary drive involved in reproduction, which lies behind individual male or femaleness.

Example: 'I was leaning over the settee with my hands cupped under my chin looking out of the window. The view was spectacular, in that it was as if the house was situated on top of a cliff overlooking a huge bay, shaped like a horseshoe, with the house in the middle. From the sea suddenly coming into the bay I could see three enormous whales making their way towards me. As I was staring in amazement they began to transform themselves and come up out of the water as three giant Viking-like figures. They were so huge that the water came up only to their knees and everything was moving so slowly, as they waded towards me. It was the most awe inspiring thing I had ever seen in my life' (Sue B). The bay, the beautiful sea, the (sperm?) whales/men show Sue touching the most primordial yet inspiring aspects of her own womanhood and urge to love.

floating On water—relaxation; being indecisive; being carried along by events. See **flying**.

flood Depression would be seen as an inundation of negative emotions; anxiety a flood of fear, an overflow of usually unconscious or uncontrolled feelings and urges into consciousness. The flood can of course be of positive feelings, like love. In any case, floods can be enriching if handled well.

flowers Sense of beauty; flowering of the feeling quality or ability; the sexual organs, depending on shape. Example: 'So for the third time I held the woman and made love. The woman's vagina was like a flower—I don't mean to look at, but in physical sensation. My penis felt like it was penetrating petals of flesh and touching with great pleasure a central receptive area. I was left with the feeling of being able to make love again and again without any negative effects. It was a very positive and healthy feeling' (John T).

Also feelings of pleasure; youthfulness; time of flowering. Bud: penis or vagina, in the sense of growing male or female qualities. Giving flowers: giving love and tenderness. Many flowers growing: feelings of well-being and relaxation. Dead flowers: death or old age; dying love or abilities. Giving dead flowers: wishing someone dead or out of one's life; dead feelings. Lotus, lily : as these grow from mud, through water to the air and light, they sometimes represent our wholeness and growth, showing our connection with the universal as we develop individually. Rose: love; femininity. Shape or number of petals is featured: a flowering of a new aspect of the self. See **colours; shapes; castrate**.

flying Example: 'During childhood I learnt to fly in a long sequence of dreams. Each linked very clearly to the last. I would go to the nearby churchyard and in the beginning I would run along as fast as I could then jump and just manage to extend the jump by a great effort of will. In subsequent practices I managed gradually to extend the jump for many yards; and eventually I could skim along indefinitely. The next stage though was to extend my height, and this took enormous effort of will and body. I made active swimming motions and climbed, but only held altitude with great and constant concentration. With further practice still, this clumsy mode of flying was left behind as I learnt to use pure motivation or will to lift me into the air and carry me easily and gracefully wherever I wished. At this stage my flying was swift, mobile and without struggle' (Jason V). The example illustrates how much will, effort and learning can be involved in flying in dreams. This aspect of flying connects with the gaining of independence and the expression of one's potential. We are all born into a certain paradigm or 'reality'. At one time, part of the 'reality' for most Britons was that anyone without a white skin was a heathen or savage. At other times the 'reality' has been that anything heavier than air could not fly. Meteors did not exist because theory discounted them. And so on. To break free of such paradigms and from the 'gravity' or hold our parental and social authority has on us to find a measure of emotional and intellectual freedom, takes the sort of will, effort and learning depicted.

Flying expresses also the dealing with our internal influences which hold us down, such as self doubt, anxiety, depression.

Example: 'I was flying. I felt nervous at first that I would fall down, but not afraid. I soon became confident and felt very happy and wanted the sensation to continue. I was flying over a building, could have been a small church, crematorium or graveyard but did not feel afraid or upset. When I woke I lay in bed and tried very hard to keep the feelings with me and, for reasons unknown, I do not wish to forget it' (Mrs SM). In flying, Mrs SM is finding a way to look at death—the graveyard—which gives her a different viewpoint, a different feeling reaction to it, and she doesn't want to lose that precious newly learnt view. In their maturing process some people learn to see their thoughts and emotions as things they experience rather than things they are, and this brings the sort of new viewpoint seen in the example.

Example: 'I was in a building with a group of people. I was being chased and suddenly flew up in the air to escape my pursuers' (Michael O). Learning independence, and the ability to make decisions despite what others feel, may be done by ignoring our own feelings. This may be achieved by always keeping busy; never having quiet moments alone; filling empty periods with entertainment or company; smoking, drinking alcohol, taking sedatives or tranquillisers; rigid positive thinking. Then, as Michael does in his dream, we fly from issues we are pursued by instead of resolving them. This may lead us to the extremes of being either rigidly materialistic, or as rigidly ethereal. In either case we lose contact with everyday human issues, and may begin to have the <u>escape</u>-type flying dream, or an <u>out of body experience</u>.

Example: 'I knew I could fly. I picked up one of the young women I felt love for and flew with her. Laughingly I felt like superman, and flew easily' (Simon W). <u>Flying alone</u> occurs most frequently, showing the independent aspect of flying. But because it often involves our positive feelings of pleasure, flying may depict our sexuality, as above, especially aspects of it expressing freedom from social norms and restraints.

Example: 'I was floating atop a tree near houses and a rising walkway. I was saying to people around the tree that I had found something wonderful. Reaching out my hand I told them they could join me if they accepted this possibility in themselves. Some thought it was a publicity campaign, but were enjoying the spectacle. A few reached out and were immediately with me, until there were about six of us, men and women. We joined hands, experiencing a most amazing sense of well-being. Then we slowly and effortlessly flew to a great height, leaving a trail of coloured smoke which could be seen for miles. It was to demonstrate the triumph of the human spirit. We then descended and were going somewhere else to show others' (Margareta H). Transcendence is also depicted by flying. The tree is Margareta's personal life. She is at the growing tip, transcending, leaving behind her past. Being <u>high in flight</u>, <u>on a hill or mountain</u> also represents the action of seeing our life as a whole, having a sense of our overall direction and destiny, our essential self. This frequently gives rise to the drive to give of one's best to others, as Margareta does in leaving behind a sign—the spire of colour.

Some researchers believe flying dreams often precede lucid dreams. See **lucid dreams; out of body experience.** See also **Hill; mountain.** <u>Idioms</u>: fly by night; flying high; send flying.

flying saucer   See UFO.

fog   Confusion; indecision; inability to see the real issues in yourself and your environment. <u>Idioms</u>: not the foggiest.

follow   Example: 'The group I followed on the underground got off. I followed them. An elderly woman friend told me they were going home, not to my destination' (Debbie T). To follow is to be influenced by; have an attraction to; pursue; seek something; look for. Debbie processed her dream and realised she was following old habits—the friend—which weren't taking her where she wanted. Nearly always suggests we are being led by an attitude, hope or habit, and not consciously assessing present needs. <u>Following animal</u>: led by basic drives, intuition or instinct. <u>Following opposite sex</u>: led by desire for satisfaction in love. <u>Being followed</u>: taking the initiative; a continued sense of hope; doom, hunch, instinct; pursued by memory, pain, guilt, ambition. <u>Followed by opposite sex</u>: memories of old love. <u>Followed by animal</u>: see **chased**.

food   There is food for the mind, food for thought, food for the body, and spiritual nourishment. We can digest information or experience, the latter being food for our growth as an individual. Food can represent any of these. Also something we might take or are taking into ourself—such as experience of a relationship, qualities of another person, sexual pleasure, social pleasure; warning about health in regard to what is eaten. Food in <u>connection with particular person</u>: being nourished by or hungry for relationship with them; enjoyment of sexuality with them. <u>Giving food</u>: giving of oneself, time, love, work, sex. <u>Stealing food</u>: dishonest about needs in a relationship; feelings of being parasite. See **eating**; **restaurant**. See also *wife* under **family** (second example).

bread   Experience; everyday life. <u>Given slice of bread</u>: sex.

cake   Sensual enjoyment.

fruits   Fruits of experience or effort and what emerges from them. <u>Soft, luscious fruits</u> such as fig or peach may represent female genitals. <u>Long fruit</u> such as banana may depict male sexuality. <u>Apple</u>: temptation; breast.

meals   Social pleasure; acceptance; social intercourse. <u>If alone</u>: independence; loss of family ties; lack of social relationships or outside stimulus.

meat   Physical or worldly satisfaction or needs.

milk   Self-giving; baby needs.

olive   Peace; kindness, because the oil can be pressed from the olive.

sweets   Sensual pleasure; pleasures in life; special love. Example: 'A lot of sweets, brightly wrapped, were being put into my open hands. All I saw of the giver were his hands. Beautiful, big, gnarled hands of a working man' (Alex U). Alex saw the hands as the holiness of everyday human experience, especially regarding self-giving, as in parenthood, love and work —the hands of Christ we forget. Alex doesn't eat sweets, so they represent pleasures he seldom allows himself, the pleasure of everyday life and love.

vegetables Basic needs; material satisfaction. If <u>long</u> as carrot, male sexuality: if a woman's dream, feelings about sex with male; if male dream, his own sexuality. <u>Onion</u>: something to cry about; also the different layers of oneself—inner self, outer self.

foreign countries Different attitude; different mental or emotional 'climate' than one's norm. One's personal associations or ideas about any particular country need to be explored. Use the questions in **dream processing**. See **abroad**.

forest See **tree**.

forgetfulness of dreams See **science, sleep and dreams**.

fortress See **house, buildings**.

fountain The process of life; flow of consciousness up into awareness; joy of collective life. <u>Drinking from</u>, <u>bathing in</u>: the separate sense of self taking in wider awareness arising from the unconscious.

Freud, Sigmund (1856–1939) When Freud, as a qualified doctor and neurologist, became interested in psychology, it was still a branch of philosophy. He gave to it a geography of the human mind, showed the influence the unconscious has upon waking personality, and brought dreams to the attention of the scientific community. His book *The Interpretation of Dreams* was a turning point in bringing concepts on dreaming from a primitive level to alignment with modern thought. With enormous courage, and against much opposition, he showed the place sexuality has in the development of conscious self awareness. Freud defined dreams as being:

1 'Thoughts in pictures'—a process of thinking while asleep.

2 'Ego alien'. They have a life and will which often appears
   to be other than our conscious will. This led older cultures
   to believe that dreams were sent by spirits or God.
3 'Hallucinatory'. We believe the reality of the dream while
   in it.
4 'Drama'. Dreams are not random images. They are 'stage
   managed' into very definite, sometimes recurring, themes
   and plots.
5 'Moral standards'. Dreams have very different moral standards than our waking personality.
6 'Association of ideas'. In dreaming we have access to infant or other memories or experience we would find very
   difficult to recall while awake.

Freud originally said that one of the main functions of a
dream was wish fulfilment, and an expression of the 'primary
process of human thinking' unaffected by space, time and
logic. Later, in considering recurring dreams which re-enact a
recent traumatic incident, he agreed that dreams were not
only an expression of the 'pleasure principle'. W.H.R. Rivers,
studying dreams connected with war neuroses, saw such
dreams as attempts to resolve current emotional problems.

   Although there is still controversy regarding whether there
can be a valid 'dream dictionary', Freud himself saw dream
symbols as having consistent meaning so frequently that one
could attribute an interpretation to them independently of the
dreamer's associations. See **abreaction; Adler, Alfred; birds;
dream analysis; displacement; door; Fromm, Erich; hallucinations and hallucinogens; hypnosis and dreams; Jung,
Carl; lucidity; plot of dreams; wordplay and puns; secret of
universe dreams; dream as therapist; unconscious.**

frog   see **reptiles.**

Fromm, Erich   A New York psychoanalyst, who stands between Jung and Freud in his view of dreams. In his book

about dreams, *The Forgotten Language,* he says they express both the wisdom and spirituality that transcends waking thought.

front   Front of <u>body</u>, <u>house</u>, etc.: the more public or expressed part of one's nature, or attitudes used to meet 'the world'; a 'front' or façade, used to create an impression; the point of stress where we as a person contact others and meet impacts, and so are more vulnerable. Also, what is in front can mean the future. Sometimes, as with the front of a <u>car</u> or the <u>front door of a house</u>, especially if <u>bonnet or door is being opened</u>, it depicts sexual nature. See **back**. Idioms: a lot of front; in front of; putting up a good front.

frozen   See **ice**.

functions of dreams   Over the years many theories to explain the 'why' of dreams have been put forward. These range from dreams being messages from spirits; being results of food eaten prior to sleep; the mind freewheeling nonsensically; the garbage disposal system of the mind; suggestions from waking experience; a computer reprogramming for the brain; to Freud's wish fulfilment and Jung's compensation theory.

If we do not argue any particular theory, however, then perhaps we see dreams as having a much wider function. The most primal drives observable are survival, growth and reproduction. Other urges, such as eating, social position, curiosity, are secondary. The human animal appears to have survived and reproduced more capably after the development of self awareness, language and reasoning. With or without these, we remain an animal with a psychobiological nature. All animals are known to dream. All animals share a certain situation. They have **an internal world**   out of which arises impulses (to eat, to mate, to avoid danger) and feeling reactions (anger, fear, anticipation). And they have **an external world** which confronts them with real survival dangers, sources of food, a mate, changes in environmental conditions. A dream lies somewhere between these two worlds.

We can think of the human personality as being like a special sort of cavity into which all these influences are dropped or are thrown. Physical sensations, internal drives and emotions, language, social rules; religious ideas; prompts to make decisions; news of war; massive media and advertising information, are all dropped in. The cavity has to deal with it, but as it is a mixture of things, many of which are in opposition, some sort of balance has to be kept. But how? And it cannot be simply a matter of throwing out all of one sort or aspect of things. Eradicating the memory of criticism might make us more calm, but it would limit the process of psychological growth, which has survival value.

Dreams can be seen to be connected with our survival and self regulating process. Because this involves all aspects of oneself and one's experience, one cannot give dreams a single definition. They probably have many secondary functions, such as an interface to balance the internal and external influences, to compensate between the inner needs and outer reality—a baby may miss its feed so, to cope with this primal need, it may dream of being fed. Traumatic or exterior dangerous events, which cannot be processed immediately, can be stored and dealt with (experimented with or abreacted) while asleep. In higher mammals, infant traumas can be stored and dealt with in sleep when, or if, a stronger ego develops. To meet 'the loneliness and isolation of consciousness' or fears of death, the dream can link the waking self with its unconscious sense of unity or God. To meet survival needs of primitive human beings prior to rational thought, the dream probably acted as a computer, synthesising experience and information, giving rise to creative solutions to hunting or social situations, presented as sleeping or waking imagery. This may explain why many primitive people say skills such as farming, weaving, writing, were told them by a vision of a god or goddess.

If we realise that the dream is an end product of a process which produces it, it enables us to see that the 'process' (the survival function which regulates, compensates, links, problem solves) can be accessed without meeting the dream. See **sleep movements; dream process as computer; Adler; Freud; Jung.**

funeral   Feelings about one's own death; very occasionally warning about health of person buried. <u>One's own funeral</u>: it is a common dream to watch one's own funeral. It depicts your own philosophy about your end. May also remind you of what you want to do while alive; desire for sympathy from family; retreat from world; a feeling of deadness in life. <u>Burying yourself</u>: leaving an old way of life or self behind. <u>Someone else's funeral</u>: a wish they were dead; a wish to be rid of them. Often unconsciously used as an easy way out of a relationship—to fantasise them dead. It avoids the responsibility of making your wishes known. See second example under **death.** <u>Parents' funeral</u>: difficulties with, or move towards independence; exploring the feeling of their loss; repressing or letting go of the painful past. See **buried; death.** See also *death and rebirth* under **archetypes.**

furniture, furnishings   Attitudes or habits developed from family or home life, especially if it is a piece of furniture from family home or past dwelling; the attitudes, beliefs we 'furnish' our mind with; notions about self; self image.

bed, mattress   Example: 'I sit on a bed. Near me, looking at a book I am holding is a woman I know, Jane. I realise as we talk that her foot is touching mine. As my wife is on my left across the room I feel uncomfortable about this. Now Jane has her left hand on my penis. I have only underpants on. The contact is pleasant and undemanding, but I feel more and more ill at ease. I feel Jane is not having any respect for my relationship with my wife and start to tell her so' (Mr BS). In the example the bed is the environment in which the action takes place. The bed is an opportunity to explore the dreamer's decisions about sex.

Bed is one of the commonest symbols in dreams. It represents, depending on the dream context, marriage; sex; rest; giving up and taking to one's bed; passivity; sensual rather than sexual contact; sickness; intimacy; privacy. Sometimes it represents sleep and meeting or unconscious—or torture, because in bed we may be tortured by insomnia, worries, physical pain. Also our lives—you've made your bed, now lie on it. Bed is an important symbol to understand. It so often shows exactly what we are doing in our subtle areas of relationship. In the example, the man is wrestling with his desire for pleasure and his sense of commitment; but also, whether he will keep his pleasure for himself, or share it with his wife. See example in **contraceptive**. Idioms: bed of nails; bed of roses; go to bed with; make one's bed and lie on it.

carpet Sometimes depicts one's financial state, bare floorboards being poverty; can be the colour or design which are important; comfort or lack of it in life (Do you feel satisfied with yourself?); a cover up; feeling of being walked on. Idioms: sweep something under the carpet; on the carpet; roll out a red carpet.

chair Passive, relaxed attitude; inactivity; receptivity or openness. Placing chair in group: sense of status. Wheelchair: an invalid situation; a sense of weakness. If pushing someone else: seeing self as carrying an invalid. See example in **autumn**.

cupboard, wardrobe Memory; resources; different roles you play or attitudes and emotions expressed if wardrobe; hidden memories and emotions, such as skeleton in the cupboard; womb. Open, closed or trapped in cupboard: whether we are 'open or closed' to other people; trapped in old feelings; sense of isolation.

187

table   Example: 'Then I was in a place where we were having a staff party. Not very big but people were sitting at tables eating, a party mood. I sat with my child, maybe youngest son, no one else at the table. I felt I didn't wish to get involved with the others, the feeling I often get at parties, just alone in a crowd' (Simeon T). Simeon's dream table shows him not feeling inclined to connect with others. So it shows how he relates socially. Generally, a table shows social connection with others; communal activity; everyday certainties which support our activities—confidence you will get paid at the end of the week; one's attitude towards the inner and exterior community, thus an altar—if table is bare, perhaps not giving much of self. Quality of table: the quality of your relationship with others. Place at table: self image of your status. Dressing table: one's attempts to create a good social image.

G

games, gambling Generally, games can be stances used to meet life; not taking life seriously—making a game of it; competitiveness; team work; life skills. Also a game can be a way of playing creatively, exploring feelings, ideas and approaches in a safe way before trying them out in life. This sort of self allowing, of letting oneself 'want' something without too much serious overtones, can be beginning of new developments in life.

Particular games suggest different 'stances'. <u>Cards, chess</u>: use of strategies and observation. <u>Ball games, athletics</u>: competitiveness; conflict within the dreamer—the two sides; sense of win or lose, success or failure; the game of love. <u>Opponent(s)</u>: what you are meeting or in conflict with. This may be a part of your nature, such as self awareness, sexuality, even your body. You might be in conflict with life itself or 'God'. <u>Gambling</u>: taking risks with your life, health, family—whatever is indicated in dream. <u>Idioms</u>: beat somebody at their own game; deep game; dirty game; fair game; game of chance; game to the end; give the game away; know what someone's game is; mug's game; name of the game; on the game; waiting game; game is up. See also *ball* under **shapes and symbols**; **doll**; **toy**.

garage Depends how you see a garage. It may be a tool-shed, workshop, frozen food store, storeroom, as well as a car park. Generally: reserves of drive, energy, motivation; abilities, personal 'tools' to meet life; resources; things you do not need but can't let go of. See **car**.

garbage   Parts of your experience, feelings, no longer useful. Occasionally one discards, or considers as useless, some aspect of self, or ability, which is actually valuable.

garden   Generally, the inner life of the dreamer; the area of growth or change in your life; what you are trying to cultivate in yourself; feelings of peace; being near to one's natural self; meditative attitude. See also second example in *wife* under **family**.

Example: 'I was working in quite a large garden by my house. A part of the garden was like a little alcove by other buildings. The garden was kidney shaped. I had dug this small plot and was considering how I might relax and sunbathe there. My daughter said I should have worked harder on it—dug it better. I felt intense emotions of resentment and anger at her criticism. I started telling her what a bad time I had in the past. How difficult it was even to work, let alone work hard' (Beatrice G). This shows the garden as depicting what one has 'worked on' or produced in life. This could mean externally, or one's own nature. The daughter is Beatrice's own self criticism, which pushes her on, though she has a tendency to want to relax 'in the sun'. This aspect of garden suggests how 'fruitful' one's life has been socially and spiritually.

Beautiful garden: suggests satisfaction at time of dream. Overgrown, weeds in garden: awareness of particular parts of your personality which need working on. Perhaps negative habits need 'weeding out'. Square, circular garden: holds a lot of your gathered wisdom and insights which would be useful if made conscious. Garden pool: childhood, or early stage in the evolution of one's self consciousness, during which there was a sense of communal awareness; sense of unity with life. See **dream processing**; *the self* under **archetypes**. Idioms: bear garden; up the garden path.

gardener   The down to earth but wise aspect of self; the wisdom or insights gathered through life, from which we can direct our own growth and life to integrate the many parts of our nature; the process in each of us—the Christ—which synthesises our life experience, and considers what love, what resonance with all life, there is in it.

gate   A threshold, like that between conscious self awareness and our total experience. Such a gate needs to open and close—open to allow selected memory, close to prevent massive flooding of impressions. The gate can also portray the passage from one period of life, or level of maturity, to another. Therefore, to stand before adolescence, parenthood, death, might be shown as facing a gate in a dream. Also similar to door—entrance to something different, or to someone else's life, as in marriage. See *door* under **house, buildings**; example in *dog* under **animals**.

geese   Freedom; our soul. See **birds**.

genitals   Direct reference to sexual aspect of self. See *penis* and *vagina* under **body**; **castration**.

gestalt dream work   See **dream processing**.

gestures   See **postures, movement and body language**.

ghost   Memories, feelings, guilt, which haunt us; parts of the wider awareness of the unconscious which attempt to communicate; the husks or influences from past traumas or events, which have been emptied of hurt and real influence, but still affect us; fantasies, hopes, longings we have given time to, and so filled with our life and sexual energy, and which now influence us. Ghost of living person: a sense of their thoughts or presence influencing one; haunted by desire for them, or a resentment or feeling about them. A ghost which feels solid: the dreamer is 'touching' aspects of their own mind or awareness existing beyond preconceived ideas and beliefs.

Example: 'So frequently do I dream of the house and the town I lived in as a child, I wonder if I do indeed haunt the house by dreaming of it. I must tell you I believe that a traumatic incident, which happened when I was 20, is involved. I was playing the piano downstairs when I heard a gun fired. On searching I found my father lying dead upstairs in an attic. He had shot his brains out. I took the scene in, never to be forgotten, in one horrified moment' (Barbara T). Some people believe that, because of such incidents as described, in their dreams the living haunt a place. Seeing a ghost while awake can still be considered as connected with the dream process. See third example under **husband**. See also **hallucination**.

giant   Childhood feelings about grown-ups, especially the frightening side of parents.

gift   Intuition; unconscious knowledge; what is received in a relationship, such as support, sense of worth, acceptance. Giving gift: giving of self; hoping receiver accepts or likes one. Receiving unwanted gift: difficulties in accepting someone, or something from within; pregnancy. See **giving**.

girl   Feelings; emotional self; young sexuality; vulnerability.
In male dream: emotions; sexual feelings; daughter. Example: 'I was away from home somewhere and was helping and encouraging a young Japanese girl, who was pregnant, to come back to England to have her baby here. I felt a lot of care for her' (Dave L). Dave processed his dream and discovered a lot of sexual pleasure in connection with the girl. He had held himself back in this area most of his life and, as he was learning to allow his sexual feelings (not simply genital sex), he found a deepening in his caring also.
In female dream: oneself at that age, whether older or

younger; feelings about sister or daughter; the aspect of one-self portrayed by the girl, as in following example: 'I was watching and at the same time I was a young girl sitting on a lawn' (Honey J).

Another girl with your man: how you deal with your sense of being wanted; anxiety about not being attractive or lovable; suspicion; a side of yourself which relates you differently to your man.

giving   Relatedness; the sort of exchange or give and take which goes on in a relationship, even the internal relationship with oneself, or the environment. One can give affection, support, sex, ideas, as well as wounds. One needs to see what the interaction is by looking at what is given. Receiving: consider what is received to define what you are accepting or rejecting in oneself or from others. The idioms show the many ways this action can be used: don't give me that; give and take; give as good as one gets; give away or give-away; give oneself away; give somebody away; don't give a brass farthing; give place; give a piece of one's mind; give them enough rope; give someone the evil or glad eye; give someone the elbow; give one's notice. See **gift**.

glass   The sort of invisible yet tangible barriers we may erect or feel around others, such as natural caution, emotional cold-ness, disinterest, fear of being hurt, or pride; social barriers; invisible aspects of ourself which nevertheless may trap us, such as fear, lack of self respect; self doubt. Frosted, smoked glass: desire for privacy; keeping parts of oneself hidden; an obscure or unclear view of a situation; occasionally relating to death—the very real yet obscure experience we all face. Breaking glass: breaking through a barrier. Breaking some-thing made of glass: breaking a relationship; shattering an illusion; broken hearted. See **break**.

glasses, spectacles   Ability to see, understand—or lack of it; a way of hiding oneself, as behind sunglasses. Terms like 'shortsighted' or 'longsighted' help to understand the use of glasses in a dream.

glove   See **clothes**.

gnome   See **dwarf**.

God   Jung says that while the Catholic church admits of dreams sent by God, most theologians make little attempt to understand dreams.

   God in a dream can depict several things: a set of emotions we use to deal with anxiety, i.e. our own belief that a higher power is in charge, so therefore we are all right in the world and are not responsible; a parent image from early infancy; a set of moral or philosophical beliefs one holds; self judgment; something/one we worship; a feeling of connection with humanity; an expression of the fundamental creative/destructive process in oneself. See *the self* under **archetypes**; **religion and dreams**. See also **individuation**.

gold   The best or most valuable in oneself or in opportunity; what stands the 'acid test' or does not tarnish with time, in terms of personal qualities, such as love, patience or care in work; something you value or want in your life. If cheap, false, tarnished: something you valued but does not deserve respect. See *gold* under **colours**.

grave   Feelings or concepts of death; feelings about someone who is dead; realisation a part of yourself is dead, buried or killed. See **cemetery**; **tomb**.

graveyard   See **cemetery**.

green   See **colours**.

grey   See **colours**.

group   See **people**.

growth of something   The changes in us which bring about new ways of relating to other people, ourself and activity. The change in personal growth may be mental, emotional or physical. Sometimes the change is one of achieving new realisations.

guillotine   Losing one's head, or threat of it; killing one's ability to think and reason, so perhaps becoming irrational.

guilt   Feeling guilt in a dream is a direct experience, but what you are feeling guilty about may well be in symbols and need clarifying. See **emotions, mood**.

gun   See **weapons**.

guru   See **God**; *the self* under **archetypes**.

H

half Example: 'I could see an older woman watching me from the road. I felt very scared at her being there. I walked to the front door, I started to walk past the front door, felt great fear and hung back, half behind the front door, for protection from her' (Pamela H). Generally it means part of; divided; incomplete; in between; conflict. Half open: opposing feelings about whether to 'be open' or not—can I, can't I, will I, won't I? Halfway up/down: indecision; faltering motivation; sometimes between the opposites, or outside one's everyday experience. Half full : may refer to half one's life used up. Cut in half: conflict between intellect and body sexuality. Half buried: something you are only partly aware of.

Hall, Calvin Author of *The Content Analysis of Dreams* and *The Meaning of Dreams*. Hall's work with content analysis—which is looking at the personality of the dreamer through a series of dreams rather than a single dream—is expressed in a popular form in *The Meaning of Dreams*. With the entrance into home life of computers, easy content analysis has become much more available. See **computers and dreams**.

hallucinations, hallucinogens Example: 'I dream insects are dropping either on me from the ceiling of our bedroom, or crawling over my pillow. My long-suffering husband is always woken when I sit bolt upright in bed, my eyes wide open and my arm pointing at the ceiling. I try to brush them off. I can still see them—spiders or woodlice. I am now well aware it is a dream. But no matter how hard I stare the insects are there in perfect detail. I am not frightened, but wish it would go away' (Sue D). Sue's dream only became a hallucination when

196

she opened her eyes and continued to see the insects in perfect clarity.

A hallucination can be experienced through any of the senses singly, or all of them together. So one might have a hallucinatory smell or sound. To understand hallucinations, which are quite common without any use of drugs such as alcohol, LSD or cannabis, one must remember that everyone has the natural ability to produce such images. One of the definitions of a dream according to Freud is its hallucinatory quality. While asleep we can create full sensory, vocal, motor and emotional experience in our dream. While dreaming we usually accept what we experience as real. A hallucination is an experience of the function which produces 'dreams' occurring while we have our eyes open. The voices heard, people seen, smells smelt, although appearing to be outside us, are no more exterior than the things and images of our dreams. With this information one can understand that much classed as psychic phenomena and religious experience is an encounter with the dream process. That does not, of course, deny its importance.

There are probably many reasons why Sue should experience a hallucination and her husband not. One might be that powerful drives and emotions might be pushing for attention in her life. Some of the primary drives are the reproductive drive, urge towards independence, pressure to meet unconscious emotions and past trauma and fears, any of which, in order to achieve their ends, can produce hallucinations. A hallucination is therefore not an 'illusion' but a means of giving information from deeper levels of self. Given such names as mediumship or mystical insight, in some cultures or individuals the ability to hallucinate is often rewarded socially.

Drugs such as LSD, cannabis, psilocybin, mescaline, peyote and opium can produce hallucinations. This is sometimes because they allow the dream process to break through into consciousness with less intervention. If this occurs without warning it can be very disturbing.

The very real dangers are that unconscious content, which in ordinary dreaming breaks through a threshold in a regulated way, emerges with little regulation. Fears, paranoid feelings, past traumas, can emerge into the consciousness of an individual who has no skill in handling such dangerous forces. Because the propensity of the unconscious is to create images, an area of emotion might emerge in an image such as the devil. Such images, and the power they contain, not being integrated in a proper therapeutic setting, may haunt the individual, perhaps for years. Even at a much milder level, elements of the unconscious will emerge and disrupt the person's ability to appraise reality and make judgments. Unacknowledged fears may lead the drug user to rationalise their reasons for avoiding social activity or the world of work. See **ESP and dreams**; dead lover in *husband* under **family**. See also **out of body experience**.

hammer   See **tools**.

hand   See *hand* under **body**.

harbour   See **quay**.

hare   See *hare* under **animals**.

harness   Directing our energy or potential; control; restraint.

hat   See *hat* under **clothes**.

hearing   See *Ear* under **body**.

hearse   Feelings about death; reminder of time left to live. See **funeral**.

heaven Compensatory feelings for difficulties in life; intuition about life after death; retreat from life; meeting one's religious concepts; one's own sense of harmony or integration. See mention of heaven and hell in **dream as spiritual guide**.

hell If threatening: emotions, anxieties which one is fearful of; one's self created misery, perhaps arising out of such things as anger or resentment we cling to, or a sense of being different or unwanted; feelings which burn in us. Sometimes people reverse the roles of heaven and hell. Hell becomes attractive, full of excitement, heaven an insipid place. See *devil* under **archetypes**; mention of heaven and hell in **dream as spiritual guide**.

hermaphrodite Example: 'I was outdoors in my underpants teaching a group of people. Looking down I saw my genitals were exposed and I had female organs. I felt OK' (Bill S). Although Bill works in the building trade, he finds it easy to cook, look after his children, cry, and accept his 'female' characteristics. Being both sexes: might also suggest feeling uncertain about our own gender, or having problems in the role of our own sex.

hero/ine If we are not the hero/ine of our own dream, we are probably still not accepting responsibility for our own drives, potentials and weaknesses. The hero/ine frequently depicts our initiative and unexpressed potential. We might see our highest ideals as coming from an exterior figure such as Christ, and so miss touching the depths of our own being, avoid responsibility for our urges or actions. What happens to the hero/ine shows how one's own creativity and expressed love fare. See *Christ, hero/ine* and *the self* under **archetypes**; **religion and dreams**.

hiding   Example: 'I was in my bedroom, I looked up and saw the top of some long curtains were on fire. I thought "My God, now my sister's setting fire to the house to hide the evidence" ' (Ms A T). The example illustrates how we may use one emotion or situation to hide what is really important.

Hiding from feeling; avoiding awareness of something we don't want to see; being protective—hiding how we really feel about someone, or our sexual feelings about someone; not knowing. Hiding from something dangerous, dangerous thing hidden: feeling threatened either by unconscious contents or exterior situation. Hiding a body, object: not facing difficult feelings connected with the body or thing. See **dead people dreams**.

high   Example: 'I must have climbed up this fire escape OK, but the building was incredibly high up and when I reached the platform I looked down and saw everything miles below. At this stage I was gripped with panic and I lay on the floor, clinging to the metal grid it was made of, and couldn't move. I was so panic stricken it immobilised me completely and I couldn't move up or even get back down' (Helen B). Being high up, as in the example, can depict having a very wide view of one's situation in life; feeling isolated, alone, or away from the known and secure—as one might in starting a new job, losing one's job, or moving to a new town; apprehension; anxiety. Looking at something high: above one's head; feeling impressed or awed; challenge. Also one's aspirations and widest view of life, therefore the spiritual. See **descend; hill; mountain; positions**. Idioms: High and mighty; high as a kite; high flown; high flyer; high minded; high places.

hill   Example: 'I am riding through thick fog. I feel I should turn back. But then I see a pale golden white glow and know that if I continue to the top of the hill I will emerge from the fog into a most beautiful place' (C B). As in this example, a hill gives a clear view of our situation; our achievement; something we have made an effort to attain; expanded awareness. <u>Going uphill</u>: difficulties; hard work or effort; the first half of our life; or life itself if it feels like an uphill struggle. <u>Going downhill</u>: feeling as if circumstances are pushing you; feeling you might lose, or have lost, control; the second half of your life, or old age.

Also hill or hills sometimes represent breasts or the belly. A <u>hole at the bottom of a hill</u>: especially if surrounded by shrubs, depicts the vagina. <u>Green sunny hillside</u>: feeling whole; a sense of heaven. See **mountain**; **high**; **descending**; last example in **flying**.

historic In some dreams we find ourselves in the past, with the feeling of those times. This nearly always depicts, not a past life, but our own feelings. So a cowboy scene might depict our pioneering spirit or sense of adventure. We need to define what feelings we derive from reading about or seeing films about such periods of history. Also our past; the person we were at some period in our life.

holding Example: 'I am a prisoner in a room with three boys aged three, five and fourteen. They seem to be my children. There are two prison warders, a man, a woman. The man was subservient to the woman who holds the keys and keeps control' (Carol J). There are five aspects to holding.

1 To control, as in controlling or 'holding one's breath'; to be able to manipulate, kill or do something with what is held; this includes holding on to something for support or protection.
2 Ownership—this is mine, to share or not.
3 In touch with; knowing; having a 'grasp' of.
4 Responsibility; left 'holding the baby'; one's situation.
5 Intimacy; taking to oneself, taking hold of oneself, as in masturbation; as in the following example: 'I was in a

large removal van with a woman sat on my lap. I held her breasts with pleasure' (Tony C).

Idioms: Get hold of; have a hold over someone; hold back; hold in.

hole Difficulty or tricky situation in life; a situation you might 'fall into'; a place to hide or feel protected in—therefore womblike feelings; an escape route; a way of 'seeing through' something; the vagina. Going into a hole: meeting feelings, urges or fears we usually keep unconscious; confronting aspects of self buried beneath our surface awareness; memories of womb existence; death, burial. Occasionally used as wordplay meaning whole. Holes in clothes, objects: faults; weaknesses; illness; 'full of holes'. Holes in body: sense of weakness; emptiness in one's life, such as loneliness, illness; negative feelings about that part of self; see **body** for appropriate part. Hole in head: letting everyone know what you think; gossiping. See third example in **dark**; first example in *son* under **family**; **tunnel**; hole in hand dream in Introduction.

holiday Sense of relaxation; being independent; satisfying one's own needs; reaching a period of one's life in which one can rest on one's laurels. See example in **clothes**; example in **crossroad**.

hollow Feeling of emptiness in one's life; womb feeling or memories; feelings about the vagina. See **hole**.

homosexuality Each of us has some element of homosexuality in us unconsciously. In one's dreams it may suggest a desire for the father or mother's love, perhaps because they were not demonstrative. So one was led to crave the love of a man/woman. Conflict or anxiety about one's own gender; feelings of sexual inadequacy or inadequacy in one's own gender; unconscious pain in regard to the opposite sex—this may be rationalised into reasons for being homosexual rather than being experienced and made conscious; depicting an introversion of one's sexual drive.

honey   The essence of one's experience; pleasure; sweetness.

horns   Protectiveness; desire to hurt; the animal in the human, as in the form of Pan; sexuality or the penis. See second example in **eating**. Idioms : pull in one's horns; lock horns with someone; take the bull by the horns; on the horns of a dilemma.

horse   See **animals**.

hose   Intestines; penis. Hosing: sex play. See **water; garden.**

hostility   Direct expression of that feeling. It is worthwhile considering who or what the dream suggests you feel hostile towards. In general the most powerful hostile feelings are towards parents, having been generated in infancy. These need to be met if one is to become an adequate sexual person in relation to an adult of the opposite sex and social authority. Unconscious hostility causes one to remain at a mystic or idealistic level of relationship with the opposite sex, causing difficulty in meeting the real individual. Meeting anger, aggression and hostility does not mean suppressing it or expressing it socially. Many of us have become, in the words of W.V. Caldwell, the author of *LSD Psychotherapy,* 'hostility cripples'. As human animals, anger and aggression are natural, but growing in a society which, although it practices the most terrible aggression at a national level, suppresses individual aggression, it is difficult for us to lead these urges towards maturity. Maturity in love is often talked about, but not maturity in hate. It helps if we can recognise whether we are repressing aggressions or hostility in our dreams. If anger is felt but not expressed in a dream, then use the technique explained in **dream processing**, in which you carry the dream forward and express in imagination the emotions held back. This should begin the process of more expressive anger in one's dreams, allowing the maturing of the aggression to begin. See Sunday school *Christ* under **archetypes**.

hot   Pleasurable 'warm' feelings; passion for someone. Very hot, burning: potentially painful emotions or passions, which may leave their mark. See **fire**. Idioms: be hot on; hot and bothered; hot blooded; hot headed; hot stuff; in hot water; in the hot seat; make it hot for someone; get the hots; hot air.

house, buildings   A house nearly always refers to oneself, depicting one's body and attributes of personality. Thus if we take a large house with its many functional rooms, the library would represent the mind, the bathroom cleansing or renewal of good feelings, the bedrooms one's sexuality or intimacy, the roof one's protectiveness or 'coping mechanisms'. Large public buildings such as hospitals, factories, blocks of flats, depict particular functions suggested by their nature. But of course, if the house or building has a personal connection—the house you live in, or place you have worked—then you need to define what are the essential feelings about such. Or see **dream processing**. If a house or building has a quality of some other type of construction, such as a library feeling like a factory, or a house a church, both aspects should be accepted as important.

attic   The mind, ideas, memories, past experience. Trapped in attic : a purely intellectual approach to life. Finding attic: pleasure at new ideas, discovering potential or wisdom from past experience. Threat from attic: disturbing thoughts. Window, turret looking out from attic: our sense of connection with the cosmos; wider awareness; intellectual view. Hiding in attic: see example in *hall* below in this entry.

basement, cellar Example: 'I know I have killed somebody and their body is walled up in the cellar. The strange thing is I haven't a clue who this person is. Various people visit my home and I am terrified the body will be discovered. In one of these recurring dreams the police actually investigate the disappearance of "the person" and go into the cellar. When I wake from these dreams I always have the most terrible guilty feeling' (Mrs P L). Usually the things we have hidden from awareness in our unconscious. The example shows how Mrs L has killed or repressed a part of herself. We might 'kill' ambition, love, sexual drive, and push them into our unconscious. But the basement or cellar is also the entrance to general memories, our biological 'unconscious' functions, archetypal patterns of behaviour, subliminal or psychic impressions, the collective unconscious. Frequently the place we keep memories of traumatic events in our life. So a dark shape or intruder might emerge from 'downstairs'. Our dark deeds or guilty memories are also in the basement. A snake in the cellar, cave: our psychobiological drive; the energy behind our growth and motivation which includes sex drive. This connects us with awareness of our evolution. Bad smell: emotions which could cause depression or illness.

castle Feelings of security or insecurity; our defensive attitudes; the way we defend ourself against 'attack'; past attitudes which may have been necessary in childhood to defend ourselves while strengthening our identity.

chimney Smoking; the birth canal; sign of inner warmth. Belching black smoke: the grim mechanised side of our culture centred on production instead of humanity.

church, chapel, temple Example: 'It was like an English church with several great spires. The whole building seemed to be built in a white and gold design. The gold parts shimmered in the sun. I gazed at this wonderful sight for some time and felt such a wonderful feeling of upliftment, my tiredness gone' (Johan E). As in the example, the powerfully re-generative side of our inner life or feelings; the world of experience we have created inwardly by our thoughts, meditation, actions; our sense of contact with life itself. Also the moral rules we make decisions from (such rules may not be 'Christian' if they kill much of our inner life); moral authority; our relationship with the community. Occasionally baptism, marriage, death, the mother or refuge.

Walking past church: not entering into contact with the best in us—or our anger towards dogma. Example: 'The priest was going to question and assault my friend in connection with some opinion he had offended the church with. I went to stand near him to give him moral support, and physical help if necessary. I hated seeing anybody degraded. The priest saw my move and sent three thug type men to shoulder me out. They surrounded me to knock me down. I went beserk and knocked them all over the place with kicks and punches' (John P). In the example John sees the dogmas of the Church as an assault and degradation of human qualities of love and moral support.

door Example: 'I find my way to a door and knock. It is at the end of a cul de sac. An old woman of about 60 comes to the door. Although old, she is healthy and well preserved. Without a word I grab her in my arms and have sex with her' (Patrick S). Freud felt that a door, a keyhole, a handle, a knocker, all depicted sex and sexual organs. The example shows this clearly. Knocking refers to the sex act, the cul de sac is the woman's legs. But the image of a door has so many other ways of being expressed in dreams and is used very frequently. In the next example it represents the experience of discovering a new feeling state. For instance, if one had always been apologetic and now became affirmative, 'new doors' of experience could well open. Example: 'I come up to a door which I'd never seen before, and on opening it, I came across another house fully furnished' (Mrs R F).

General meanings, depending on the dream, are a boundary; the difference between one feeling state and another; such as depression and feeling motivated; the feelings or attitudes, such as aloofness, we use to shut others out of our life to remain independent or private; being open or inviting; a sense of leaving an environment or relationship—escape; entering into new work or relationships. Someone at a door: opportunity; the unexpected; new experience. Front door: public self; confidence; our relationship with people in general; a vagina. Back door: our private, family life; our more secret activities; the anus. Side door : escaping from a situation, or being indirect. Shutting a door: privacy; trying to find 'space' for oneself; the dismissing attitudes or tension we use to shut others out of intimate contact; end of a relationship. Door to strange landscape or world: finding entrance into unconscious. Doorknob: see **knob**.

Example: 'I am being strangled from behind by a faceless man! I had gone down to lock my flat door for the night when I noticed the door was open. I hastily bolted it and ran upstairs, but unknown to me the intruder was already in the flat' (Miss H). Here the door represents the censorship the dreamer places between her conscious self and her sexual drives. In 'strangling' our own life drive, we ourselves feel cut off from life.

fortress See *castle* above in this entry.

hall Public or dance hall: how you relate to groups or the public; meeting sexuality; a place of initiation, maturing beyond old habits, ways of life and views—perhaps because civic ceremonies such as marriage, trials, social rewards, take place in hall-like environments.

Hallway: the way one meets other people or allows them into one's life or intimacy; the receptive female reproductive function; connecting link with aspects of oneself. Example: 'I find myself in the entrance hall of a very large house. The hall is very large with curved staircases at either side meeting at the top to form a balcony. There is nobody about and I am frightened. I start to walk up the stairs but then find myself hiding in the roof with very little space above my body' (Mrs B). The hall is probably Mrs B's childbearing ability and her image of herself as a woman. The words 'little space above my body' suggest her main area of life has always been her childbearing function or physical attractiveness as a woman, and she had not developed her mental self. See also **corridor**; *white* under **colour**.

home Example: 'I was sitting in the living room at home and my mum was sitting there like we do when we're relaxing in the evening. From nowhere in particular my dad was there. He held his girlfriend in his arms and displayed her in front of us. She was stark naked. My mum tensed up, tightened her lips, and tried to look away. I felt acutely embarrassed for me, mum, dad and his girlfriend' (Lynsay S).

Generally, one's basic needs such as shelter, warmth, nourishment—but usually in the sense of what we have created as our basic way of life; the values, standards, goals we have accepted as normal, or are 'at home' with; as in the example, the situation or state in our home, which here means family atmosphere.

Example: 'I am walking down a busy street when I realise that all I have on are my bra and pants. Everyone is staring at me and I try to appear unconcerned but feel more and more embarrassed as I go on. Eventually the street and the people fade and I am alone in my own home and a great sensation of relief comes over me. I do not bother to put any more clothes on but wander about the house secure in the comfort people are no longer looking at me' (Mrs S C). Here home is the sense of being oneself, or absence of concern over other people's criticism.

In a past home: depicts the part of our character or experience which developed in that home environment. Someone else's home: what we sense as the attitudes and atmosphere or the situation prevailing in that home. So a young woman going to the home of her lover and his wife shows her facing the fact of her lover's home and commitment in marriage. Future home: The direction you would like your life to take, or fear it might. See *house* below in this entry. Idioms: bring something home to someone; close to home; come home to roost; home and dry; broken home; home truth; home is where the heart is.

hospital   Example: 'I was a prisoner in a hospital, although there were no locked doors or bars. It was a psychiatric hospital, but we were allowed to believe we had a physical illness. I had been very ill, but was trying to escape' (Joan P). At the time of her dream Joan was feeling trapped in depression and also attending a therapy group. Hospital represents needing or being involved in a healing process of body or mind; worries about one's health.

hotel   Temporary attitudes or way of life; a short term situation; relaxation; escape or separation from family or home; sexual activity outside home life.

house   If the house is one we know, live in now or in the past, what is said about *home* applies. If it is a house created by the dream: one's body and personality in all its aspects.
    Inside the house: within oneself. Outside the house and garden: extroversion or the relationship with environment. Ground floor: practical everyday life; sexuality; hips and legs. Basement : unconscious: see **basement, cellar.** First, other middle floors: internal needs, rest, sleep, hungers; the trunk. Top floor, attic: thinking; the conscious mind; memory; the head: see *attic* above in this entry. Front of house: our persona; facade; social self; face. Things in house: aspects of one's feelings and makeup. Other people in house: different facets of dreamer. Windows : one's outlook on life; how you see others: see larger entry on *window* below in this entry. People, things coming from downstairs: influences, fears, impressions

from unconscious or passions, or from everyday worries. People, things from upstairs: influence of rational self. Attackers, intruders from outside: social pressures or response to criticisms. Repairs, enlargement, renovation: reassessment or change of attitudes or character; personal growth. Damage, structural faults: faults in character structure; hurts such as broken relationship; bodily illness. House falling down, burning: big changes in attitudes; leaving old standards or dependencies behind; sickness: see last example in **falling**. Cramped house: feeling of need for personal change; feeling restricted in home environment or in present personal attitudes. Kitchen: creativity; nourishing oneself; mother role; diet: see **cooking**. Living room: personal leisure; 'space' to be oneself; everyday life. Dining room: appetites; social or family contact; mental or psychological diet. Bedroom: privacy; sex; intimacy; rest: see *bed* under **furniture**. Study, library: mental growth; mind. Larder: hungers; sensual satisfaction. Toilet: privacy; release of tension; letting go of emotions, fantasies or desire which we need to discharge: see **toilet**. Nursery, child's bedroom: feelings about your children; one's own childhood feelings and memories. Floor : basic attitudes and confidence; what supports you, such as health and good will of others. Ceiling: boundary of ideas or awareness. Row of houses: other people. See *room; stairs; wall; attic* in this entry.

hut Childhood family feelings; basic uncomplicated situation or relationship.

lift Mood shifts or movement of attention, as when we move from being involved in physical sensation and shift to thinking; rise or drop in status or work; our emotional highs and lows—the lift going out through the roof could show tendency towards being manic, going underground meeting influences from the unconscious; being 'uplifted' or feeling 'down'. Example: 'I was in a lift with a young woman. She intimated there was some difficulty about getting the lift to work. I felt this was not so and pushed the button. The doors closed and the lift began to ascend. As it did we moved close together and kissed. But the main feeling was of being accepted and liked. This moved my feelings so much I felt a great melting feeling in my abdomen, and a lot of body sensation against her body' (Anthony F). Here the lift shows Anthony 'being moved' emotionally and sexually—the lift can depict sex and the energy flowing up the trunk in love or meditation.

mansion Although a house represents all the aspects of self in which our identity lives—a body, emotions, creativity, etc. —a mansion is depicting the same thing with a different emphasis. It is ourself as we are, plus features still latent, possibilities not yet developed or explored. See *house* in this entry.

public house Social, free and easy side of self; alcohol dependency.

roof The philosophy, beliefs or coping strategies we use to protect ourself from stress. Standing on roof: heightened awareness, see **dream as spiritual guide**. Mending roof: developing new coping strategies. Leaking roof: need for new coping strategies. Roof garden: spiritual or mental growth or flowering of new ideas, insights or abilities, see last example in *window* in this entry.

room A particular feeling state—for instance the room might feel sinister, warm, spacious, cold, etc., so depicts such. Sometimes a room, because of its spaciousness, represents the amount of potential or opportunity one has. The 'containing' quality of a room may also depict involvement in one's mother. Finding extra rooms: a common dream theme—recognition or discovery of previously unnoticed aspects, abilities, fears, or traits in oneself. Example: 'There was a room in my house I had never been in before. It was filled with water and had three kittens submerged in it. While in the room I didn't need to breathe' (Audrey P). The room here represents Audrey's childbearing function—her womb. The room can therefore depict mother or qualities of mothering. See descriptions of various rooms under *house* in this entry.

stable The natural urges you have.

stairs Taking steps towards something; going up or down in life in your own estimation. <u>Running up</u>: escaping from urges arising from lower down in the body; so, a movement of attention towards the abstract or mental, away from fears arising from unconscious or sexuality. Example: 'I go up the first flight of stairs, then the next, and there is my ex husband's Nan who is dead and whom I have never met. I don't see her face but I know it's her. She is a blinding white light and I run down the stairs' (Mrs H). The example shows how going upstairs can be an opening or widening of awareness to include areas of experience usually avoided. In fact Mrs H takes her awareness down to more everyday levels to escape meeting the light.

Example: 'I climb a few flights of stairs. As I go up, the stairs start wobbling and breaking up. At the top the last flight breaks away from the landing and I am left to cross a gaping hole with a few bits of debris to cling to. It is very frightening, but I see other people passing me on the caved in stairs and on to the landing as if nothing has happened' (Maureen). Lack of confidence, a fear of failing or not being capable is also a common feeling in connection with stairs. Maureen sees life as full of pitfalls.

wall Codes of behaviour, belief systems, attitudes—often unconscious—you live within, or are protected by; the boundaries of behaviour or thought you keep within, are fearful of extending beyond, or are trapped by, thereby what one feels to be barriers or restrictions; one's feelings of confidence which protect against anxiety or social 'knocks'; the feelings or attitudes you keep people away with—the walls we put up between us to maintain privacy, stop being hurt, or to maintain a role or status. Also a special feeling which you have created, such as developing a sense of one's own value.

Example: 'I realised T had been in Bill's room and not respected his need for privacy, so Bill had torn down the wall as a protest and made the room, which now appeared about four times its usual size, into a public sitting room' (Cyril A). Sometimes what the wall depicts is obvious, as in the example, where it is shown as the way Cyril maintains his separation from others and thus is a private individual. The fall of the wall shows how 'exposed' one might be. The description of private areas of our life in a newspaper might be an example of just such a wall coming down. Idioms: drive up the wall; go to the wall; writing on the wall; back to the wall; knock one's head against a wall. See **wall, fence.**

warehouse Memories; past experience; aspects of self put in storage, such as ambition while bringing up children.

window Example: 'I was looking at a little matchbox shaped thing and one looked into it like a window. I looked at my arm through the window, then my vision was full of patterns of my energy going up and down my arm. It was very beautiful, leaflike shapes with glass-like balls and clear liquid but even the liquid making patterns on the move up and down' (Wendy O). In general one is either looking out of, looking into, or going through a window. This makes them largely connected with what we see in the sense of perception or being aware of things, either within ourself, as in the example, or in regard to other people. So they can depict our eyes or awareness also.

Looking out of a window: your 'view' of or feelings about what you perceive in your environment or life; looking for a way out of a situation. Looking into a window: what you feel or 'see' in regard to someone else if you see another person; what you are aware of when 'looking' at or giving awareness to yourself. Climbing out of window: possibly your way of avoiding difficult feelings, i.e. by giving attention to exterior things—television, a book—rather than what we feel. Climbing in window: looking within oneself or seeing what makes someone else 'tick'. Opening window: letting others see your feelings or opinions; allowing other people's influence on yourself. No windows: not seeing what is going on around you; introversion; attention held by internal feelings, thoughts or concerns. Height of windows, such as first floor: suggest what area of your experience you are looking at the world through. You might only look at life through a basement window, which suggests being influenced by one's sexuality or unconscious feelings; see levels of *house* within entry above. Example: 'Presently I come to another domed window and stand looking at sea and sky. I am filled with serenity and peace' (JD). Domed window, window in roof: depicts our head or mind. We each have a cosmic sense—a synthesis of experience in which we develop a personal view of what life is about in the largest sense; looking through the domed or roof window depicts this cosmic sense. Idioms: window dressing; window on the world; a room with a view.

housework   The cleaning out of non-functional, negative attitudes, thoughts and experience; keeping our internal house in order, perhaps by taking time to clarify or define motives, opinions and feelings about others.

Humphrey, Nicholas   Sees human beings as needing to learn and modify strategies for social survival and interaction. He says of the human animal, 'It depends upon the bodies of other animals not merely for immediate sustenance in infancy and its sexual fulfilment as an adult but in one way or another for the success—or failure—of almost every enterprise it undertakes. In these circumstances the ability to model the behaviour of others in the social group has paramount survival value.' We know that cats, while dreaming, practise stalking and hunting. Humphrey speculates that in dreams humans practise and modify social behaviour.

hunger   Our needs, or demands, physically, emotionally or mentally. We may feel the need for success or fame just as acutely as the need for sex or food. See **eating; food.**

hunter, huntress   The aspect of ourself which is either killing out our 'animal', or gaining sustenance from it; the urge to get away from everyday responsibility; our breadwinning qualities.

hypnosis and dreams   Many experiments have been done using hypnosis in connection with dreams. In the early part of this century Carl Schroetter hypnotised Miss E, a pharmacist, in an attempt to test Freud's theory of symbol formation. He suggested Miss E would dream of having homosexual intercourse with a female friend, L. The dream she subsequently reported was 'I sit in a small dirty cafe holding a tremendous French newspaper . . . A woman with a strong Yiddish accent—L is Jewish—asks me twice, "Don't you need anything?" I don't answer . . . she comes a third time . . . I recognise her as my acquaintance. She holds a threadbare suitcase with a sticker on it that reads "For ladies only!" I leave the cafe with her . . . she hangs onto me which I find unpleasant but suffer it . . . Before her house she pulls out an enormous bunch of keys and gives one to me. "I trust only you with it; it is the key to this case. You might like to use it. Just watch that my husband doesn't get hold of it." ' The dream contains several of the classical Freudian symbols of sex, such as the suitcase, the key and the phrase 'For ladies only'. Miss E had not, according to Schroetter, heard or read of Freud's ideas.

Roffenstein, suspecting Miss E may have known something of Freudian ideas, chose 'a 28-year-old, totally uneducated nursemaid of lower than average intelligence, who grew up and still lives in an uneducated milieu'. He suggested she dream of intercourse with her father. She reported: 'I dreamt about my father, as if he had presented me with a great bag and with it he gave me a large key. It was a very large key. It looked like the key to a house. I had a sad feeling. I opened the bag. I snake jumped out against my mouth; I shrieked aloud.'

More recent experiments are reported by Woods and Greenhouse in *New World of Dreams*. The suggestion was made to one subject that as a child she had wet the bed and her mother scolded her. That night she dreamt she fell into a pond in winter and her mother was angry. An interesting aspect of these experiments is that another subject under hypnosis was told the dream and asked what it meant. Without hesitation she said, 'Oh, that girl must have wet the bed.' This and other experiments suggest humans have an inherent, although perhaps unconscious, ability to understand the language of dreams.

I

I See **dreamer**. See also **identity and dreams; individuation**.

ice Being cold or emotionally or sexually. It depicts what is meant by the term cold shoulder, where we shut off any display of warmth or compassion. It also therefore shows the dreamer as having 'frozen assets' in a personal sense. Icicle: frozen male sexual feelings. Iceberg: similar to ice, but may suggest frozen potential. Body locked in ice, perhaps dead: deadening of all our feeling reactions and enjoyment or motivation. Idioms: break the ice, cut no ice; put on ice; tread on thin ice. See **cold**.

identity and dreams To have a sense of personal existence distinct from others may be unique to human beings, and in large measure due to the learning of language. Jung and Neumann's studies of the historical development of identity suggest, in an evolutionary sense, that having an 'I' is still a very newly acquired function. This makes it vulnerable. It is also noticeably something which develops during childhood and reaches different levels of maturity during adulthood. Although it is our central experience, it remains an enigma—a will o' the wisp, which loses itself in dreams and sleep, yet is so dominant and sure in waking.

In dreams, our sense of self—our ego, personality or identity—is depicted by our own body, or sometimes simply by the sense of our own existence as an observer. In most dreams our 'I' goes through a series of experiences, just as we do in waking life, seeing things through our physical eyes, touching with our hands, and so on. But occasionally we watch our own body and other people as if from a detached point of bodiless awareness. If we accept that dreams portray in images our conception of self, then dreams suggest that our identity largely depends upon having a body, its gender, health, quality, the social position we are born into, and our relationship with others. In fact we know that if a person loses their legs, becomes paralysed, loses childbearing ability or is made redundant, they face an identity crisis. But the bodiless experience of self shows the human possibility of sensing self as having separate existence from the biological processes, one's state of health and social standing. In its most naked form, the 'I' may be simply a sense of its own existence, without body awareness.

Dreams also show our sense of self, either in the body or naked of it, as surrounded by a community of beings and objects separate from the dreamer, and frequently with a will of their own. If we place the dreamer in the centre of a circle and put all their dream characters, animals and objects around them; and if we transformed these objects and beings into the things they depicted, such as sexuality, thinking, will, emotions, intuition, social pressure, etc., we would see what a diverse mass of influences the ego stands in the middle of. It also becomes obvious that our 'I' sees these things as outside itself in nearly all dreams. Even its own internal urges to love or make love may be shown as external creatures with which it has a multitude of ways to relate. If we take the word psyche to mean our sense of self, then in our dreams we often see our psyche at war with the sources of its own existence, and trying to find its way through a most extraordinary adventure—the adventure of consciousness. One of the functions of dreams can therefore be thought to be that of aiding the survival of the psyche in facing the multitude of influences in life—and even in death.

See **Individuation; dreamer**.

idol See **statue**.

igloo A cold and perhaps unloving home environment. Also the womb; frigidity; a sense of uncaring parental influence. See **ice**.

illness If one has painful memories which are never cleared, or feelings of anger or resentment which are held within, these will often be shown in a dream as an illness or infection; a collapse of one's confidence, or the uprising of fears and depression can also be shown as illness. Also occasionally depicts the way we attempt to get love or attention, by being ill; sometimes relates to our actual physical body, but quite rarely; also may show our intuitions about the physical condition of someone else. See **infection; body**.

imprisoned We are often imprisoned by a state of mind, by a fear, or by ignorance. In attempting to develop a relationship, we may be trapped by feelings of dependence upon what our parents want us to do. If we fear failure, we will not meet the challenge of the new, and so can be imprisoned by the fear. Such feelings as being an outsider, unwanted, resentful, can also imprison us in particular situations. See **escape**, **trapped**.

incest Such dreams very seldom refer to physical incest, but to the desires we carry from infancy to possess or be in control of the love and body of our parents. As a baby we have a sense that nothing exists outside ourself; therefore everything should obey our desires. That it does not—that parents do other than what we need of them—is a shock which is a part of maturing. Our infant emotions, uncensored by social rules and self consciousness, are enormously powerful, and wherever unsatisfied or unresolved are stored unconsciously. If we are to integrate the potential energy locked in these areas, we must meet some of the incestual desires and transform them into adult love.

219

incubation   As can be seen from the entry on **hypnosis**, the dream process is quite amenable to suggestion and conscious influence. It is probably most helpful to think of this action as similar to the process of memory. In seeking information from memory we hold a question or idea in consciousness, the resulting associated memories or information being largely spontaneous. The question held directs what information is taken from the enormous pool of memory. A question might even call together scattered pieces of information which are then put together into a new composite, a new realisation. So the process is not only recall of existing memory, but also creative. It may also access skills, such as the ability to subtract one number from another. Because of these factors our conscious queries can influence the process of dreaming, causing them to respond. As dreams have access to our full memory, our creative potential as well as learnt skills, such response to concerns or queries are often of great value.

   To make use of this, first consider the query as fully as possible while awake. Look at it from as many viewpoints as possible, talk it over with others. Make note of the areas that are already clear, and what still remains to be clarified. Just before going to sleep, use imagery to put your question to your unconscious resources. Imagine standing before a circle of gentle light—a symbol of one's total self—and ask it for the information sought. Then, as if you have asked a question of a wise friend, create a relaxed state as if listening for the considered reply. In most cases, dreams which follow will in some way be a response to what is sought, though not necessarily in the way imagined. See **dream process as computer; creativity and problem solving in dreams.**

Indian   An aspect of your own desires or needs which you do not usually identify with or acknowledge. See **aborigine**.

individuation   One of Carl Jung's most interesting areas of thought is that of individuation. In a nutshell the word refers to the processes involved in becoming a self-aware human being. The area of our being we refer to when we say 'I', 'me' or 'myself' is our conscious self awareness, our sense of self, which Jung calls the ego. The autobiography of Helen Keller has helped in understanding what may be the difference between an animal and a human being with self awareness. Helen, made blind and deaf through illness before learning to speak, lived in a dark unconscious world lacking any self awareness until the age of seven, when she was taught the deaf and dumb language. At first her teacher's fingers touching hers were simply a tactile but meaningless experience. Then, perhaps because she had learnt one word prior to her illness, meaning flooded her darkness. She tells us that 'nothingness was blotted out'. Through language she became a person and developed a sense of self, whereas before there had been nothing.

The journey of individuation is not only that of becoming a person, but also expanding the boundaries of what we can allow ourselves to experience as an ego. As we can see from an observation of our dreams, but mostly from an extensive exploration of their feeling content, our ego is conscious of only a small area of experience. The fundamental life processes in one's being may be barely felt. In many contemporary women the reproductive drive is talked about as something which has few connections with their personality. Few people have a living, feeling contact with their early childhood; in fact many people doubt that such can exist. Because of these factors the ego can be said to exist as an encapsulated small area of consciousness, surrounded by huge areas of experience it is unaware of.

In a different degree, there exists in each of us a drive towards the growth of our personal awareness, towards greater power, greater inclusion of the areas of our being which remain unconscious. A paradox exists here, because the urge is towards integration, yet individuation is also the process of a greater self differentiation. This is a spontaneous

221

process, just as is the growth of a tree from a seed (the tree in dreams often represents this process of self becoming), but our personal responsibility for our process of growth is necessary at a certain point, to make conscious what is unconscious.

Because dreams are constantly expressing aspects of individuation it is worth knowing the main areas of the process. Without sticking rigidly to Jungian concepts—which see individuation as occurring from mid-life onwards in a few individuals—aspects of some of the main stages are as follows. Early babyhood—the emergence of self consciousness through the deeply biological, sensual and gestural levels of experience, all deeply felt; the felt responses to emerging from a non-changing world in the womb to the need to reach out for food and make other needs known. Learning how to deal with a changing environment, and otherness in terms of relationship.

Childhood—learning the basics of motor, verbal and social skills; the very basics of physical and emotional independence. One faces here the finding of strength to escape the domination of mother—difficult, because one is dependent upon the parent in a very real way—and develop in the psyche a satisfying sexual connection. In dream imagery this means, for the male, an easy sexual relationship with female dream figures, and a means of dealing with male figures in competition (father); see **sex in dreams**. The dream of the mystic beautiful woman precedes this, a female figure one blends with in an idealistic sense, but who is never sexual. The conflict with father—really the internal struggle with one's image of father as more potent than self—when resolved becomes an acceptance of the power of one's own manhood. Women face a slightly different situation. The woman's first deeply sensual and sexual love object—in a bonded parent-child relationship—was her mother. So beneath any love she may develop for a man lies the love for a woman. Whereas a man, in sexual love which takes him deeply into his psyche, may realise he is making love to his mother, a woman in the same situation may find her father or her mother as the love object. In the unconscious motivations which lead one to choose a mate, a man is influenced by the relationship he developed with his mother; a woman is influenced by both mother and father in her choice. Example: 'I went across the road to where my mother's sister lived. I wanted to cuddle her and touch her bare breasts, but we never seemed to manage this. There were always interruptions or blocks.' (Sid L).

At these deep levels of fantasy and desire, one has to recognise that the first sexual experience is—hopefully—at the mother's breast. This can be transformed into later fantasies/dreams/desires of penis in the mouth, or penis in the vagina, or penis as breast, mouth as vagina. For most of us, however, growth towards maturity does not present itself in such primitively sexual ways, simply because we are largely unconscious of such factors. In general we face the task of building a self image out of the influences, rich or traumatic, of our experience. We learn to stand, as well as we may, amidst the welter of impressions, ideas, influences and urges, which constitute our life and body. What we inherit, what we experience, and what we do with these creates who we are.

One of the major themes of individuation is the journey from attachment and dependence towards independence and involved detachment. This is an overall theme we mature in all our life. In its widest sense, it pertains to the fact that the origins of our consciousness lie in a non-differentiated state of being in which no sense of 'I' exists. Out of this womb condition we gradually develop an ego and personal choice. In fact we may swing to an extreme of egotism and materialistic feelings of independence from others and nature. The observable beginnings of this move to independence are seen as our attempt to become independent of mother and father. But dependence has many faces: we may have a dependent relationship with husband or wife; we may depend upon our work or social status for our self confidence; our youth and good looks may be the things we depend upon for our sense of who we are, our self image. With the approach of middle and old age we will then face a crisis in which an independence from these factors is necessary for our psychological equilibrium. The Hindu practice of becoming a *sanyassin,* leaving behind family, name, social standing, possessions, is one way of meeting the need for inner independence from these in order to meet old age and death in a positive manner. Most people face it in a quieter, less demonstrative way. Indeed, death might be thought of as the greatest challenge to our identification with body, family, worldly status and the external world as a means to identity. We leave this world naked except for the quality of our own being.

Meeting oneself, and self responsibility, are further themes of individuation. The fact that our waking self is a small spotlight of awareness amidst a huge ocean of unconscious life processes creates a situation of tension, certainly a threshold or 'iron curtain', between the known and unknown. If one imagines the spotlighted area of self as a place one is standing in, then individuation is the process of extending the boundary of awareness, or even turning the spotlight occasionally into the surrounding gloom. In this way one places together impressions of what the light had revealed of the landscape in which we stand; clues to how we got to be where we are, and how we relate to these. But one may remain, or choose to remain, largely unconscious of self. The iron curtain may be defended with our desire not to know what really motivates us, what past hurts and angers we hide. It may be easier for us to live with an exterior God or authority than to recognise the ultimate need for self responsibility and self cultivation. To hide from this, humanity has developed innumerable escape routes—exteriorised religious practice, making scapegoats of other minority groups or individuals, rigid belief in a political system or philosophy, search for *samadhi* or God as a final solution, suicide. This aspect of our maturing process shows itself as a paradox (common to maturity) of becoming more sceptical, and yet finding a deeper sense of self in its connections with the cosmos. We lose God and the beliefs of humanity's childhood, yet realise we are the God we searched for. This meeting with self, in all its deep feeling of connection, its uncertainty, its vulnerable power, is not without pain and joy. Example: 'On the railway platform milled hundreds of people, all men I think. They were all ragged, thin, dirty and unshaven. I knew I was among them. I looked up at the mountainside and there was a guard watching us. He was cruel looking, oriental, in green fatigues. On his peaked cap was a red star. He carried a machine gun. Then I looked at the men around me and I realised they were all me. Each one had my face. I was looking at myself. Then I felt fear and terror' (Anon.).

The last of the great themes of individuation is summed up in William Blake's words 'I must Create a System, or be enslav'd by another Man's; I will not Reason and Compare: my business is to Create.' A function observable in dreams is that of scanning our massive life experience (even a child's life experience has millions of bits of information) to see what it says of life and survival. Out of this we unconsciously create a working philosophy of what life means to us. It is made up not only of what we have experienced and learnt in the general sense, but also from the hidden information in the cultural riches we have inherited from literature, music, art, theatre and architecture. The word 'hidden' is used because the unconscious 'reads' the symbolised information in these sources. It is, after all, the master of imagery in dreams. But unless we expand the boundaries of our awareness we may not know this inner philosopher. If we do get to know it through dreams, we will be amazed by the beauty of its insight into everyday human life.

In connection with this there is an urge to be, and perhaps to procreate oneself in the world. Sometimes this is experienced as a sense of frustration—that there is more of us than we have been able to express, or to make real. While physical procreation can be seen as a physical survival urge, this drive to create in other spheres may be an urge to survive death as an identity. Dreams frequently present the idea that our survival of death only comes about from what we have given of ourself to others.

infection Ideas or thoughts which cause irritability or negative internal states. Thinking one's job is not secure might create disinterest and loss of motivation in work, even if in reality the job is secure; taking in negative attitudes from others; warning about physical health; sexual impregnation. See **illness; body.**

injection Feeling other people's opinions or will forced on and influencing one; internal influence of something exterior; social pressure to conform or be obedient; sexual intercourse. If a sedative is given: return to non-responsibility, as in infancy. See **syringe.**

insects Example: 'I have to keep walking because there is something I am afraid of behind me. When I am pressed up against the ceiling being crushed I look down and the stairs and bannister rail are swarming alive with a black moving wave of crawling things, like some awful insects. In the hallway is a swamp with crocodiles and other hideous things. My terror is terrible. The person who actually lived in this part of the house was the owner's mother. She treated me badly but no one knew as she was artful in her abuse. She pulled me along by my hair, locked me in a cupboard, and once locked me in the orchard—four high walls and a hidden door' (Rita). The example shows memories of pain and anger are still irritating or 'bugging' Rita. The swamp shows these feelings undermine her confidence.

Generally insects represent irritations or feeling something 'bugging' one; feeling insignificant—the ant in the mass of

other ants; sexual urges, especially with cockroaches. As
Jiminy Cricket suggests, insects can represent our conscience
and guilt which remind us of feelings we might sooner forget;
perhaps insects represent these areas because they live their
life in our house and garden largely unseen, so depict
thoughts and feelings occurring on the edge of consciousness.
Also one's children; if flying off, children leaving home. Wasp,
hornets: painful emotions; feeling stung by remarks. Lice, parasites: thoughts or sexual habits which are purely selfish or
carry a health risk; feeling others are parasitical. Spider: often
the dependent emotions and conflicts one feels 'caught in'
connected with mother; any emotions you don't want to 'handle', such as those surrounding a spouse leaving.

intercourse   See **sex in dreams**.

interpretation of dreams   Although mind and body may be
a total unity, and the separation in language merely a conve-
nience, despite its unity our being has a number of interacting
systems. The action of the heart on the other systems is obvious, and the influence of emotions on the organs is also becoming obvious. What is not so well established is the importance of the feedback occurring when we gain insight into our
own functioning through understanding a dream. Although
our being is already a self regulating system, the ability to turn
consciousness inwards to make clear aspects of unconscious
function appears to increase the efficiency of self regulation.
This is shown in the first example of **reptiles, lizards, snakes,**
where David finds a long-standing neck pain and goes
through insight into its cause. In this way we might be seen as
a conscious organism which not only reprogrammes mental
patterns or habits, but to some extent can renovate or change

227

body efficiency as well. See **dream analysis; dream processing**; the Introduction.

intruder   See **burglar, intruder**.

inventor   Creative aspect of oneself; personal insights; the self.

invisible   Becoming invisible or appearing out of nowhere suggests something emerging from or relating to the unconscious, being forgotten; hidden influences, as when touching dimensions of experience (states of consciousness) usually unknown.

iron   Strength; the material side of life; unbending emotions. Idioms: iron fist in velvet glove; iron curtain; man of iron; rule with rod of iron.

Iroquoian dream cult   The Iroquois (Huron and Seneca) American Indians, as early as the 17th century (first European contact and study), had developed a deeper psychological understanding than the white races of the time. They had no divinity but the dream—so wrote Father Fremin, who studied their customs. They clearly described the conscious and unconscious, and said that through dreams the hidden or unconscious area of the psyche makes its desires known. If it does not receive these desires it becomes angry. The Iroquois therefore developed a system of allowing the dreamer to act out their dreams socially. Although a moral and disciplined group, during such acting out the dreamer was allowed to go beyond usual social boundaries. This included receiving valuable objects and making love to another person's spouse. This was to allow unconscious desires to be expressed, thus avoiding sickness of body or mind. Such hidden desires were seen as the basis of social as well as individual problems.

island   Feelings of isolation or loneliness—the loneliness could be as one might feel when retired from work, isolated from a situation you once knew; feeling trapped; feeling safe from the world by introversion. Swimming, getting to an island: move to independence. Desert island: attempt to 'get away from it all'. Island in stormy sea: personality traits which give strength amidst difficult emotions and turbulence. Large island with other people: isolating oneself by involvement with a particular belief or group of people.

ivory   Something precious or beautiful, such as an insight or personal quality, which has grown out of the push and shove of life.

J

jailer May be any of a range of attitudes, such as guilt, self criticism, sense of alienation, intellect, restricting the expression of other parts of one's nature. See **prison**.

jellyfish See **fish, sea creatures**.

Jesus In a general sense, free from institutional dogma, Jesus can represent the human experience of life in the body, in which we meet conflict, temptation, and meet death—life itself becoming conscious. See *Christ* under **archetypes**.

jewellery May represent the giver of the piece, or one's feelings about them—love given or received; something valuable in a 'quality of our life' sense, such as something we have learnt through hard experience and ought to value; a woman's honour, self respect, sexuality. If the jewellery has a particular history, such as a family heirloom, the first piece of jewellery given by spouse, then it represents what we feel about family tradition, spouse, etc. See **jewels; ring**.

jewels Things we, or our unconscious, treasures; our integrity or sense of wholeness; the lasting parts of our nature, even the eternal aspect of self or the essential core of our life. For instance, ability to work creatively with others is not just valuable in general, it also expresses the powerful symbiotic force in nature; it connects one with the universal.

Because of the different colours in jewels, some of them may have slightly different meanings. Amethyst: healing; influence of dreams. Diamond: human greed; hardness of nature; what one values; the aspects of one's life that are lasting and valuable, not only in an everyday sense, but in a cosmic sense. Emerald: personal growth and awareness of connection with the natural in life. Opal: the inner world of fantasies and dreams; psychic impressions. Pearl: inner beauty and value that has arisen from the irritations or trials of life. Ruby: emotions, passion, sympathies; extending self to others. Sapphire: religious feelings; expansion of thinking boundaries.

jokes in dreams   See **wordplay, puns**.

journey   How we are feeling about our life and its ups and downs, goals and destinations, challenges and opportunities; undertakings we embark on, or experiences being met. In our life we have lots of journeys, such as through schooling; marriage and perhaps divorce; work; parenthood; and the overall journey of life and death. See (where applicable) **day and night** for time of journey; **car; train; boat; hill; airplane**. See also **individuation**.

judge   Sense of guilt or self judgment; conscience; decision making. May depict the 'shoulds' and 'should nots', we apply to ourself, or our moral code. Sometimes, the way we judge others becomes a harsh judge of ourself. Feeling what a failure our parents were in raising us becomes a difficult judgment of our own state as a parent. Idioms: judge not, that ye be not judged; sit in judgment.

jump   See **postures, movement and body language**.

Jung, Carl (1875–1961)   Son of a pastor, his paternal grandfather and great grandfather were physicians. He took a degree in medicine at the University of Basle, then specialised in psychiatry. In early papers he pioneered the use of word-association, and influenced research into the toxin hypothesis regarding schizophrenia. Jung's addition to modern therapeutic attitudes to dream work arose out of his difference of view with Freud regarding human life. Jung felt life is a meaningful experience, with spiritual roots. His interest in alchemy, myths and legends added to the wealth of ideas he brought to his concept of the collective unconscious. The subject of symbols fascinated him and he devoted more work to this than any other psychologist. He saw dream symbols, not as an attempt to veil or hide inner content, but an attempt to elucidate and express it. It is a way of transformation where what was formless, non-verbal and unconscious moves towards form and becoming known. In this way dreams 'show us the unvarnished natural truth'. By giving attention to our dreams we are throwing light upon who and what we really are—not simply who we are as a personality, but who we are as a phenomenon of cosmic interactions.

Jung recommended looking at a series of one's dreams in order to develop a fuller insight into self. In this way one would see certain themes arising again and again. Out of these we can begin to see where we are not balancing the different aspects of ourself. See **abreaction**; **active imagination**; **amplification**; **archetypes**; **black person**; **collective unconscious**; **compensatory theory**; **creativity and problem solving in dreams**; **dream analysis**; **Fromm, Erich**; **identity and dreams**; **individuation**; **lucidity**; **mandala**; **dream as spiritual guide**; **unconscious**.

jungle   Eruption of urges and feelings from the unconscious —could be negative or positive depending on dream; confusion; area of 'uncivilised' or unconscious, maybe non-socialised, feelings and urges, therefore may contain unmet anxieties (snakes and lions) or sexual urges (native men and women). <u>Idioms</u>: law of the jungle.

jury   Decision-making; conscience. See **judge**.

K

keel See **boat**.

key An attitude, thought or feeling opening up areas of memory, experience or motivation previously 'locked up'; realisation or information allowing solution to a problem; depicts an effective way of doing something. Also, often the penis or sexual intercourse.

kick Self assertion; self expression; protectiveness; aggressiveness. Idioms: for kicks; kick over the traces; kick in the teeth; kick the bucket; alive and kicking. See **hostility**.

kill Example: 'When inside the house I dream of recurrently, I am terrified of someone, a man who is trying to find and kill me' (Barbara T). As a young woman Barbara discovered the dead body of her father (he had shot himself) in the house of her dream. Being killed shows Barbara feeling overwhelmed by the feelings about her father—the man. Being killed: an interior or exterior influence which you feel is 'killing'—undermining, making ineffective, strangling, choking—one's self confidence or sense of identity. Killing: repressing or stopping some aspect of oneself, as when we kill our love for someone. Killing parents, animals: see **family; animals**.
Example: 'Some two weeks before my dear wife died of cancer of the oesophagus, at about three a.m. in the morning, she shot up in bed screaming "No. No! No!" On questioning her she said her mother, who had died in November 1981, was trying to kill her' (Gerry B). In this unusual dream the wife feels the approach of death, depicted by her mother. As dreams suggest, death is as much a new area of experience as

adolescence was, it would have helped the dreamer if she had taken time to develop a more positive relationship with her mother as described in **dream processing**. See **death**.

king   One's father; what you are ruled by; feelings of inferiority/superiority. Also in times past the king represented the group, the overall collective psyche of the people. He became synonymous with God, as the Pope is today. The word God was here equivalent to 'the collective psyche'. So the king or queen may represent our relationship with our fellows. See **people**.

kiss   Example: 'The cat came in, as it fed I had a strong urge to touch it, such strong feelings of love were pouring out of me. The animal looked up at my face as I wanted to kiss it. The lips had pink lipstick on. I kissed it. Its paw came up around my arm, I could see the black claws. We were rolling around on the floor, it felt very sexual' (Pat A). Acceptance of what is being kissed—Pat accepts or allows her sexuality, depicted by the cat; sexual agreement; tenderness; movement towards unity. Idioms: kiss of life; kiss of death; kiss something/somebody goodbye.

kitchen   See *house* under **house, buildings**.

knapsack   The resources and difficulties we carry in life; our past experience or karma; a burden—perhaps of nursed anger or other negative feelings—we carry; our child, if we feel parenthood a heavy load.

kneel   See **postures**.

knife   See **weapons**.

knitting   Something you are concentratedly working at in your life; knitting a relationship together; consider what garment is being made and refer to **clothes**.

knob   Penis; one's hold on a situation. <u>Doorknob</u>: turning point in opportunity, sexual or otherwise.

knock   One's attention called to whatever is knocking. Some aspect of self, or a realisation, is asking to be let into consciousness. <u>Knocking</u>: trying to get attention; wanting to be allowed into someone's life; sexual act.

knot   Tangle of feelings or tension; relational tie; a problem; the ties we have to work, family, mother's apron strings, or views.

Krishna   See *Christ* under **archetypes**.

L

label Self image; how you feel others see you; your view of what is labelled; definition of your feelings if labelled to someone else.

ladder Your feelings—whether anxious or secure—about reaching situations or opportunities in life which are new or not easily attained; attainment through effort and daring; the heightening of insecurity or feelings in sex—getting up, getting it up. Rungs: the separate stages or efforts necessary to 'climb'. Idioms: top of the ladder. See also *stairs* under **house, buildings**.

lagoon, lake The inner world of our feelings and fantasies; the unconscious. Sinking into: becoming introverted; giving up on trying, or expressing oneself. Looking into depths: self awareness; looking into oneself. Dirty water: difficult feelings; being unsure of oneself; depression. See **water**.

lamb See **animals**.

lame Feeling uncertain about how one stands in life; loss of confidence or strength expressing oneself or being motivated. Left leg: weakness in the feelings and ideas out of which we gain support. Right leg: weakness in our external activities.

landscapes Our moods and attitudes, but particularly the set of habitual feelings we meet life with. As we create our surroundings in dreams, landscapes depict what feelings we ourself generate and live in. Gloomy: pessimism; self doubt; depression; a gloomy view of life. Sunny: hopeful; optimistic;

something to look forward to. Recurring scenes: habitual attitudes with which you approach situations. Recurring scenes of past residence: a stance you developed from that period of your life. See countryside.

lane   See road.

language, foreign or strange   One function of dreams is to bring aspects of our thinking or feeling, which may be ill defined, towards clarification. Foreign or strange language may therefore illustrate something which is being communicated to us from within, but is still not clear. The unconscious, as in speaking in tongues—glossolalia—and of course in dreams, frequently moves towards clear awareness in stages. The strange language is a halfway house, as is a dream. If we bring focused attention to these, as explained in dream processing, the next step, clear verbal expression, can be reached. Speaking in language we are learning: the language is becoming habitual, making it possible to think in it. See speaking.

larder   See *house* under house, buildings; food.

large   See size.

late   See time of day.

laugh   Release of tension; attempt to put others at ease; ridiculing or feeling embarrassed by some aspect of self; taking things lightly. Sometimes much laughter can hide tears or sadness. Idioms: don't make me laugh; laughing stock; laugh in somebody's face; hollow laugh; laugh up one's sleeve; laugh on the other side of your face.

lava Deeply buried past experience which has pushed to the surface; heated emotions and sexuality; sometimes physical illness such as fever.

lavatory See **toilet**.

lead Heavy hearted; a weighty situation; materialistic attitudes.

leader See **roles**.

leaf See **tree**.

leak Wasted or lost energy; or something being allowed out or expressed. <u>Idioms</u>: leak out (be revealed).

learning while asleep There have been many claims that one can learn while asleep—possibly with the aid of a recorded series of suggestions or information being spoken from a speaker under one's pillow. Different research projects have arrived at a variety of conclusions. The major scientific conclusion is that we do not learn from what we hear while asleep. Sleep is important in the process of learning, however. If one learns a list of nonsense words, memory of them eight or twenty-four hours later is better if we have slept; memory eight hours later without sleep is not as efficient as twenty-four hours later with intervening sleep. This suggests memory traces are strengthened during sleep.

That we do learn, in the sense of creating new information or perception, while we sleep is generally accepted. Albert Einstein suggested that the creative scientists are those who have access to their dreams. He meant that in order to be innovative we must be able periodically to leave behind the practical everyday path of commonsense and rational thought. The rational tends to move in areas of thought connected with what is already known. To create something new, to find a new direction, we may need to be capable of retrieving apparently irrational ideas, sift them and reconstruct them in practical ways.

Dreams have this ability to fantasise, to look at and experience the irrational, to take an idea and move it completely out of its old setting or viewpoint. Because our mind can do this in sleep, we can touch not only our creativity, but also our ability to problem solve. As a personal test of this, try the following experiment. At the end of this explanation a problem will be set. It is one that requires no special training or information to solve. The solution is simple and will be seen as correct when reached. But do not even begin to think about the problem until you go to bed! It would discount the experiment if you did. On going to bed, think about the problem for no more than 15 minutes. If you solve the problem note how long it took. If not, stop thinking about it and go to sleep, making the resolve to remember any dreams. It is likely that you will dream the answer. If not, on waking spend a further 15 minutes trying to reach the answer.

The letters O,T,T,F,F,–,–, form the beginning of an intelligible series. Add two more letters which make it obvious that an infinite number of letters could be added.

left behind   Example: 'In my dream I woke up and had the feeling that a lot of time had passed. I felt I had lost all this time. A group of friends I was with had gone ahead, left me behind, and I wondered if I would ever catch up' (Patience C). Oneself left behind: feelings of rejection or inadequacy; sense of waking up to what you have not done or experienced in life, as Patience does in her dream. Leaving something, someone behind: leaving the past behind, breakup of relationship. Idioms: fall behind; put it all behind me. See also **bag**.

left, right   Left: if we are right handed, the left represents the less dominant or expressed side of oneself, or the parts of

239

our nature we try to hide or suppress. If we write or knock in a nail using our right hand, we will hold the paper or nail with our left. So left leg or arm frequently has this sense of representing the supportive but less dominant functions in us. Our confidence may support our activity as a salesperson, so may be depicted as being on the left. Right: the dominant, confident, conscious, exterior or expressed side of self; rightness; correct social behaviour; moral.

Dreams can also use a play on what is right and left to illustrate a polarity or opposites. Our internal world of feelings, memories and values—the left; our external world of activity and environment—the right. A secondary choice—left; the 'right' choice at the time—right. Parts of self unconscious or shadowy—left; our conscious known self—right. The immoral, selfish, wrong action—left; the moral, right action—right.

Example: 'On my right are three monks, on my left sits a beautiful, shapely blonde. I am in the centre and I see a road, which leads to the right and a beautiful sunlit valley in the distance' (from *Dreams Your Magic Mirror* by Elsie Sechrist). Here right and left represent not only choice between sexual pleasure and religious discipline, but also the polar opposites of spiritual and material. Although in the dream there is a movement to the right, to find equilibrium we often have to take a way between the opposites.

Idioms: two left feet; keep on the right side of somebody; in one's right mind; in the right; mister right; set somebody right; right hand man; right in the head; start on the right foot; give one's right arm.

legs   See *legs* under **body**.

lens   Focusing attention on an area of experience, realisation or intuition.

letter Thoughts about or intuitions concerning person letter is from; unrealised feelings about sender; hopes, perhaps to have contact with person. Opening letter: realising something; receiving news; sexual intercourse. Unopened letter: unrecognised intuition; virginity. Black edged: news of or feelings about death. Idioms: French letter (condom); red letter day.

library One's life experience; the wisdom and skills we have gathered; the intellect; research. Huge library: collective unconscious; cosmic mind. See **book**.

lice See **insects**.

life after death See **philosophy of dreams; death; murder; out of body experience**.

lift See *lift* under **house, buildings**.

light Generally, being aware; waking as opposed to sleeping; being able to understand and have insight; to see; lightness of heart; release from dark feelings.

Example: 'I am alone in the house. It begins to grow dark, so I switch the light on, but the light is very dim. So I go to another room and try another light, but this light is even dimmer. I carry on like this all over the house until I am in virtual darkness and very frightened' (JW). JW was six at the time of the dream, and here light depicts feelings of sureness or confidence, which gave way to anxiety. The light is the opposite to the emotions of fear which arise from within. Flickering dimming lights: also feelings about death.

Example: 'My husband was laying on top of me, his feet on my chest and was giving me sexual pleasure by kissing, licking, sucking my fanny. He reached over to turn the light on, he wanted to look at my body. I felt OK about him looking but saw the blinds were partly open and felt anyone walking past in the street would see as well, I felt very uneasy about that' (Heather C). Here light represents becoming aware of how others might see one.

Very bright light: intuition; the Self; mega concept; see **aura**. Spotlight, searchlight: focusing attention on what is shown. Idioms: bright lights; cold light of day; come to light; hide one's light; in its true light; lighter side; in a good light; see the light; light at the end of the tunnel; throw a light on. See **dark**; **day**.

lighthouse   Warning of danger of unconscious elements that may wreck areas of your life unless avoided. Use the light to become aware of what the danger is. See **light**.

lightning   Unexpected changes; discharge of tension, perhaps destructively; expression of wider awareness; intuition; conscience. Killed by lightning: life changes occurring. Lightning struck tree: death in some form.

Sometimes information leading to a realisation builds up over time, but in a flash is put together forming a new, perhaps life-changing, insight which may be depicted by lightning. See **aura**.

limp   See **lame**.

liquid   Because feelings are often felt to flow within us, as when we listen to rousing music, or notice a feeling in the chest which moves to the throat, then may become crying or other expressed emotion, they may be shown in a dream as fluid. Liquid in bottle: a change of feelings, as when we drink wine or medicine; influenced by exterior emotions. White liquid: milk of kindness, self-giving or sperm, the magic fluid out of which life emerges.

little   See **size**.

liver   Irritability; suggestion for health or diet changes, perhaps in connection with alcohol. See **body**.

lizard   See **reptiles, lizards and snakes**.

lobster   Male sexuality when it appears aggressive and protective. See **crab**.

lock, locked   Generally, the emotions or physical tensions we use to keep others from 'getting at us', or to prevent our own urges or fears from being experienced; desire to keep something safe or protected, such as one's honour or emotions; feeling trapped; vagina; sexual tension. Occasionally a problem which needs a specific solution, the key; our ability to choose, whether to let someone into an intimate relationship.

looking   See **seeing, saw, sight**.

lorry   Similar to car—drives such as ambition, what motivates one—but usually connected with work or our more commercial relationship with people. For instance, one's personal motivations meeting the influence of big unified groups such as the police or large businesses.
  Example: 'I was a passenger in a very large eight-wheeled lorry, my husband being the driver. We stopped at a pedestrian crossing in our town and my husband got out of the driving seat and went into the local town hall near a crossing. I waited in the lorry for what in my dream seemed hours. The next thing I remember is that I was then riding a bicycle on the other side of the crossing and cycled away up the road' (Diann R). Her husband's involvement with social and work activities—the lorry and hall—make Diann decide to become more independent rather than wait for her husband to be 'with her'.

losing something   A lost opportunity; forgetting something which is important. Depending on dream, might also suggest actual, or feelings about, loss of virginity; loss of health; losing a lover/partner; or whatever the lost thing depicts.

lost   Being lost depicts confusion; loss of motivation or ability to make clear decisions. Sometimes suggests issues in your life have arisen and not been noticed and you are being negatively influenced, in which case consider the environment in which you are lost. <u>Lost in unknown place</u>: it suggests you are in a new area of experience, a new situation or period of your life. You need to take stock calmly and get your bearings.

loudspeaker   Something we have heard; something which is trying to gain 'a hearing'; how we receive aural information—in one ear and out the other, or is it received and understood?

love   Like most emotions, love in a dream is usually a direct expression of that feeling, or a compensation for not receiving it. So one question to ask is whether we are trying to compensate for a lack in our life. Apart from that it may be helpful to see in what way the love is being expressed in the dream. The following stages of love may help in defining this.

baby love   Completely dependent upon the loved person for one's needs, physical, emotional and social. Great anger, jealousy or pain if the loved one relates to anyone else. Wants to be always with the loved one. Will have sex, but the emotional bond and cuddling is more important.

adolescent lover   Initial uncertainty or clumsiness concerning emotional and sexual contact. Desire to explore many relations. Still finding out what one's boundaries are. Great sexual drive. Partner will probably be loved for dreamer's own needs —for example, the dreamer wants a family and uses the partner to gain that end; the dreamer loves the partner because in that way they can get away from parental home. Great romantic feelings and spontaneous love which are difficult to maintain in face of difficulties.

adult love   Growing sense of recognising needs of partner. Ability to be something for the partner's sake without losing one's own independence or will. Becoming aware of the issues which colour or influence relationship, and meeting them as partners. Independence and closeness together. Caring sexual partners through discovering each other's needs and vulnerability.

lucidity, awake in sleep   Sometimes in the practice of deep relaxation, meditation or sensory deprivation, our being enters into a state akin to sleep, yet we maintain a personal waking awareness. This is like a journey into a deep interior world of mind and body where our senses no longer function in their waking manner, where the brain works in a different way, and where awareness is introverted in a degree we do not usually experience. It can be a frightening world, simply because we are not accustomed to it. In a similar way a measure of waking awareness can arise while dreaming. This is called lucid dreaming. During it we can change or wilfully direct what is happening in the dream in a way not usual to the dream state.

Example: 'I had backed my car into a big yard, a commercial area. My wife, two of my sons and I got out of the car. As we stood in the yard talking I realised there was a motorbike where my car should be. I said to everyone, "There was a car here a moment ago, now it's a motorbike. Do you know what that means? It means we are dreaming." Mark my son was now with us, and my ex-wife. I asked them if they realised they were dreaming. They got very vague and didn't reply. I asked them again and felt very clearly awake' (William V). William's is a fairly typical lucid dream, but there are features which it does not illustrate. During the days or weeks prior to a lucid dream, many people experience an increase in flying dreams. The next example shows another common feature.

Example: 'In many of my dreams I become aware that I am dreaming. Also, if anything unpleasant threatens me in the dream I get away from it by waking myself' (Alan). Lucidity often has this feature of enabling the dreamer to avoid unpleasant elements of the dream. The decision to avoid any unpleasant internal emotions is a common feature of a person's conscious life, so this aspect of lucidity is simply a way of taking such a decision into the dream. Some writers even suggest it as a way of dealing with frightening dreams. Avoidance does not solve the problem, it simply pushes the emotion deeper into the unconscious where it can do damage more surreptitiously. Recent findings regarding suppressed grief and stress, which connects them with a higher incidence of cancer, suggests that suppression is not a healthy way of dealing with feelings.

Another approach to lucidity is that it can be a sort of playground where one can walk through walls, jump from high buildings and fly, change the sofa into an attractive lover, and so on. True, the realisation that our dream life is a different world and that it does have completely different principles at work than our waking world is important. Often people introvert into their dream life the morals and fears which are only relevant to being awake in physical life. To avoid a charging bull is certainly important in waking life. In our dream life, though, to meet its charge is to integrate the enormous energy which the bull represents, an energy which is our own but which we may have been avoiding or 'running away' from previously. Realising such simple differences revolutionises the way we relate to our own internal events and possibilities. To treat lucid dreams as if they offered no other attainable experience than to manipulate the dream environment, or avoid an encounter, is to miss an amazing feature of human potential.

Example: 'In my dream I was watching a fern grow. It was small but opened out very rapidly. As I watched I became aware that the fern was simply an image representing a process occurring within myself which I grew increasingly aware of as I watched. Then I was fully awake in my dream and realised that my dream, perhaps any dream, was an expression of actual and real events occurring in my body and mind. I felt enormous excitement, as if I were witnessing something of great importance' (Francis P). It is now acceptable, through the work of Freud, Jung and many others, to consider that within images of the dream lie valuable information about what is occurring within the dreamer, perhaps unconsciously. Strangely, though, it is almost never considered that one can have direct perception into this level of internal 'events' without the dream. What Francis describes is an experience of being on the cusp of symbols and direct perception. Considering the enormous advantage of such direct information gathering, it is surprising it is seldom mentioned except in the writings of Corriere and Hart, *The Dream Makers*.

Example: 'After defining why I had not woken in sleep recently, i.e. loss of belief, I had the following experience. I awoke in my sleep and began to see, without any symbols, that my attitudes and sleep movements expressed a feeling of restrained antagonism or irritation to my wife. I could also observe the feelings were arising from my discipline of sexuality. Realising I did not want those feelings I altered them and woke enough to turn towards her' (Francis P). After the first of his direct perception dreams, Francis attempted to use this function again, resulting in the above, and other, such dreams. Just as classic dream interpretation says that the dream symbols represent psychobiological logical processes which might be uncovered by dream processing, what we see in Francis' lucidity is a direct route to self insight, and through it a rapid personal growth to improved life experience. Such dreams provide not only psychological insight, but very frequently a direct perception of processes occurring in the body, as the following example illustrates.

Example: 'Although deeply asleep I was wide awake without any shape or form. I had direct experience, without any pictures, of the action of the energies in my body. I had no awareness of body shape, only of the flow of activities in the organs. I checked over what I could observe, and noticed a tension in my neck was interfering with the flow and exchange of energies between the head and trunk. It was also obvious from what I could see that the tension was due to an attitude I had to authority, and if the tension remained it could lead to physical ill health' (Tony C).

An effective way to develop lucidity is frequently to consider the events of waking life as if they were a dream. Try to see events as one might see dream symbols. What do they mean in terms of one's motivations, fears, personal growth? What do they suggest about oneself? For instance a person who works in a photographic darkroom developing films and prints might see they were trying to bring to consciousness the latent—unconscious—side of themselves. A banker might feel they were working at how best to deal with their sexual and personal resources. In this way one might actually apply what is said in this dream dictionary to one's outer circumstances. The second instruction is, on waking, at a convenient moment, imagine oneself standing within one's recent dream. As you get a sense of this dream environment, realise that you are taking waking awareness into the dream. From the standpoint of being fully aware of the dream action and events, what will you now do in and with the dream? Re-dream it with consciousness. For example the things you run from in your normal dreaming you could now face. See **dream processing** for further suggestions.

luggage   The habits or attitudes, or the emotional environment we have created in our life; a baby or our feelings about being a parent. See **bag**; **knapsack**; **suitcase**; example in **clothes**.

luminous   Unity of many aspects of one's nature. See **aura**.

M

machine Example: 'I see a little girl humming an innocent tune, plucking daisies in a vast lush green field. Suddenly a huge machine or monster comes ploughing through the field over the girl' (Debbie H). Debbie sees life itself as a machine, unfeeling, mechanical, blind in its functioning. The word juggernaut is from Sanskrit *Jaganatha,* lord of the world. Devotees formerly threw themselves under a huge cart as it moved.

Generally, a machine represents the body's automatic functions and drives, such as breathing and ageing; the mechanical forces of nature; habitual or mechanical behaviour. <u>Intricate machine</u>: brain or the thinking process in its mechanical habitual form; the habitual, almost mechanical fantasies we have or things we do.

Example: 'I am in charge of a life machine which keeps the world going. Unless I tend it all the time it may stop, and I am terrified. I hear a pulsating noise, or imagine I do' (Mr P E). Here the machine represents the heart, and the dreamer's anxious relationship with the body's functioning and processes. <u>Idioms</u>: cog in the machine. See **engine**.

mad A dog running across a busy road to chase a bitch isn't acting rationally according to human standards. But he is still acting on old drives which have not integrated fresh information or environment—the traffic. <u>Confronted by a mad person or people</u>: meeting parts of ourself which have not been integrated with our present situation; cultural fear we have about meeting the unconscious. <u>Being mad</u>: feeling threatened by the irrational and perhaps dis-integrated aspects of the unconscious.

249

maggots   Impurities in body; sickness, feelings about death. See **body**.

magic   Might be the wish to accomplish something without effort or difficulty; desire to control situations; without knowing the underlying processes, our mind and emotions do things which appear as magic. To the child mind in us all, growth from a cellular speck to becoming a person is pure magic. Magic also represents the power of unconscious sexuality and how it can be hurt, bewitched, or controlled.

magician   See **roles**.

magnet   The influence—to attract or repel—we have on others or they have on us.

make-up   Our ability to change the impression we make on others; cover-up for our real feelings or situation. See **cosmetic**.

man   Example: 'I was walking down the steps of a house, leading into the front area of the basement. I was with a man, perhaps a friend. At the bottom of the steps a psychiatrist was talking to a male client. They were having a session there in the open. I sensed the man's feelings of embarrassment and exposure. But I felt it was necessary to be thus exposed, i.e. the psychiatrist was purposely holding the session in the open so the man could learn to relax' (Bernard O). Bernard, a practising therapist, is all of the men in the dream. It portrays the interaction between different parts of himself. The 'I' walking down the steps is the active, fairly adventurous person Bernard sees himself as; the man following—a friend—is a man Bernard knows who has sexual difficulties, and represents Bernard's own sexual hesitations; the psychiatrist is Bernard's therapeutic skill used in his own life; the male client is Bernard's difficult feelings when dealing with groups of people—the public—which he is trying to 'expose' or get to know and transform.

Generally, a man depicts an aspect of self—even in a woman's dream—depending on the activity and character of the man in the dream. Any indication whatsoever in the dream gives a clue to what aspect of self. In the example, the character of the friend, the role of the psychiatrist and the feelings of the client indicate which aspects of Bernard's character are being dealt with. Therefore a man trying to rape a woman would be her fears about sex; a homosexual would depict those feelings; a businessman, one's work or business abilities; a loving man, one's feelings about love, and so on.

Older man: father or one's accumulated experience and wisdom; perhaps even wisdom from the unconscious if man is white haired or holy. Wild, ape, half animal man: urges which have not yet been integrated and socialised, usually pertaining to sexuality in today's social attitudes or natural social feelings at odds with present attitudes.

Man in woman's dream: in general, a woman's ability to question conventional behaviour and social habits; her strength to look with insight into her own life and change it thereby—but not her feeling values, emotions and intuitions; her creative or business ability in the world, and power to be competitive and challenging; her defence against 'just knowing' out of the power of her emotions and inbuilt prejudices. Man she knows or loves: feelings, worries about relationship. Dreaming the man is looking at other women or leaving is usually fears about same. Two men: might be a triangle.

Idioms: man to man; be a man; front man; hit man; make a man of; odd man out; right hand man. See **family; woman;** and other entries pertaining to particular roles or age.

mandala   If one could produce a graphic image of the whole of human nature, many different forms might be integrated within an overall shape, perhaps a circle or square. Also, if it were possible to have a visual presentation of a person's inner world of mind, weaknesses, strengths, order, confusion and quality, each person would appear differently. Some would be internally jumbled, divided and ugly; others symmetrical, integrated and beautiful.

Because the unconscious produces dreams, and because dreams are imagery which give form to the otherwise abstract elements of internal human nature, there arise in some dreams shapes or patterns which depict an overall view of one's own inner condition. Carl Jung drew attention to the circle and square designs in some dreams, calling them mandalas, and seeing them as representing the nucleus of the human identity. Although we are, in our everyday life, the magical and mysterious process of life, it is difficult for us actually to answer the question 'Who am I?' or 'What am I?' with any lasting conviction.

The mysterious essence of ourself is met in dreams as a circular or square object or design; as the sun, a flower, a square garden with a round pond in the middle, or a circle with a square or quartered design within it, a circle with a cross within, a revolving or flying cross-shaped object. Classical symbols from all nations use this theme; and we can find it in the round table of King Arthur, in the centre of which the Holy Grail appeared; the healing sand paintings of the Navaho Indians; the zodiac; circle dances; stone circles; the Buddhist wheel of birth and death; and so on.

The circle usually symbolises a natural wholeness, our inner life as nature has shaped it. The square shows wholeness we have helped shape by conscious cooperation with our inner world. There are two main reasons why one produces this theme in one's dreams. It occurs in children or people meeting internal or external shocks, and produces a strengthening of the vulnerable identity in meeting the varied influences they face. It arises in people who are meeting and integrating the wider life of their being existing beyond the boundaries of their usual interests, or what they allow themselves to experience. The contact with the self is then part of an extending of awareness into what was dark or unknown, not only in our own unconscious, but in external life. In touching the nucleus of one's being in this way, one becomes aware in some measure of the infinite potential of one's life. There is often an accompanying sense of existence in eternity and the many different 'mansions' or dimensions of experience one has within the eternal. See *the self* under **archetypes**; **shapes**.

mansion   See **house, buildings**.

manure   In some ways our personality or identity is like a plant which feeds from the most unlikely material to produce beautiful leaves and flowers. The plant can transform manure into living leaves and petals. Our identity feeds on experience and information, some of which may appear uninviting, painful or unwholesome. In fact our experience may be all of these, and be depicted in dreams as manure, and if not put to our roots—our process of becoming aware of things in an intensely felt manner which links feelings with intellectual insight—remain a disintegrating influence. Learning processes which pile intellectual information on children or adults without helping them to allow their deep feeling responses, are piling manure on the psyche while cutting off its roots. Personal disintegration is the result.

map   Clarification of a direction in life, or how best to direct ambition or motivation.

market   Reality of everyday life; the push and shove, give and take of relating to people in general, but particularly 'the public'; the wide range of experience one meets in exposing oneself to more than one's close family and friends.

marriage, wedding   One's marriage or feelings about marriage; uniting two different aspects of dreamer such as intellect and feelings, practical and intuitive self; the 'marriage' between conscious and unconscious self—any children of the marriage would be the flowering of new abilities or qualities; sometimes is about what our energy or drive is uniting us with, such as a new business venture or creative scheme—any children of this marriage suggest our intuitive assessment of the likely outcome. Also in some cultures dreaming of a wedding signifies a death in the family.

Example: 'I am at the wedding of my best friend. The groom doesn't turn up and she decides to marry the first person who comes along. I wonder whether this is a good thing to do' (Mary T). Dreaming of <u>wedding if single</u>: Mary could equally as well have dreamt she was the bride, but being in her 30s and unmarried it is easier for her to consider or experiment with the idea of marriage using the image of her friend. Should she marry whoever offers? When single one often dreams of marriage as a way of clarifying. What would it be like? Could one succeed in it? Is the present partner OK? How will one achieve it?

Example: 'When I was engaged to my present husband I dreamt we were married and I looked down at my wedding ring. It was twisted and bent. In fact I now see it as a warning because we have not made a good marriage' (SW).

marsh, swamp   Feeling bogged down, held back, losing ground, perhaps due to lack of self confidence or emotional support; may show the emotional dependence one gets stuck in between child and parent; or feeling unable to move because of relationship with an overbearing person.

Mary, Virgin   Motherhood; positive feelings about one's mother; religious openness or receptivity. Also Mary represents the human soul or psyche and its possibility of dropping preconceptions—virginity—and thus being receptive to the unseen or unconscious side of self—the holy ghost. Her child is the union between the receptive conscious self and wider awareness.

mask Our false self we put on in meeting others. Latent qualities we can express or don when needed—a mother might be a tigress when her children are threatened, but a meek person otherwise; her tigress would not be 'false'. Ego less.

mass The approach of our individual self to the sense of wholeness, the communal whole or collective mind, or to the Christ. See *Christ* under **archetypes**.

masturbation This may be represented in a dream by such things as using a pump, beating a drum, or any rhythmic movement. If there is a tendency to repress the sexual need, it may happen that one masturbates during sleep, in an attempt to release sexual pressure. Because the person has consciously decided not to allow sexuality, this might give rise to a feeling of being possessed by another will. In fact our unconscious will to express our needs has overridden the conscious decision during sleep. Out of such a split in the person, ideas about devils and possession probably arose. Although Christianity at a fundamental level appears to teach the love and acceptance of all sides of human nature—therefore integration through love thy neighbour as thyself, so love thyself—in practice it becomes tight morality which creates devils through rejection and splits in human nature. In many Christians, there are enormous conflicts between sexuality, love, work and spirituality.

mattress Similar to bed—the situation, comfortable or otherwise, one has created in life. You made your bed, now lie on it. Also comfort; sexuality; relaxed feelings.

maze Confusion of ideas and feelings; conflicting urges and opinions; the difficulty in finding our way through the mass of apparently irrational emotions and images arising from within. Sometimes we need to admit we are lost and need help. Occasionally the circuitous and often confusing route we take to meeting self; the unconscious.

meal   See **food**.

measurement   Might refer to wondering how long—days and weeks—something will be; comparisons; how 'big' something is in life.

meat   See **food**.

mechanic   See **roles**.

medicine   Healing influence; meeting experiences we might not like but need in order to change a negative situation. Idioms: taste of one's own medicine; take one's medicine.

meditation   Being self responsible for state of mind; listening to intuition and unconscious. For people involved in any form of personal growth, they occasionally have a dream in which some form of instruction is given as an aid to their unfolding. Such dreams are worth following as the unconscious has the ability to sift and consider our collective experience, and present what applies to our need.

Example: 'While recovering from a major operation and experiencing enormous pain I dreamt my father—dead—appeared standing at the end of the bed, and he said in a very matter of fact voice, "Think of five pink bouquets." My father would never have used those words, so the scene impressed itself on me. I therefore woke and tried to visualise the five bouquets. I managed to get three in a row, four, but I could not manage five until I had formed them into a diamond with one in the middle. When I achieved that my pain subsided, and did so each time I used the image—why I do not know' (Ken S). Ken's experience suggests a psychosomatic effect from his dream-proposed meditation. Such meditations often show ways to alter character attitudes or help find strength to make necessary changes in life.

medium   Intuition, but perhaps in an obscure way; contact with the unconscious or the dead in its symbolic form. See *the dream as extended perception* under **ESP in dreams; symbols and dreaming**.

melt   A change; emotions softening.

menhirs   The eternal or universal aspect of self emerging into consciousness. See **rock**.

menstruation   Emerging sexuality; procreative drive; mystery of life; acceptance of life working in oneself if menstruating, non-acceptance of basic life drives if not menstruating. Problems with menstruation: problems with relationship between what life needs of personality, and what personality wants of life; might refer to physiological problems which need attention. In man's dream: one's receptive nurturing nature; the aspect of the male self which can 'conceive' creative ideas. If ill, problems in sexuality, creativity, emotions or in letting go of 'I want'. See **premenstrual tension**.

mermaid, merman   The link between the deep forces of the unconscious and the waking self. The unconscious image or idealised sense of womanhood (mermaid) or manhood (merman); love of one's image of someone rather than the reality of them as a human being.

metal   Hardness of feelings; the restrictions of the real world or of one's own imagination; strength of will or obstinacy; reality.

microscope   introspection; extended cellular perception; making mountains out of molehills.

milk Human kindness; mother love; self-giving; sperm. Idioms: milk and water; milk of human kindness; milk somebody, cry over spilt milk. See **food, drink**.

mill Process of extracting what is useful from one's gathered experience. Can be painful, as it needs intense self awareness; crushing or painful experiences of life.

mines For many a place of work; otherwise the unconscious and its resources; bringing to consciousness one's potential and innate wisdom. Entrance to mine: feelings about the unconscious; vagina. See **ore**.

mirror Concern over one's 'image' or how others feel about one; self examination; self love, negative only if the love is not shared with others; anxiety about changing or ageing.

Example: 'Getting ready for a wedding in an upstairs room, feeling a bit unsure of what to wear. I look in a mirror and see I have on stockings and suspender belt with a very short frilly petticoat. It looks very sexy. I am aware that the door is open and have an urge to close it, but then feel OK about looking sexy and people seeing me' (Nora). Nora is looking at how she may appear to others if she allows her natural feelings to show.

Also self awareness in the sense of insight into behaviour or character traits; the mirror is similar to water and can depict looking into the unconscious to see who one is. Change face in mirror, multiple selves: becoming aware of aspects of one's character which are usually unknown or not accepted.

miscarriage May be an attempt to heal the experience, if dreamer has had miscarriage or abortion. From the viewpoint of the unconscious it is at times important to name the baby;

fear of miscarriage; loss of new idea, project or growing aspect of self.

mist   See **fog**.

moat   The 'I've got a headache' type of defence against another person's approach to intimacy. See *castle* under **house, buildings**.

money   What we value; one's potential, energy or personal resources; personal potency, therefore links with sexuality and self-giving; what we pay for our desires or actions—'I told my husband a few home truths last night, but he certainly made me pay for it'; opportunity, because money buys time to explore or try the new. Holding on to money: feeling insecure, or being 'tight' emotionally or sexually. Not enough money: sense of being inadequate or failing potency. Dud money: not giving of oneself or feeling cheated.

Example: 'A small Indian boy stole a 50 pence piece from me. I had an internal struggle about whether to take it back. The hesitation was that it was "manners" to make out nothing had happened, not to blame someone for something "not nice". Because of these unspoken rules the boy could laugh at me. I decided to take the money back and accuse him of theft' (Stephen Y). Stolen money: Stephen is considering what his 'values' are, how he wants others to relate to him, and whether to state his needs instead of being 'nice'. Also, feeling others are taking us for granted; giving oneself cheaply in sex or relationships.

monk   See **roles**.

monkey   See **animals**.

monster   Our own internal emotions or drives we are frightened of. Use the approaches in **dream processing** to change the monster into usable personal resources; dread of death; a monstrous deed done or lie lived; our negative relationship with the power which moves us to growing, mating and dying.

moon Love; romance; intuitions arising from the unconscious; one's inner world of fantasy, imagination, the psychic. Because of its connection with the tides, the deep inner movements caused by the subtle side of our nature, the tides of feeling, even madness; the pull and attraction of mysterious dark desires; a woman's strange, sensual, overpowering attraction. New or old moon: female sexuality; change; intuition. Moon's changes: life, death, rebirth; the tides in our affairs. Full moon: power of the inner drives. Flying to moon: trying to escape reality or responsibility; attempting to break free of limitations. Moonlight: romantic view of the world; not seeing things too clearly; looking within self.

morning See **time of day**.

mortuary Feelings about death; parts of self dead but not buried, may be brought to life by being used.

mosaic Our life, its pattern and what we manifest by it through the many separate acts and events; our view of life when we put all the pieces of experience together.

moth The self we assume in our dreams or fantasy; the unconscious urge our being has to survive personal death.

mother See **family**.

motorbike Youthful drive and motivation; physical energy; restlessness, sexual drive; daring.

mountain Something big in one's life; reaching a wider awareness of our life or situation; something which stands above the commonplace. Example: 'I was on top of a mountain with my sons, but was terrified I was going to fall' (John A). John feels alone caring for his children and fears failure. Also attainment achieved by facing the difficulties of life. See **hill**; last example in **flying**.

mouse   See **animals**.

mouth   See **body**.

mud   The fundamental, primordial, sensual, slimy basis of life and how we relate to it; emotions which cause us to feel bogged down; past experience which may hold us back, but has enormous growth potential in it; the healing possibilities of our body and its minerals. Body dirty with mud: ill health; one's life needs 'cleaning up' morally. Sinking into mud: sexual difficulties; feelings of hopelessness or despair. Idioms: mud slinging; drag somebody through the mud; a name is mud; stick-in-the-mud.

mummy, Egyptian   The dead; feelings we have buried about a dead person; our mother; a part of self which might be reborn; attempt to preserve a way of life which is dead—mummification—instead of facing change and the new.

murder, murderer   Each of us are implicated in killing—by denying, repressing, controlling some part of our own nature. These denied areas of our own sensitivity or potential can fortunately be resurrected through self awareness of our deed. If we flee from a murderer, it depicts a fear that is threatening our confidence or something we feel threatened by. Murderous rage in dreamer: it is observable that repressed sexuality leads to feelings of murderous rage which may not be expressed socially, but do appear in dreams; may also express

261

childhood anger linked with emotional bond with mother being damaged.

muscle See *muscle* under **body**.

museum Memory; family and cultural heritage; the living past within us.

music The play of subtle feelings and forces in our being; realisations difficult to define; the influence of wider awareness in our life. Playing music: self expression; expressing our essential self which might be overlooked in general activities. Idioms: music to one's ears; face the music.

musical instrument Often one's sexual organs; one's skills in self expression. Large complex instrument: the mind and its influence in the rest of our being. See **organ**.

N

nail   Bonding; holding power, male sexuality. <u>Nail in body</u>: consciousness painfully bound to physical reality. <u>Idioms</u>: hit the nail on the head; tough as nails; nailbiting; bed of nails; nail in one's coffin.

name of person, place   Our name represents our sense of self, our essential 'I'. <u>If name is altered</u>: suggests a sense of change in the way we see ourself. <u>Other people's names</u>: our feelings for that person; the quality we feel in regard to someone else with the same name; or wordplay or associations with the name. A woman dreamt a friend asks her 'Do you know where Chris is?'; she replied he was on the back seat. On waking she realises she is being asked 'Where's the crisis?' Two weeks later she had a kidney infection—in the back seat. Names also suggest qualities, as in Peter, the rock; or one's friend Pat may be pleasure loving, so we use the name or person to represent that quality. See **wordplay, puns**.

<u>Place names</u>: these can represent our feelings about the place, or be similar to personal names in their suggestion of something. Example: 'On the other side of the road was a window with my wife's ring and watch and other trinkets. I went to pick them up but a stranger put his hand over them. I then crossed the road to get a bus to Andover' (Arthur P). Arthur's dream wants to make sure he gets the message by saying hand-over and Andover.

<u>Idioms</u>: call someone names; clear someone's name; have a bad name; not a thing to one's name; in name alone; in the name of; make a name for oneself; name dropper; one's middle name; name is mud; somebody who shall be nameless; or

name of person, place

my name's not . . . ; worthy of the name; name in vain; lend one's name to; name the day.

narrow   Narrow minded; limited choices or view; feeling restricted.

natives   Natural feelings; being uncivilised. See **aborigine**; **black person**.

navel   Dependency, especially upon mother; the way we connect our deepest self with the outside world.

near   The nearer something is to you in a dream, the closer it is to becoming conscious in a direct way rather than as a symbol. See **positions**.

necklace   Display of special qualities; rich feelings; feelings connected with giver; may represent 'millstone' around neck.

needle   Penetrating insight; male sexuality; power to mend ills; irritations. Needle in body: sickness in body. Needlework: what one has made of oneself. Idioms: get the needle; needle in a haystack.

negro   See **African**; **black person**.

neighbour   One's relationship with other people; the qualities we see in our neighbour.

nest   Emotional dependence upon parents; home life; not being independent; female sexuality; nest egg. Idioms: foul one's own nest; hornets' nest; feather one's nest; cuckoo in the nest.

264

nettle Feeling stung by remarks; irritation, feeling nettled; sickness in the body; a difficult situation you may try to avoid, as in 'grasping the nettle' or 'stung into action'.

new Whatever is new in one's life—a relationship, opportunity, scheme. If contrasted with old, an attempt to decide, contrasting what we already know from the past/old, and what is arising.

newspaper Something that is news to you, or you have just become, or need to be, aware of; something conscious rather than unconscious; something publicly known about yourself.

night See **day and night; time of day; dark**.

nightmares Many dreams lead us to feel an intensity of emotion we may seldom if ever feel in waking life. If the emotions felt are frightening or disgusting we call the dream a nightmare. One of the common features of a nightmare is that we are desperately trying to get away from the situation; feel stuck in a terrible condition; or on waking feel enormous relief that it was just a dream. Because of the intensity of a nightmare we remember it long after other dreams; even if we seldom ever recall other dreams, even worry about what it means.

As so many dreams have been investigated in depth, using such varied approaches as hypnosis, exploration of associations and emotional content, and LSD psychotherapy, in which the person can explore usually unconscious memories, imagery and feelings, we can be certain we know what nightmares are. They arise from six main causes.

1   Unconscious memories of intense emotions, such as those arising in a child being left in a hospital without its mother. Example: see second example in **dark**.
2   Intense anxiety produced—but not fully released at the

time—by external situations such as involvement in war scenes, sexual assault (this applies to males as well as females, as they are frequently assaulted). Example: 'A THING is marauding around the rather bleak, dark house I am in with a small boy. To avoid it I lock myself in a room with the boy. The THING finds the room and tries to break the door down. I frantically try to hold it closed with my hands and one foot pressed against it, my back against a wall for leverage. It was a terrible struggle and I woke myself by screaming' (Terry F). When Terry allowed the sense of fear to arise in him while awake, he felt as he did when a child—the boy in the dream—during the bombing of the Second World War. His sense of insecurity dating from that time had emerged when he left a secure job, and had arisen in the images of the nightmare. Understanding his fears, he was able to avoid their usual paralysing influence.

3   Childhood fears, such as loss of parent, being lost or abandoned, fear of attack by stranger or parent, anxiety about own internal drives.

4   Many nightmares in adults have a similar source, namely fear connected with internal drives such as aggression, sexuality and the process of growth and change, such as encounter with adolescence, loss of sexual characteristics, old age and death. Example: see third example in *doors* under **house, buildings**.

5   Serious illness. Example: 'I dream night after night that a cat is gnawing at my throat' (male from *Landscapes of the Night*). The dreamer had developing cancer of the throat. These physical illness dreams are not as common as the other classes of nightmare.

6   Precognition of fateful events. Example: 'My husband, a pilot in the RAF, had recently lost a friend in an air crash. He woke one morning very troubled—he is usually a very positive person. He told me he had dreamt his friend was flying a black jet, and wanted my husband to fly with him.

Although a simple dream, my husband could not shake off the dark feelings. Shortly afterwards his own jet went down and he was killed in the crash' (Anon.).

Understanding the causes of nightmares enables us to deal with them. The things we run from in the nightmare need to be met while we are awake. We can do this by sitting and imagining ourselves back in the dream and facing or meeting what we were frightened of. Terry imagined himself opening the door he was fighting to keep closed. In doing this and remaining quiet he could feel the childhood feelings arising. Once he recognised them for what they were, the terror went out of them.

A young woman told me she had experienced a recurring nightmare of a piece of cloth touching her face. She would scream and scream and wake her family. One night her brother sat with her and made her meet those feelings depicted by the cloth. When she did so she realised it was her grandmother's funeral shroud. She cried about the loss of her grandmother, felt her feelings about death, and was never troubled again by the nightmare. The techniques given in **dream processing** will help in meeting such feelings. Even the simple act of imagining ourselves back in the nightmare and facing the frightening thing will begin the process of changing our relationship with our internal fears.

no Unless we can say 'no' effectively, our 'yes' in life may be acquiescence rather than agreement. Therefore, saying no in our dreams is an important expression of our needs and ability to make decisions in face of disagreement. It is important to understand what it is you are saying no to, however.

noon See **time of day**.

noose Fear of getting 'hung up' on something or somebody; fear of a trap—or desire to trap.

north   The head, as opposed to south, the genitals; unconsciousness; coldness, suggesting a situation which leads us to seek the light and warmth; death; frozen emotions.

nuclear explosion   Fear about the future. See **atom bomb**.

nude   Dropping the facade, attitudes or feelings we may mask our real emotions with in everyday life—a child may scream if someone it dislikes gets near it, but an adult will probably tolerate the nearness, or refrain from expressing displeasure; desire to be seen for what one is; expression of natural feelings or desire to be intimate; revealing one's true nature. Anxiety about being nude: fear that others know what you really feel and desire; feeling vulnerable and one's weaknesses are exposed; guilt about being a human animal with sexual characteristics and urges.

numbers   Numbers can have a personal or symbolic significance. For instance we may have had three children, so the number three in a dream about children could be connected with our feelings or fears about them—although three has generally been seen as the troublesome triangle in love, or the child, mother, father threesome. So a number may refer to a particular year of one's life, the number of a house, the months or years that have passed since an important event, your family group, or merely have a general significance.

one   One-self; a beginning; the first; unity; being alone; independence. Just one left: near the end. Idioms: it's all one to me; one up; at one with; one and only; one off.

two   Duality; indecision; balance; male and female; two sides to an argument—or a way of comparing; opposition; the opposites, such as light and darkness; parents and reproductive possibility. Chased by, fighting with two people: two against one feeling, as may have happened with child and parents;

feeling odds are against one. Idioms: put two and two together; two's company; two timer; in two minds.

three Triangle; mother, father, child; synthesis; creativity— the child springing from the two opposites—therefore sometimes represents the solution to opposition. Confronting three people, out with two others: facing collective will of others; non-sexual friendship. Idioms: three's a crowd.

four Physicality; the earth; stability and strength; the home or house; reality; down to earth, yet at the same time the spiritual within the physical; the four sides to human nature —sensation, feeling, thought, intuition; earth, air, fire and water. Idioms: four square; on all fours; four letter word. Four or more people: feelings about meeting group decisions and feelings; someone's opinion or will backed by others; supportive feelings.

five The human body; human consciousness in the body; the hand; sometimes called the number of marriage because it unites all the previous numbers—$1+4$ and $2+3$; the five senses.

six Harmony or balance; sex. Idioms: sixes and sevens; six of the best; hit for six.

seven Cycles of life—7, 14, 21, etc.; a week; spiritual meanings—seven candles, seven churches, seven chakras, seven colours, seven notes in music—so represents human wholeness. Idioms: seventh heaven.

eight Death and resurrection; infinity; old fonts and baptistries are octagonal because of the association with regeneration.

nine Pregnancy; childbirth; the end of a cycle and the start of something new; cycles. Idioms: nine days wonder; nine times out of ten; nine to five; cloud nine; nine points of the law.

zero   The female; unconscious; the absolute or hidden; completeness.

other numbers   Ten: a new beginning; the male and female together—ten to one. Eleven: eleventh hour. Twelve: a year; time; a full cycle or wholeness, as in the zodiac or 12 disciples. Thirteen: bad luck. Big numbers: a lot; impressive; much of oneself involved.

nun   Sexual restraint; religious feelings or morals; idealism.

nurse   Healing process; someone you know who is a nurse; job of work for many; sister.

nut   Feeling a 'nut'; inner nourishment or wisdom which needs work to get at its kernel.

O

oak   See **trees**.

oar   The personal energy and skill used to direct our way through the 'waters of life'; wordplay for whore; phallic because of its in and out motion. Idioms: stick one's oar in; rest on one's oars.

oasis   The life-giving influence of emotions and life processes within the 'desert' of intellectualism or materialism.

oats   Sexual energy; sexual satisfaction. Idioms: have one's oats; off one's oats; sow wild oats.

obelisk   One's creative energy leaving its mark in the world —it is sexual in the sense the snake is sexual; how one has shaped one's basic nature through personal effort. See also **reptiles, lizards and snakes**.

obesity   See **fat person**.

obscene dreams   It is reasonable and healthy for all of us to have a dream which surprises us or shocks us occasionally. As dreams partly deal with aspects of our urges and fantasies which we do not allow in waking life, such occasional dreams are safety valves. It is healthy to be able to allow a wide range of dream experience, from the holy to the deeply sexual; from outright aggression to tender love. In fact we gain an idea of the depth and broadness of our own soul—whether or not our psyche is narrow—from the range of dreams we experience. If obscene dreams assail and worry us again and again, however, then there is a problem in the way we are relating to ourself and the exterior world. Psychotherapeutic counselling might help.

obsessed   We are each obsessed in some degree. Few of us could walk down our road nude, or maybe even without shoes and socks. We take such obsessions for granted and accept them as norms, so we do not feel mentally unbalanced. When a similar power of feeling leads us to behaviour outside the norm we face our own doubts about ourself. Obsession in dreams may illustrate some anxiety, drive or desire which is leading us beyond our accepted norm; or the obsession may be used to escape the real feelings, such as childhood pain, or adult conflict and entrapment.

In past cultures the ideas or fears which obsess us would have been described as an evil spirit or ghost taking over the person. This is because the irrational obsession takes hold of us against our will, so this is quite an accurate image. The obsessing factor may still appear in present day dreams in the form of a spirit or demon.

obstacle   Depicts something which causes uncertainty or withdrawal of enthusiasm, creativity or love. Such might be produced by someone's criticism which evokes our own self doubts; indecision; our own inhibitions or anxieties; maybe even a hidden form of not wanting to succeed because it would confront us with the new—we might fail.

Example: 'I have this recurring nightmare. I see my mother standing by my bedroom door, blocking it as if I am being trapped and stopped from getting out. I often call to her "Let me out Mum" but she just stands there staring with no expression on her face at all. I end up getting out of bed and switching my bedroom light on and then she disappears. Sometimes I will see her standing by my wardrobe. It seems as if she is always standing by a door and trying to trap me' (Natalie S). Natalie is 14 and the obstacle she faces in choosing her own clothes—the wardrobe—and making her own decisions—her mother—is her own dependence upon her mother, and the need to develop a new relationship with her.

Example: 'As I was driving along I turned my car over. I wasn't hurt but could not now get to my destination. I didn't feel at all upset about the car being damaged' (Tim K). The example shows a subtle and self-made obstacle, the damaged car. In fact Tim admitted ruining his own work opportunities —the car—because he was frightened of failure. The obstacle, obstruction, barrier or interference can be a person, wall, river, animal—or it might be an internal thing like paralysis or a lump in the throat. Refer to the entry on the appropriate subject to define what it is acting as an obstacle. See first example in **failure**; **fence**; **wall**.

ocean   See **sea**.

octopus   See **fish, sea creatures**.

odour   See **perfume**.

office   Feelings about or relationship with work; feelings about authority.

officer, official   Relationship with authority or officialdom; one's father; how we authorise our own activities; our sense of right and wrong; a coordinating or directing function in ourself; a sense of sureness out of wider awareness or experience.

ogre   Feelings developed in relationship with one's father; lack of sympathy or understanding; being inconsiderate; feelings about authority.

oil   Attitude which removes friction in oneself or in a relationship; flattery; unctuousness; fat in one's diet. Idioms: well

oil

oiled; oil the wheels; strike oil; oil on troubled waters; burn midnight oil.

ointment   Care; healing.

old, ancient, antique   *old* The past; the different lives we have lived—baby, youth, lover, parent, provider; what is established and well worn; tradition and wisdom of folklore.

Example: 'I am standing in a bookshop. It is a long established business. As I look at the books I find two which are about the life of Christ. They are leather bound and handwritten—quite ancient. Both seem to me to be about the author's own inner life. I believe one is written from a religious viewpoint and the other from a more occult one. I am not attracted to either' (Bill O). Bill is looking back on past attitudes, one religious, one occult, which had been big parts of his life. Old people: wisdom; mother or father; past experience; traditions; old age; death. Old building: past way of life; former life with family or another person. Old things, furniture: past or outworn ways of life or activities.

ancient   Usually suggests contact with parts of ourselves which are older than the development of the conscious self, such as cellular wisdom; life processes; accepted traditions or ways of life; wisdom of the unconscious.

antique   Elements of our past experience which might be worth keeping; wisdom of unconscious.

olive   See **food**.

onion   See **food**.

opal   See **jewels**.

opera   Dramatisation of inner feeling situations. See **arena**; **stage**; **film**.

operation   Memories regarding actual operation; a sick inner attitude which needs attention; fear of illness; physical fitness.

oracle   Intuition; unconscious hopes or desires; attempt to manipulate. See **ESP in dreams**.

orange   See **colours; food**.

orchard   Efforts may be bearing fruit; one's growth. See **garden**.

orchestra   The working relationship between the different aspects of oneself—mind, body, spirit; one's sense of social cooperation or harmony in the cosmos. Conductor: the self; whatever is directing one's life. See **music; musical instruments**.

ore   One's potential; new ideas or energy; resources needing work to make usable. See **mines**.

organ   The different aspects of self, different ideas, feelings, abilities, weaknesses and strengths which can be played or called upon; the whole range of our being as it responds to decisions and activity; sexual organs. See **music**.

orphan   Feeling abandoned or unloved; feeling rejected or misunderstood—or part of self rejected and misunderstood; vulnerability in independence and consciousness. See **abandoned**.

ostrich   Because of folklore, may represent avoidance of seeing what is happening around one.

otter   See **animals**.

out of body experience   Example: 'At about two or three in the morning my wife Brenda and I were suddenly awoken from sleep by a noise. As we lifted our heads to listen we identified it as the handle on our children's bedroom door being turned. The house only had two bedrooms, and the children's room was directly opposite ours. Both of us had had the same thought—"Oh no, it's the children again." Much to our annoyance they had been waking in the middle of the night claiming it was morning and time to play. We had tried to suppress it, but here it was again.

'As these thoughts went through our minds we heard the sound of feet clomping down the stairs. This was strange as the children usually stayed in their room. Brenda got up, determined to get whoever it was back into bed. I heard her switch the light on, go down the stairs, switch the sitting room light on, and I followed her via the sounds of her movement as she looked in the kitchen and even toilet—we didn't have a bathroom. Then up she came again and opened the children's door—strange because we had assumed it had been opened. When she came back into our room she looked puzzled and a little scared. "They're all asleep and in bed" she said.

'We talked over the mystery for some time, trying to understand just how we had heard the door handle rattle then footsteps going down the stairs, yet the door wasn't open. Also, the door handles on our doors were too high for the children to reach without standing on a chair. There was a stool in the children's bedroom they used for that, yet it wasn't even near the door when Brenda opened it.

'Having no answer to the puzzle we stopped talking and settled to wait for sleep again. Suddenly a noise came from the children's bedroom. It sounded like the stool being dragged and then the door handle turning again but the door not opening. "You go this time" Brenda said, obviously disturbed.

'I opened our door quickly just in time to see the opposite door handle turn again. Still the door didn't open. I reached across, turned the handle and slowly opened the door. It stopped as something was blocking it. Just then my daughter Helen's small face peered around the door—high because she was standing on the stool. Puzzled by what had happened, I was careful what I said to her. "What do you want love?" I asked.

'Unperturbed she replied, "I want to go to the toilet." The toilet was downstairs, through the sitting room, and through the kitchen.

'Now I had a clue so asked, "Did you go downstairs before?"

' "Yes," she said, "but Mummy sent me back to bed." ' (Tony C).

This is an unusual example of an out of body experience (OBE). Mostly they are described from the point of view of the person projecting, and are therefore difficult to corroborate. Here, three people experience the OBE in their own way. From Tony and Brenda's point of view what happened caused sensory stimuli, but only auditory. Helen's statement says that she was sure she had physically walked down the stairs and been sent back to bed by her mother. Tony and Brenda felt there was a direct connection between what they were thinking and feeling—get the children back to bed—and what Helen experienced as an objective reality.

OBEs have been reported in thousands in every culture and in every period of history. A more general experience of OBE than the above might include a feeling of rushing along a tunnel or release from a tight place prior to the awareness of independence from the body. In this first stage some people experience a sense of physical paralysis which may be frightening (see **paralysis**). Their awareness then seems to become an observing point outside the body, as well as the sense of

277

paralysis. Then there is usually an intense awareness of one-self and surroundings, unlike dreaming or even lucidity. Some projectors feel they are even more vitally aware and rational than during the waking state. Looking back on one's body may occur here. Once the awareness is independent of the body, the boundaries of time and space as they are known in the body do not exist. One can easily pass through walls, fly, travel to or immediately be in a far distant place, witnessing what may be, or appears to be, physically real there.

Sir Auckland Geddes, an eminent British anatomist, de-scribes his own OBE, which contains many of these features. Example: Becoming suddenly and violently ill with gas-troenteritis he quickly became unable to move or phone for help. As this was occurring he noticed he had an A and a B consciousness. The A was his normal awareness, and the B was external to his body, watching. From the B self he could see not only his body, but also the house, garden and sur-rounds. He need only think of a friend or place and immedi-ately he was there and was later able to find confirmation for his observations. In looking at his body, he noticed that the brain was only an end organ, like a condensing plate, upon which memory and awareness played. The mind, he said, was not in the brain, the brain was in the mind, like a radio in the play of signals. He then observed his daughter come in and discover his condition, saw her telephone a doctor friend, and saw him also at the same time.

Many cases of OBE occur near death, where a person has 'died' of a heart attack for instance, and is later revived. Be-cause of this there are attempts to consider the possibility of survival of death through study of these cases. In fact many people experiencing an OBE have a very different view of death than prior to their experience.

Early attempts to explain OBEs suggested a subtle or astral body, which is a double of our physical and mental self, but able to pass through walls. It was said to be connected to the physical body during an OBE by a silver cord—a sort of lifeline which kept the physical body alive. This is like the concept that the people we dream about are not creations of our own psyche, but real in their own right. Whatever one may believe an OBE to be, it can be observed that many people in this condition have no silver cord, and have no body at all, but are simply a bodiless observer, or are an animal, a geometric shape, a colour or sound (see **identity and dreams**). The person's own unconscious concepts of self seem to be the factor which shapes the form of the OBE. If, therefore, one feels sure one must travel to a distant point, then in the OBE one travels. If one believes one is immediately there by the power of thought, one is there. If one cannot conceive of existing without a body, then one has a body, and so on.

This approach explains many aspects of the OBE, but there is still not a clear concept of what the relationship with the physical world is. The many cases of OBE which occur during a near-death experience also suggest it may be connected with a survival response to death; not necessarily as a way of trying to transcend death, but perhaps as a primeval form of warning relatives of death. If there is survival of death, then the OBE may be an anticipatory form, or a preparatory condition leading to the new form. See **hallucinations, hallucinogens**.

oval   The womb; female qualities or sexuality.

oven   Because of the idiom 'one in the oven', may depict pregnancy or the womb; the human ability to transform character qualities—from being a sulky, irritable person, one can change to being self-giving and open. It depicts this because the oven transforms inedible substances or objects into delightful food.

owl   See **birds**; second example in *wife* under **family**.

oyster   See **fish, sea creatures**.

P

packing Depends on dream. <u>Already packed case</u>: readiness to meet change. <u>Packing and wondering what to take</u>: decisions about what stance or attitudes are suitable to meet present situation or change; sense of an end in sight; attempt to be independent. <u>Can't pack in time</u>: anxiety about details; feeling unready for change. <u>Idioms</u>: pack off; pack up; send somebody packing; pack one's bags.

paddle See **oar**. <u>Idioms</u>: paddle one's own canoe.

padlock See **lock**.

painting The unconscious frequently senses things, or synthesises out of our experience views of things, we have not been consciously aware of. A dream may depict this as a painting; subtle feelings or realisations; a view we have of or about something. <u>Any form of artistic expression</u>: self expression; expressing one's feelings or intuitions; one's inner situation; creative ability. <u>Painting, decorating</u>: expressing feelings; the impression we give to others; what 'colour' we are painting things, in the sense of painting a very black picture; a cover up. We can paint the town red; paint too rosy a picture. Or we might be working at changing our appearance or lifestyle. See **photographs**.

pan, pot Receptive state of mind and feelings, perhaps connected with creativity (cooking), family life, or providing for one's needs. <u>Chamberpot</u>: feelings and values connected with excretory functions; female sexuality. <u>Idioms</u>: flash in the pan.

paper   Blank writing paper: unexpressed sentiments or ideas; opportunity; feeling a lack of communication with someone else. Wrapping paper: depending on the colour and quality, how you feel others see you; the exterior impression of what you are getting or giving in a relationship; the outward appearance of your own potential. Idioms: commit to paper; not worth the paper it's written on; on paper; paper tiger; pen to paper; paper over the cracks.

parachute   Depicts whatever life skill one uses to deal with anxiety about failing/falling; achieving a more down-to-earth practical attitude after flying high, or retreating into flights of fancy.

paradise   Experience of being in the womb; feeling in harmony with self. See **heaven**. Idioms: fools' paradise.

paralysis   Example: 'It starts as a dream, but I gradually become aware that I cannot move. The harder I try to move the worse it gets and I become very frightened. I can neither move nor wake myself up. Sometimes I feel as if I am leaving my body. But to deal with the fear I have learnt—it's a recurring thing—to stop struggling, knowing that I will eventually wake' (Susan Y). This is a common experience which may be due to the fact the body is paralysed during periods of the dream process; all brain signals to the voluntary muscles are inhibited. This is not sensed as a problem if we are unconsciously involved in a dream. If enough self awareness arises in the dream state, then awareness of the inability to move may occur, along with the anxiety this can arouse. Another factor is illustrated by what Susan says—the harder she tries to move the worse it gets. Our unconscious is very open to suggestion. If this were not so we would lack necessary survival responses. In a dimly lit situation we may mistake a shape for a lurking figure. Our body reactions, such as heartbeat, react to the mistake as if it is real, until we gain fresh information. Whatever we feel to be real becomes a fact as far as our body reactions are concerned. The fear that one cannot move becomes a fact because we believe it. When Susan relaxes, and thereby drops the fear of paralysis, she can be free of it. This applies to anything we feel is true—we create it as an internal reality.

Dreaming one is paralysed is similar. It depicts the paralysing effects, either of fears we have or of what we have imagined as real in the way described; we may be 'paralysed' by feelings of guilt or inadequacy; internal conflict paralyses us. The healing of the paralysed man by Christ represents this removal of guilt, shame or fear by contact with the self.

parasites   Lice, fleas, bugs: things said, thought or done which make you feel uncomfortable or ashamed; feelings that one is, or someone else is, a parasite in a relationship.

Example: 'I was practising relaxation and went into a dream state. I saw a dark shape attached to my body near my heart. I felt very frightened as I saw it. But as I watched it broke away and left me' (John W). John had experienced a heart attack, and the dark shape was an embodiment of his fears about his heart, sucking his energy and well-being. In relaxing he was able to let go of these feelings. Because the dream process shows such internal processes in imagery, the fears are shown as an incubus or dark parasite, which falls away.

parcel, package   Something we have experienced but not explored the import of. A parent may die, for instance, but we may not 'unwrap' the feelings evoked enough to see we have taken something to heart. If we did we might find a regret at not expressing the love we felt while Mum or Dad was still alive, and we now want to be more daring in giving love. Also, one's potential or latent skills; impressions or 'gifts' received from others—such as support, love, their example—but not made fully conscious.

Parliament   The many aspects of self involved in decision making; one's feelings about social situations.

parrot   Repeating without judgment what others have said; accepting or copying something without evaluating it.

party   Example: 'Then I was in a place where we were having a staff party. Not very big but people were sitting at tables eating in a party mood. I sat with my child, maybe youngest son, no one else at the table. I felt I didn't wish to get involved with the others, the feeling I often get at parties, just alone in a crowd. I left with my son. Some young men tried to dissuade us but I pushed away' (Simeon T). Simeon finds groups of people difficult to relate to. The dream shows this is a feeling which started in his childhood—his youngest son. Generally, our feelings about groups; social skill or lack of it; social pleasure. <u>Dreamer as host of party</u>: our relationship with the different aspects of self. <u>Dreamer as main guest</u>, say at a birthday party: wanting family or social acclaim and love, or feeling loved.

passage   A sense of being 'in between' regarding work, love or life; change, as in a rite of passage—so, the movement between stages or phases of life; the back passage, rectum; or front passage, vagina, and so the birth passage. See **corridor**. <u>Idioms</u>: work one's passage.

passenger   <u>Being a passenger</u>: feeling that circumstances are carrying you along, either because you are passively allowing them to or because you feel powerless to change; sense of being carried along by the process of life, such as ageing. <u>Passenger in car</u>: being motivated or moved by someone else's viewpoints, opinions or enthusiasm; being dependent, perhaps on the person who is driving the car; allowing a secondary part of self, such as indecision, pride or stubbornness, to direct decisions. Carrying passengers: feeling you are taking the responsibility in work or family. See **car**.

passive   See **active/passive**.

passport   One's sense of identity, with its connections with racial, national and family background; feelings about travel.

past lives   While there may be some evidence for reincarnation in the work of Dr Ian Stevenson, dreams which clearly state reincarnation in their theme most likely represent present life situations.

Example: 'I dream of living in China, a long time ago. I was married to a man with whom I had two children. He began to tire of me and brought concubines into our household. I hated him. When I woke I realised I had dreamt about a past life' (Patricia L). Patricia had in fact been married to a man in this life who, after her two children were born, began to bring other women home. This broke up their marriage. From Patricia's point of view, this happened because in a past life her husband and she had not resolved their difficulties, so had to meet them again in this lifetime—whatsoever ye sow, so shall ye reap. Where such dreams have been thoroughly explored, I have found that their imagery arises from emotions and trauma which the dreamer finds difficult to meet. Placing it in a past life enables one to avoid the difficulty of experiencing present life pain. Patricia says she hated her Chinese husband. The dream process can create a drama to represent our present situation using any form of structure. It is, after all, the master dramatist. This function of the unconscious explains many 'past life' memories elicited by hypnotic regression. Most of them are explainable in terms of present life trauma or situation. See **hallucination, hallucinogens**.

path   The approach or attitudes one uses regarding life in general, in relationships or in work; the direction one has decided on or is following; the way a relationship or marriage is going; a line of thought or enquiry. <u>Well-worn path</u>: a well-established or habitual way of doing something. Also the path sometimes represents one's overall direction or experience of life within the process of growth and change. <u>Losing partner on path</u>: fear or intuition that the relationship will end or partner die first.

pearl   See *pearl* under **jewels**; *oyster* under **fish, sea creatures**.

pedestal   To feel special or to make special; to place above other things; to idolise or worship.

Pegasus   See *horse* under **animals**.

pen, pencil   Desire to communicate; occasionally male sexuality because of shape.

pendant   See **necklace**.

penguin   Suggests feeling isolated by cold emotions.

penis   See *penis* under **body**; **castrate**.

pentacle   See *five* under **numbers**.

people   <u>Several people in dream</u>: not feeling lonely; involvement of many aspects of oneself in what is being dreamt about; social ability. <u>Large crowds</u>: enormous involvement of self in issue; one's relationship or feelings about the social environment one lives in; in groups we have a feeling of being looked at or on view—how we relate to that may be depicted by what we are doing in the dream group. See **party**; **roles**.

Example: 'I was outdoors with a group of people acting as leader. We were in the middle of a war situation with bullets playing around us. Maybe aeroplanes were also attacking. I was leading the group from cover to cover, avoiding the bullets' (Paul W). Despite feeling attacked, either by external events, or from inner conflicts, Paul is using leadership skills to deal with his own fears and tendencies. If a friend told us he had just had an argument with his wife and was going to leave her, we might sit down and counsel them by listening and helping them to sort out the hurt feelings from their long-term wishes. We might point out they had felt this way before, but it passed—in other words give feedback they had missed. In a similar way, our various emotions and drives often need this sort of skill employed by ourself. This unifies us, leading to coping skills as in Paul's dream.

Example: 'Walking alone through a small town. I was heading for a place that a group of people, in a street parallel to mine, were also heading for. A person from the group tried to persuade me that the right way to get to the place was along the street the group was walking. I knew the street did not matter, only the general direction. The person was quite disturbed by my independence. It made him or her feel uncertain to have their leader apparently questioned. I felt uncertain too for a moment' (Ivor S). A group of people, as in Ivor's dream, can also depict how one meets the pressure of social norms. As social relationship is one of the most important factors outside personal survival—and survival depends upon it—such dreams help us to clarify our individual contact with society. Human beings have an unconscious but highly developed sense of the psychological social environment. Ivor's dream shows something we are all involved in—how we are relating to humans collectively. Are we in conflict with group behaviour and direction? Do we conform, but perhaps have conflict with our individual drives? Do we find a way between the opposites? Much of our response is laid down in childhood and remains unconscious unless we review it.

In some dreams, a group of people represent what is meant by the word God. This may sound unlikely, but the unconscious, because it is highly capable of synthesis, often looks at humanity as a whole. Collectively humanity has vast creative and destructive powers which intimately affect us as individuals. Collectively it has performed miracles which, looked at as an individual, appear impossible. How could a little human being build the Great Pyramid, or a space shuttle? The Bible echoes this concept in such phrases as 'Whatever you do to the least of one of these, you do to me.'

pepper   Warming up one's emotions; livening up the situation; irritation.

perfume, scent, smell   Example: 'I went back in time in circles, almost as if going unconscious. I went back and back and then there came this awful smell such as I've never experienced. I always felt it was the smell of death. I would wake terrified. One night my husband, a practical and down to earth man, said he would read me to sleep to see if it helped me not to have the dream. It made no difference, I still had the nightmare. Imagine my surprise though. He said "I knew you'd had the dream again for there was an awful smell in the room for a minute" ' (Mrs E C). A smell can remind us of a particular situation or person. Odour attracts, repels, relaxes or offends, and so depicts feeling responses and intuition, and may summarise what we feel about a person or situation. Frequently in dreams a smell expresses an intuition of something rotten in one's life if the smell is bad—rotten might mean 'bad' emotions felt in a relationship; a hunch or feelings about something, as in the example; memories. Good smell: good feelings; non-verbalised intimations or love.

Also explainable by the large number of idioms regarding smell. Idioms: on the right scent; throw someone off the scent; in bad/good odour with; odour of sanctity; smell a rat; smell of greasepaint; smells fishy; something stinks to high heaven;

perfume, scent, smell

like stink; raise a stink; what you did stinks. See *nose* under **body**.

perspire, sweat Mostly fear. As we get near to experiencing areas of our memory or inner feelings which disturb us, rapid heartbeat and perspiration are some of the first signs. Occasionally pleasurable exertion. Idioms: in a cold sweat; no sweat; sweat blood; sweat of one's brow; old sweat; sweat it out.

pet Our natural drives and feelings—such as procreation or desire to be 'petted'—which have been 'house trained' or caged, depending on dream. The dream will indicate what one is doing with this side of one's nature. Feelings of being like a pet, only being able to do what the person you are dependent upon wishes; receiving or giving affection. Baby pets: if in a woman's dream, may signify her maternal drive, her desire for children; one's own dependent self and feelings. See **animals**.

petrol Energy; explosive or dangerous emotions.

petticoat See **clothes**.

philosophy of dreams In attempting to put together the information gathered from viewing thousands of dreams—not simply at face value, but explored in depth through the emotions and direct associations of the dreamer—a philosophy or view of life arises. It suggests that our birth as a physical and psychological being is a paradox. We are unique, and at the same time a common undifferentiated person. Psychologically we have our identity out of the lives of thousands of humans who preceded us and left the gift of language, of music, art, of concepts and information. Our mental life, our consciousness, is in some very real way formed out of what they left from their life. Our consciousness has been hewn out of the rock of possibilities by the love, the struggle and pain, the endeavour and wit of their lives. Particularly our psyche has been shaped by or modelled on our parents, and the traces in their life, unknown though they may be, of their parents, backwards for many generations.

Our identity is given to us by the humans who raise us. This sense of self arises because we are treated as if we were a self. This, with language, is the creative matrix of our self awareness. The giving of a name is therefore a miracle which acts as a nucleus around which the many mental connections can be made which form our self image. Perhaps this is why giving the name in baptism is seen as a holy rite in Christianity.

Our conscious personality can live without ever becoming aware of its connections with other lives except as it meets them in everyday affairs. That its existence has depended upon what was given by countless other lives—that humans constantly create each other, consciously and unconsciously, through the dynamic flux of communication—might never be realised. That one's own life is also a part of this creative process, this sea of living consciousness, might never be known. Nevertheless, each individual life constantly takes part in the collective, negatively or positively. This is not a mystical thing, but is plainly observable. From the point of view of dreams, if our life has given nothing in deed, in love, in rearing of children, in ideas or art, or in common humanity, we are dead—during life and afterwards. Giving and receiving, kinship and symbiosis, growth and decay are the fundamentals of the living process according to dreams.

At death, we face a very real end, a real death. There is no magical escape from this. All that we have been, all we have become, all we gathered and won is lost—finished. But the paradox occurs again. Dreams suggest that out of all we gave of ourself, out of all we received from the being of others, we are recreated in a realm of consciousness. This may mean that we continue as living influences in the lives of those who still live. But the suggestion is that something more than this occurs.

phoenix   See **birds**.

photos   Memories; wanting to be remembered or noticed; looking at some aspect of oneself. Looking at <u>family photos</u>: realisation of past influences in one's life; family environment, mentally and emotionally. <u>Taking photos</u> : capturing a realisation; taking notice of something; remembering. <u>Photo of oneself</u>: one's self image; need to look at oneself or get an objective view. <u>Photos which come to life</u>: the living influence of past experience; our continuing involvement in what the picture depicts; something which we held as a thought, which is taking shape and becoming real. <u>Developing photos</u>: bringing to consciousness what was latent or unrealised before.

physician   See **roles**.

piano   See **musical instrument**.

pictures   See **painting; photos**.

pig   See **animals**.

pill   An experience you need, or are making yourself meet because you think it is good for you; something we 'swallow' because we think it is right—we may 'swallow' lies or excuses; an attempt to deal with internal feelings by external means. <u>Pill we are actually taking</u>: may link with feelings or physical reactions to the drug being taken. <u>Idioms</u>: sugar the pill; bitter pill.

pillow   Comfort; support. <u>Hugging pillow</u>: feeling alone and needing contact.

pimple   Character blemishes, if on face; sense of not being inwardly clean; feelings about one's spots.

pin   Small ideas, actions or information which, connected, help create something or hold things together; one's connection or emotional bond with things. If <u>stuck in</u>: irritation or hurts; irritating or painful sexual intercourse. <u>Idioms</u>: for two pins; don't care two pins; on pins and needles; pin back one's ears; pin one's hopes on; pin someone down; pin something on someone; pin money.

pipe   Unconscious connections with others; emotions, or things which you feel are 'on tap'; a difficult way out of a situation; sometimes refers to the experience of being born, especially if accompanied by panic or fear; the 'pipes' in one's body—see 3 in *the dream as extended perception* under **ESP in dreams**. <u>Crawling into pipe</u>: sexual intercourse—sex creates unconscious links with partner; experiencing unconscious connection with others.

pirate   See **roles**.

piston   Sexual drive or activity.

pit   Feelings or situations one finds it difficult to get out of; feelings about death; feeling trapped or forgotten.

place, environment   See **setting**.

placenta   Dependence; being depended upon; how one gains nourishment from another.

plait   Plaited hair: girlhood. See *hair* under **body**. Plaiting rope, etc.: weaving together different influences in one's life; uniting conflicting feelings or people; a triangle of people.

plane   See **airplane**.

planets   The influence of the abstract or subtle in one's life; desire for the strange or alien. If dreamer has any inkling of astrology, the planet can depict the traditional 'planetary' qualities. Sun: vital energy; the self; consciousness or awareness. Moon: see **moon**. Mercury: intuition and the mind. Venus: love; motherhood and femininity; receptivity. Mars: energetic activity; aggressive action or fire in one's life and feelings; masculinity ruled by passions. Jupiter: growth; expansion in self and activities; preservation; freedom from limitations. Saturn: fate; the past catching up with us; retarding influence; emotional coldness; lessons of life which shape our growth; time. Uranus: sudden changes; fluctuation. Neptune: the unconscious influence in daily life; psychic impressions; awareness of death. Pluto: the deep unconscious and death; beyond the ego.

plank   Depends what it is used for in dream. Can be security for life if flooring, or sense of losing basic support if a rotten floor. See *floor* under **house, buildings**. If for making something: one's potential; the materials you have for undertaking a project of 'making something of oneself'. If nailed above one: feeling of being trapped, fear of death; setting up one's own death, in the sense of killing one's chances in work or relationship. See **fence; coffin; wood**.

plants   Areas of progressive change in one's life; emerging personal qualities; occasionally one's children being helped in their 'growth'. Dead, dying plants: loss of vital enthusiasm; dying pleasure. See **weeds**.

plate   Example: 'I am at a wedding at which we are being served a celebratory chicken lunch. Whilst my back is turned for a moment one of the other guests on the table (who is female but whom I do not know) removed my plate and substitutes it with a plate of food which doesn't contain chicken. When I challenge this, I am told that there is no more. At this I rather petulantly decide to leave the wedding' (Brian Y). Brian uses a plate of food to represent the good things he feels are rightfully his in life; but his negative emotions in a relationship with a female rob him of this. If food on plate: what one has a sense of ownership about; what one has received or hopes to receive from others, or from one's own efforts; what you have created and now face. Communal plate: what is available to you but you may have to compete for or share—in work, relationship, life. Empty plate: one's needs; appetites; receptivity; perhaps status, as in the past only the rich had plates. Idioms: handed to one on a plate; on one's plate. See **food**.

play   See **film; theatre**.

playing   Depends on what the 'game' is. Whatever we 'play' at in a dream might just be fun or suggest great seriousness. As humans we use an enormous number of strategies to gain our ends, as explained in the book *Games People Play*. The idioms define some of these 'games'. Idioms: come into play; foul play; make a play for; make play of; play a part in; play along with; play at; play cat and mouse; play dead/possum; play down; played out; play fair; play false; play for time; play hard to get; play it cool; play no part in it; play on words; play safe; play people off against each other; play something down; play the field; play up; play upon a weakness/fear; play up to someone; the state of play; play somebody at their own game; child's play; play ball with; play it by ear; play fast and loose; play gooseberry; play havoc with; play merry hell; play into their hands; play one's ace; play one's cards right; play second fiddle; play the fool; play the game; play the white man; play to the gallery; play with fire; two can play at that game.

plot of the dream   In attempting to understand our dreams, it is important to honour their drama or plot. Dreams appear to be very specific in the way they use the characters, objects and environs occurring in them.

Example: 'I was walking up a steep hill on a sunny day when my husband came running down the hill with blood pouring from his right arm. He couldn't stop running. As he passed me he called to me for help. I was happy and peaceful and ignored him. I calmly watched him running fast down the hill, then continued on my way' (Joyce C). Out of the infinite number of situations Joyce could have dreamt about, this was the one produced. Why? There are many factors which appear to determine what we dream. How events of the day influenced us; what stage of personal growth we are meeting—we might be in the stage of struggling for independence; problems being met; relationships; past business such as childhood traumas still to be integrated. And so on. If Joyce had dreamt she and her husband were walking up the hill the whole message of the dream would have been different. If we can accept that dream images are, as Freud stated, a form of thinking, then the change in imagery would be a changed concept. If the language of dreams is expressed in its images, then the meaning stated is specific to the imagery used.

In processing our dreams, it is therefore profitable to look at the plot to see what it suggests. It can be helpful to change the situation, as we have done with Joyce's. Imagining Joyce walking up the hill on a sunny day, arm in arm with her husband, suggests a happy relationship. This emphasises the situation of independence and lack of support for her husband which appears in the real dream. Seeing our dreams as if they were snatches from a film or play, and asking ourself what feelings and human situations they depict, can aid us to clarify them. As a piece of drama, Joyce's dream says she sees, but does not respond to, her husband's plight.

Our internal 'dream producer' has an amazing sense of the subtle meanings of movement, positioning, and relationship between the elements used. And some of these are subtle. A way of becoming more aware of what information our dream contains is to use visualisation. Sit comfortably and imagine yourself back in the dream. Replay it just as it was. Remember the whole thing slowly, going through it again while awake. As you do so, be aware of what it feels like in each scene or event. What do the interactions suggest? What does it feel like in the other roles? We can even practise this with other people's dreams. If we imagine ourself in Joyce's dream, and replay it just as she describes it, we may arrive at a feeling of detachment from the husband. If we stand in the husband's role we may feel a great need which is not responded to as we go 'down hill fast'. In this way we gather a great deal of 'unspoken' information from dreams.

Looking at our own dreams in this way can be more difficult, simply because we do not always want to see what is being said about ourself. See **amplification; dream processing; postures, movement, body language; word analysis of dreams; settings**.

ploughing   Working at preparing or changing oneself or a situation; making way for new growth; using past experience for future growth. Plough: means of 'ploughing'; male sexuality in its move towards parenthood—sowing the seeds.

plumbing   The way we direct emotions or the flow of feelings; our internal 'plumbing'. See **pipe; water**.

plunge   Taking a risk; facing uncertainty; going into something unknown or untried.

pocket   One's personal secrets or thoughts; self; sense of ownership or possession; vagina. Trouser pocket: can refer to sexuality. Idioms: be in somebody's pocket; in/out of pocket; pocket one's pride; burn a hole in one's pocket; dip into one's pocket; line one's pocket.

point   Anything pointed can refer to male sexuality; reaching a point—arriving at a culmination or change; a meaning, a decision to be made.

pointing   Drawing one's attention to something; feeling at the receiving end of someone's emotions or suggestions.

poison   Warning to avoid something; something that will not be good for us; attitudes, emotions or thoughts which can harm us; warning against business deal or relationship; possibly related to foods we are eating which are not suitable. Idioms: what's your poison; poison one's mind; poison pen letter; avoid it like poison.

pole   The penis; male sexuality; life force in its positive expressive aspect.

policeman/woman   See **roles**.

pool   Our inner world of thoughts, fantasies and feelings; sometimes a sense of union with living beings—collective consciousness.

Pope   Father; code of behaviour arising from religious beliefs; God. See **dream as spiritual guide**.

positions   One's stance or position in life; the way one is relating to what is depicted, or the way we feel we are relating to it.

above   What is superior or has a wider view or possibility than our present standpoint; sense of inferiority in relationship to what is above us; what we strive for. If we are standing above, high up: having a wider viewpoint; being intellectual; feeling superior or in a position of advantage. Idioms: above all; above and beyond; above asking; above oneself; above board; above one's station; risen above oneself. See **high; hill; mountain; flying**.

behind   The past; what you have chosen to or want to forget – left behind; what one is unaware of, as talk behind one's back; what has been learnt or dealt with. People behind dreamer: taking the lead in relationships; being decisive. Idioms: behind the scenes; behind the time; fall behind; put something behind me.

below   Something you feel is 'beneath you'; what is 'below' in the body—so the nonintellectual aspects of self; something one can now look back on from a detached viewpoint. If below something else, see *above* in this entry. Idioms: beneath my contempt; it's below my standards.

close   Intimacy; being made aware of; what one feels connected with or has ties with; near to, in the sense of making a decision—near to leaving home; close to, as 'close to finding the solution'; a situation which is near at hand or being confronted or realised now. Idioms: at close quarters; close fisted; close on; close to home; that was close.

distant   Barely conscious of; a long time off; something one does not identify with strongly.

in front   The future; what is seen and understood; what is being confronted.

opposite   Meeting or 'facing' a situation; opposition or resistance to decided direction.

297

positions

side   Supportive feelings as 'by one's side'; as well as; indication of choice, as 'What side are you on?' or 'Who's on my side?' Idioms: from all sides; let the side down; on every side; on the wrong side of 30; on the right/wrong side; on the side; pass by on the other side; pick sides; put to one side; side by side; side with somebody; take sides; take to one side; the other side (death); safe side; bit on the side; seamy side.

poster   Something the unconscious is trying to show you.

postures, movement, body language   Even in everyday life, the way we hold and position our body, the inclination of chest and head, the movement of hands, are a means of communication. The apparently intuitive information in some dreams, when investigated, can be traced to an unconscious insight into the language of the living body. We all have this ability to understand body language, but it seems to be something which is inherited from past times before verbal language. It therefore remains a largely unconscious ability. In our dreams, however, it is a major factor in how the dream is structured.

If you cannot find a satisfying description below, imagine yourself making the movement or posture in the dream to see if you can define what the feeling quality is, or what you are saying non-verbally. It can often be of value to make the movement or take up the posture physically instead of in the imagination. By comparing the movement/posture with another one, it can help to clarify its quality.

Example: 'Marilyn was experiencing emotional pain connected with her impending divorce. Marilyn had dreamt of seeing a dinosaur standing in her path, devouring all who approached it. We explored it by having Marilyn find a body posture and movements which for her expressed the feeling of the dinosaur. In doing so Marilyn did not sense anger or aggression, but she did feel like a predator which always had to take to gain her own needs. This feeling immediately reminded her of her family life as a child. She remembered when she was sent shopping as a very young child of three or four; as well as buying what she had been asked, she purchased some sweets for herself. When she arrived home she was treated as if she had done a terrible thing, and that was where she began to feel like a predator. It seemed to her as if her own needs were always gained at the expense of someone else.

'With this awareness, she could now see that the dinosaur standing in her path clearly related to her present situation. Bargaining to gain a realistic share of the house and property jointly owned by her husband and herself, felt to her as if she were gaining her needs at his expense, like a predator. That made her feel so awful, she was almost ready to allow her husband to take all, leaving her without house or money to start again. Her awareness of where the feelings arose from, and the unrealistic part they played in her life, allowed her to relate to the situation with less pain and more wisdom' (from *Mind and Movement,* Tony Crisp).

jump   Daring; taking a risk; sometimes connected with **flying**. Jumping to avoid: feeling of threat; anxiety, evasion tactics. Jumping off: getting out of a situation. Jumping at dreamer: unexpected; irritations. Idioms: one jump ahead; the high jump; jump at; running jump at yourself; jumping down one's throat; jumping off place; jump out of one's skin; jump the gun; jump the queue; jump to it; jump on the bandwagon; jump to conclusion.

kneel   Humility; acknowledgment of dependence or cooperation; sense of awe; defeat.

prone   Relaxation; letting go of activity; introversion; sex. Or retreat from the world; feeling injured; afraid to stand up for oneself; non-involvement; negative introversion; weakness; death. Idioms: lie low; lie at one's door; lie in wait; take it lying down. See *squatting down; standing,* both in this entry.

run Exuberance; flowing life energy; strong and easy motivation. Running away: avoiding one's own emotions or sexuality; not meeting problems in a way that will resolve them;
anxiety about what you are running from; feelings of guilt.
Running to: anxiety; responsibility and self-giving; sometimes
running towards danger. Running as if made of lead: held
back by one's own hesitations. Example: 'There followed a
nightmare of running along streets, round corners, knowing I
was being followed and trying to get away. Then I met a
friend who was also running away. She took me down a narrow street full of down and outs and prostitutes' (Pauline B).
  Idioms: run for one's money; run of the house; out of the
running; on the run; run along; run down; run for it; run out
of steam; run out on someone; run up against; run wild. See
second example in **emotions, mood**; *Am I meeting things I
fear?* in **dream processing; nightmares; chased**. See also **lucidity**.

sit One's situation at time of dream; status, depending on
where one is sitting; being relaxed; inactive waiting. Sitting
up: becoming more involved. Idioms: sit back; sit for; sit in on
something; sit on; sit out; sit something out; sit tight; sit at
someone's feet; sit in judgment; sitting target; sit on the fence.

squatting down The down expresses sleep; rest; withdrawal;
non-involvement. Idioms: feel down; down and out; do someone down; down at heel; down hearted; down with. See *prone*
above in this entry.

standing Our involvement in the exterior world of change,
opposites, and needs which require expenditure of effort; our
'standing' in society; what one 'stands' for; being active; confrontation; cooperation with others. Idioms: know where one
stands; left standing; make a stand against; stand alone; stand
aside; stand by; stand corrected; stand down; stand firm; stand

in someone's way; stand up for; stand up to; stand one's ground; stand on ceremony or dignity.

turn A change; making a new decision.

walk Motivation and confidence; where you are walking is what you are meeting in life, or where you are going; personal effort in trying to get somewhere; changing one's relationship with things; a period of experience you are passing through. Walking up a lane: as above, but may be memory lane. Idioms: walk over somebody; walk away with; walk off with; walk on air; walk tall; walk the streets; walk out on; walk out with.

potter The drives you are shaping your life with, or being shaped by; the self.

poverty Feelings of being inadequate; negative emotions depriving one of well being; sense of deprivation; being tight emotionally and sexually.

prayer Depending upon feelings in dream, looking for certainty in face of anxieties; seeking approval or authority for one's desires; expression of pleasure and thanks; seeking co-operation of unconscious faculties to aid one's everyday activities; attempt to channel the forces of the unconscious. See **dream as a spiritual guide**.

precipice If at the top: fear of failure; on the edge of losing confidence; near to a leap into the unknown or great change. If precipice drops into a void: death; the unconscious or unknown. If at bottom: sense of insurmountable obstacle in life.

precognition As a part of the human survival ability, the capacity to predict the future is a well-developed everyday part of life—so much so we often fail to notice it. When crossing a road we quickly take in factors related to sounds, car speeds, and our own physical condition, and predict the likelihood of being able to cross the road without injury. Based on information gathered, often unconsciously, we also attempt to assess or predict the outcome of relationships, job interviews, business ventures, and any course of action important to us. If detailed observations were made of the habits of ten people, one could predict fairly accurately what they would be doing for the next week, perhaps even pinpointing the time and place. For instance some would never visit a pub, while others would be frequently there.

Because the unconscious is the storehouse of millions of bits of observed information, and because it has a well-developed function enabling us to scan information and predict from it, some dreams forecast the future. Such predictions may occur more frequently in a dream rather than as waking insight, because few people can put aside their likes and dislikes, prejudices and hopes sufficiently to allow such information into the consciousness. While asleep some of these barriers drop and allow information to be presented.

Ed Butler's dream is about his work scene. Each detail was real and horrifying. Shortly afterwards, Rita was burnt just as in the dream. Example: 'I was startled by the muffled but unmistakable sound of a nearby explosion. While unexpected, it wasn't entirely unusual—the high energy propellants and oxidisers being synthesised and tested in the chemistry wing were hazardously unstable. When I heard the screams I froze for an instant, recognising that they could only be coming from Rita, the one woman chemist in the all male department. I rushed to the doorway of her laboratory. Peering through the smoke and fumes I saw a foot sticking out of the surrounding flames. I was only in my shirt sleeves, unprotected, not even wearing my lab coat, but I had to go into the flames. I grabbed Rita by the foot and noticed with horror that her stockings were melting from the heat. I pulled her back into the doorway and tugged at a chain which released gallons of water on her flaming body. When satisfied the fire was quenched, even though my own clothes still smouldered, I ran for the emergency phone' (from *Dream Network Bulletin,* June 1985).

Some precognitive dreams appear to go beyond this ability to predict from information already held. So far there is no theory which is commonly accepted which explains this. A not too bizarre one, however, is that our unconscious has access to a collective mind. With so much more information available, it can transcend the usual limitations when predicting from personal information. The next examples are all from Shirley G. Because of space, only three of the dreams are quoted. Nevertheless, they are typical of dreams which do not seem to fall into the category of precognitive dreams arising from unconscious scanning or information already known. Example: 'I set out to dream the winner of a horse race each day for a week. 1 Was driving down a country road and suddenly saw a glimpse of Emmerdale Farm down a side road. Following day: chosen horse Emmerdale Farm came in first. 2 Was working in a room when a man popped his head around the door and shouted excitedly "John, John, your uncle's here" and disappeared. I carried on working. Chosen horse: Uncle John. Came in first. 3 Was walking down a road, called into a house by a friend to have a chat. On the way out she opened the door and I saw a completely empty room except for a huge black fireplace. Door closed and I left the house. Chosen horse Black Fire—which I insisted would only be placed due to a fireplace. Came in 2nd.' See **ESP in dreams**.

pregnancy   A new area of one's potential or personality developing; a deepening relationship with one's unconscious is producing a new area of experience—still unexpressed, but developing. In a woman's dream: may refer to desire for a child.

If pregnant at the time of dream: anxieties, feelings or intuition regarding pregnancy and birth. Carolyn Winget and Frederic Kapp researched on the dreams of 70 pregnant women.

Those women whose dreams included a high percentage of anxiety themes were the ones who delivered their babies in the shortest time—less than ten hours. The conclusion was that by allowing feelings of anxiety in our dreams we are less influenced by anxiety in waking, and we can deal with situations more confidently.

Someone else pregnant in dream: an aspect of oneself about to bring forth new characteristics; an intuition about that person. See example under **girl**; **cave**; third example under *penis* in **body**; second example under **baby**. See also **birth**.

prehistoric   Our own primeval urges and drives, such as fear, territorial aggression, mating rituals, survival—many of these urges have not been transformed. Many of our social rituals, such as the father giving the daughter in marriage— possibly out of the need to allay aggression between males, and break the father's sexual bond with the daughter—arose from these basic drives. Also our babyhood or prenatal life.

premenstrual tension   Dr Ernest Hartmann carried out studies in connection with people who have stable sleep patterns. His aim was to define whether waking events influenced people's need for sleep. For instance, a loss of boyfriend or stress caused many young women to have an increased need for sleep. Some people who had undergone successful psychotherapy for their emotional difficulties, and some meditators, found their sleep need was decreased.

Wanting to know more about why these situations changed sleep need, Hartmann went on to study dream sleep in a group of women who suffered premenstrual tension (PMT). This group were prone to depression and irritability during PMT—records show there is an unusually high rate of murder, suicide and admission to psychiatric hospitals during this time. Although Hartmann found this group needed a little more sleep time than a control group, the main feature of change was their increased need for dreaming. Their length of time spent in dreaming increased in relationship to their depression. The conclusion reached was that one of the functions of dreaming is to help deal with difficult states of emotion or anxiety.

presents Receiving: being affirmed; feeling recognised or loved; gaining something from a relationship. Giving: giving of self, negative or positive; making love; if it is a present actually received in life, probably relates to giver and circumstances of giving. See **parcel, package**.

priest, priestess One's religious beliefs; one's relationship with religious beliefs; a sense of sin; sympathy; a sense of community; a non-sexual relationship.

prince The best aspect of the dreamer if male; one's brother or lover/boyfriend if female.

princess The best aspect of the dreamer if female; one's lover/girlfriend if male.

prison See **imprisoned**; *wolf* under **animals**; **cage, cell; escape; holding; trapped**.

prize May reflect people having praised dreamer; feeling rewarded; occasionally intuition.

propeller One's driving force or interest.

prostitute Dire sexual need unconnected to feelings of care or respect; sexuality breaking out of deadening moral restrictions. Woman's dream: unacknowledged sexual longings; feelings of 'cheapness' or guilt in sex; desire to be more free sexually. Woman dreaming another woman is prostitute: one's own hidden desires; feeling the other woman is promiscuous or might be in competition with her; uncertainty about her own sexual value. <u>Man's dream</u>: wishing a woman was more available; wish that sexual relationships were as simple as an exchange of cash; being ill at ease about his sexual practices; feeling unable to break free of sexual dependence on partner/mother.

psychodrama and dreams   In psychodrama there is no 'interpretation' of a dream. The dreamer unravels the meaning of the dream by acting it out with the help of others. The dreamer acts the main role of him or herself, and directs the helpers in the other roles. In dramatising and exploring the dream in this way, the obvious as well as the hidden meaning, associations and emotions are made clear. To finish, the dreamer is encouraged to take the dream forward, altering it to what feels more adequate and satisfying. This gives the person opportunity to express and enact what was absent in the dream, and provides release from recurring dreams, and catharsis where necessary.

pub   See **barroom**.

pulling   Doing something about a situation; positive action or expression of will. <u>Being pulled</u>: being influenced by someone or something else; being influenced by aspects of your nature which you feel at odds with; being pulled by your emotions—perhaps attracted to someone. <u>Idioms</u>: have pull; pull one's socks up; pull out; pull through; pull something off; pull strings; pull the women; pull together; pull up one's roots; pull rank.

pulse   Feelings about health; life in us; anxiety about death.

punishment, torture   Depicts the internal pain, or fear of retribution, that occurs inside us due to conflict between our social training and internal drives. The more rigidly moral we are, the more hell and punishment we dream about.

puns See **wordplay, puns**.

puppet Manipulation or feeling manipulated; feeling powerless against what feels like an external influence—the power of alcohol and drugs.

puppy See **animals, pet**.

purse Something in our nature we value and try not to lose; a woman's sexual feelings; the vagina.

pus Emotions infected by fears, self doubts, jealousy, etc.; occasionally sign of physical illness.

pushed, pushing Pushing: being positive in what you want; exerting one's will or effort of will. Being pushed: feeling coerced or taken for granted. Idioms: give someone the push; when it comes to the push; push off; push/press on; pushover; push one's luck.

pyjamas Being casual or intimate; sexuality; difficulty in facing life.

pyramid The self; wider awareness; integration of self; death.

Q

quarrel Conflict within the dreamer. See **people**—it describes some of the main areas of human conflict.

quartz Deep internal process, such as those shaping the body—consciousness can influence these, so the dream may show what relationship exists; the self. See **jewels**.

quay Departures; meetings and partings; leaving a phase of life behind, or meeting a new one, and how we encounter such changes. See also **beach**.

queen See **king**.

quicksand Feelings of insecurity; emotions which take away our confidence or sense of value or adequacy.

R

rabbit See *rabbit* under **animals**.

race One's life or taking part in life and the human race, perhaps acknowledging one's position in the 'race'; competitiveness, or feelings of competition. Racing car, bike: competitive drive; sexual energy; daring. See example in **failure**.

radar Intuition; one's subliminal sense of other people, or of what feelings or 'signals' other people are giving out.

radio Our sense of what is 'in the air'—messages we are picking up from other people or our environment. Being on radio: feeling valued; having a sense of something worth communicating.

railway Lines, tracks: a communal or generally accepted direction; habitual pathways of thought or action; rigidly fixed to certain attitudes or way of life, inflexibility. Station: moving towards something new; changing scenes, i.e. from family to work environment; leaving something behind—a relationship, one's youth; one's ability to change; effort to get somewhere in life or experience something new. Engine: the energy which takes us through life; libido. Carriages: the compartments of our life. Train journey: the aspect of our journey through life which has connections with other people and has a predetermined end, limiting our individual will; journey into self awareness; can refer to ageing and death, especially where there is a feeling of 'departing' or 'time of departure'; the train of thought or experiences which carry us through life. Leaving someone behind, being left behind: feelings about loss of spouse; or breakup of relationship. <u>Missing train</u>: feeling left out of opportunity; sense of inadequacy; held back by one's own hesitations; hidden desire to avoid change or to make one's individual journey. <u>Idioms</u>: go off the rails; lose track of something; make tracks for; on somebody's track. See **airport; ticket**.

rain   Depending on dream setting, depressed feelings or difficulties; emotions which take away enthusiasm and act as a barrier to action; tears and emotional release—an outpouring; other people's emotions 'raining' on one. Also return of feelings after a dry intellectual or unfeeling period; something which gives life or heals. <u>Idioms</u>: come rain or shine; it never rains but it pours; saving for a rainy day.

rainbow   A sense of better things to come; illusion; an awareness of the beauty and value of life in the midst of difficulties. <u>Idioms</u>: chasing a rainbow.

raincoat   See **clothes**.

rape   Example: 'I tried to turn but my legs were like lead. The man caught me and I fought. He tried to rape me but couldn't do it. As I talked to him I began to feel sorry for him and not frightened. I realised that inside he was a nice person. In the end I found I liked him so much I began to kiss him myself' (Mrs JB). Rape in dreams is very different from rape in real life, as we create our own dream, so why introduce rape? Perhaps in the above example Mrs JB discovers her own power in the situation as she realises the weakness of the male.

Example: 'A man is trying to make love and at the last moment I repel him as I know it will cause a pregnancy. When I was about 10 I was raped and for many years had a fear of men' (Anon.). This is the other side of rape. Rape in this dream may be memories, the effects of which are still visible in the life of this dreamer, causing her difficulties in warm sexuality.

Example: 'The devil attacked a woman. He was invisible. The woman turned black as he raped her. She didn't die. At this point I woke and went to the toilet. On returning to bed I continued the dream, particularly wondering what I was in conflict with in the image of the devil. I found it disturbing and frightening to be confronted by such a powerful opponent. Partly because of the rape, I realised it was repressed sexuality. I then approached the "black" woman with tenderness and this transformed the devil into available sexual or emotional energy. I tried this again and again. Each time it worked, and I could observe the devil was my sexual warmth and love which had become negative through restraint' (Neil V). In this male dream, it is the conflict with his sexuality which causes the 'devilish' rape. When he can find tenderness, the negative aspect disappears. Rape also depicts the real evil of another person disregarding our personal needs and feelings, abusing not only the body, but particularly the 'person'. Being raped by someone known: feeling anxious about sex with them; fighting off desire for them.

raven   See **birds**.

rat   See *rat* under **animals**.

reaching out   The desire for something; attempt to grasp, control or manipulate something or someone, depending on dream; extending or giving oneself. Being reached towards: feeling of being asked for something, or demands of other people.

reading   Realisation; recall from memory; scanning internal memory for information.

receptacle   For example, a jar, cup, bottle or kettle: receptive state of mind; our body and what we put into it; what feelings or thoughts we 'contain' or pour out; the womb—see first example under **fish, sea creatures**.

record, cassette, CD, computer disc   Can simply be the sort of pleasure we feel on listening to music; the impressions left on us by events, people, and therefore memory, but often memory integrated by the unconscious into insights; the impression we might leave behind at death—what remains of us; the impression we would like to give others. Idioms: for the record; track record.

recurring dreams   If we keep a record of our dreams it will soon become obvious that some of our dream themes, characters or places recur again and again. These recurrences are of various types. A certain theme may have begun in childhood and continued throughout our life—either without change, or as a gradually changing series of dreams. It might be that the feature which recurs is a setting, perhaps a house we visit again and again, but the details differ. Sometimes a series of such dreams begin after or during a particular event or phase of our life, such as puberty or marriage.

Example: 'This dream has recurred over 30 years. There is a railway station, remote in a rural area, a central waiting room with platform going round all sides. On the platform mill hundreds of people, all men I think. They are all ragged, thin, dirty and unshaven. I know I am among them. I looked up at the mountainside and there is a guard watching us. He is cruel looking, oriental, in green fatigues. On his peaked cap is a red star. He carries a machine gun. Then I looked at the men around me and I realise they are all me. Each one has my face. I am looking at myself. Then I feel fear and terror' (Anon.). The theme of the dream can incorporate anxious emotions, such as the above example, or any aspect of experience. One woman, an epileptic, reports a dream which is the

312

same in every detail and occurs every night. In general such dreams recur because there are ways the dreamer habitually responds to their internal or external world. Because their attitude or response is unchanging, the dream which reflects it remains the same. It is noticeable in those who explore their dreams using such techniques as described under **dream processing** that recurring themes disappear or change because the attitudes or habitual anxieties which gave rise to them have been met or transformed.

A recurring environment in a dream where the other factors change is not the same. We use the same words over and over in speech, yet each sentence may be different. The environment or character represents a particular aspect of oneself, but the different events which surround it show it in the changing process of our psychological growth. Where there is no such change, as in the examples above, it suggests an area of our mental emotional self is stuck in a habitual feeling state or response.

Some recurring dreams can be 'stopped' by simply receiving information about them. One woman dreamt the same dream from childhood. She was walking past railings in the town she lived in as a child. She always woke in dread and perspiration from this dream. At 40 she told her sister about it. The response was 'Oh, that's simple. Don't you remember that when you were about four we were walking past those railings and we were set on by a bunch of boys. Then I said to them, "Don't hurt us, our mother's dead!" They left us alone, but you should have seen the look on your face.' After realising the dread was connected with the loss of her mother, the dream never recurred. Another woman who repeatedly dreamt of being in a tight and frightening place, found the dream never returned after she had connected it to being in the womb.

Recurring dreams, such as that of the railings, suggest that part of the process underlying dreams is a self regulatory (homoeostatic) one. The dream process tries to present troublesome emotions or situations to the conscious mind of the dreamer to resolve the trauma or difficulty underlying the dream. An obvious example of this is seen in the recurring nightmare of a young woman who felt a piece of cloth touch her face, and repeatedly woke her family with her screams. Her brother, tiring of this, one night woke her from her screams and made her talk about her feelings. His persistence gradually revealed that she associated the cloth with the burial shroud of her grandmother. This brought to the surface grief and feelings about death she had never allowed herself to feel before. The nightmare never returned. See **nightmares; dream processing**.

reflections   Present view or opinion of ourself. Because few of us define how we really see ourself, the self image may be largely unconscious, therefore shown as a face which might be different to what we are used to seeing; how we feel others see us; may also be aspects of ourself the unconscious is showing us which we may not have been aware of.

refrigerate   To cool down our emotions or sexuality; to be cold emotionally or sexually; a romance which is cooling off; something we have put in 'cold storage'.

relatives   See **family**.

religion and dreams   In most ancient cultures, consideration and even veneration of dreams played a great part. Some groups felt that dream life was more real and important than waking life. Not only were dreams looked to for information about hunting (Eskimo groups), but also for ways of healing physical and psychological ills (Greek dream temples) and insights into the medicinal properties of herbs, barks and clays (African tribal witchdoctors). Common to most of these groups, and evident in the Old Testament, was also the sense that through dreams one had awareness of the transcendental or supersensible. St Peter's dream of the sheet and unclean animals was a turning point in the history of western society —as was Constantine's dream of his victory if he used the symbol of Christianity.

At its most fundamental, the human religious sense emerges out of several factors. One is the awareness of existing amidst external and internal forces of nature which cause us to feel vulnerable and perhaps powerless. Such natural processes as illness, death, growth and decay, earthquakes, the seasons, confront us with things which are often beyond our ability to control. Considering the information and resources of the times, one of religion's main functions in the past was the attempted control of the 'uncertain' factors in human life, and help towards psychological adjustment to vulnerability. Religions were the first social programmes aiding the human need for help and support towards emotional, mental, physical and social health and maturity. Even if primitive, such programmes helped groups of people to gain a common identity and live in reasonable harmony together. Like a computer program which is specific to a particular business, such programmes were specific to a particular group, and so are outdated in today's need for greater integration with other races. Religions also offered some sort of concept of and connection with the roots of being.

Example: 'For two nights running I have dreamt the same nightmare. I am in a chapel walking down the first flight of several flights of steps when I hear loud noises behind me. I am told to run, being warned of the soldiers who ride the cavalry horses right down the steps, and who run you over if you are in their way. The horses are fierce and they absolutely race down the steps at the same time every day, and you literally have to lock yourself away in a nearby room which is a long way down the chapel. I ran into the room hearing the pounding of the horses' hooves. It was a terrible pandemonium in that chapel. In the room were school children the same age as me and some perhaps younger' (Maria H). Maria, who is 16, in describing her dream says she had recently been confronted with whether to have a sexual relationship with her boyfriend. Religion, represented by the chapel, is Maria's way of locking out her powerful sexual urges. Many dreams show that religion, as a set of beliefs, is used as a way of avoiding anxiety in the face of life's uncertainties. For many people, the rigid belief system helps them to avoid uncertainty in making decisions.

Dreams also portray and define the aspect of human experience in which we sense a kinship with all life forms. This is the side of spiritual experience through which we find a connection with the roots of our being. While awake we might see the birth of a colt and feel the wonder of emergence and newness; the struggle to stand up and survive; the miracle of physical and sexual power which can be accepted or feared. In looking in the faces of fellow men and women we see something of what they have done in this strange and painful wonder we call life. We see whether they have been crushed by the forces confronting them; whether they have become rigid; or whether, through some common miracle, they have been able to carry into their mature years the laughter, the crying, the joy, the ability to feel pain, that are the very signs of life within the human soul. These things are sensed by us all, but seldom organised into a comprehensive view of life, and an extraction of meaning. Often it is only in our dreams, through the ability the unconscious has to draw out the significance of such widely divergent experiences, that we glimpse the unity behind phenomena which is an essential of spiritual life, i.e. we all have a life, we breathe, we have come from a mother, so share a universal experience.

Example: To quote J.B. Priestley from his book *Rain Upon Godshill:* 'Just before I went to America, during the exhausting weeks when I was busy with my Time Plays, I had such a dream, and I think it left a greater impression on my mind than any experience I had ever known before, awake or in dreams, and said more to me about this life than any book I have ever read. The setting of the dream was quite simple, and owed something to the fact that not long before my wife had visited the lighthouse here at St Catherine's to do some bird ringing. I dreamt I was standing at the top of a very high tower, alone, looking down upon myriads of birds all flying in one direction; every kind of bird was there, all the birds in the world. It was a noble sight, this vast aerial river of birds. But now in some mysterious fashion the gear was changed, and time speeded up, so that I saw generations of birds, watched them break their shells, flutter into life, mate, weaken, falter and die. Wings grew only to crumble; bodies were sleek, and then, in a flash bled and shrivelled; and death struck everywhere at every second. What was the use of all this blind struggle towards life, this eager trying of wings, this hurried mating, this flight and surge, all this gigantic meaningless effort? As I stared down, seeming to see every creature's ignoble little history almost at a glance, I felt sick at heart. It would be better if not one of them, if not one of us, had been born, if the struggle ceased for ever. I stood on my tower, still alone, desperately unhappy. But now the gear was changed again, and the time went faster still, and it was rushing by at such a rate, that the birds could not show any movement, but were like an enormous plain sown with feathers. But along this plain, flickering through the bodies themselves, there now passed a sort of white flame, trembling, dancing, then hurrying on; and as soon as I saw it I knew that this white flame was life itself, the very quintessence of being; and then it came to me, in a rocket burst of ecstasy, that nothing mattered, nothing could ever matter, because nothing else was real but this quivering and hurrying lambency of being. Birds, men and creatures not yet shaped and coloured, all were of no account except so far as this flame of life travelled through them. It left nothing to mourn over behind it; what I had thought was tragedy was mere emptiness or a shadow show; for now all real feeling was caught and purified and danced on ecstatically with the white flame of life. I had never before felt such deep happiness as I knew at the end of my dream of the tower and the birds.'

Some North American Indians developed the totem out of similar processes. In one generation a person might learn to plant a seed and eat the results. Later someone might see that through fertilisation more food was produced. Still later someone found that by irrigating, still more improvement was made. No one individual was responsible for such vital cultural information, and the collective information is bigger than any one person, yet individuals can partake of it and add to it. The totem represented such subtle realities, as it might in a modern dream; as Christ might in today's unconscious. That older cultures venerated their collective information, and that modern humans seem largely apathetic to it, shows how our 'religion' has degenerated. Yet utilising the power of the unconscious to portray the subtle influences which impinge upon us, and building the information gained into our response to life, is deeply important.

With the growth of authoritarian structures in western religion, and the dominance of the rational mind over feeling values, dreams have been pushed into the background. With this change has developed the sense that visionary dreams were something which 'superstitious' cultural groups had in the past. Yet thoroughly modern men and women still meet Christ powerfully in dreams and visions. Christ still appears to them as a living being. The transcendental, the collective or universal enters their life just as frequently as ever before. Sometimes it enters with insistence and power, because a too rational mind has led to an unbalance in the psyche—a balance in which the waking and rational individuality is one pole, and the feeling, connective awareness of the unconscious is the other.

Although it is tempting to think of the transcendent as ethereal or unreal, the religious in dreams is nearly always a symbol for the major processes of maturing in human life. We are the hero/ine who meets the dangers of life outside the womb, who faces growth, ageing and death. The awe and deep emotions we unconsciously feel about such heroic deeds are depicted by religious emotion.

See **angel**; *Christ, rebirth* and *Devil* under **archetypes**; **church**; **evil**; **fish, sea creatures**; example in *whale* under **fish, sea creatures**; **heaven**; **hell**; *sweets* under **food**; **dream as spiritual guide**. See also **hero/ine**; **mass**; **masturbation**; **old**; **paralysis**; **colours**; *sheep* under **animals**.

religious themes   See **angel**; *Christ* and *Devil* under **archetypes**; **church**; **evil**; **heaven**; **hell**; **religion and dreams**; **dream as spiritual guide**.

remembering dreams   Considering that each of us has four or five periods of dreaming each night, most of our dreams are forgotten. But for people who observe family or friends regularly remembering a dream, and yet themselves are seldom if ever able to recall one, the question arises as to why such a wide divergence occurs.

There are many different reasons why dreams may be forgotten. The most obvious is that we do not give enough attention to our dreaming process. When people become intrigued by what they might be dreaming, and develop a motivation to remember, they frequently start recalling several dreams a week. From this standpoint, the reason why some people have always remembered might be that they have always been either intrigued or anxious about their nightly dramas.

The way we rise in the morning has an effect upon this type of memory. If our attention is immediately turned outwards on waking, there is little hope of recalling a dream unless it has great power, as might a nightmare. Spending a few moments leaving our mind open to memory aids recall. Any visual, or even muscular activity, will fill consciousness with new and powerful impressions which might obliterate the subtler impressions of dreaming. Rorschach suggested not opening the eyes, and remaining physically still. Tests also showed that passage of time, even a few minutes, between dreaming and attempting to remember causes many dreams to fragment and be lost. So any attempts to remember need one to record the dream quickly, by speaking it to one's bedmate, using a tape recorder by one's bed, or writing it down.

Some dreams have rather misty or fragmentary imagery and theme, while others are clear, concise and dynamic. These latter are more easily remembered. There may be times when we sleep with longer periods of wakefulness, perhaps due to feeling cold, or uncomfortable in a strange bed, which cause us to remember as we are nearer consciousness. Because dreams occur in cycles during the night, if something wakes us during a dream cycle the memory is easier, if only because less time has elapsed since occurrence. So another method of capturing a dream is to have one's alarm gently sound prior to the time one usually wakes. The last hour or so of sleep includes a long period of dreaming, so waking in this period with intent to remember can often capture the quarry.

There are also psychological reasons for forgetfulness. Dreams often deal with past areas of experience which we do not wish to remember, or would rather not be aware of. If we find it difficult to feel emotions, or feel uncomfortable with them, it is highly likely we repress dream memory, as dreams have a base of high feelings. Experiments have shown that during dreaming our heartbeat, body movements and breathing frequently reflect intensified emotions. Also, research into what areas of the brain produce dreaming suggest that dreams may be from the 'visceral brain', which is largely non verbal. If temperamentally we find feeling qualities a foreign language, connecting with a dream would need to be a learnt skill.

rent Interpersonal responsibility; what we 'pay' for what we have or want. <u>Collecting rent</u>: what we want from others, or what we are getting from them in the way of feelings, influences.

reptiles, lizards, snakes   Our basic spinal and lower brain reactions, such as fight or flight, reproduction, attraction or repulsion, sex drive, need for food and reaction to pain. This includes the fundamental evolutionary ability to change and the urge to survive—very powerful and ancient processes. Our relationship with the reptile in our dreams depicts our relatedness to such forces in us, and how we deal with the impulses from the ancient part of our brain.

Modern humans face the difficulty of developing an independent identity and yet keeping a working relationship with the primitive, thus maturing/bringing the primitive into an efficiently functioning connection with the present social world. The survival urge at base might be kill or run, but it can be transformed into the ambition which helps, say, an opera singer meet difficulties in her career. Also the very primitive has in itself the promise of the future, of new aspects of human consciousness. This is because many extraordinary human functions take place unconsciously, in the realm of the reptile/spine/lower brain/right brain/autonomic nervous system. Being unconscious they are less amenable to our waking will. They function fully only in some fight or flight, survive or die, situations. If we begin to touch these with consciousness, as we do in dreams, new functions are added to consciousness. See *The dream as extended perception* under **ESP and dreams**.

frog   Unconscious life or growth processes which can lead to transformation (the frog/prince story); the growth from childhood vulnerability—tadpole to frog—therefore the process of life in general and its wisdom. Frogspawn: sperm, ovum and reproduction.

lizard   Example: 'My wife and I saw a large lizard on the wall near a banana. It was there to catch the flies. The lizard turned so it was facing away from us—head up the wall. We then were able to see it had large wing-like flaps which spread from its head in an inverted V. With amazement we saw on these flaps wonderful pictures, in full colour, of birds. In fleeting thoughts I wondered if the bird "paintings" were to attract birds, or were some form of camouflage. But I felt certain the lizard had "painted" these wonderful pictures with its unconscious art' (David T). Generally, a lizard is very much the same as a snake, except it lacks the poisonous aspect; awareness of unconscious or instinctive drives, functions and processes. In the above dream, the banana is both David's pleasure and sexuality, while the lizard is the creativity emerging from his unconscious through the attention he is giving it—he is looking at the lizard. <u>Chameleon</u>: either one's desire to fade into the background, or adaptability.

snake Example: 'A small snake about a foot long had dropped down my shirt neck. I could feel it on the left side of my neck. Fearing it was poisonous and might bite me, I moved very slowly. At one point I put my head on the ground, hoping the snake would wish to crawl away. It did not. Then I was near an elephant I loved, and hoped it would remove the snake. It did not. Even as I slept I felt the snake was an expression of the attitude of not sharing myself with anybody except family' (David T). For months prior to the above dream David had experienced a great deal of neck pain. After discussing the dream with his wife, and realising much of his thinking and feeling was inturned, the pain disappeared. So the snake was both 'poisoner' and 'healer'. This may be why snakes are used as a symbol of the medical profession. The Hebrew word for the serpent in the Garden of Eden is Nahash, which can be translated as blind impulsive urges, such as our instinctive drives.

So, generally, snakes depict many different things, but usually the life process. If we think of a person's life from conception to death, we see a flowing moving event, similar in many ways to the speeded up films of a seed growing into a plant, flowering and dying. The snake depicts the force or energy behind that movement and purposiveness—the force of life which leads us both to growth and death. That energy —like electricity in a house, which can be heat, power, sound and vision—lies behind all our functions. So in some dreams the snake expresses our sexuality; in others the rising of that energy up our body to express itself as digestion—the intestinal snake; as the healing or poisonous energy of our emotions and thoughts.

Example: 'I was in a huge cathedral, the mother church. I wanted to go to the toilet/gents. As I held my penis to urinate it became a snake and reached down to the urinal to drink. It was thirsty. I struggled with it, pulling it away from the unclean liquid. Still holding it I walked to a basin and gave it pure water to drink' (Bill A). Here the connection between snake and sexuality is obvious. But the snake is not just Bill's penis. It is the direction his sexual urges take him he is struggling with. Out of his sense of love and connection with life— the cathedral—he wants to lift his drive towards something which will not leave him with a sense of uncleanness. Snake in connection with any hole: sexual relatedness.

A snake biting us: unconscious worries about our health, frustrated sexual impulse, our emotions turned against ourselves as internalised aggression, can poison us and cause very real illness, so may be shown as the biting snake. Snake biting others: biting remarks; a poisonous tongue. A crowned or light-encircled snake: when our 'blind impulses' or instinctive or unconscious urges and functions are in some measure integrated with our conscious will and insight, this is seen as the crowned snake or even winged snake. It shows real self awareness and maturity. In coils of snake: feeling bound in the 'blind impulses' or habitual drives and feeling responses. Instincts and habits can be redirected, as illustrated by Hercules' labours. Snake with tail in mouth: sense of the circle of life—birth, growth, reproduction, aging, death, rebirth; the eternal. Snake coiling up tree, pole, cross: the blind instinctive forces of life emerging into conscious experience—in other words the essence of human experience with its involvement in pain, pleasure, time and eternity; the process of personal growth or evolution; healing because personal growth often moves us beyond old attitudes or situations which led to inner tension or even sickness. Snake in grass: sense or intuition of talk behind your back; danger; sneakiness. Colours: green, our internal life process directed, perhaps through satisfied feelings, love and creativity, into a healing process or one which leads to our personal growth and positive change; white, eternal aspect of our life process, or becoming conscious of it; blue, religious feelings or coldness in relations. See **colours; anxiety dreams;** *death and rebirth, the self* under **archetypes; dreams and Ancient Greece;** *cellar* under **house, buildings; hypnosis and dreams; jungle; paralysis.**

toad Deeply unconscious drives and processes, such as the biological activities to do with intestines and cells, so what we might feel squeamish about—might therefore connect with abortion; the power of life in us; a cold-blooded or ugly part of ourself.

rescue Intervention in our life by someone else's action or emotions; something which changes the situation one is in, or changes mood. Rescuing someone else, or animal: the effort we make, or what we have put into dealing with a relationship difficulty or an internal feeling state. Also can relate to one's desire to do something admirable or noble, such as saving souls, helping someone in distress, and thus having power in life. Rescuing someone of opposite sex: breaking the bonds of emotion, sexuality or dependence which tie us to parents or others.

restaurant, cafe Sociability; search for emotional or sexual satisfaction; hunger for company or sexuality. See **food.**

riding   Idioms: along for the ride; a rough ride; ride something out; let it ride; ride roughshod; take somebody for a ride; riding high. See **car**; **horse**.

right   See **left, right**.

ring   One's wholeness; one's essential self. Wedding, engagement ring: the state of the relationship, as in example below, where Mary is 'choking' on or 'can't swallow' her relationship. Example: 'If I swallow I am going to swallow and choke on my engagement ring. I seem to be trying to stop a ring going down my throat' (Mary S). Heirloom, parents' ring: psychological influence of the family or parent, even if dead. Idioms: have a hollow ring; have a true ring; run rings round someone. See **shapes**, **symbols**.

ritual   See **ceremony**.

river   The images used in drama of rivers helps us understand their symbolism. The river can be calm, in flood, or even dried up, representing our state of feeling about our energy, sexuality and emotions—the energy which as anxiety can cause illness, or as pleasure sustain health. Similarly we can drown in the river (drown in despair), float on it, be carried along by prevailing feelings, or cross over, suggesting change or even death. Generally, then, it depicts the feelings which flow through us or we are immersed in; the process of life in our body, connecting with emotions, sexuality and changes of mood; the flow and events of our life or destiny. Being in river: being influenced by or immersed in one's internal flow of feelings and energies. Crossing river: making great changes. If one is in the water to cross, it means meeting a lot of emotions in the process of change. Seeing someone cross river: feelings about death; same as falling in river. Going against current: resisting one's own feelings; going against prevailing influences or attitudes; going back to the womb.

<u>Directing a river</u>: channelling one's emotional or sexual energy. <u>Stagnant river</u>: restrained feelings or sexuality; holding oneself back.

road One's prevailing direction in or approach to life. This direction/approach can be either self created out of one's own actions or decisions or arise out of other people's or social influence; one's predispositions; any direction you are taking, such as a love affair, a business, a new attitude; one's public activities.

Example: 'My dream is of an eternal journey, which takes a road that turns into a circle or maze that is endless. Behind me is a large fat young man with blond hair. I can't get along and he catches up with me, I say "We can't go back we must struggle on." He takes my wrist. I am trying to hide my fear of him and the pathway, when I wake up' (JP). JP feels her life is something she must 'struggle on' with, but it is an endless circle of confusion in which she gets nowhere. This illustrates the road as a symbol of one's approach to life. Perhaps it is her fear which creates this sense of life for her.

Example: 'Janet my wife was cycling beside me. We came to the end of a short road. I said we should turn left, but Janet thought we ought to turn right. We got out into the middle of the road without turning either way' (Arthur P). <u>Crossroads, deciding which road to take</u>: Arthur's dream shows crossroads as depicting our many choices. Arthur's choice involves his attempt to include his wife's needs. The size, richness, cleanliness, amount of people, situation of the road shows how you inwardly see either the direction chosen, or the choices confronting you. See **crossroads**.

Example: 'Walking alone along a road through a small town. I was heading for a place that a group of people, in a street parallel to mine, were also heading for. A person from the group tried to persuade me that the right way to get to the place was along the street the group was walking. I knew the street did not matter, only the general direction. The person was quite disturbed by my independence. It made him or her feel uncertain to have their leader apparently questioned. I felt uncertain too for a moment. Then I walked on and came to an open stretch of ground' (Tony C). Tony's dream shows how roads can represent different sorts of social behaviour. To choose one's individual 'road' may be difficult, because others are so sure they know best. Patterns of behaviour such as needing an authority figure to follow are also here depicted as a road.

Road behind: the past; what you have already achieved or done. Road ahead: the future; aspects of self not yet expressed; new areas of endeavour. Fork in road: something to decide; parting from accustomed way or relationship. Unpaved road, track off to one side: going off the beaten track or being side-tracked. Lane: individual direction. Known road: one's associated feelings with that road. Running out into road: danger. Going wrong way up one way street: going against prevailing attitudes. Going out from house into road: how others see you; being in public view. Idioms: on the road to recovery; road hog; end of the road; take to the road; middle of the road; the high road to. See **track**.

rock Reality, but not just physical reality; the physical world; the eternal as it is met by our waking self; stability; a remembrance of something or someone important to us. If the rock is sculpted: what our life has expressed to enrich our own spiritual or eternal nature. A small rock, stone: the unconscious sees our personal existence as a part of the material the cosmos is made of—another pebble on the beach. The rock portrays how we shape the material of our nature through our life—similar to the parable of the talents. See **stone**.

rocket Male sexuality; energy to gain greater awareness of oneself.

roles   The different people in our dreams, such as doctor, lawyer, business person or tramp, in general represent the different abilities, weaknesses or interests we have ourself. Even if we know the 'role model', it still depicts that person's quality or skill in ourself. The only difference might be that our personal reactions to that particular doctor or school-teacher, say, will also play a part. Roles often play an important part in our self image. Without an appreciated social role we may feel uncertain and ineffective. Maturity might require the acceptance that we are nothing, but can be many things. See **baker; beggar; chemist; gardener; inventor; nurse; potter; victim; waiting**.

actor/actress   Depending on context, can represent yourself wanting public acclaim, or not expressing real self, acting a role. Just as someone's life may be 'acted out' on stage or in a film, so actors may represent a showing of facets of your own life, especially inner life; the false image we may be expressing; our attempt to impress others, or act a part. Idioms: act a part; act on (impulse or information); acting up; caught in the act; as the actress said to the bishop. See **theatre**.

astrologer   Intuitions, thoughts or concern about your future; intuition concerning your innate abilities or qualities, and where they might lead.

authority figure   Might depict what has arisen in your life out of relationship with father; one's relationship with authority; a view of how one uses power or authority.

bus conductor   How we give someone authority in a group, although we may be more capable than they; the part of self concerned with paying our way; feelings helping or standing in the way of reaching our goal.

captain   The daring, doing, positive side of self; how we relate to father figures or dominant male authoritative men; the side of our nature which is capable or is in touch with the wider issues in our life, and makes decisions out of comprehensive awareness.

captive, prisoner Many emotions, anxieties, moods or ideas 'captivate' us, or act as means of denying free expression to our own talents, sexuality or well being. Fear of illness might stop us going on holiday, thoughts that only the privileged can make it in business might stop us developing ideas we have. In this sense we, or areas of our potential, can be imprisoned or made captive. Using **dream processing** and the allied methods can help to define what is restraining us and find freedom from such restraints. See **imprisoned**; *wolf* under **animals**; **cage, cell**; **escape**; **holding**; **trapped**.

carpenter The creative but practical part of us; the side of us which tends to create with old ideas and attitudes (the wood) but which perhaps is not very radical; sometimes the self. See *Christ* under **archetypes.**

conjurer Depending on dream, might be the ability to change our moods or attitudes easily, which is a commonplace yet at the same time magical ability humans have—in this way we might pull out of a deep depression and suddenly become creative; or perhaps the youthful side of self which forever wants magical or idealistic answers to life and its relationships.

convict See *captive, prisoner* above in this entry.

cook The active and practical side of our nature which, by working at it, can transform inedible aspects of a relationship or situation into something which satisfies us; the sense of responsibility which 'feeds the family'; female reproductive ability—puts one thing in the oven (sperm and ovum) and out comes something else (baby); need or ability to nourish oneself and provide for physical, emotional, mental and spiritual needs. Idioms: cook the books; cook someone's goose; cook up; what's cooking.

cripple Emotional hurts; parts of us injured by trauma or twisted by such withheld feelings as anger or jealousy.

dentist Depends on your relationship with dentists. Fear of being hurt; the courage and ability to deal with painful areas of experience; father's distressing sexual attentions—or rape feelings; need for care of what comes out of our mouth, such as things we say, opinions, criticism.

doctor Our dependence upon authority figure for a sense of wholeness, or to deal with anxiety; the healing process within us—or the unconscious wisdom we have concerning our body's needs and well being. The doctor might give us advice, for instance; anxiety about health; desire for intimacy or to be looked at. Idioms: doctor something; have an animal doctored; doctor the accounts.

farmer Feeling easy with sexuality and material world; practical down-to-earth feelings; care of 'animal' side of self; earthy wisdom. See **farm, farmyard**.

fireman How we deal with our passions or outbursts of emotion or anger; dealing with misplaced energy.

judge Feelings of guilt; self criticism or judgment; how we are relating to someone whose judgment means a lot to us.

leader Our relationship with authority figures, or the generally accepted ideas which people take to guide their life; the relationship with the leader might show how much responsibility we are taking for our own life; feelings of being responsible, as in parenthood or professional capacity.

lover One's lover: present feelings or fears about the relationship. Dream lover, someone else: your sexual desires or needs; sexuality which is either not accepted or not expressed in present relationship. See **affair**.

magician Sometimes the self—the magical abilities the unconscious has which are seldom tapped; one's potential. Black

<u>magician</u>: the negative or selfish ways we might use our power or internal insights and wisdom. See **conjurer**.

monk   Influence of religious teachings; difficulty in meeting sexuality and emotional and financial independence; awareness of spiritual.

nun   Sexual purity; fear of sex; religious feelings; one's sister.

pirate   Our own piratical or plundering urges or what we feel plundered by; sense of having someone else take what is important to us.

policeman/woman   Sense of what is socially right or wrong—our feelings of what others would dislike or punish us for; our social rules of conduct rather than our innermost sense of rightness, therefore inhibitions; feelings of guilt or shame. <u>Policewoman</u>: more emphasis on moral issues connected with feeling values.

sailor   One's ability to meet the storms and calms of life.

salesman   Someone seeking to influence you; opportunity; one's business sense. <u>In woman's dream</u>: perhaps a hint of things you want—a lover, a new romance—that you are not admitting to yourself.

scientist   Creative rational mind; intellectual curiosity; in some dreamers the fear of rational critical people—or of looking at oneself analytically.

secretary   The other woman; practical business side of self supporting creative action.

seductress, seducer   One's sexual drives which have not matured into satisfactory expression in relationship with real person; sexual longings unattached to present partner; fantasy of being loved.

331

servant Social roles—top dog/underdog feelings; feeling you are treated like a servant, or treating someone else as a servant.

shepherd Being in contact with instinctive or feeling reactions in self; the Self. See *farmer* within this entry; *Christ* under **archetypes**.

shopkeeper May relate to work if dreamer works in shop or store; relates to how one supplies one's needs or who supplies one's needs—therefore might show feelings about parents. It might throw light on how you gain your needs from other people.

soldier If <u>dreamer in opposition with soldier</u>: things we feel in conflict with; our internal conflicts and involvement with the 'wars' or trauma we have experienced. If <u>dreamer is soldier</u> or <u>united with soldiers</u>: our willingness or ability to face internal conflicts and hurts. <u>Military service</u>: feeling bound by social or personal disciplines or restrictions; learning strengths and self discipline to meet internal conflicts.

stranger Unknown aspect of oneself; part we avoid 'meeting' in everyday life.

teacher Relationship with authority figure; learning situations; something to learn or teach.

thief Fear we might lose something, or that what we have gained will be taken; unacknowledged desires; desire to take from others; conflict of will. See **stealing**.

victim <u>Being the victim</u>: feeling victimised; often depicts the chip on our shoulder. We may have been hurt at some time and go on bemoaning our fate. The 'chip' may be useful in avoiding real responsibility or in hiding from trying out one's positive creativity or sexuality. Thus we avoid possible failure or further hurt. <u>Other person as victim</u>: may still be as above; the hurts and damage received from relationship with others;

passive anger—by being the victim we get someone else to be a bastard and can thus sneer at them because we have manipulated them; hidden desires to avoid success, perhaps as a way of hurting parent. See **victim**.

waiter/waitress Wanting to be waited on; feeling you are being made to wait on others; wordplay for waiting around for someone else.

room   See **house, buildings**.

root   See **tree**.

rope   <u>Tied by</u>: what is holding us back from expressing; strength turned against oneself. <u>Tying someone else</u>: restraints we use to hold back particular parts of our feelings or drives; sometimes sexuality.

rose   See **flowers**.

round   See **shapes, symbols**.

ruins   See **house, buildings**.

running   See **postures, movement, body language**.

rust   Negligence; sense of ageing; seeing how transitory worldly things are.

S

sack   The womb; death; getting the sack.

sacrifice   May refer directly to feeling someone is or will make you a scapegoat; sometimes connected with decision making—we cannot have all things at once, so we are willing to sacrifice one thing for another; occurs in some dreams where a change is occurring in one's personality—parts of our nature we once identified with can now be allowed to die to the process of growth. Also sacrifice depicts a strange fact of human psychology. Some aspects of oneself grow in strength and maturity by letting them 'die'. While we maintain a behaviour pattern or belief, it stays in its habitual form: when we let go of it, a new approach can emerge.

saddle   Influencing something or somebody by our will; feeling constrained to support someone else; in control. If thrown from saddle: out of control.

sadism   Anger from childhood hurts; sometimes the inability to face the real emotional pain of one's own hurts as a child; lack of real sexual satisfaction, perhaps because of lack of emotional development.

sailing   How we are handling or feeling about our life. The images in sailing lend themselves to depict human endeavours to work with the tides and influences of life. Dealing well with wind, waves: suggests being able to meet internal and external pressures, emotions and drives, and using them to advantage. Being overwhelmed, sinking: finding emotional, sexual drives and anxieties too much to cope with. See **boat, ship**. Idioms:

plain sailing; sail against the wind; sail close to the wind; sail into something; sail under false colours; set sail; trim one's sails; take the wind out of someone's sails.

sailor   See **roles**.

salad   Sometimes a direct reference to the body's need for such foods; lack of meaty (sexual) experience.

salt   The subtle qualities we bring to our activities which transform them from empty trivialities into meaning or savour; zest; may sometimes refer to the body's reaction to salt. Idioms: above/below the salt (in or out of honour); salt mine; salt something away; with a pinch of salt; worth one's salt; salt into a wound; salt of the earth.

sand   Lack of security; passage of time; lack of emotion or nourishment. See **desert**. Idioms: built on sand; sands of time are running out; bury one's head in the sand.

Satan   The things in self, or in the world, which we feel frightened of, or feel we cannot control; the influence of dry intellectualism or materialism. See *devil* under **archetypes**.

satellite   Communication between the more global awareness of the unconscious and our everyday waking self. If in satellite: might suggest loss of a down-to-earth attitude; global view. Being attacked from satellite, UFO: thinking and feeling has been split from realistic evaluation, perhaps because internal pain is scrambling communications.

sausage   Penis or male sexuality; down-to-earth experience. Idioms: not a sausage.

335

savings   Sense of security; what we have not expressed; one's potential.

saw   See **tools**.

scales   Justice; conscience; trying to make a decision—weighing the information; fair play; trying to find a balance.

scar   Influences still remaining from past hurt.

school   The learning process; what we learnt at school—not lessons but interrelationships, class structure, competitiveness, authority, mortification, group preferences, etc.; habits of behaviour or feeling reactions developed during those years—puberty occurs at this time, and confronts us with many new feelings, choices and drives. Schoolfriend: your own attitudes developed in school, as you are 'meeting' them in the present. School clothes: social attitudes or moral rules learnt at school.
   Example: 'I am back at school on the first day of the new school year. At this point it can vary slightly, but I always feel out of place, usually because I am older than the other girls now or—most common—because my uniform is incorrect and it is time for assembly—I went to a very strict convent school. There is always some feeling of panic and quite often loneliness' (PH). PH is still uncomfortable about who she is as a person. The influence of the school years still nags at her, that she ought to be other than she is. Not having a nature that easily conformed, she was led to feel isolated and an alien.
   Places in school: particular abilities we have. Library: our knowledge and learning ability; stored information. Gymnasium: taking risks in learning something new; daring; physical health. Classroom: study; relationship with authority.
   Example: 'In the bathroom area, a school class was being held, so I had to wait for my bath, steam would be bad for the books. I didn't have any soap with me but I was going to

wash my hair and could use the shampoo' (Leonie K). Leonie is getting rid of attitudes or a self image developed at school, shown as shampooing her hair. The new attitudes of letting off steam would not have been acceptable at school.

Idioms: of the old school; tell tales out of school; old school tie; well schooled. See *schoolteacher* under **roles**.

science, sleep and dreams   In 1937 through the use of the electroencephalograph (EEG) measuring tiny electrical brain impulses, Loomis and his associates discovered that the form of brainwaves changes with the onset of sleep. The next leap forward in understanding came when Aserinsky and Kleitman found rapid eye movements (REM) in 1953. In 1957 the REM were linked with dreaming. This defined sleep into two different observable states, REM sleep, and NREM (non-rapid eye movement or non-rem) sleep. Within NREM three different stages have been identified. These are defined by the different EEG patterns of electrical activity in the brain. They are measured by the height (amplitude) of the brain waves and frequency of up and down movement. There are also electrical changes occurring in the muscles (measured using an electromyograph or EMG), and in movement of the eyeballs (measured using an electro-oculograph or EOG).

While awake the height is low and frequency fast. As we relax prior to sleep the EEG shifts to what are called alpha waves, at 8 to 12 cps (cycles per second). Stage one of sleep is the transition between this drowsy state of alpha waves to sleeping, in which theta waves occur, at 3 to 7 cps. In this first stage we experience random images and thoughts. This lasts about 10 minutes, followed by stage two, in which 'sleep spindles' occur which have 12 to 14 cps on the EEG. These last from 1/2 to 2 seconds, with K complexes following, which are slow large EEG waves. About half our sleep period is spent in this second stage of sleep. Deep sleep is reached when our brain exhibits delta waves, with 1/2 to 2 cps.

After approximately an hour and a half from falling into

deep sleep, an exciting change occurs. We return to level two and REM occur. Suddenly the brain is alert and active, though the person is asleep and difficult to wake. This level has been called paradoxical sleep because of this fact. Voluntary muscular activity is suppressed and the body is essentially paralysed. Morrison has pointed out that, although the brain is transmitting full muscular activity messages, these are usually suppressed by an area of the brain in the pons. But bursts of short actions occur, such as rapid eyeball jerks, twitches of the muscles, changes in the size of the pupil, contractions in the middle ear, and erection of the penis. It may be that similar excitation occurs in the vagina. Also, 'autonomic storms' occur during which large erratic changes occur in heart rate, blood pressure, breathing rate and in other autonomic nervous system functions. These are the changes accompanying our dreams.

If we slept for eight hours, a typical pattern would be to pass into delta sleep, stay there for about 70 to 90 minutes, then return to stage two and dream for about five minutes. We then move back into delta sleep, stay for a short period and shift back to level two, but without dreaming, then back into level three. The next return to stage two is longer, almost an hour, with a period of dreaming lasting about 19 minutes, and also a short period of return to waking. There is only one short period of return to stage three sleep which occurs nearly four hours after falling asleep. From there on we remain in level two sleep, with three or four lengthening periods of dreaming, and returns to brief wakefulness. The average amount of body shifting is once every 15 minutes.

1 In undergoing 205 hours of sleep deprivation, four healthy males showed various physiological and psychological changes. Some of these were headache, lack of concentration, hallucination, memory loss, tremor and, in some, paranoia. In all cases one night's sleep restored normal functioning.

2 One in ten people who complain of excessive daytime drowsiness suffer from sleep apnoea, which is a stoppage of breathing while asleep.

3 A condition called narcolepsy causes sufferers to fall asleep at inappropriate times—while making love, walking, playing tennis, working.

4 As we age we usually sleep less. Our REM sleep in particular decreases sharply.

scissors   Cutting remarks; cynicism; sharp tongue; anger; fear of or feelings about castration (female castration expresses in cutting off breasts)—the cutting off of developing sexual characteristics in body and mind; sometimes refers to separation or independence, as in cutting umbilical cord, or death; cutting something or someone out of one's life; cutting off or cutting out feelings.

screw   Male sexuality; intercourse; security. Idioms: got a screw loose or missing; put the screw on someone; have a screw; screw you.

scurf   Thoughts; ideas; opinions.

sea   Most activities which underlie our physical and mental life are beyond our awareness. Occasionally something—an ache in the chest, a strange emotion which unsettles us—may emerge into consciousness, then disappear. The sea, with its surface and hidden depths, lends itself to depicting this human experience of known and unknown regarding self. The enormity of the sea is also a visible image of the enormity of our own inner world, most of it unknown, and also the relationship we have with the universe, which we exist in yet know so little about. The sea holds vast treasures, curiosities, and our history—not simply because life emerged from the sea, or our blood is as salt as the ancient sea, but because so many ships and shorelines are now beneath the waves. Sometimes these can be recovered, and this depicts our remembering or making conscious.

Example: 'My husband and I were standing looking at the sea's surface. It was just falling night. I saw a mass of dark shapes, thought it would be a school of fish. Then we were looking at water birds, maybe ducks, again dark shapes as the light had almost gone. Then there was a hole in the sea, like a belly button, I was wondering what it was, how was it being made, was there something under the water? Something very big was coming up to the surface very close to me. It shot me to wake' (Ginny Q). Ginny and her husband had been exploring the content of their dreams. The image of the sea shows Ginny sensing there are enormous depths to her own being, and something big—a previously unconscious complex of insights and feelings—is becoming conscious.

So, generally the sea represents the boundary between unconscious and conscious; our processes of life and the origins of our life; the wisdom, still unverbalised because locked in process rather than insight, of our existence; source of the huge life drives, such as that which urges us towards independence, mating and parenthood; a symbol of infinite energy or consciousness, in which human existence is only a tiny part. Example: 'A small speed boat was at sea. But the sea dissolved anybody who fell in. One man fell in but held himself together as a blob of water and jumped back to the speedboat. I remember the words "The sea is a great solvent" (Tim P). Tim is aware of his unconscious sense of being a part of the huge sea of life or energy. In it one might lose one's sense of identity. In the end, identity is 'held together' by one's own belief in oneself.

Going under the sea: bringing internal contents to consciousness; remembering the womb experience; letting our ego surrender a little; looking at death. If there is a sense of hugeness, depth: going beyond the boundaries of experience usually set up by our conscious self or ego. Waves: impulses, feelings and emotions, such as sexuality, anxiety, anger. Tide:

rising and falling of feelings such as love, pleasure or sexuality; may refer to aging when going out; tide in our affairs. Example: 'I am either standing at the edge of the sea or near, when suddenly enormous tidal waves appear in the distance and are coming closer. I know they will engulf me, I turn and run away. Sometimes they do overtake me, other times I wake up' (Mrs AV). We can run from pleasure and wider insight, just as much as from pain or fear. Idioms: all at sea; plenty more fish in the sea; lost at sea. See **beach; fish, sea creatures**.

seance   Meeting the unconscious as if it were spirits; concern about death or the dead; intuition.

searching   Usually indicates an attempt to find: a past way of life, like wanting to have childhood lack of responsibilities, a lover from the past; an answer to a pressing problem; one's identity or sense of value in a particular setting. May also indicate a feeling of having lost something—youth, sexual appeal, creativity, motivation. See **looking**. Idioms: searched high and low; a searching look; search me.

searchlight   Focused attention; concentration; insight.

seasons   Times of life. See **spring; summer; autumn; winter**.

secret of the universe dreams   Writers commonly quote the experience of William James who, while under anaesthetic, dreamt he found the secret of the universe. What he was left with was the doggerel 'Higamus Hogumus women are monogamous—Hogumus Higamus, men are polygamous.' The conclusion is that dreams cannot be truly revelatory. While it may be true to say that some such dreams contain little which adds to the dreamer's understanding, some dreams give in-

341

sights which profoundly alter the dreamer's future attitudes or actions.

Revelatory dreams are more common to men than women. This may be because more men concern themselves with questions of what the universe is. If the dreamer creates a mental or emotional tension in themselves through the intensity with which they pursue such questions—and we need to accept that often such intensity arises out of anxiety regarding death and one's identity—then the self-regulatory process of dreaming might well produce an apparent revelation to ease the tension. On the opposite tack, research into mental functioning during dreaming, or in a dreamlike state as in research using LSD, shows that there is an enormously increased ability to access associated ideas, allow feeling responses and achieve novel viewpoints. Freud pointed out that dreams have access to greater memory resources and associated ideas. P.H. Stafford and B.H. Golightly, in their book dealing with LSD as an aid to problem solving, say that this dreamlike state enables subjects to 'form and keep in mind a much broader picture . . . imagine what is needed—for the problem—or not possible . . . diminish fear of making mistakes'. One subject says 'I had almost total recall of a course I did in thermodynamics; something I had not given any thought to in years.'

Although humans have such power to scan enormous blocks of information or experience, look at it from new angles, sift it with particular questions in mind and so discover new connections in old information, there are problems, otherwise we would all be doing it. The nature of dream consciousness, and the faculties described, is fundamentally different to waking awareness, which limits, edits, looks for specifics, avoids views conflicting with its accepted norm, and uses verbalisation. A nonverbal, symbolic scan of massive information is largely lost when translated to waking consciousness.

My experience is that the content of revelatory dreams is

almost wholly lost on waking. If the individual explores the dream while awake, however, and dares to take consciousness into the realm of the dream, then the enormous waves of emotional impact, the massive collection of details, the personality changing influence of major new insights, can be met. The reason most of us do not touch this creative process is in fact the same reason most of us do not attempt other daring activities—it takes guts. See **creativity and problem solving in dreams**.

sedative   Attitudes we use to stop ourself feeling anxiety or emotions. This may be dangerous to our health if feelings such as guilt or grief remain unfelt.

seed   Sperm or ovum; new idea arising out of past experience; a suggestion; a new possibility or potential.

seeing, saw, sight   This is one of the major aspects of dreaming. Unless we are born blind, virtually every dream shows us looking at, seeing or viewing the events, objects, environment and people of the dream. In a word count from a sample of 1,000 dreams, the words see, saw, look, looking occurred 1,077 times. This is the highest occurrence of any words in the sample. Next were feel, feelings, felt with a score of 855, and house, houses with 412.

This suggests that dreams are almost entirely about giving attention to, being aware of, being confronted by, considering or realising some aspect of the enormously wide range of experience which human consciousness meets. Therefore, whatever appears in the dream shows we are giving some thought to, feeling or confronting what is depicted. During each day we meet, in sensory impressions, in memory, in emotion, in thought, a huge variety of things. It is therefore of great interest what comparatively few subjects our spontaneous dream response chooses to give attention to out of all the range. It seems likely these chosen areas are important to us.

Looking at something implies our attitudes or response to what is seen. Being looked at by someone else in the dream suggests seeing oneself from a viewpoint which is not our norm. By actually attempting to stand in the role of the other person, as described in **dream processing**, we can become conscious of this different viewpoint. By standing in our own role in the dream, and actually taking time to consider what it is we are 'seeing', and the impressions involved, we can 'see' or become aware of what the dream is getting us to look at regarding ourself. Idioms: from the look of things; look after; look askance at; look at; look before you leap; look blue; look down on; look for; look forward to; look into; look out; look over something; look small; look the other way; look up to; look for a fight; not like the look of; as far as I can see; as I see it; do you see what I mean; I'll see about that; I see; see over something; overseer; see eye to eye; see life; see red; see which way the wind blows; catch sight of; get out of my sight; in sight of; lose sight of; out of sight, out of mind; second sight; at first sight. See **searching**.

semen   Essence of masculinity; the sense of one's personal identity, but also the potential one has as an individual. Thus the withholding of sperm in the dream might be the non-giving of self, warmth, emotion, bonding.

settings   The environment in which the action of the dream takes place signifies the background of experience which supports the situation dealt with in the foreground.

Example: 'I was in a crowd around a church' (Efrosyni G). If we looked at the rest of Efrosyni's dream we might lose the impact of this very first 'scene setting' statement. If we look up **crowd**, we find under, Talking to, leading, or part of crowd at a central event, 'an impulse or idea which unifies many parts of one's own nature'. So here is something which Efrosyni is deeply interested in. Many of her feelings are involved in it. Looking up **church** we find 'religious feeling or beliefs, including moral code, or our feelings about organised religion'. So it is against Efrosyni's religious beliefs that the rest of the dream drama unfolds.

Example: 'I was in a house with old clothes and was washing up' (Mrs PR). The entry on **house** says it is P's everyday feeling state, her general image of herself. The old clothes are a sense of being old or unattractive. Washing up suggests she feels there are things to clear up concerning what is happening in her life. But it also suggests she sees herself as unexciting. Having clarified that—she feels old and uninteresting, and this needs to be cleaned up or dealt with—the very next part of the dream explodes into view with meaning. 'My daughter's husband to be came in. I admired the way he dressed and he turned his back on me.' At the end of her dream P feels 'lost and rejected'. By clarifying the opening scene, it seems likely P looks at her daughter in her new romance (P being 50, a divorcée, and at the tail end of a 'whirlwind romance') and feels jealous. Maybe she even hopes to attract her daughter's man away from her, but he indicates there is no hope. Basically, after her romance, P feels unwanted and rejected. The helpfulness of the dream, however, is that the first scene shows P the sort of feelings about herself that she is living with daily—feelings of being old and uninteresting. Shifting those feelings can change the way others react to her.

sewing   Creating a new attitude; changing old habits; healing a hurt, or tear in a relationship if mending.

sex in dreams   Although sex is symbolised in many dreams, where it appears directly it shows that the dreamer is able to accept their sexual urges and hurts more easily. What is then important is to attempt an understanding of what setting or drama the sexual element occurs in. Our psychological and sexual natures, like our physical, never stand still in development unless a pain or problem freezes them at a particular level of maturity. Therefore our sexual dreams, even if our sex life is satisfactory, show us what growth, what new challenge, is being met.

Example: 'My lover was standing behind me, and John, my husband, was standing in front of me. I was asking John to have sex with me and at the same time thinking, "Oh, hell, if he does he will think we have something going between us." I felt no flow towards John but felt somehow I was trying to tell my lover that I was desirable' (Sally A). Sally's dream needs no interpretation. Such clear dreams show that Sally is ready to be directly aware of what she is doing in her relationships. If the sex in the dream is deeply symbolised, it suggests the dreamer is less willing to be aware of their motivations or connected painful feelings. Even though Sally's dream was clear, it was still dealing with an area of her sexuality she was not clearly conscious of. If she had been aware, it is doubtful whether she would have dreamt it.

Example: 'I was in a farmyard. A small boy climbed all over the bull. It became terribly angry. It had been chained without attention too long. Now it tore away and sought the cows. The gates were closed, but the bull smashed through the enclosing fence. I rushed to the fence and sat astride it, but on seeing that the bull smashed it like match wood, I looked around for some safe place. The bull charged the first cow to mount it, but so terrible was its energy and emotion that it could not express as sex. It smashed the cow aside as it had done the fence. Then it rushed the next and tossed it over its head, charging and smashing the next. I climbed into somebody's garden, trying to get out of the district' (Arthur J). Although this dream depicts Arthur's 'chained' sexual drive using the bull, it is still fairly obvious. If we consider the setting and plot of the dream, as suggested above, we see that Arthur is desperately trying to avoid responsibility for, or trying to escape, his own sexual drive—figuratively 'sitting on the fence'.

Example: 'My husband and I were walking down a road. We were going in the same direction together. I started to sing with a very happy feeling but then felt I should stop because he would say the happiness was because I had had sex. I sensed he knew what I was thinking as I walked along. He then quietly began to sing and the dream ended with me smiling to myself. We had sexual cut off for four weeks but had made love that afternoon' (Joan W). In talking about this dream Joan said she felt it slightly embarrassing to admit that sex gave her feelings of happiness. She liked to believe she was perfectly happy without it. It is probably out of the slight conflict between her conscious attitude and her feeling of well-being after sex that the dream was produced. See **animals**; **adolescent**; **affair**; *devil, Christ, Shadow* under **archetypes**; **bag**; **banana**; **bed**; example in **bite**; **black person**; *breasts* and *penis* under **body**; **bud**; **candle**; **cane**; **castration**; **ceremony, ritual**; **clothes**; **compensatory theory**; **cuckoo**; **cup**; **dam**; **dance**; third example in **danger**; **defence mechanisms**; **dragon**; **drum**; **emotions, mood**; **ejaculation**; second example under **evil**; fourth example under *husband* in **family**; **feelings**; **homosexuality**; **horns**; **hostility**; example in *door* under **house, buildings**; **hypnosis and dreams**; **insects**; **jungle**; **kiss**; **left, right**; **lift**; second example under **light**; **man**; **masturbation**; **mirror**; **murder**; **nest**; **oval**; **pole**; **prostitute**; **purse**; **rape**; **refrigerate**; **religion and dreams**; first example under **reptiles**; **sadism**; **sex while asleep**; **wordplay, puns**.

sex while asleep   Example: 'Many times in my adult life I have woken to find I have made love to my wife while asleep. Or I wake to discover myself in the middle of the sexual act. At such times I have usually been avoiding my sexual drive and it has burst through to fulfil itself while I was asleep or under the sway of dreams. For instance most times this happened I have been in the middle of a dream in which there is a sense of absolute imperative that I must make love/have sex.

347

It is like being lost in a storm of glamour and fantasy or vision in which I am totally involved. The whirl of the "dream" is towards the wonder, totality of the need to have sex. As this imperative is expressed in my still spontaneous, dreaming physical action, the experience of sex is also visionary and enormous' (Charles W).

This fairly common dreaming experience demonstrates powerfully how dreams are an expression of a self regulatory or compensatory action in the psyche and body. Charles says that he had been restraining his sexual activity. This shows the enormous gulf which can exist between what we will to do as a conscious personality, and what our being needs to do or wishes to do outside conscious decision making. The 'glamour and fantasy' Charles describes are regular features of how these deeper needs make themselves known, or attempt to coerce the conscious mind, into fulfilling the need. If we reject the fantasy, the unconscious processes will attempt a more radical approach, as in actual physical movement while we sleep. This may have given rise to ideas about possession or devils in past ages, when it was not understood that we can split our mind by such conflicts. Fear of the 'possessing' influence actually heightens its power through suggestion. It is much better to understand what one's needs are, and seek an acceptable fulfilment. See **abreaction**.

shade, shadow Feeling 'put in the shade'; feelings still overshadowing one from past experiences or relationships; feeling inferior; protection; occasionally a sense of the dead or fear of the unknown. Idioms: afraid of one's shadow; shades of; shadow of one's former self; worn to a shadow. See **shadowy figure**.

shadowy figure Example: 'A shadow thing came very quickly up the stairs, along our corridor and into the bedroom, over to the bed to bend over me. I felt fear as I never felt it before and I started to make a noise. It was also the shadow making the noise and it was frightened, and moved towards the window. I felt sorry it was frightened too, but then it was too late as it had gone. I woke up making a howling noise, my husband said, he felt the fear in the room strongly too' (Gloria F). In the example, Gloria is meeting her own feeling of fear. This is obvious because the shadowy thing felt the fear also. In fact it is the feeling of fear. Such shadowy figures are our own rejected emotions or potentials. See *the Shadow* under **archetypes**.

shampoo   Attempt to clear away thoughts or attitudes which are not useful, or interfere in clear thinking. See **hair**; second example under **school**.

shapes, symbols   These are a visual presentation of our own internal or psychological structure. Because the mind and emotions in some ways appear so abstract, it is difficult to have a clear image of our differences compared with other people; or to see changes which occur through maturing. Shapes, symbols and patterns give us a clear image of our inner world. See example in *spiral* below.

centre, middle   Emphasises the importance of the thing, person or animal in that position; conflict, where the middle is between opposites; obstruction when something might be in the middle of the road, corridor, etc.; feelings of being involved, when in the middle of a crowd for instance. When something is in the middle of a circle or square can represent the self. Idioms: middle of the road; piggy in the middle; centre of attention.

circle   Wholeness, it suggests a good harmony between all the aspects of our being, physical, mental and spiritual; may be used to depict the self; female sexuality. If the circle is irregular, suggests imbalance or lack of harmony. Idioms: go round in circles; come full circle; vicious circle; circle of influence/friends.

crescent Femininity; the vagina; the process of feminine creativity. Crescent moon: the beginning or ending of something to do with one's feelings or inner life.

cross Difficulties or tribulations we carry, perhaps unnecessarily; human life and its whole spectrum of experience, physical, sexual, mental, emotional, cosmic—painful and delightful; wrongness, as with tick being correct, cross being wrong or forbidden; completion as when crossed off list; the body, upon which consciousness is nailed or fixed during life.

diamond Choices or direction, like the compass needle.

mandala This is any circle or square within which shapes, objects or other symbols appear. The mandala can be a square garden with round pond in it—square with circle in, etc. It depicts what we have done with our life, what qualities or balance we have achieved through our own effort or self responsibility. It shows whether we have dared meet the darkness and light in our nature and bring balance; whether we have found the courage to have our boundaries of thought and viewpoint split asunder by a greater vision or despair, and what we have done with the pieces of wonder and pain we have found. See *spiral* below in this entry.

oblong An area of our experience—might be sex, mind, etc.; boundaries of our awareness or what we dare let ourselves experience; physical reality.

patterns Concepts or realisations, made up of interblending pieces of information and experience; the order or chaos of our inner world of thoughts and feelings; the patterns we live by, such as habits, and beliefs; insight into the cycles or patterns underlying human and animal life.

sphere, ball Wholeness; an 'all round' view or a rounded character. Ball: interaction between two people, sexual and otherwise (the 'ball' is in your court), in that throwing the ball may show someone trying to get one's attention and response. Ball games, being thrown a ball: challenges, prowess, competition in the game of life; having and letting go; sex play; masturbation; a man's 'balls'; wholeness. Idioms: have a ball; ball at one's feet; one's eye on the ball; start the ball rolling; new ball game; play ball with someone; he has/hasn't the balls. See *the self* under **archetypes**.

spiral Things we repeat over and over, like habits; movement towards greater awareness or insight.

Example: 'We walk around, go upstairs, and I notice a staircase leading to a room or rooms. The stairs are painted in the green too, and they go up square, about eight steps in a flight, but round and round—spiral. I am scared by them, don't want to go up, but am curious. We move in and nobody but myself has really taken any notice of the stairs. Nobody has been up. Half way up I can see there is a glass roof, the wooden frames painted green. I am terrified but have to go on. Then I wake. Next dream I got up there. It smelt very musty. Lots of draw sheets covering things. I bent to lift a sheet. It was raining. I could hear it thrashing on the glass. Then I woke' (Ann H). In this example we have the spiral and the square combined in the stairs. In this way the dream manages to combine many different ideas such as climbing to the unknown, spiralling or circling something, and the squareness or down-to-earth nature of what is being discovered. There are things we have learnt, yet not realised consciously. Like a jigsaw puzzle, we have all the pieces, and we sense the connection, but we have never formed it into a conscious thought or verbal idea. It therefore remains as a feeling sense or hunch, but not a rational idea. Ann is spiralling towards, or circling around, such a realisation. She is frightened because it may be difficult—one may realise that all the years of marriage point to having been used as a doormat.

square   Down to earth; reality; the physical experience; stability; the materialising of an idea, feeling or plan. Leonardo da Vinci's diagram of the man in the circle within the square represents a complete balance of the various aspects of human nature—as he may have achieved himself. See *mandala* above in this entry.

star   Six pointed: personal harmony between physical, mental and spiritual. Five pointed: one's body, oneself and one's sensed kinship with all life.

triangle   The three major aspects of human nature—body, personal experience and impersonal consciousness; similar to the number three—see **numbers**. Triangle with point upwards: depicts the physical aspects of human nature moving towards the personal or conscious. Triangle with point downwards: the areas of consciousness moving towards physical expression. Triangles linked in star of David: complete balance in human nature. Sometimes the points of the triangle are used to represent three stages of human development of awareness. The first is the undifferentiated or preconscious stage; the second is the sense of individuality, feeling 'otherness' in regard to the world; and the third is the relationship of the self to the 'other' in people and the world.

sheep   See **animals**.

shell   The defence we use to avoid being hurt emotionally, or to defend the integrity of our identity. See **fish, sea creatures**.

shine   Containing a lot of our personal energy. See **aura; light**

ship   See **boat, ship**.

shit   See **excrement; toilet**.

shiver   Fear or conflict; excitement. Idioms: give one the shivers; send shivers up one's spine.

shoes   See **clothes**.

shop   Desires, something we are looking for or want—love, fame, sex; place of work or business. Idioms: shop around; set up shop; shut up shop; talk shop; closed shop. See *shopkeeper* under **roles**.

shot, shooting   To be shot: a traumatic injury to feelings, often out of parental or other close relationship. It need not be something dramatic like being assaulted, but can be a quiet injury like not bonding emotionally with parents. Someone, something else shot: still usually refers to dreamer. Dreamer shooting someone, something: anger; fear or defence against meeting feelings or insights; aggressive sexuality. Idioms: get shot of; shot across the bows; shot in the arm; all shot to pieces; shot in the dark. See example in **abreaction**.

shovel, spade   Introspection; the work of digging into our memories; uncovering our past experience.

shrink   dreamer or people shrink: return to a childhood feeling state or point of view; losing face or feeling 'small'. Other things shrink: they are becoming less threatening or interesting or play less important part in one's life; are seen as connected with the unconscious, aspects of which are often seen as of 'little' significance, yet are full of the sort of power which motivates or undermines our resolves.

sick   Bad feeling you are discharging; feeling sick of a relationship or situation; being pregnant. <u>Idioms</u>: fall sick; make one sick; sick and tired of; sick as a dog; sick to death of.

sight   See **seeing, saw, sight**.

signature   Agreement; what you will.

silence   Uneasiness; unspoken feelings; expectancy; being unable to voice one's feelings; condoning; absence of life—death.

sing   Expressing one's inner feelings, one's real self; touching the flowing feelings of our life; other people's self expression and daring.

sinking   Despairing; losing ground; loss of confidence. <u>Idioms</u>: be sunk; sinking feeling; sink or swim; sink to someone's level. See second example in **falling**.

sister   See **family**.

size   How important we see something, or what feeling impact it has on us, or how we feel in relationship to the person or object.

big, large   Importance, relationship, as when we feel small beside somebody with a 'big' reputation. <u>Idioms</u>: big of somebody; big brother; big fish/noise/wheel/shot; big guns; big head; go down big; big time; too big for shoes; big time.

little, small   Of little importance; feeling 'small'; relating to childhood. See also **shrink**.

skeleton   Feelings about death; part of your own ability, feelings or talent you have 'killed off' or allowed to die at some time.

sky The mind; our potential. Dream scenes such as the sky opening and people or objects appearing, or threatening things falling from the sky, are graphic descriptions of how suddenly a new thought or viewpoint or event appears from nowhere; or for no apparent reason anxious or depressing thoughts occur 'out of the blue'. Floating, flying in sky: avoiding anxiety; escape into daydreaming or the mind; having a wider awareness of a situation; exploring potential. Colour, mood of sky: our view of life at the moment. Idioms: sky's the limit; sky high; pie in the sky; out of the blue. See **flying**; **space**.

sleeping Not being aware; avoidance of feeling or looking at something; surrender of waking self. Idioms: lose sleep over; sleep around; put it to sleep; sleep in; sleeping partner; sleep like a log; let sleeping dogs lie; sleep off; sleep on something; sleep together; sleep with; sleep rough.

sleep movements Adrian Morrison at the University of Pennsylvania, investigating narcolepsy, a condition producing sleep in the middle of activity, found that a small area of the brain, the pons, suppresses full muscular movement while we dream. If this area is damaged or suppressed, humans or animals make full muscular movements in connection with what is dreamt. He observed that cats would stalk, crouch and spring at imaginary prey. These very important findings suggest a number of things. The unconscious process behind dreaming, apart from creating a non-volitional fantasy, can also reproduce movements we have not consciously decided upon. This shows we have at least two centres of will which can direct body and mental processes. Christopher Evans, linking with the work of Nicholas Humphrey at Cambridge University, sees the movements of dreaming cats as expressions of survival 'programs' in the biological computer. These 'programs' or strategies for survival need to be replayed in order not only to keep in practice, but also to modify them in connection with the influx of extra experience and information. In the human realm, our survival strategies and the way we relate to our social, sexual, marriage and work roles may also be replayed and modified in our dreaming.

Such movements are not linked simply to survival or social 'programs'. An important aspect of dreaming is releasing painful emotions or trauma, and moving toward psychological growth. Also, the process producing these movements does not keep strictly to the realm of sleep. It is observable that many muscular spasms, ticks, or unwilled waking movements arise from this source—the 'will' of the unconscious—attempting to release trauma or initiate a necessary programme of psychological growth. That such 'dream' activities as spontaneous movement or verbalisation should occur during waking would appear to suggest that a dream must occur with them. Research shows this is unlikely. It does however show that a dream may be imagery produced to express this mental, muscular, emotional 'self regulation'. The imagery may not be necessary if the process is consciously experienced.

Because the self-regulatory process produces spontaneous movements, emotions and verbalisation, it is likely there is a connection between it and many ancient religious practices such as pentecostalism, *shaktipat* in India, *subud* in Indonesia and *seitai* in Japan. These are forms of psychotherapy practised by other cultures. They create an environment in which practitioners can allow spontaneous movement and fantasy while awake. Because consciousness is then involved, and can co-operate with the self-regulating or healing activities of the unconscious, such practice can lead to better health and utilisation of unconscious functions. The older religious forms of this practice relied on belief systems of spirits or gods. Once the connection between these practices and the dream is realised, much in them which was obscure becomes understandable. In my book *Mind and Movement* I explain the connection between the dream process, self regulatory healing, extended perception and waking consciousness. See **abreaction; sleep walking; dream as therapist and healer**.

sleep rocking   Ian Oswald (as related in his book *Sleep)* observed active rocking in some children and adults during sleep. These rocking movements were very powerful, occurring at a rate of one per second during REM sleep. They occur more frequently in the blind or to people institutionalised during childhood. As rocking is a movement used by primates and humans to comfort themselves during stress or unhappiness, it is possible that the rocking accompanies disturbing dreams. The dream probably evokes unhappy feelings or conditions from the past; as the person used rocking to cope with their past distress, it occurs as an habitual accompaniment of the distressing dream.

sleep walking   Very common with some people, especially during adolescence or times of stress. Sometimes accompanied by hallucinations. Sleep walking is normal as an occasional event in children. If the child is agitated, excited or acting in a manner to injure themselves during the sleep walking, then it may be a sign of emotional distress.

The same applies to adults. Many sleep walkers perform complex acts without coming to harm. A young Portsmouth boy drove his father's car 27 miles before waking in Southampton. The police checked his story and did not charge him. But sometimes severe injury is inflicted either upon themselves or others. During a dream phone-in on London Broadcasting Company, a man told me his experience of smashing through a glass window, cutting an artery and nearly bleeding to death. In America and England homicidal acts have been committed while the person claimed to be sleepwalking, and the people involved were acquitted of murder.

Because of such powerful activity during sleep, many people who experience this type of sleep walking are worried about what they might do to a partner sleeping next to them.

In most cases one wakes as the contact is made, or the involved person wakes one, but the element of risk cannot be denied. Where such worry exists, hope can be gained by understanding what was observed with many men who began to sleep walk after war combat. In their cases the movements, speech and emotions were observably connected with trauma occurring during their war experience. The self regulatory process in dreams was thereby attempting to release the tension, horror or emotional pain of the events. Where these emotions could be met consciously, perhaps with the help of a psychotherapist, the sleep movements stopped. This suggests that dramatic activity while sleep walking has similar roots, and can be dealt with.

smell   See **perfume, scent, smell**.

smoke   Intuition of danger or anxiety about danger; smouldering passions or emotions. Idioms: go up in smoke; put up a smoke screen; no smoke without fire. See **fire**.

smoking   Anxiety; something controlling our decisions— habits; sometimes connects with hidden sexual desires.

snail   Vulnerability, its shell depicting our defence against being hurt; feelings of repulsion for some people. Probably repulsion regarding 'squirmy' feelings regarding their body or sexuality.

snake   See **reptiles, lizards, snakes**.

snow   Depending on feeling reaction to the snow, it can depict emotional coldness or frigidity; pureness; beauty. Skiing, winter sports: freedom, relaxation.

soap   Feeling one needs to 'clean up one's act' in some way, or 'come clean'; sense of grubbiness; guilt or conscience; clearing away negative emotions.

soldier   See **roles**.

son   See **family**.

soup   A hunger being satisfied. See **food**.

south   The genital area of self; warmth, lightness, feelings.

space   Space in a building: one's potential or what has not been used up in activity yet; opportunity; sense of independence and freedom. Cosmic space: beyond thinking or limited concepts and ego boundaries; beyond what is established already; being out of touch with reality.

spectacles   See **glasses**.

speed   Intensity of feelings; growing anxiety; feelings of not being able to cope with events.

spice   Sex; pleasure.

spider   See **insects**.

spirits   Feelings or intuitions about the dead or death; fears concerning one's own unconscious memories or feelings; intuitions arising from one's own mind and awareness, as it exists beyond the preconceptions and boundaries of prejudice or fear. Idioms: be with someone in spirit; high/low spirits; public spirit; spirit away; spirit is willing. See **ghosts**. See also *devil* under **archetypes**; **masturbation**; **sex while asleep**.

splinter   Minor irritation; hurtful words or ideas; harboured ideas which bring negative feelings or pain.

spring   New growth; what was latent emerging; a new start in business or relationship; childhood or youth. Spring of water: free-flowing feelings; rejuvenating energy. See **water**.

stab   Feeling 'wounded' by someone else's remarks, actions or attitude; aggressive sexuality. See **weapons**.

stage   See **theatre**.

stairs   See *stairs* under **house, buildings**.

stars   Intuitions about the cosmos; the perhaps almost unnoticeable promptings or motivations which occur through life leading us in a particular direction—destiny; hopes or wishes. See *star* under **shapes, symbols**.

starvation   Something in oneself not given due attention; the impoverished and ignored aspect of self; attempts to deny the body because there is anxiety about its needs and urges.

station   See **railway**.

statistics   In the following box are figures based on a word count of 1,000 dreams. If we look at the entry on 'man', for example, the number 304 appears beside it. This means the word 'man' appeared 304 times within the 1,000 dreams. The word beside it, 'men', appeared 91 times. These are totalled to make the next figure, 395, which is the number of times reference to man/men appeared in the dreams. The figure 1 in the next column shows that within the group headed 'People and family', the words man/men had the highest score. The word 'people' came second, scoring 345. The figure in the third column shows the position regarding all the headings, making man/men the sixth highest score, with 'see, seeing, looking' the highest.

NUMBER OF TIMES SUBJECTS APPEARED IN DREAMS			
	No. of times appeared	Ranking in group	Overall ranking
People and family			
Baby 85, Babies 4	103	9	
Boy	70	14	
Child 71, Children 111	182	6	
Daughter	64	15	
Father 69, Dad 10	79	12	
Friend 136, Friends 60	196	5	
Girl	85	10	
Husband	197	4	
Man 304, Men 91	195	1	6
Mother 122, Mummy 3, Mum 12, Mother's 22	159	7	
People	345	2	
Person	76	13	
Son	80	11	
Wife	106	8	
Woman 175, Women 41	216	3	
Objects			
Bus	51	6	
Car	124	4	
Clothes 54, Wearing 48, Dressed 53	155	2	
Fire	44	8	
Table	50	7	
Tree 32, Trees 36	68	5	
Water	164	1	
Window 103, Windows 32	135	3	

Doing

Driving	80	11	
Fall 41, Falling 30	71	12	
Finding, Found, Finds	297	2	12
Flying, Fly, Flew	98	10	
Hold, Holding, Held	142	8	
Give 44, Gave 23	67	13	
Ran 83, Run 61, Running 64	208	4	
Sleep, Sleeping, Slept	106	9	
Sat 47, Sit 112, Sitting 20	179	7	
Standing 141, Stood 52	193	6	
Swim, Swimming, Swam	59	14	
Take, Took, Taking	248	3	
Wait, Waiting, Waited	56	15	
Walking 165, Walk 68, Walked 134	367	1	
Work, Worked, Working	194	5	9

Body

Arm 43, Arms 67	110	2
Body	79	5
Breast, Breasts	36	8
Ear, Ears	5	12
Eye 20, Eyes 46	66	6
Face	97	3
Hand 107, Hands 62	169	1
Hair	41	6
Head	96	4
Leg, Legs	56	7
Mouth	30	10
Nose	9	11
Teeth, Tooth	34	9

House and Home

Bed	153	4
Bedroom	66	8
Door, Doors, Doorway	311	3
Floor	103	6

House and Home			
Home	134	5	
House, Houses	412	1	4
Room, Rooms	390	2	8
Stair, Stairs, Steps	98	7	

Psyche			
Decide 9, Decided 41, Decision 6	56	18	
Fear 58, Terrified 45, Scared, etc. 86	189	9	
Feel(s) 187, Feeling(s) 244, Felt 424	855	2	2
Happy	63	17	
Heard, Hear	97	13	
Keep, Kept	102	12	
Knew 177, Know 106	283	6	
Realise	38	19	
Remember 104, Remembering 13	117	11	
Say 69, Saying 99, Talk(ing) 113, Talk 113	394	3	7
See 293, Seeing 411, Look(ing) 373	1077	1	1
Sex, Sexual, Sexuality	94	14	
Take, Taking	174	10	
Tell, Told	193	8	
Think 72, Thinking 41, Thought 226	339	4	10
Tried, Trying	298	5	11
Want, Wanting, Wanted	200	7	
Watch, Watching	71	16	
Wonder 47, Wondering 26	73	15	

Orientation and size			
Above	46	10	
Behind	100	9	
Bottom	44	11	
Down	404	2	5

Orientation and size *continued*			
High	100	9	
Large, Big	296	3	13
Left	166	5	
Low	21	13	
Right	130	7	
Side	149	6	
Small	171	4	
Top	115	8	
Under	40	12	
Up	424	1	3

Life events		
Birth, Born	23	3
Death, Dying, Dead, Died	276	1
Married, Marriage, Wedding	65	2

Animals		
Bear 15, Bears 4	19	4
Bull	14	5
Cat	24	3
Cow	9	6
Dog 51, Dogs 14	65	1
Elephant	19	4
Horse 30, Horses 16	46	2
Lion	5	8
Monkey	4	9
Mouse	2	10
Pig	1	11
Wolf	7	7

Colours		
Red	52	5
Orange	2	9
Yellow	13	8
Green	59	4
Blue	61	3

Colours *continued*		
Violet	1	10
Gold	26	6
Silver	14	7
Black	86	2
White	101	1

statue, idol   An unfeeling or 'dead' part of self; feelings that someone is unresponsive or cold. Idol: values you have erected, false or otherwise.

stealing   Taking love, money or opportunity under false pretences; not giving as good as you get; feeling you are undeserving or unloved, and what you get is stealing because it is given unwillingly. Being stolen from: feeling cheated or not respected; may refer to sexuality or love—do you give it, or does it feel as if it is taken from you? Can also refer to death—that life is being 'stolen' from one. Idioms: steal one's heart; steal someone's thunder; steal the show.

steam   Emotions under pressure; expressed emotions; something transitory. Idioms: getting steamed up; full steam ahead; get up steam.

steeple   A landmark in one's life; may also refer to the body, as 'bats in the belfry' suggests. The top of the steeple is the mind and wider awareness; male sexuality.

steps   Effort made, or to make, to get somewhere. See *stairs* under **house, buildings**.

sterilise   Fear of illness; reference to infection in the body.

stiffness Sensing that you are either holding yourself back in relationships or endeavours, or you are too formal; anxiety or tension.

stone Hardness, loss of feeling or unfeeling. Idioms: cast the first stone; leave no stone unturned; stone dead; stone deaf; blood out of a stone; stony broke; heart of stone; stoned. See **rock**.

storm Anger; emotional outburst; feeling battered by events or emotions. Storm is approaching: a sense of difficult times ahead; anger or passion building up. Idioms: bend before the storm; storm in a teacup; take by storm; weather the storm.

strangle Holding back feelings; trying to kill emotions or sexuality. Most of our feelings create sounds such as laughter or crying, a sigh, words of anger or love, cries of pain. The attack on the neck is therefore usually an attempt to stifle these. See also **danger**; third example in *door* under **house, buildings**.

string Attempts to make something secure; mending a situation or relationship; trying to hold something together—a business, a marriage; connection with others. Idioms: have someone on a piece of string; hold the purse strings; string along; string someone along; strung up; no strings attached; pull strings; apron strings.

submarine Ability to meet the depths of feelings in the unconscious, as well as functioning all right in the everyday world.

sucking Emotional hunger; experiencing childhood longings, dependence or feelings. Being sucked at: if other than child-parent relationship, feeling one's energy drained; having a sense of another person, or an aspect of oneself, being parasitical—not giving as well as receiving—or having baby needs. Idioms: suck up to someone; bloodsucker.

sugar Pleasure; substitute for relationship or love; may refer to body health. Idioms: All sweetness and light; be sweet on someone; a sweet tooth; the sweets (rewards) of.

suicide Remembering that most people in dreams depict an aspect of oneself, this may be illustrating that we lack pleasure in life or have little to live for in the way of satisfaction; suicide may also be a sign of interiorised anger, where instead of admitting our anger, we destroy parts of our own feelings; may depict business or relationship suicide. Someone we know: often shows us hoping person will get out of our life; intuition.

suitcase Example: 'In last night's dream the baby I dream about incessantly had been locked in a suitcase but was quite unscathed when taken out, except that it was very dirty, but still not crying. I do not have any memories in connection with these babies and the only feelings I have are those of remorse that I have neglected the baby. I have had four children of my own, none of whom were ever neglected in this way' (Mrs C). Mrs C uses the suitcase in at least two ways. One is her womb, or reproductive ability. Although she has had four children, this does not stop her unconsciously desiring more. The second is what 'luggage'—emotional feelings, urges, thoughts—she carries.

Generally, it depicts the womb; what one carries inside oneself, such as longings, attitudes, fears; how we see ourself socially—the luggage might be a sign of status, how we rate ourself; also a symbol of independence or going somewhere. See **bag**.

summer   Mid life; success; fruitfulness; pleasure; warmth.

sun   Warmth; vitality; conscious awareness; the self or source of one's life energy. Sunlight: being aware; warmth; positive feelings in body and mind; health. Sunbathing: allowing the flow of inner energies to give pleasure. Sunrise: realisation; a new start; childhood; hope and energy to grow. Midday: maturity; middle life; time to be working at one's life. Sunset: old age; death; return to latent period prior to a new birth. See **time**; *rebirth* under **archetypes**.

surgery   A surgery: one's health, emotional or physical. Having surgery: feeling 'got at' by someone; having someone 'get under one's skin'; difficult but healing changes in self; feelings about surgery if imminent.

swallowing   Holding back emotions; swallowing words or anger; taking in something. Idioms: swallow one's pride; he/she swallowed it.

swamp   Feelings which undermine confidence and well being; might depict feelings about a relationship, perhaps with mother. See example in **insects**; **sink**.

sweeping   Clearing away outmoded attitudes, anxieties or emotions; getting feelings about someone out of one's life. Idioms: make a clean sweep; sweep someone off their feet;

sweep something under the carpet; sweep the board; sweep the floor with.

sweets   Pleasure; rewards. See **sugar**.

swimming   Example: 'I looked at a large pool where a river surfaced. A woman swam in it and was going to enter tunnels leading away from it. As I watched I saw some huge crocodiles swim towards her. With great speed and confidence she swam away, obviously being able to match the threat' (Laurie V). Laurie explored the dream and found the swimming expressed his growing confidence in meeting feelings which in past years had led to depression.

Generally, swimming shows confidence in dealing with the sort of impacts, anxieties or emotions which cause some people to 'go under', either in relationships, running a family or business, being able to meet the many influences, urges and thoughts in which we exist; expressive motivation; trusting oneself, life, and our sexuality. Swimming against current, tide: meeting opposition, either from within or others; moving against general opinions; feeling difficulties. Swimming underwater: taking awareness into what was unconscious. Swimming with other people: sharing common feelings, goals, etc.; connections with others. Diving in: taking the plunge in a new activity, relationship or way of life. Hanging about, not getting in: hesitation about a change or something new in life. Idioms: in the swim; swim against the tide; sink or swim. See **pool**.

swing   Like rocking, may refer to way we relax ourself when facing stress—see **sleep rocking**; self gratification, sex or masturbation; feelings of pleasure; daily ups and downs. Idioms: Get into the swing of things; go with a swing; in full swing.

symbols and dreaming   Words are themselves symbols of objects, ideas, or feelings. Whether we look at mathematical equations, a film, a novel, or a business logo, each involves the use of symbols. When we look at a thermometer we lose sight of it as a real object, and see it as temperature. Throughout our everyday life we use things symbolically without noticing. A name on the label of goods may depict quality to us. A face can represent love or brutality. In the struggle towards human awareness, and its increasingly subtle use of symbols such as language to think and express with, there must have been stages of development. This is a side of 'history' seldom given attention, yet very important. Perhaps our dream 'thinking' is using an earlier form of using symbols, one which might have been more an everyday event prior to language.

Even though we exist as an individual integrated with today's world, our earlier levels of thinking still exist. Unconsciously we still see the thermometer as temperature; the car as status, independence or ease in getting to work; inside our house as an expression of ourself—if we didn't we would not take pains to make it nice for guests. Through these unconscious feeling connections or symbolic views we have of things, dreams create their store of images and scenes. Processing a dream is an attempt to discover what values we ourself unconsciously place upon the people, animals, objects and situations around us. See **unconscious.**

syringe   Intercourse; a sense of what influence other people's opinions or criticism is having on us; for some, drug dependence. See **injection.**

T

table   See **furniture**.

tablet   See **pill**.

tadpole   Sperm; a baby, so perhaps pregnancy; our feelings about prenatal life. See *frog* under **reptiles, lizards, snakes**.

tail   As the tail can be raised and lowered, can refer to sexual excitement; the penis; what we are carrying with us from the past.

talisman   Feelings or beliefs we use to ward off anxiety, loss of confidence, or sense of inadequacy.

talking   Sense of being in contact with whatever is depicted; expressing what one feels and thinks; standing up for what one believes or feels strongly about. <u>Difficulty in speaking, not speaking</u>: restrained anger or difficult feelings; anxiety or lack of confidence; absence of real contact or communication. <u>Speaking and not being understood</u>: feeling of not being listened to; frustration. <u>Idioms</u>: on speaking terms; know someone to speak to; nothing to speak of; speak as one finds; speak for someone; speak out; speaks for itself; speak volumes; speak with forked tongue; speak one's mind. See also *mouth* under **body**; **silence**.

talking in sleep   Most people who have kept a dog have witnessed it bark while it is obviously dreaming. Calling out during a disturbing or active dream is common to humans also. Some people sleep talk very frequently, however; so

371

much so they worry in case they disturb the sleep of others, or say things they regret. In some cases they will even respond to questions. One such person told me that she went to her mother's room and asked her about whether or not to get married. The dreamer was single, so the subject of the talk may have been bothering her. Perhaps the most prolific and creative of sleep talkers was Edgar **Cayce**.

tame   Developing a relationship with the animal aspect of self; taking away sexual drive.

tangled   confusion. <u>Bodies tangled together pleasurably</u>: intimacy; acceptance.

tank   Defensive aggression. <u>Water tank</u>: the womb, especially if fairly small and containing fishes or tadpoles; one's inner feelings and processes.

tap   Emotions, turning them on and off; tapping one's resources; depicts how well we can get our needs.

tapestry   Reflection of one's inner condition or history; the tapestry of life, its richness and symmetry. See *patterns* under **shapes, symbols**.

target   One's aims or motivations; the self; vagina. <u>Idioms</u>: sitting target.

taste   Likes, dislikes, desires and standards. The words used to describe taste often refer equally as well to feelings—bitter, sweet, sour. <u>Idioms</u>: bad taste; taste blood; have a taste for; leaves a nasty taste; acquired taste.

tattoo   Indelible memory of an experience or relationship—might relate to pain also; tribal or group identity.

tax Feeling 'taxed'; what we owe to life and society for our existence; how much of self we want to give.

taxi Desire for help. See **car**.

tea Sociability; uplift or energising influence; allowing oneself time to 'drink in' one's surroundings or experiences. See **drink**.

teacher See **roles**.

teddy bear Desire for comfort; wanting sympathy and love which cannot hurt us or respond negatively; childhood state of relationship.

teeth See *teeth* under **body**.

telepathy See **ESP and dreams**.

telephone Desire or attempt to communicate; attempt to make contact with an aspect of oneself or someone else. Dreamer not answering phone: avoiding contact or communication; someone is trying to 'get through' to you. No reply to dreamer's call: feeling someone is out of contact with you, not aware of your feelings. 999 call: Probably a crisis in your relationship or life; reaching out for help; moral dilemma. Telephone number: if it is of someone known, most likely an attempt to communicate with that person—see **numbers**.

telescope Taking a 'closer look' at whatever is being viewed; making something bigger than it is.

television TV set: the function of seeing what is going on, or what is the news from within oneself. Watching TV: watching one's activity, values, politics. Television personality: see **famous people**.

temple See **church**.

temptation Conflict between different aspects of self—perhaps sexual urges and social fears, or personal boundaries.

tennis See **games**.

tent One's relationship with natural forces in self; feeling of being on the move, not putting down roots; getting away from everyday responsibilities.

tests Measuring oneself against others; self assessment; feelings of being compared or criticised, or self criticism; stress caused by competitive work, or need for qualifications. Medical tests: concern about health.

thaw Change in emotional responses; forgiveness; melting of frigidity or emotional distancing through withdrawal of feelings.

theatre Observing the 'play' of one's own thoughts and feelings, hopes, fears and fantasies. On stage: feeling in the public eye, or wanting to be noticed; going through a 'stage' of one's life. The stage: a situation you are meeting or in the midst of, perhaps demanding you play a particular role. Looking at stage: what is claiming one's attention at present; looking within oneself; experimenting with or exploring an idea; role or situation. Idioms: set the stage for; stage fright; stage-manage; act a part; act of God; act on; catch somebody in the act; get in on the act; get one's act together; act one's age; play the fool.

See **cinema**.

thermometer   Concern about health if medical thermometer; one's emotional warmth or lack of it.

thirst   To have an inner need for something; to long for satisfaction, probably in regard to one's emotional or spiritual needs, but can be sexual too. See **drink**.

throat   Self expression. Idioms: at each other's throats; cut-throat competition; cut one's own throat; lump in the throat; jump down someone's throat; ram something down some-one's throat; stick in one's throat. See *neck* under **body**.

thunder   Repressed emotions being released; warning of emotional outburst; external difficulties. See **storm**.

ticket   The price we pay to achieve something or get some-where; sense of right to something, therefore confidence; sometimes ability or correct view of something. Idioms: that's the ticket; just the ticket; meal ticket; work one's ticket.

tickle   Attempt to release tension, to break down barriers of reserve; prelude to sexual intimacy; sexual pleasure.

tide   See *tide* under **sea**.

time of day   The passage of time in our life; our age; our sense of ease or pressure.

the daylight hours   Our conscious waking life; our area of choice and ability to make decisions. Most dreams deal only with one day. Where several days pass in the same dream, or even longer periods: the dream is expressing periods of change; different stages of growth in one's life; or very different conditions through which one has lived or might live. Being late: feeling we have left something too late or we have missed out on something; realising we have not acted quickly enough to avert something; avoidance of responsibility.

afternoon, evening The end of life, middle or old age; the more subtle feeling areas of experience or relationship.

hours of the day May refer to age; period of life, 12 noon being midlife; something that happens at that time of the day; 11 may be eleventh hour. See **numbers**.

midday Midlife; fully awake, as opposed to the unconscious.

morning Our youth, or the first part of our life; energy; enthusiasm.

night Example: 'Three of us were on our way to a lively night out and I suggested a short cut through Richmond Park' (Jasmine C). In Jasmine's dream the night depicts her feelings of relaxation, pleasure and sexual encounter. This aspect of night also suggests feeling the absence of the workaday world; time for reflection and being by oneself; intimacy with others; introspection.

Example: 'It was a very dark night with thunder and lightning, heavy rain and high winds. I am in a waiting room at Heathrow airport' (Mrs W). Night in this dream shows a period of difficult change in the dreamer's life. It represents a period of darkness or depression; loneliness; difficulties; sometimes negative feelings about old age and death.

Example: 'I was creeping through a field at night. In darkness I and others were trying to accomplish some secret act, rather as spies or underground agents might. I also remember another where I was near a house at night. There was some special reason for getting to the house. Again an "agent" sort of feeling'.(Sam K). Sam is experiencing areas of his unconscious or unknown self, thus the secrecy, as he probably has hidden something from himself. This aspect of night suggests turning our attention inwards to an extent where we discover insights, memories or mysteries which were previously unknown to us. These can be painful areas of our experience, or very positive and life enhancing realisations. It depicts the times in life when feelings arise from within when we are alone, or in a receptive mood—or go in search of who we are.

Idioms: it's about time; all in good time; at one time; do time; for the time being; half the time; gain time; have no time for someone; lean times; time after time; time flies; behind the times; big time. See **dark; light; sun.**

toad   See **reptiles, lizards, snakes.**

toilet   Privacy; our need for time where we are not always considering what others need or want of us, but can do what we want. If it is a bathroom and toilet: possibly includes the need for cleaning up one's sexual attitudes or general attitude to others and self.

Example: 'I am in a toilet and people can see me. Sometimes the walls fall down. Once I looked around and everyone was watching me.' (Ms JR). This relationship with the toilet usually shows that one needs more privacy and time to oneself.

Example: 'I go to the toilet and it is full up to the brim. It is disgusting, and I can't go' (Alan). Alan went on to say he is often awake in his dreams and if anything unpleasant happens he wakes himself to avoid it. Alan shows great difficulty in meeting the very biological, blood and guts, and sexual side of himself. This may lead to living a very intellectual or sweetness-and-light sort of life; occasionally suggests the body needs cleansing. Not being able to go to the toilet: as with Alan, a difficulty in expressing the more natural and down-to-earth aspects of self; holding back sexuality or emotions; being selfish and not sharing or 'giving' of oneself.

Example: 'I was watching my teddy bear go to the toilet. It fell down and disappeared' (Jackson S). Jackson was very young and just learning to sit on the toilet by himself. His dream shows him meeting the fear of falling down it. He has seen things disappear for ever, and this disturbs him. He uses his bear as himself. This aspect of the toilet can depict the magical, hidden, or unseen world into which we disappear in sleep—the unconscious.

Toilet bowl: the part of us which can deal with the body wastes, and the emotions we need to discharge; female sexual organ; 'sexpot'. Going to the toilet: expressing oneself; releasing feelings, often creative; letting go of tightly held attitudes or sexuality; acceptance of one's own natural drives and needs. What we put down the toilet: what we consider to be the least important or most unpleasant aspects of ourself or our experience; what we want to get out of our life. My small son, who had depended for long years on a pacifier, one day decided he no longer wanted to have that dependency, or be seen as needing it. He took the pacifier out of his mouth, put it down the toilet and flushed it away.

tomato passion; sexuality; if dream shows body reactions, may show personal reaction to tomato as food. See **eating**; **fruits**.

tomb Feelings or insights about death; fears we face when beginning the meeting with contents of our own unconscious; unconscious family influences. Bodies in tomb: our own potential; aspects of self which 'died' in the past, or were buried, perhaps by the immediate needs of bringing up children, or some other aspect of outer life. Trapped in tomb: illustrates a withdrawn or autistic aspect of self—a part trapped by fears or pain; how we bury our living potential by withdrawing from difficulty, pain, or life. See **grave**; **cemetery**.

tools Practical abilities we have; suggestion of things we might need to do in our life—hammer out a situation with someone, cut away old attitudes, drill through resistances to discover our real feelings, etc.; male sexuality in different aspects.

drill Working through the emotions and fears which resist our insight; sex when there is little feeling contact or there are fears preventing intimacy.

hammer Aggression; desire to hammer home one's point; energy to break through resistances or break old patterns of behaviour.

saw Energy to reshape old attitudes; wordplay on see; sex as the relationship meets hesitations; masturbation.

torch Confidence in meeting the dark or unknown aspects of self; insight. See **searchlight**.

tornado Emotions and urges against which we feel power-less, and which may become obsessive. See **storm; wind**.

torpedo Unconscious or unadmitted sexual drive which could be destructive; unconscious aggression.

tortoise Our vulnerable feelings or hurts which hide be-hind a defensive shell, perhaps of shyness, introversion or withdrawal—could be anger. See also **crab; shell; snail**; example of the unofficial Christ in *Christ* under **archetypes**; *shellfish* under **fish, sea creatures**.

touching Being aware of; becoming conscious; meeting and becoming intimate; contacting. Touching also sometimes shows a linking up with something, as when a person touches a power line and gets shocked. This suggests we have 'touched' feelings or drives which are a shock to us.
  Example: 'Now I sit on a bed. Near me, looking at a book I am holding is a woman I know. I realise as we talk that her foot is touching mine. As my wife is on my left across the room I feel uncomfortable about this. Now the woman has her left hand on my penis.' (Anthony B). Often directly or indirectly sexual, as in the example. The absence of touching

379

touching

<u>in otherwise intimate scene</u>: can suggest lack of ability to reach out or express one's needs for contact; a passive attitude in which you want the other person, or a more automatic aspect of oneself, to take responsibility and risks.

Active <u>avoidance of touching</u>: as illustrated in the following example, shows feelings of anger. The anger may be passive, but such avoidance of contact is as vicious as hitting. The dreamer moves towards a healthier state by expressing her anger. Example: 'My husband came over to me with his arm out to touch me but I was so angry I put my arm up to shield myself from his touch and then began to throw things at him to express how angry I was feeling' (Susie R).

Example: 'The man was so superior in his attitude, and patronisingly arrogant about the lost children, that I cursed him with a touch, saying "May you lose children of your own" ' (Albie G). Touching is also a means of communicating our emotions or intentions. This can be love, anger, sympathy or, as with Albie, a statement which attempts to break down insularity. Albie's dream also shows another aspect of touching, which is its use to produce a change. Albie wanted to leave a mark, make a change in the man, who is an aspect of himself. <u>Idioms</u>: get in touch; keep in touch; lose touch; lose one's touch; out of touch; touch and go; touch someone; touched up; touch something off; touch upon; common touch; Midas touch; touch bottom; soft touch; touch wood.

tower Something we have built or created in our life. As such it can be an outer achievement or erection of inner attitudes such as defensiveness, isolation, insularity, or an attempt to reach the heights of awareness or recognition. Also male sexuality and drive which may not be expressed satisfactorily, and thus be the source of aggression towards females and society. This also has the elements of insularity and defence. Occasionally heightened awareness, as in the lighthouse dream of Priestley in the entry **religion and dreams**.

Example: 'The Devil was trying to force me to make love to

a girl. I wanted to leap off the tower and fly away, but it was high, and I was frightened I would fall' (Quentin C). Quentin is 15 and facing his emerging drive of love and sex. The woman in the tower is here his idealised relationship with the opposite sex. Actual intimacy is threatening and he wants to 'fly' from it but feels this would be failure. The Devil is his own life pushing to grow, but felt as threatening.

town   See **city, town; capital**.

toy   Childhood attitude to life or people; not taking something or someone seriously, just 'playing' at life or love; can also show an attitude of play that is positive and creative, not killing one's creativity by being too serious; the toy dream may be a way of 'playing' with emotions and sexuality which allows the dreamer to explore and mature these areas in a safe way. Toy animal, cuddly toy: a childhood attitude to one's natural drives; one's desire for a non-threatening emotional or sexual relationship. See **doll; games, gambling**.

track   A little used, unconventional, or more natural way of going about something. Idioms: off the beaten track; in one's tracks; lose track of something; make tracks for; hard on someone's track; on the right/wrong track; track record; on the track of; blaze a trail. See **road; railway** for railway track.

train   See **railway**.

tramp, drop out   The ignored or little expressed side of oneself; the 'yes but' syndrome—I would make an effort in life, but I'm broke, people put me down, others are against me, I come from a broken home, I've had a hard time in life, life owes me a living feeling. In a woman's dream: may refer to the negative feelings and thoughts connected with your urge towards personal identity and success—a woman can't make it in the world, it's a man's world, my husband puts me down feelings and attitudes.

transformation   Any dream in which an obvious change occurs in one of the dream figures shows transformation. Each of us go through major transformations during growth— not just physically, as when we change from a toothless baby to a walking, toothy child, but also psychologically.

Example: 'On a hot summer day I was walking with a beautiful black woman through countryside. She stopped and told me she had a problem. To show me she pulled down the strap of her dress. On her shoulder the black skin was peeling to reveal golden white skin underneath. She said that if she kept seeing me she would become completely white. She was going to ask advice from her mother about what to do. As we walked on two black men fought with me. They wanted to take her back to the village. I woke feeling I was winning' (paraphrased from *The Way of The Dream,* Fraser Boa). Here the dreamer is relating well to his own feelings of sexuality and sensuality. However, he is beginning to see a female partner as a real person, not just as his sexuality paints her. Also, the reference to seeking advice from the mother suggests his ability to love is still not freed from emotional and erotic connections with his mother, and needs transforming. One often hears people, even in their 40s, saying 'It is difficult (developing a relationship) with that person because my mother doesn't like them.' The dreamer 'fights' the opposing drives, which want to take the man's love back to the village, his childhood level of love—thus he moves towards becoming independent in love and life. The transformation is towards mature love and relatedness.

For a further description of the major areas and themes of transformation, see **individuation**.

transparent   Available to insight and awareness; something we can 'see through'—therefore suggesting gaining discernment; may also show us feeling vulnerable because others can see parts of our nature usually hidden, or that we are revealing more of self.

trapped   Example: 'After our first baby was born I had such nightmares my doctor gave me a tranquilliser to take before going to sleep. I have taken one at bedtime for 36 years! I am too afraid not to take it. But I still have dreams' (Margaret S-W). Although this is not a dream about being trapped, Margaret is trapped by fears which she never faces. Such fears can stay with us a lifetime, so it is much more economical and satisfying to meet the difficulties they represent. In a dream, Margaret's fears might be represented by a trapped dream, such as the next example.

Example: 'I am trapped in a small brick room with no way out. I shout for someone to help me. Then either a huge bird or creature with arms tries to catch me and I scream myself awake' (Karen S). Karen had lived through a divorce, an unhappy love affair, the loss of a baby. In the dream the figure who comes after she has called for help might save her, but her fears make her reject it. Perhaps Karen's feelings about men paint them as monsters. Whatever her past males may have been like, with such feelings it is Karen herself who is the prisoner and suffers loneliness. Trapped dreams can also depict feelings we have about work, about lack of opportunity, and so on. It must be remembered that the dream puts into images one's own feelings about the situation, not the external thing itself. See **imprisoned**; **cage**; **cell**; *wolf* under **animal**; **escape**; **holding**.

travelling   What you are doing with your life. Thus your destiny or direction in life; the direction or function of your personal growth at time of dream; the movement of life through the aging process. <u>Travelling without goal</u>: having no aim in life; confused about direction; taking life as it comes. <u>Going on holiday</u>: moving towards giving yourself more free time; growth towards allowing yourself to fulfil your needs instead of always considering other people. Travelling to an island: becoming more independent; isolating oneself. Travelling alone: independence; loneliness. Travelling with others: one's social relationships; how you compare yourself with others; what feelings and attitudes influence you. See **railway**; **boat**; **road**; **airplane**.

treasure   The riches of the self—the wonder, wisdom or value of our own life in its wholeness; something we have had to face difficulties to gain, such as personal achievement, mature love, self realisation, wholeness; something which is enormously valuable in bringing wholeness and health to oneself—such as a balancing of dry intellectual achievement with deeply felt love, or an introverted personality with outward activity.

trees   The tree depicts the living structure of our inner self. Its roots show our connection with our physical body and the earth; its trunk the way we direct the energies of our being—growth, sex, thought, emotion. The branches are the abilities, directions and many facets we develop in life—varied and yet all connected in the common life process of our being. The tree can also symbolise new growth, stages of life and death, with its spring leaves and blossom, then the falling leaves. The top of the tree, or the ends of the branches, are our aspirations, the growing vulnerable tip of our personal growth and spiritual realisation. The leaves may represent our personal life which may fall off the tree of life (die) but what gave it life continues to exist. The tree is our whole life, the evolutionary urge which pushes us into being and growth. It depicts the force or process which is behind all other life forms —but seen as it expresses in our personal existence.

In some old manuscripts pictures show a man lying on the ground and his penis growing into a tree, with fruits, birds, and perhaps people in its protective shade. This illustrates how one's personal life energy can branch out from its source in the basic drives, and become creativity, fruitfulness, something given to others. The tree can also represent the spine, and the different levels of human experience—physical, sensual, sexual, hungers, emotions, relatedness, communication, thought, awareness.

Example: 'I was about eight years old when I had this dream. In it I was sitting in a large garden. I believe there was a big house nearby which was our family house—not our real house. With me were other members of my family, and there was a baby boy too. Nearby was a large tree. We climbed this tree, the baby as well, to see what was at the top. The baby fell out of the tree. We climbed down and took the baby to a room and lay it on a bed. It seemed to be asleep and didn't wake up. Later we went back to the room to see the baby but it had gone. In its place was a bluebird. As we looked the bluebird flew away' (told to author on LBC radio programme). The tree in this dream depicts the child's sense of her life as it might develop or grow in the future. Climbing it shows her exploring what it might be like to grow up. At about eight most children unconsciously develop a philosophy which enables them to meet the difficulties of meeting the growth of self awareness, which includes the knowledge of death at the end of life. The dreamer looks at this by having the baby fall out of the tree. Death is seen as the bluebird which flies away.

Example: 'I flew low over small trees which were just coming into leaf. They had beautiful soft green leaves. I knew it was autumn and the leaves were only just coming out because it had been a cloudy, overcast summer. I felt the leaves would have time to mature because the sun would be out in the autumn, and the trees would not die' (Colin C). Colin dreamt this in his early 50s, at a time when he felt frustrated by not being able to achieve a regular source of income or, more important, feel satisfied with what he had achieved in life. The flying shows him taking an overview of his situation. The poor summer is his feelings that the years of his life which should have been most productive had been poor—literally, the sun had not shone on his endeavours. But he feels encouraged because he senses that his personal 'summer' is still to come, and his many endeavours—the trees—would not prove unproductive.

A <u>wood, collection of trees</u>: the natural forces in one's own being, therefore one's connection with or awareness of the unconscious; other people's personal growth and connection with self. <u>Dead tree</u>: past way of life; something which was full of life for you in the past, but is now dead; dead relative. <u>Falling tree</u>: sense of threat to one's identity; loss of relative. <u>Christmas tree, other evergreen</u>: the eternal aspect of our transitory experience. <u>Human, animal hung on tree</u>: personal sacrifice; the death of some part of self so further growth can occur—death of dependence so independence can arise; the pains and struggles, the sense of crucifixion occurring in the maturing process. <u>Oak</u>: strength; masculinity. <u>Flowering tree</u>: fertility; femininity. <u>Idioms</u>: top of the tree; family tree; bark up the wrong tree. See *death and rebirth* and *the self* under **archetypes**; second example in *wife* under **family**; fifth example in **flying**. See also **individuation**.

trespassing   Feeling that you are not respecting someone else's boundaries or wishes—or vice versa.

tunnel   Pathways you have created into your unconscious; ways you have evolved to deal with innermost feelings and memories; vagina or being in the womb; strategies developed to reach our inner resources and bring them to the surface. See last example in *death and rebirth* under **archetypes**; second example in *penis* under **body**; **corridor**; examples in **dark**; **enclosed**; **end**; **swimming**.

U

UFO Example: 'A flying saucer dropped a man on our lawn. He was 7 feet tall and stood in a ring of light. The sky was vivid pink and a peculiar aeroplane flew over. It was the shape of a cross' (Mrs A). The circle, the light, the shape of the cross and the big man, are all symbols of the Self. Our mind has the ability to view our experience as a whole, rather than in parts. What we sense unconsciously in this way is presented to the conscious mind as images such as UFOs or circles of light.

The <u>ball of light or fire</u>: this is a common waking experience as well as a dream image, which occurs when the person touches their sense of wholeness as described above. We see this mentioned in the description of Pentecost—the flame on top of the head—and may account for cases of people seeing flying saucers. See **hallucinations, hallucinogens**; **satellite**; **dream as spiritual guide**; **unconscious**.

umbilical Dependence upon others for one's needs; emotional tie to mother; prenatal life.

umbrella The coping skills we use to ward off difficult feelings and changes in circumstance.

unconscious As dreams apparently emerge from what has been named the unconscious, it is helpful to understand ideas regarding it, and something of its nature.

In ancient cultures we occasionally find hints regarding the unconscious, but not definite statements as were presented by Freud. In the dream theories worked out by the Iroquois American Indians, they believed that through dreams the hidden or unconscious area of the psyche makes its desires known (see **Iroquoian dream cult**). The Greek stories of the Underworld also clearly depict common unconscious activities.

In general, however, many ancient peoples developed concepts of exterior agents such as devils, angels, spirits and God to account for phenomena which today we connect with the unconscious. The first philosopher to talk clearly of an aspect of the mind being unconscious was Leibnitz. He observed that one often recalled at a later date some detail of experience which at the time one was unaware of. One must therefore have observed it unconsciously. So in general the word means anything we are not generally aware of in our being.

Freud's concept of an unconscious element of human nature which influenced conscious behavior was strongly resisted. It was disturbing to many people and questioned the idea of humans being the 'captain of their soul'. The Freudian slip has become one of the popular examples of the influence of the unconscious. Saying to guests arriving at one's house, 'I'm so sorry—I mean glad—you could come' suggests one's real feeling was sorrow at their arrival, not gladness. There is a story of a faculty member of Oxford University who asked the guests at a function to toast the queen, but his actual words were 'Let us toast our queer dean.' However such slips might be seen as attempts to conceal our real feelings, rather than evidence of unconscious motivations.

Taking into account not only Freudian and Jungian approaches to the unconscious, but something of more recent research, the term unconscious must be taken to represent many functions and aspects of self, rather than something we can neatly define. Therefore, we might think of the term as being like the word 'body', which means a whole spectrum of organs, functions, chemical processes, neurological events, systems, cell activities, as well as one's experience of these.

memory Penfield's experiments with memory, along with the experiential side of humanistic psychology, suggest that most if not all of our experiences are retained in a level of memory we seldom have access to. Our everyday experience of accessing parts of our memory, and only occasionally touching other parts, is an example of this. Even prenatal life has been shown to leave memory, although it is not verbal. The word unconscious can refer to the memories which we have little access to, or have not been able to recall since their inception, but which can be recalled under special circumstances.

communication Careful research into speech shows that we constantly use a miracle of mental functioning in communicating with each other. Each sentence we hear spoken undergoes enormous forms of analysis. Each word is taken and a meaning sought. This is compared with other meanings, depending on context in sentence, conversational direction, speaker and speaker's tone. At unbelievable speed, we formulate our response, with similar search and comparisons, as well as filters controlling social situation, mood, status of person being addressed, and so on. All this takes place with almost no awareness, so we can think of it as a process of the unconscious. Factors which govern subjects spoken and choice of words are also largely unconscious.

information processing According to modern theory, the amount of information the human brain can hold is more than is held in all the books in the Library of the British Museum. Gradually it is becoming recognised that information gathered is not simply what we 'learn' from vocal communication, or read, or set out to learn. In fact an unimaginable amount of information gathering has gone on prior to speech, and goes on at an unimaginable speed prior to school years. Consider a small preschool child walking into the garden. It has learnt gradually to relate to muscular movement, balance and its own motivations and feeling reactions in a way enabling it to walk. It has already grasped thousands of bits of 'information' about such things as plants in the garden, the neighbour's cat, the road outside, possible dangers, safe areas. Stupendous amounts have already been absorbed about interrelationships. An idea of 'reality' in the sense of what is probable, and what would be dangerously out of norm, has been formed. We gather information in ways little recognised. How our parents relate to their environment and to other people is all recorded and learnt from, bringing about enormous 'programming' affecting how we act in similar circumstances.

As explained in the entry on the **dream as spiritual guide**, we have great ability in 'reading' symbols, ritual, art, music, body language, architecture, drama, and extracting 'meaning' from them. So we have immense stores of information from these sources. Work done with people exploring their dreams over a long period suggests that some of these information resources are never focused on enough to make conscious what we have actually learnt. Sometimes it is enough simply to ask oneself a question to begin to focus some of these resources. Such questions as what social attitude and response to authority did I learn at school? What feeling reaction do I get when I am in the presence of someone I know well? These may help to bring to awareness aspects of information gathered but remaining unconscious. These unfocused, or unconscious, areas of information can explain why we have apparently irrational feeling responses to some people or situations.

the body A lot of what we call the unconscious are basic physiological and psychological functions. For instance in a modern house, when we flush the toilet, we do not have to bring a bucket of water and fill the cistern again. A self regulating mechanism allows water to flow in and switches it off when full. This is a clever built-in function that had to be done manually at one time. Nowadays we have built into some dwellings fire sprinklers or burglar alarms. Through repeated actions over thousands or millions of years, many basic functions, or functions only switched on in emergencies, have been built into our being. We do not need to think about them, just as we do not have to give awareness to the fire sprinkling system or toilet each time we walk through a room or flush the toilet. They are therefore unconscious.

Research with animals in connection with rewards and conditioned reflexes has shown that by gradually leading an animal towards a certain performance by rewarding it each time it gets nearer to the goal, it can do the most amazing things. It can increase the circulation of blood to its ear, slow its heart, and in fact influence body functions which were thought to be completely involuntary. Where human beings have learnt to use some of these techniques—such as raising the temperature of an arm at will, or helping to increase the efficiency of the immune system—the actual processes still remain unconscious. In general, however, the body's functions are thought to be outside our awareness, and so are one of the areas of the unconscious.

species behaviour and habits   As a species, humans have certain norms of behaviour, many of which we share with other animals. We tend to find a partner of the opposite sex and produce children. We care for our children. We have strong feelings about territory. In groups this becomes nationalism and, like ants or some group animals, we fight to defend our territory. We elect leaders, and have complicated rituals regarding group status or personal 'face'. We seek outward signs of our status, and wherever possible show them.

Talking to individuals, these drives are often hardly recognised. Yet they are powerful enough when manipulated to gather huge armies of people who then march to their death. They are behind enormous hostility between neighbours and nations. Although irrational, and not in our best interest to be influenced by, millions of us are moved by them as if we had little will of our own. The feelings behind them, although seldom acknowledged directly by our conscious self, are often

391

raised to religious status. The procreative drive, the election of leaders, the parental and child raising urges, are all to be seen in the Christian religion as the bones behind the robes and rituals. Why does Catholicism ban the condom and divorce, make a giant figure out of the Pope, worship a woman with a baby in her arms, if it is not based on these mighty urges and biological drives?

Dreams reveal that much of human life arises out of these patterns. The patterns are in us unconsciously. We often venerate the 'norm' of these patterns and raise them, religiously or politically, to a level of tremendous importance. The problem is that many of these patterns are no longer serving us well. They are habits developed through thousands or millions of years of repetition. While they remain unconscious we find it difficult to redirect them or even admit to their influence in our life.

There are, of course, many other aspects of the unconscious, such as memories of childhood trauma, the dream process, the image formation process and sensory apparatus. It is enough to begin with if we recognise that a lot of ourself and our potential remains unknown to us because it remains unconscious, or a part of our unconscious processes.

under/underneath   The person we are beneath our social mask; the feelings and urges we have but may not admit to others or even ourself; the less expressed or capable side of our nature; something we hide. If dreamer is under something, someone: feeling suppressed; feeling weighed down or worried about something; feeling the underdog. If dreamer sees something under them: feeling the top dog; seeing one's inferior (not as capable) functions or self; looking down on others; having a wider view. Idioms: come under; down under; under one's wing; under the weather; under the thumb; under one's hat; under a cloud; under one's nose; under the counter; under the influence. See **above**.

underground   Under the ground: the usually hidden side of ourself; our unconscious depths of experience—ancient strata of psychological and physiological processes in us; parts of self we have ignored or buried. Underground/subway: our journeys into what is usually unconscious in us, such as realisation of childhood traits still active in us as an adult, meeting repressed sexuality, discovery of unexpressed potential or insight. See **tunnel**.

undress   Reveal one's real feelings; reveal one's sexual feelings; be intimate. See **clothes**.

unearth   Bring to consciousness; reveal to oneself or realise; become aware that you have buried feelings about a past love, old hurts, etc.

uniform   Identification with a role, such as soldier or nurse; identification with, or conformity with, collective likes and dislikes—being 'in' with the group; social pressure to conform; feeling a sense of being accepted by a group or at work; social correctness. See first example in **school**.

university   Individual potential and learning ability; something important you are learning; something important you have to offer. See **school**.

up, upper   Example: 'When I was very small probably even pre-school I often dreamt of flying. I was mostly dressed only in my short vest and usually floating upwards to escape adults who were clawing at my legs to pull me down' (Miss GC). Looking through dreams in which the words 'up', 'upwards', 'upper' or 'upstairs' are used, again and again one sees the same feeling as expressed in the example—getting away from being 'pulled down' by difficult feelings, by depression, by everyday duties, by difficulties in relationships, and so on. It expresses the technique we use when worried, such as reading a book, being entertained, having a drink—anything to take our attention away from the difficult feelings. Moving upwards of course also depicts positive change; shifting towards mental activity; gaining a wider view of things; promotion. Idioms: one up on; on the up and up; up a gum tree; up and down; ups and downs; up the pole; up the wall; up the spout; up to the hilt.

urine/urinate   Release of sexual feelings; other people's sexual attitudes, or their negative sexual attitudes; the flow of life through us. Dreams in which we try to go to the toilet but it is mysteriously locked or closed, may be due to the need to pee during the night.

utopia   Escape from our difficulties or internal pains; sense of one's own wholeness.

V

vacation   See **holiday**.

vaccination   Ideas or feelings received from someone else—depending upon how you feel in the dream, what has been received can aid in meeting negative influences in life; influence of other people in your life; may be similar to injection and suggest sexual intercourse. See **injection**.

vagina   See *vagina* under **body**.

valley   Being down to earth; outward activity; fertility; depression or gloominess; female sex organs—*cwm* in Welsh means the valley between the hills; occasionally associated with death—valley of the shadow of death.

vampire   The fear associated with emotional or sexual relationships; feeling that someone is too demanding; the sense of not being able to be independent of one's parent/lover, and feeling any personal independence or will is sucked away by them. We create this creature out of our own doubts or fears. If a man is afraid of sex—afraid his mother/lover will disapprove if he has any sexual feelings of his own—the fear and perhaps anger will sap any good feelings about sexual relationship. Such a man or woman, every time they have sex—because they still do not really wish to give of themself—feel bad after sex, perhaps sucked dry, even 'dead'. The fear or anger about not having a will of their own, and still emotionally dependent on mother/father, turns back upon them, depicted as the vampire.

vanish Thoughts and feelings constantly appear and then disappear, sometimes never to be seen or captured again. This is the magical world of mind and emotion, where things emerge out of the vast world of the unconscious, and vanish again. Therefore suggests one is losing awareness of something. Person, animal who vanishes: love for someone which has gone; something we realised or learnt which we have lost sight of; an autonomous part of self which we cannot yet direct. See **autonomous complex**.

vase Womb; receptivity; our ability to contain something. With flowers: sense of beauty and growth emerging out of receptivity; could be brothers and sisters.

vault The womb; our store of resources; sexual potency; memories; unrealised wisdom.

VD Sense of uncleanness in sexual life or an unhealthy sexual attitude; feeling infected by another person's sexual attitudes; awareness of the fears and hurts that infect one's sexual life.

vermin See **insects**; *mouse* and *rat* under **animals**.

victim Feeling victimised; having a passive relationship with others, or one's own internal aggression; the aspect of self which one has injured or murdered by repression or moral condemnation. See *victim* under **roles; murder; aggression**.

village One's childhood; quiet homely feelings; rural or unsophisticated in a business or commercial sense; past values. Village of one's birth, childhood or home: the values and attitudes which prevailed at that period. See **town**.

vine   One's connections with family and ancestors; growth or fruitfulness of parts of self; the spiritual in one's life. Idioms: clinging vine. See **tree**.

violin   Innermost feelings; heartfelt feelings or urges. See **music; musical instrument**.

virgin   State of being which is free of preconceptions; receptivity; girlhood or innocence. In woman's dream: oneself if still a virgin; a daughter. That one has had sex doesn't mean that one's girlhood feelings actually were met and mated with; these might very well reappear in a new relationship or in a phase of one's marriage. In man's dream: one's feeling self which is receptive; one's soul or psyche; the aspect of oneself which can connect with awareness because it can rid itself of preconceptions.

visions   See **hallucinations, hallucinogens; religion and dreams; unconscious; ESP in dreams**.

vitamin   Intuition about health needs; anxiety about health —hypochondria; thoughts or feelings which are healthy, for instance the confidence which one might gain by taking vitamins might be healthier for one than the vitamins themselves.

voice   Expression of oneself, not simply ideas, but subtle feelings or realisations. Spontaneous speech, voice that speaks through or to one: our personality or mind is not a totally unified whole. Some aspects of self we may not identify with. Because we disown them, they become split from our main expression. Contacting them may be like meeting a stranger— thus in dreams they are shown as exterior to self, or a separate voice, perhaps disembodied. Also some aspects of self express spontaneously—see **autonomous complex**. The voice may therefore be one's intuition; expression of unconscious but not integrated parts of self; fears; the Self being met in the dream.

Example: 'I was going mad. I was crawling around on my hands and knees and wailing and behaving in a most peculiar manner. I actually felt mad. But inside my head a tiny voice kept saying, "You aren't completely insane yet—there's still a chance." People around me kept saying to each other, "We think she's possessed by devils." My sane voice then said "Make the sign of the cross, cast out the evil spirit." I kept trying to do that but my hands wouldn't or couldn't complete the sign. I woke still feeling disturbed' (Margaret F). Margaret has fears about her sanity. The voice here is that of her unconscious, speaking from a more whole view of her being. Such a voice might very well be the voice of one's fears and confusion, however.

Example: 'My present lover, Tony, and a man I had loved years before were standing side by side. A voice was telling me to go to Tony' (Miranda L). Here Miranda's unconscious is summarising her feelings and helping her transfer her feelings of love connected with the past to her new lover.

void   See **abyss**.

volcano   Long held emotions or hurts. If <u>erupting</u>: emotional release—possibly hurts from many years past will surface and, if allowed, express in a healing way.

vomit   Discharge of feelings and ideas that one's system finds irritating or poisonous to well-being.

voyage   A new undertaking, relationship or way of life. Sometimes the voyage of discovery into one's inner life. See **traveling; boat**.

vulture   See **birds**.

W

waiter/waitress   See **roles**.

waiting   Looking to others or circumstances for your cue. Idioms: waiting in the wings; lady in waiting; wait on someone hand and foot; a waiting game; lie in wait. See *waiter/ waitress* under **roles**.

wake up   To realise something; to 'wake up' to one's situation; to come out of a period of withdrawal. Idioms: rude awakening; wake up to something; wide awake.

walking   See **postures, movement, body language**.

wall   Our defensive attitudes; feelings of security; social barriers; boundaries created by anxiety or view of life—a nationalistic attitude might act as a barrier to seeing other viewpoints on history. Our dependence upon our physical senses gives a boundary to our awareness, and a wall may symbolise such a frontier of our awareness.
  Example: 'I went to the top of the turret and saw all the men getting ready to defend the castle if attacked. They had arrows and a lot of men were standing on little ledges on the outside of the wall, with no protection and I knew they were very brave to face an attack as sooner or later they would have been hit' (Anna R). Here the wall is obviously to do with defending the dreamer against attack. Such a wall might be made out of our aggressive feelings, with religious dogma which might defend us against fears and uncertainty, or from tightly controlled behaviour and emotions.
  <u>Walls of favourite house</u>: might be our feelings of security

wall

in our marriage or family which give us defence against the 'storms' of life. Wall of prison, trap: fear; pain; ignorance; prejudice; anger; sense of being an outsider. Idioms: drive somebody up the wall; go to the wall; writing on the wall; back to the wall; head against a brick wall; fly on the wall. See *wall* under **house**; **fence**.

wallpaper   Surface appearance of things; the surface layers of your own feelings and awareness; cover up.

wand   personal influence over others; power of suggestion; spell we cast over another's feelings or decisions; male sexuality. Idioms: wave one's magic wand.

wanting   Wanting is a primal drive which, through socialisation, we may crush and thereby lose contact with what we want from our own feelings and needs. In doing so we may also lose much of our decisiveness and creativity.

Example: 'I still want him all to myself. We never touch or kiss or anything in the dreams, and I want him to, but would never let on I wanted this. I am a bit coy in my dreams' (Pauline B). Pauline is dreaming about a past lover whom she has tried to forget, but when we pick out the 'wants' we see how strong her feelings are. Looking at dreams in this way helps us define what our desires are.

Example: 'The older man still wanted something from me. I didn't want to be involved with him at all and yet had to be polite, etc., so he wouldn't hit out at me/us. We needed some kind of contact with this man, I lent forward and kissed him on his face and drew back quickly as I didn't want to give any more than that, I had a fear that he would want more' (Sandra O). Sandra had divorced an older husband, and was living with a younger man. The complication of her 'wants' is shown in the dream. When it is a 'don't want' in the dream, it is helpful to change it to a positive. 'I didn't want to go with my mother' could become 'I wanted to do my own thing.'

Because what we want is complex and often in conflict, our dream characters may want something which we oppose, as in the following example. Example: 'To escape from a man chasing me, I decided I must get a taxi home. Got in one driven by a woman who wanted to take me to the man who was chasing me. Woke up sweating' (Ann G). The urge to integrate the male part of herself, seen as the taxi driver, is in conflict with Ann's fear of it.

war Internal conflicts. There might be a bloody battle between one's moral code and sexual needs, for instance; or between what we allow ourselves to feel and the self healing process which attempts to release childhood pain; or between intellect and body needs or emotions. Idioms : in the wars; on the warpath; war of nerves; declare war. See **attack; fight;** *soldier* under **roles; bomb; air raid;** unofficial Christ in *Christ* under **archetypes.**

warehouse See *warehouse* under **house, buildings.**

warmth Often appears alongside sunlight and comfort in dreams; physical comfort and wellbeing; supportive family feelings; love, cheerfulness or hopefulness; feeling of emotional situation 'warming up'.

warning Warning bell, voice, signal: intuition that something needs attention in our life, internally or externally. Being warned by someone else or voice: sense of not living up to our own standards; something we have noticed unconsciously but need to become consciously aware of.

washing Getting rid of negative feelings such as despair or self doubt; fears about health—neurotic phobias about one's own wholeness. Washing hair : changing one's attitude; altering the way one thinks about something or one's viewpoint. Washing vagina, penis: clearing negative sexual feelings; dealing with the results of pent up sexuality or reproductive drive. Hanging up washing: allowing change to come into one's life; letting other people see one's new attitudes. In a mother's dream: may refer to caring for the family emotionally. Washing hands: getting rid of feelings about something you have done or been involved in. Idioms: all come out in the wash; lost in the wash; it won't wash; wash dirty linen in public; wash one's hands of. See **soap**; **bath**.

wasp See **insects**.

watching Being aware of; observing something—perhaps something you have noticed from everyday events but not made conscious, or something about self; watching out for what other people are doing to you—suspicion; learning something or trying to understand. Idioms: be on the watch for; watch out; watch one's step; watch over; watch someone like a hawk. See **seeing, saw, sight**.

watch (wrist) If a present probably relates to giver or circumstances of giving. See **time**; **presents**; **clock**.

water Emotions, moods and flow of feeling energy. Because of the nature of water it lends itself to depicting aspects of how we relate to emotions; for instance, one can 'drown' in or feel swept away by some emotions, at other times we can feel cleansed and refreshed. It also represents our potential to experience many emotions because water can take any shape or move in so many ways. How we relate to the water shows how we are meeting our emotions and moods.

Example: 'I am in deep water, no evidence that it is the sea. I am wearing my heavy brown coat. I have no fear, no feeling of cold and I pleasantly just sink' (Mrs B). Mrs B is in her 80s, and is preparing for death in her dreams. The water in her dream has the feeling of being womblike, suggesting that she senses death as a return to a womblike feeling state, with possible rebirth.

Example: 'I was then standing in front of a series of glass water tanks. I had apparently written an article about the balance between intellect and emotion, which had presented emotion in a way to show its equal value with intellect. The tanks had water flowing through them with a series of valves. This demonstrated the different relationships between intellect and emotion. Some tanks were beautifully clear and colourful, showing the right balance. The unbalanced ones had weed growing in them. I was then in a lift with a young woman. We moved close together and kissed. This moved my feelings so much I felt a great melting feeling in my abdomen, and a lot of body sensation against her body' (Anthony F). Anthony's dream perfectly illustrates how water refers to the emotions and flowing body feelings.

Example: 'I was in a hospital ward—maybe for children. I was there to help them. In the ward was a large oblong tank full of water. I got into the water. I realised all the sick people in the ward bathed in the water—not soap, just immersion. This produced feelings of revulsion. I felt I would take into myself their sickness. I also thought that if I drank the water it would show the patients a positive attitude towards their sickness. They would no longer be afraid, and this would be a factor in their healing' (Anthony F). Another of Anthony's dreams in which he is looking at how to meet anxious feelings about his health. He sees that a more positive conscious attitude heals the childhood fears.

Entering water: entering into strong feelings such as might arise in a relationship or new job; sexual relationship; emotions which might stand in one's way—as a deep lake might, or turgid water. Deep water: the deeps of one's inner life. Hot water: strong emotions—see example in Introduction. Electricity and water: emotions which can generate very powerful reaction to a situation, such as jealousy or anger. Idioms: make water; muddy the waters; tread water; water something

403

down; turn on the waterworks; water under the bridge; hold water; in hot water; head above water; pour cold water onto something. See **fluid; river; rain.**

water creatures See **fish, sea creatures.**

weapons Guns, rockets, knives, spears, etc., depict our desire to hurt someone or, if we are being shot or hurt in the dream, how we have internalised our own aggression or past hurts or fear of being hurt; also defence against fears or being hurt. If we shoot or stab someone or something, we need to consider what part of ourself we are turning our aggression upon. If we kill or injure a recognisable person, we may be harbouring the desire to hurt or kill that person, even if only in reputation. All weapons can represent male sexual drive or aggressive sexuality. The situation in which the action takes place: defines what the weapon expresses. Ineffective weapons: feelings of inadequacy. A work tool used as a weapon: our skill or authority turned against ourself or someone else, as might happen if a doctor got sexual favours through his position.

arrow Something that has really got into us, like hurtful words or actions; or being pierced by a powerful emotion such as love; turning our attention inwards in a wounding way; sometimes a message, perhaps of love or endeavour.

gun Penis; male sexuality; anger; confidence in defending oneself against criticism, etc.; fears or anxieties; attitudes we use as a defence against our own emotions or realisations—a man might feel depressed about growing old, and defend himself against this with positive thoughts; also the bulldozer emotions we sometimes use against others, like a pistol held to their head. When shot by gun: feeling hurt, wounded; fear of sex. Idioms: shot in the arm; shot across the bows; shot to pieces; shot in the dark; long shot.

knife Penis, cutting intellectual insight, aggression, depending on how used in the dream; an attempt to wound someone. Idioms: get one's knife into someone; on a knife edge; under the knife (surgery); cut it out; cut the air with a knife.

sword Because it often has a cross as a handle, has mixed meanings. Erection; social power; justice; spiritual strength. Sword hanging by a thread: threats hanging over one. When sheathed: the soul or self in the body. Heirloom: a heritage of attitudes from one's family; willpower or discrimination. Consider background of dream for meaning. Idioms: cross swords with someone; double-edged sword; sword of Damocles. See **cross; fight; attack; war**.

weather Changing external situations, or internal response to situations; our moods and emotions. The following idioms give indications of the meaning. Idioms: sunny disposition; things don't look so bright; things will brighten up; it never rains but it pours; like living under a cloud; things are a bit rough/stormy/overcast. See **rain; flood; cloud; snow; lightning; thunder**.

web A sticky situation you feel yourself in; feeling caught up in something that might trap you; a web of lies; the symmetry of the Self. See *spider* under **insects**.

wedding See **marriage, wedding**.

weeds Things you have developed in your life which are not contributing much, or might even be stopping more positive personal growth; misplaced endeavour or energy. See **plants**.

weight Seriousness; sense of a burden or responsibility; importance. Weight of someone on dreamer: feeling they are being too dependent or a burden in one's life. Idioms: carry

weight

weight; pull one's weight; throw one's weight around; worth one's weight in gold. See **fat**.

well   Access to one's deepest resources of life; the source of one's 'well-being'; the vagina; a view into one's depths. See **water**.

werewolf   See **vampire; animals**.

west   Where the sun sets—death or the end of something; physical life; down-to-earth self.

whale   See **fish, sea creatures**.

wheat   Wisdom of experience; the harvest of life experience; fruitfulness.

wheel   The ability to meet changes, to be mobile. Large water wheel or fun fair wheel: the ups and downs of life; the wheel of life—birth and death. Idioms: behind the wheel; set the wheels in motion; take the wheel; wheeling and dealing; wheels within wheels; oil the wheels; spoke in one's wheel. See **shapes, symbols**.

whip   Hurtful remarks; angry feelings; sexuality which has as its base a desire to hurt; desire to control through threats or pain. Idioms: whip hand; whipping boy.

white person   Depends on skin colour of dreamer. If black: feelings about whites; or if known, what you feel about them. If white: same as any person dream.

widow   <u>Married woman dreaming of being a widow</u>: fears of losing husband; desire to be free of husband.

wife   See *wife* under **family**.

wig   False ideas; unnatural attitude. If <u>dreamer wears wig</u>: feelings about being bald. See *hair* under **body**.

wind   The movement of consciousness or mind; the hidden influences in our life; ideas and conceptions which move us. <u>Flying with the wind</u>: uplift of sexual energies into the mind to become a wider view or an integration of experience; upliftment. See **tornado**.

window   See *window* under **house, buildings**.

wine   See **alcohol**.

winter   Emotional coldness; an unfruitful period of one's life; old age; death.

wireless   What we listen to or hear going on around us or inside us; company; other people's 'noise'. <u>Inside wireless</u>: our mind; inside oneself.

wise man   Father; the self; what we have learnt from our active experience. See *the self* under **archetypes**; example in **cliff**.

witch   Example: 'I talked about my mother, she was standing before me in full anger and blaming me for bringing out the witch in her. She said "Look at my eyes", they were horrid to see, all red and angry and she was dark' (Lesley M). The fears or difficult feelings and habits we have developed in relationship with our mother. Because these feelings are now part of ourself, if female, we can of course become the witch in relationship to someone else. Also vindictiveness, jealousy, etc.

wizard   See *magician* and *conjurer* under **roles**.

woman   Example: 'I gave birth to a baby girl I named Charlotte. I had mixed emotions about this, uncertainty, excitement. I wanted to share the news with my friends. I phoned one, a woman in Australia. I told her with enthusiasm, but she listened quietly and remained silent. I felt uneasy, then she said "We lost Luke"—her son—"the week before." I then woke with muddled feelings' (Mo).

A woman in a woman's dream: an aspect of herself, but often a facet of herself she is not immediately identifying with. The above example helps make this plain. Mo explored her feelings about the dream characters. It all fell into place when she asked herself what she had 'lost' recently. She had left a lover of some years' standing. This gave her a lot more freedom and new opportunity, depicted by the baby, but also muddled feelings of loss. Her Australian friend represents her feelings of grieving for the 'death' of her relationship. Her muddled feelings arise because she both loves the new life which opens up, but grieves for the death of her romance.

A woman's sister, female children: particularly used to represent herself. The character of the dream woman, loving, angry, businesslike, lazy, sexual, gives a clue to what part of the dreamer it is referring to. If the dream woman is a person known well, the above can still be the case, but the woman may represent what the dreamer feels about that person. A woman younger than the dreamer: oneself at that age. An older woman: could be the dreamer's mother; her feelings about aging; her sense of inherited wisdom. Two women and the dreamer: conflicting feelings or drives. One woman, one man: behaviour patterns arising from parental relationship. A goddess or holy woman: the dreamer's highest potential; what she is capable of but may not yet have lived.

Man dreaming of a woman. Example: 'On a raised mobile platform a goddess stood. I loved her and flew to her, skimming above the heads of the people. I talked to her. She told me the only love I could receive from her was that which I gave to a human woman. Inasmuch as I gave love to a human female, she would love me. She was all women' (Andrew P). The example shows Andrew meeting his archetypal conception of a woman, his ideal. But he understands that you cannot love an ideal. His love must find a real woman. Through a real love he would call love from out of himself, out of his unconscious reserve.

In a man's dream: his present relationship with his own feelings and intuitive self; his sensitivity and contact with his unconscious through receptivity; or how he is relating to his female partner. The latter is especially so if the woman in the dream is his partner; how capable he is of loving a woman. An old woman: usually the dreamer's mother. The woman, because she is his feelings, is obviously also his sexual desires and how he meets them. A younger woman: can depict his desires for a woman of that age, or his more vulnerable emotions. Two women and the dreamer: an 'eternal triangle'; conflicting feelings. If one woman and one man: pattern of behaviour developed in relationship with parents.

The conditions or situations of the woman, see under appropriate entries, such as **illness**; **murder, swimming**; etc. See *anima* and *the Great Mother* under **archetypes**.

womb   The state of existence or consciousness from which we have grown; the state or condition prior to our development of personality—this can be personal, but it also relates to all human creatures, so is historical or evolutionary. It is a condition without ego, with a sense of being life itself. Going back to the womb, to the condition of withdrawal or autism: regression to the 'womb' state of awareness—therefore perhaps a time of not being able to meet the stress of having a personality with self awareness, a time of gaining respite and perhaps touching one's roots of being in order to gain new strength.

So much of our foundations of experience are connected with our experience of prenatal life and birth that we may need to touch these experiences to heal or free parts of our nature for further growth. See *vagina* under **body**; **individuation**; see also **balloon**; *nest* under **birds**; **breath**; **catacomb**; *blue* under **colour**; **dark**; **deep**; **descending**; **hole**; **hollow**; example in *room* under **house, buildings**; **igloo**; **receptacle**; **recurring dreams**; **river**; **sack**; *under the sea* under **sea**; **suitcase**; **tank**; **tunnel**; **water**.

wood   Wooden things: the past, or structures of thought or behaviour we have built, which originally had life but are now habitual; being 'wooden'—lacking life or feeling. Wooden room, house: a part of our nature which has been carefully cultivated or created out of past experience. For woods see **tree**.

wool   Warmth, gentleness; motherhood; protective fuzziness of thought and feeling; ideas. Knitting wool: creativity; ideas or thoughts we knit together. Idioms: woolgathering; woolly thinking; pull the wool over someone's eyes.

word analysis of dreams   Having written a dream down, by using highlighting pens to make all matching words the same colour, one can immediately see the main issues in some dreams.

Example: 'We walk around, go upstairs, and I notice a staircase leading to a room or rooms. It goes up square, about eight steps in a flight, but round and round—spiral. I am **scared** by them, don't want to go up, but am curious. We move in and nobody but myself has really taken any notice of the stairs. Nobody has been up . In one dream I try to go up but the children are **scared** for me. They plead, "Don't go up Mum, just forget them". Then I wake. In the next dream I wait till they are asleep. Half way <u>up</u> I am **terrified** but have to go on. Then I wake. Next dream I got <u>up</u> there. Then I woke' (Ann H). Ann's dream theme recurs, so is important to her. In marking just some of the words we see that the 'up' or 'go up' is important. Childhood fears hold Ann back for a while, but she dares to climb. If we look at the entries for climb and stairs, we see they depict taking steps towards exploring the unknown, daring to explore one's potential or opportunities.

By marking the words in this way we might also highlight certain statements otherwise hidden in the dream. Particularly watch out for the connections with the word 'I', such as I want, I do, I will, I have, I know, I cannot, etc. Example: 'I want to withdraw.' 'I was full of sadness but was trying not to show it.' 'I felt keyed up and ready to fight.' Taking such statements out of context and looking for connections with everyday feelings or situations often throws considerable light on the dream. If what you realise is then considered in connection with the plot of the dream, the viewpoint your unconscious has on the situation might become evident. For instance, the statement 'I felt keyed up' occurred within a classroom, and helped the dreamer understand the anger generated at school. See **amplification**; **plot of the dream**; the comments on dream processing in the Introduction; **dream processing**; **postures, movement, body language**; **settings**; **symbols and dreams**.

word play, puns   According to Freud, one of the major processes of the unconscious is condensation. This means that within one element in a dream, such as the strange room we dream we are in or the unusual name a person has in the dream, are condensed many associated emotions, memories or ideas. Talking about a peapod which appeared as part of her imagery, Constance Newland shows how it represented her father's penis. The pea associated with pee or urine, and the pod with a seed carrier, the testicles. Freud gives the ex-

ample of a patient who dreamt he was kissed by his uncle in
an 'auto'. The patient immediately gave his own association as
auto-eroticism. A psychologist whose patient dreamt she was
going on a trip on a boat called *Newland,* correctly inferred
that the patient was getting better, because the name suggested new territory traversed. One woman dreamt about a
busy intersection, and realised it was referring to inter-sex-on.

So we need to consider how unconsciously we might be
playing with words, then check if this helps us gain insight.
Also, phrases are used in the same way. We might see such
words as 'I felt a prick', 'keeping it up was difficult', 'dead
end' and so on, in writing down our dream. See **names of
people**; introduction to **colours**.

work   At work: concerns or issues connected with one's
work or lack of it. Working: actively trying to change a situation in one's life—one might be working at one's marriage or
learning something, depending on dream surroundings.

Example: 'I am working in a hospital in outpatients. Nobody is there. My two children appear. I know I have to find
them somewhere to sleep. I lay them on seats, tell the only
nurse I can find that I am going to find them a bed. I know
where the children's ward is but I can't find it. When I eventually find it all the side rooms are filled. I know I have been a
long time so I start to panic, worried my children are missing
me, and worried night sister will have found them. I pass a
military meeting. As I continue the men come out and I get
caught in the cross fire and am shot in the leg. I am now
terrified. I have to get back to the children. Night sister must
have found them by now and if not what will they be doing.
When I got back they are there with night sister' (Laramie F).
Laramie works as a nurse, was divorced just prior to the
dream, and was obviously concerned how her work affected
her children. This internal conflict (the crossfire) injures her
confidence (the shot leg). Idioms: have one's work cut out; set

to work; worked up; work like a horse; work off; work out; dirty work; donkey work; spanner in the works.

world   The sphere of one's experience; one's own world of awareness and activity; the way one experiences the world/life. End of the world: end of the way you have been experiencing or relating to life; fears or feelings about death; anxieties about external events; big change in one's personal growth. Other worlds, dimensions: new ways of experiencing oneself and life; new paradigm; breakthrough to new realisations. Idioms: a world of; on top of the world; out of this world; think the world of; best of both worlds; small world.

worm   Feeling insignificant or ineffective; something you treat as insignificant, the penis. Worms: ill health; health worries. Idioms: even a worm will turn. See **maggots**.

worship   Worshipping: opening oneself to the influence of what is being worshipped—an idea, a person, an object. Worshipped: inflated sense of self.

wound   Hurt feeling; trauma from the past. If wounding someone: desire to hurt someone, or to destroy some aspect of oneself. If pierced: apart from hurt feelings, may also show one being opened by new experience, even love.

writing   Thinking about something; sorting out one's ideas and decisions; leaving one's mark in life; expressing one's inner feelings and ideas; one's personal history. What someone you know has written: what you feel about them; their influence in your life and mind.

X Y Z

X   Sometimes represents an error; X marks the spot; 10; the cross; an unknown quantity.

X-rays   Something influencing your life unconsciously; seeing into a situation or oneself; fear of illness.

yacht   See **boat**.

yawn   Boredom; tiredness; unconsciously trying to say something—yawning is a movement arising from the self-regulatory process. See **sleep movements**.

yeast   Ideas or intangible influences which can yet change one's life or situation.

yes   Whenever we say yes to a person or situation in a dream, we are opening to the influence of that aspect of ourself. It is important to define what leads us to agreement in the dream. Is it that one says yes because of feelings that one ought, one should, or it was expected? Was the yes out of anxiety? Was it said because that was what you agreed with, or was it the most useful response? See **no**.

yogi   The Self; withdrawal from outward activity.

youth   Oneself at that age; the attitudes and responses developed at that age. If <u>dreamer younger than youth</u>: one's potential of growth and change; the part of self growing towards that age. See **boy, girl**.

zero See **numbers**.

zip Connections with others; one's ability to be 'open' or 'closed' with others.

zodiac Where an animal or figure of one's birth sign—such as a lion in a Leo's, bull in Taurean's, twins in Geminian's dream—appears, this frequently represents the dreamer's basic personality traits. Often it depicts the natural urges the personality meets in itself, but which may not be expressed. How one deals with the animal or figure shows one's relationship with what is felt to be one's basic self and potential. See **planet**.

zoo One's natural urges and instincts, such as sexuality, parental caring, social grouping. What is happening to the animals shows how one is relating to the natural side of oneself—and how it is responding to one's conscious attitudes and activities. Life processes in us are not inert: they constantly respond to what we do and what we are. See **animals**.

Bibliography

Adler, Gerhard, *Studies in Analytical Psychology,* International Universities Press, 1967.
Adler's view of dreams.

Becker, Raymond De, *The Understanding of Dreams,* Hawthorn, 1968.

Bro, Harmon, *Edgar Cayce On Dreams,* Warner Books, 1970.

Brook, Stephen, *The Oxford Book of Dreams,* Oxford University Press, 1983.
A dream anthology, from pre-Christian to present times.

Caldwell, W.V., *LSD Psychotherapy,* Grove Press, 1969.
Caldwell travelled widely in the USA and Europe, visiting and studying results in the practices or clinics of psychiatrists using LSD as a psychotherapeutic tool. In the book he gives an excellent synthesis of the mass of information and experience gathered. In doing so he maps the heights, depths and fantasies of the human psyche, in a way that is beyond any particular school of thought. Such a map is of great use to anyone seriously investigating dreams.

Campbell, Joseph, *Myths To Live By,* Paladin 1988.
Wonderful reading, although not directly about dreams. Campbell shows how human beings create certain myths, no matter what their culture or historic period. This myth creating faculty is obviously linked with dreaming, and portrays life and death as the unconscious sees them.

Chetwynd, Tom, *Dictionary for Dreamers*, Paladin, 1974.
Good dictionary.

Corriere, Karle, *Dreaming and Waking*, Peace Press, 1980.
Exploring the idea of whether, if we meet the feeling content of dreams, they gradually cease to be symbolic. A landmark in dream theory.

Crisp, Tony, *The Instant Dream Book*, C.W. Daniel Co. Ltd., 1984.
Explains techniques which can be used to transform the fears and emotions of dream without analysing them. It also considers the different areas of dream activity, such as body dreams, problem solving, extra sensory and sexual dreams.

Crisp, Tony, *Mind and Movement*, C.W. Daniel Co. Ltd., 1987.
Considers the problem-solving or self-regulating psychological and physiological process underlying dreaming. It also considers how the process which produces dreams underlies many other puzzling phenomena such as ESP, abreaction and flashbacks to past events.

Diamond, Edwin, *The Science of Dreams*, Eyre & Spottiswoode, 1962.
A fascinating collection of researched information on dreams.

Evans, Christopher, *Landscapes of the Night*, Victor Gollancz, 1983.
The computer theory of dreaming, with excellent survey of other theories.

Fagan & Shepherd, *Gestalt Therapy Now*, Harper Colophon, 1970.
Contains an explanation of Fritz Perls' approach to achieving insight into one's dreams.

Faraday, Ann, *Dream Power,* Hodder and Stoughton, 1972.
Good basic textbook, written for laypeople, but intelligently.

Freud, Sigmund, *The Interpretation of Dreams,* Allen & Unwin, 1955.
The first of all modern dream books.

Fromm, Erich, *The Forgotten Language,* Allen & Unwin, 1952.
Subtitled An Introduction to Dreams, Fairy Tales and Myths.

Garfield, Patricia, *Creative Dreaming,* Ballantine, 1974.
Clear description of taking dreams to satisfaction.

Green, Celia, *Lucid Dreams,* IPR, 1968.
The foundation research on lucidity in dreams.

Hadfield, J.A., *Dreams and Nightmares,* Penguin 1954.
Hadfield proposes a biological theory of dreams, which stands between Freud, Jung, and more modern theories.

Hall, Calvin S., *The Meaning of Dreams,* Harper & Row, 1953.
Hall worked with series of dreams, and with content analysis. This is the result of his research, written in an easily readable form.

Heyer, G.R., *Organism of The Mind,* Kegan Paul, 1933.
Although Heyer is not writing directly about dreams, the book is an interesting commentary on what was being discovered by Analytical Psychology in the early part of the 20th century.

Jacobi, Jolande, *The Way Of Individuation,* Hodder and Stoughton, 1967.
Explanation of Jung's concept of the stages in becoming a person.

Jung, Carl, *Dreams,* Ark Paperbacks, 1986.
Very technical consideration of the subject.

Jung, Carl, *Man and His Symbols,* Aldus, 1964.
The breadth and depth of dreams. Excellent reading.

Jung, Carl, *Modern Man in Search of a Soul,* Kegan Paul, 1933.

Jung, Carl, and Richard Wilhelm, *Secret of the Golden Flower,*
   Kegan Paul, 1942.
Jung's commentary on this ancient Chinese book on meditation is wonderful reading for those seriously interested in their
own inner life.

Langs, Robert, *Decoding Your Dreams,* Unwin Hyman, 1989.
A good basic handbook on learning to discover the wealth of
information and wisdom in one's own dreams.

Lincoln, J.S., *The Dream in Primitive Cultures.*

Martin, P.W., *Experiment in Depth,* Routledge & Kegan Paul,
   1964.
Martin was one of the early pioneers, along with Rev. Leslie
Weatherhead, who started helping people to adequately explore their own dreams, i.e. without the psychiatrist.

Newland, Constance, Frederick Muller Ltd, 1963.
Suffering frigidity, Constance Newland successfully under-
went a number of psycho-analytical sessions using the drug
LSD. The connections with dreaming lie in the enormously
rich and potent fantasies she met and dealt with during her
analysis. The book is therefore a powerful description of the

world one meets in dreams, and the personal fears and forces which underlie the strange imagery of the unconscious.

Oswald, Ian, *Sleep,* Penguin, 1966.
The great landmark in researched basis of sleep and dreams.

Rawson, Wyatt, *The Way Within,* Vincent Stuart, 1965.
Interesting results of a dream group working together over some years. Arising from the work of P.W. Martin.

Rennick, Teresa, *Inner Journeys,* Turnstone Press, 1984.
Handbook on the use of visualisation and fantasy in problem solving and personal growth. It is useful to work with dream images in this way, especially in taking the dream forward towards satisfaction.

Sechrist, Elsie, *Dreams: Your Magic Mirror,* Cowles, 1968.
Expressive of the Edgar Cayce view of dreams.

Shohet, Robin, *Dream Sharing,* Thorsons, 1985.
Working as a dream group.

Stevens, William Oliver, *The Mystery of Dreams,* Allen & Unwin, 1950.
Examples of different types of dreams.

Tart, Charles, *Altered States of Consciousness,* Doubleday Anchor, 1969.
Has a whole section on dreaming and self induced dreams.

Ullman & Krippner, *Dream Telepathy,* Turnstone, 1973.
Researched results of telepathy during dreaming.

WHEN YOU WANT TO KNOW HOW TO

- say it
- spell it
- master it
- remember it

These are the books that have the answers you need!

21ST CENTURY BOOKS

☐ **AMERICAN HERITAGE DICTIONARY (3rd Edition)**
$5.99 21861-6

☐ **ROBERT'S RULES OF ORDER**
$5.99 21722-9

☐ **GUIDE TO IMPROVING YOUR WRITING**
$5.99 21727-X

☐ **GUIDE TO INCREASING YOUR READING SPEED**
$5.99 21724-5

☐ **MANUAL OF STYLE**
$5.99 22074-2

☐ **OFFICE ASSISTANT'S MANUAL**
$5.99 21725-3

☐ **DICTIONARY OF COMPUTER TERMS**
$6.99 21557-9

☐ **DICTIONARY OF QUOTATIONS**
$5.99 21447-5

☐ **DICTIONARY OF SLANG**
$5.99 21551-X

☐ **GRAMMAR HANDBOOK**
$5.99 21508-0

☐ **ROGET'S THESAURUS**
$5.99 21555-2

☐ **GUIDE TO BUILDING YOUR VOCABULARY**
$5.99 21721-0

☐ **SYNONYMS & ANTONYMS FINDER**
$5.99 21323-1